C000259339

THE FOREIGN POLICY OF GEORGE W. BUSH

In remembrance of:

Adriaan Moens, Professor, March 29, 1922-May 5, 2003

My father wrote at the end of his curriculum vitae the simple words
that I wish to copy and follow: *Soli Deo Gloria*

The Foreign Policy of George W. Bush

Values, Strategy, and Loyalty

ALEXANDER MOENS
Simon Fraser University, Canada

ASHGATE

© Alexander Moens 2004

All rights reserved. No part of this publication may be reproduced, stored in a retrieval system or transmitted in any form or by any means, electronic, mechanical, photocopying, recording or otherwise without the prior permission of the publisher.

Alexander Moens has asserted his right under the Copyright, Designs and Patents Act, 1988, to be identified as the author of this work.

Published by
Ashgate Publishing Limited
Gower House
Croft Road
Aldershot
Hants GU11 3HR
England

Ashgate Publishing Company
Suite 420
101 Cherry Street
Burlington, VT 05401-4405
USA

Ashgate website: http://www.ashgate.com

British Library Cataloguing in Publication Data
Moens, Alexander, 1959-
    The foreign policy of George W. Bush : values, strategy, and loyalty
    1. Bush, George W. (George Walker), 1946- 2. Iraq War, 2003
    3. United States - Foreign relations - 2001 -
    I. Title
    327.7'3'09051

Library of Congress Cataloging-in-Publication Data
Moens, Alexander, 1959-
    The foreign policy of George W. Bush : values, strategy, and loyalty / by Alexander Moens.
        p. cm
    Includes index.
    ISBN 0-7546-4274-7
    1. United States--Foreign relations--2001- 2. Bush, George W. (George Walker), 1946- I. Title.

    E902.M625 2004
    327.73'009'0511--dc22

Reprinted 2005

2004013268

ISBN 0 7546 4274 7

Printed and bound in Great Britain by TJ International Ltd, Padstow, Cornwall.

Contents

Acknowledgments

Brock Stephenson, a graduate student at Simon Fraser University, has been my research assistant throughout this entire project. His sharp eye and analytical mind has helped me find excellent sources and avoid numerous pitfalls.

The students in Political Science 449 in the Spring of 2004 read and critiqued all my chapters. Steven Molnar also read the entire manuscript and gave me many good tips.

John Bryson, at the Department of National Defence, Ottawa, and Carl Hodge, professor at Okanagan University College, read chapters and gave me their perceptive insights and critical comments.

Dean of Arts, John Pierce, gave me extra time to finish the book. The Social Sciences and Humanities Research Council of Canada and Simon Fraser University's Discovery Parks Grant provided financial help in the research.

Ben Fishman, a former student and now in the publishing business himself, did the final editing and formatting of the entire manuscript.

Most of all, thanks to my dear Marsha for her unfailing love and patience.

Introduction: A Foreign Policy of Values, Strategy, and Loyalty

People had a difficult time understanding George W. Bush when they first heard of him in the 2000 election campaign. He spoke in simple terms (often haltingly) and exuded strong Texan and Christian values. It was easier to stereotype and belittle him than get a handle on his personality and background.

Never have so many negative books appeared so early about a president so little known. Some pictured Bush as lazy, inarticulate and as a 'lunkhead.'[1] Others dismissed the son of George Herbert Walker Bush as "Shrub," and called his achievements as Governor of Texas, except for education, 'political hooey.'[2] A media critic argued that 'a callow and illiterate president' now occupied the White House, 'gamely fronting for a far-right oligarchy...'[3] One aspiring biographer published a slanderous account based on bogus sources, falsely accusing him of racism, drug use and white-collar crime.[4]

So was born the image in America and around the world of Bush as a spoiled son of a political dynasty, a representative of powerful lobbies, a candidate who lacked the necessary qualifications and a man who cannot think for himself. Bush was portrayed as a Texas *bon vivant*, uncommitted to any political purpose. He became the 'accidental candidate,' who came 'ambling into history,' as a result of political operators around him, such as Karl Rove.[5] Even though a *Washington Post* study published in late 2001 showed Bush would have won the Florida election in a hand count, he was accused of stealing the vote and manipulating the Supreme Court. He was called the 'Thief-in-Chief.'[6]

After the terrorist attacks of September 2001, and especially after the war in Iraq, this river of literature became murkier yet, taking on a sinister quality. Revenge of his father's political fortunes turned into dynastic conspiracy theories.[7] 'Lies,' the deliberate manipulation of public policy, 'warmongering,' and dark schemes of American attempts at world domination became the lead explanations for all Bush did.[8] *Fahrenheit 9/11* became the first explicit movie to slam Bush.

There were attempts by insiders such as David Frum and admirers like Bill Sammon to show Bush in a more favorite light.[9] Bob Woodward's first book on President Bush, *Bush at War*, made the case for a decisive and hands-on war leader with a clear view ahead.[10] Just as the early appraisals of academics and policy analysts began to appear,[11] the first wave of 'kiss-and-tell' memoirs showed up. Ron Suskind, a reporter with *Vanity Fair*, who had embarrassed the President's Chief of Staff, Andy Card, with an interview about Karen Hughes, and then written negatively about Karl Rove, lined up with disgruntled former Treasury Secretary Paul O'Neill to write a highly critical account of Bush's decision making and policy process.[12] Richard Clark, the counter terrorism czar, followed with his account of how Bush allegedly fumbled the ball on the Al Qaeda attacks. Based on inside interviews, Woodward published his second book on Bush, but this time was critical of his decision to go to war with Iraq.[13]

What has been missing in all these accounts is a systematic attempt to explain Bush's person, his presidential style and decision-making process, and to link these to his presidency and foreign policy. The following chapters try to fill this gap by arguing that the person, character, and style of this president are the most important factors in understanding his presidency and foreign policy. To put it in plain words: the policy is the person.

Values, Strategy, and Loyalty

Three features describe this person, his presidential style and the substance of his foreign policy. First, Bush thinks and acts in terms of values; second, he has a natural talent for political campaign strategy, a skill he improved all his life. Finally, for this President all politics are personal and the glue is loyalty, trust and mutual responsibility between him and his advisers in the inner circle, key Congressional players, as well as foreign leaders.

In both domestic and foreign policy, Bush believes ardently in several key values and pursues them consistently. Abstract issues and public policy that are not grounded on these values cannot capture his interest. Compassionate conservatism is not a political ploy or campaign spin but contains the key principles he sought in Texas and pursues in the White House. The term includes values of personal responsibility and traditional family, faith-based communities helping the needy, and the quest to rebuild an American society and culture that respects faith and favors life. He is unwavering in these, but also unhurried. He knows from personal experience that simple, honest ideals are what matter most. Neither policy expertise nor intellectual insight can compete with that moral compass.

At the same time, Bush is a master strategist. He has always thought about politics from the vantage point of the race. He worked for years with two of the all-time best Republican strategists: Lee Atwater and Karl Rove. Bush is neither a simple idealist nor a pragmatist. His values are packaged inside a political strategy that is primed to invest and spend political capital with an acute sense of timing. Of course, values and political interests often clash, which explains the inherent tension in some of Bush's decisions.

Political loyalty is the third element of his presidential style. Loyalty to faith values, to family and to political teammates are all part of one continuum. This loyalty builds true relationships of trust from which flows a team effort and which makes people accountable to each other. Presidential advisors, Congressmen, and foreign leaders do not have much influence on Bush unless they become part of this loyalty circle.

This book starts with the argument in Chapter 1 that the 'pop' version of Bush has hampered understanding of the man. His personality and background are not straightforward, but form a study in contrasts. He became a politician in his own right in Texas and brought his political formula of values, strategy and loyalty to the national scene in 2000. Chapter 2 describes Bush's campaign for the White House, the first circle of loyal advisers, his message discipline and his way of connecting with the people. It explains why he delegated foreign policy to second place and how he became president-elect with zero political capital. The whole Florida episode rendered his Electoral College victory a 'diminished thing,' as he admitted.[14]

As Chapter 3 explains, when Bush came to the White House, he had to earn the respect of Congress and the American people. 'What,' he was asked prior to his inauguration in January 2001, 'did you learn about being President from watching your father?' His answer: 'I learned how to earn political capital and how to spend it.'[15] To earn that respect, he turned to the top themes of his campaign; tax cuts and education, applying strong leadership qualities and clear values. His tight White House organization and finely honed political game plan prevented him from becoming a lame-duck president on Day One.

Chapter 4 makes the case that Bush's early foreign policy showed strong values, but unlike the domestic counterpart, lacked a game plan for action. Foreign policy could not compete with the domestic agenda, for in terms of concrete foreign and defense plans, only two made it on the priority list. Bush sought an amicable end to the Anti-Ballistic Missile Treaty in order to speed up plans for missile defense and launched a plan for military transformation. As he gained a reputation in domestic politics in mid 2001, the President remained without much political capital and vulnerable in foreign policy.

When Al Qaeda attacked America on September 11, 2001, Bush had as little foreign policy respect as he had domestic capital after Florida. Chapter 5 describes his patient, focused and determined rout of Al Qaeda and the Taliban, and how his launch of the war on terror abroad and at home turned around his perception in a matter of weeks. The certainty of his faith and the emotional comfort of his loyal relationships gave him the clarity to respond. The war on terror flipped his agenda from domestic to foreign and President Bush began pursuing his values worldwide – to fight evil and promote freedom.

Chapter 6 explains Bush's decision to go on the offensive in the war on terror by removing Saddam Hussein, and by putting pressure on the remaining rogue states. The President and his advisers perceived an acute threat environment in the fall of 2001 that made them willing to take enormous risks. If his immediate actions after 9/11 were his 'finest hour,' Iraq was the most controversial. The decision to topple the most threatening rogue forms the big case study of this chapter, showing how Bush combines strong values with a consistent strategy. It also reveals growing tension in the decision-making process between values, loyalty and diversity of views.

What kind of presidency and foreign policy do you get when you combine a confident, activist, and moralist president who also has a sharp political game plan and who sticks as loyally to personal relations as he wants his advisers to stick to him? The analysis that follows is an attempt to explain Bush's foreign policy by understanding the complexities in the man and how this particular personality and style bore so heavily on the final outcome of his policy.

Notes

1   Paul Begala, *'Is Our Children Learning' The Case Against George W. Bush* (New York: Simon & Schuster, 2000), p. 108.
2   Molly Ivins and Lou Dubose, *Shrub: The Short but Happy Political Life of George W. Bush* (New York: Random House, 2000), p. 179.
3   Mark Crispin Miller, *The Bush Dyslexicon: Observations of a National Disorder* (New York: W.W. Norton & Company, 2001), p. 259.
4   James H. Hatfield, *Fortunate Son: George W. Bush and the Making of an American President* (Brooklyn, New York: Soft Skull Press, 2002).
5   Gail Sheehy, 'The Accidental Candidate', *Vanity Fair*, October 2000: Frank Bruni, *Ambling into History: The Unlikely Odyssey of George W. Bush* (New York: HarperCollins, 2002). The thesis that Bush is merely the product of behind-the-scene handlers is developed in Lou Dubose et al., *Boy Genius: Karl Rove, the Brains Behind the Remarkable Political Triumph of George W. Bush* (New York: Public Affairs, 2003), and James Moore and Wayne Slater, *Bush's Brain: How Karl Rove Made George W. Bush Presidential* (New York: John Wiley & Sons, 2003).
6   Michael Moore, *Stupid White Men* (New York: Regan Books, 2001), p. 2.
7   Elizabeth Mitchell, *W: Revenge of the Bush Dynasty* (New York: Hyperion, 2000), p. 132. See also Kevin Phillips, *American Dynasty: Aristocracy, Fortune, and the Politics of Deceit in the House of Bush* (New York, Viking Press, 2004).
8   See David Korn, *The Lies of George W. Bush: Mastering the Politics of Deception* (New York: Crown Publishing Group, 2003); Molly Ivins and Lou Dubose, *Bushwhacked: Life in George W. Bush's America* (New York: Random House, 2003
9   David Frum, *The Right Man: The Surprise Presidency of George W. Bush* (New York: Random House, 2003), Bill Sammon, *Fighting Back: The War on Terrorism from Inside the Bush White House* (Washington, D.C.: Regnery Publishing, Inc., 2002); Stephen Mansfield, *The Faith of George W. Bush* (New York: Jeremy P. Tarcher/Penguin, 2003).
10 Bob Woodward, *Bush at War* (New York: Simon & Schuster), 2002.
11 Fred Greenstein (ed.) *The George W. Bush Presidency: An Early Assessment* (Baltimore: Johns Hopkins University Press, 2003); Gary L. Gregg II and Mark J. Rozell (eds.) *Considering the Bush Presidency* (New York: Oxford University Press, 2004); Ivo H. Daalder and James M. Lindsay, *America Unbound: The Bush Revolution in Foreign Policy* (Washington, D.C.: Brookings Institution Press, 2003); John Newhouse, *Imperial America: The Bush Assault on the World Order* (New York, Knopf, 2003).
12 Ron Suskind, *The Price of Loyalty: George W. Bush, The White House, and the Education of Paul O'Neill* (New York: Simon & Schuster, 2004; Richard A. Clarke, *Against All Enemies: Inside America's War on Terror* (New York: The Free Press, 2004).
13 Bob Woodward, *Plan of Attack* (New York: Simon & Schuster, 2004).
14 Bruni, p. 219.
15 Walter Isaacson and Jim Kelly, 'Bush Speaks', *Time Magazine*, December 2000-January 2001, p. 75.

Chapter 1

The Background and Personality
of George W. Bush

Both Bush and Texan

Born on July 6, 1946, George Walker Bush is the oldest son of a President and a member of one of America's most famous political families.[1] It is a family that traces its roots to the Pilgrims coming on the Mayflower and who are distantly related to the Queen of Great Britain. The Walker's and Bush's were banking and steel magnates whose members included personal advisers to Herbert Hoover and Franklin Roosevelt. Bush's mother, Barbara Pierce, is a descendant of President Franklin Pierce. The Walker and Bush families stand for business accomplishment, Republicanism, conservative family values and service to the country both in terms of the military and politics.[2] Given the wealth, fame, connections and strong social code of such a powerful family, Bush in his early years gained a perspective on life that was larger than his immediate nuclear family and his boyhood surroundings in Texas.

Just as important, and especially in the period from 1950 to 1959, when his father was developing his Zapata Oil Company, Bush lived in Midland, Texas as a fairly average middle-class kid. At that time his father was neither rich nor famous. From age four to thirteen, Bush lived a predominantly 'normal' life in Midland. It consisted of going to a public primary school, playing little league baseball, and roaming around with other middle class kids. While there would be periodic trips to family gatherings at estates in Maine, Florida, New York or South Carolina, George W. Bush equally enjoyed going to summer camp in East Texas. When Prescott Bush, his grandfather and a US Senator from Connecticut visited the family in Midland, a political world would open to the young Bush. During trips to visit his grandparents in New York, Bush would see something of the old patrician way of life, including the opportunity to visit professional baseball players at spring training camp, as one of his father's uncles was co-owner of the New York Mets. So it was back and forth between the 'bigness' of the 'Bush-Walker world' and the 'smallness' of day-to-day life in Midland.

Midland is not a typical American town, but was then a booming small city in a large rural environment, having grown in spurts along with the oil industry. Most of the families of friends, both for young Bush and his parents, were connected to the oil industry. Bush's Midland experience was thus a mixture of the egalitarianism of backyard barbeques, church gatherings and sports activities, *and* the risk-taking, adventurous culture of oil drilling. Bush saw his father 'making it on his own' out in Texas with the help of ready investors from the family and its network of friends.

Bush's father had chosen the oil industry in the Western Texas area called the Permian Basin in 1948. He had been offered a job in one of his uncle's oil equipment industries and had literally started at the bottom of the totem pole in West Texas. When he formed his first company, called Bush-Overbey with one of his neighbors in 1950, he tapped back into the family network to gather some $350,000 in investment money, thereby blending his own accomplishment with the strength of the Bush-Walker family connection. The elder Bush soon merged his company with Hugh and William Liedtke, who later formed Pennzoil, to create Zapata Oil. The Liedtke brothers helped him find some of the most consistently producing wells in the area. By 1959, Bush's father branched out to try his hand at offshore oil drilling and moved the family to Houston.

The move to Houston in 1959 was a major change for the thirteen-year old George. Now the world of private schools, upper-class tony neighborhoods, and big downtown businesses opened up. The young Bush had only two years to make the adjustment as more changes were in store. Both his father and grandfather had attended Phillips Academy in Andover, Massachusetts and had gone on to Yale University in New Haven, Connecticut. That path had served them well and it was natural for Bush's parents to consider the same opportunity for their son. Being barely two years in Houston, the move to Andover was a complete shock for Bush as he did not know 'Andover from Adam.'[3] In his campaign biography, he later remembered it as 'a hard transition.'[4] Some friends thought he had done something terrible to be sent away to a school they jokingly nicknamed, 'Bendover.' It is of note that none of Bush's younger brothers (Jeb, Neil and Marvin) went to Andover after him. Perhaps, Bush's parents belatedly felt the fit between their Texas kids and Andover was not a good one.

The tenure at Andover and then Yale made him a stronger Texan at heart. Aside from his regular visits home, he helped his father campaign in Texas for a seat in the US Senate in 1964, in which the elder Bush lost to the Democrat Ralph Yarborough. He later helped him run successfully for the US House of Representatives in a Houston district in 1966 and again in 1968. His summer work was usually back in Texas and he dated Cathryn Wolfman in Houston in his last years at Yale.

After graduating from Yale in 1968, it was no surprise that Bush chose the Texas Air National Guard as his way to avoid being sent as an infantryman to Vietnam. It required a two-year full time and a four-year part time commitment. But for Bush it was a win-win situation: First, going back to Texas and becoming a pilot, as his father had been during World War II, was high on his wish list. Second, the six-year commitment was not a problem as Bush was unclear about what he wanted to do. Although he was repulsed by the 'Sixties Generation' and the counterculture movement his peers started, George W. was a member of the Baby Boomers. He did not rebel against the rigid discipline and academic demands of Andover, but he also did not get as much 'structure' out of it as had his father.

The next major change in Bush's early life came in 1970 when his father lost his second try at the US Senate to Lloyd Bentsen. Richard Nixon, who had pushed the elder Bush to run, then appointed him US Ambassador to the United Nations. That effectively ended the Bush parental home in Houston as the home base for George. After having been in and out of Texas on various training programs with the National Guard, he now was on his own in Houston. He moved into a large rental complex called the Chateaux Dijon, and for the next three years, he alternated between National Guard duty, short-lived jobs and working on election campaigns. Throughout, Bush was involved in a rambunctious social life with lots of parties, social drinking and girlfriends. These so-called 'nomadic'[5] years did not end until he enrolled in Harvard's Business School in September 1973.

His Harvard years again reinforced his identity as a Texan, both culturally and politically: he wore his bomber jacket and cowboy boots and spit tobacco into a Styrofoam cup. He stayed away from campus politics as he had done at Yale. In his last year at Harvard in 1975, he met up with his old Midland friend, Joe O'Neill, and seeing that oil prices had sky-rocketed after the 1973 Arab oil embargo, set out with the leftover $13,000 from his education fund to start in the oil business for himself. In the following eleven years, Bush reaffirmed his old Midland identity. He blended back into his hometown with some of his old friends, like O'Neill, with some old business friends of his father who were also eager to help him, and with the new generation of oil businessmen, such as Don Evans who later became CEO of Tom Brown Inc. Bush set up his own company and then pursued the Bush-Walker family connections to find investors, adding to this list the contacts he had made at Andover, Yale and Harvard.

After two years in Midland, George married Laura Jane Welch, the daughter of a developer and contractor, who had also grown up in Midland. Although they did not remember each other, they had been in the same junior high school, and had even lived in the same housing complex in Houston in 1970. Laura worked in Austin as a school librarian and would from time to time visit her parents and friends in Midland. They knew of each other as Laura's friend Jan Donnelly had married George's friend Joe O'Neill, but they had not actually met, and at first Laura was reluctant to do so. It was the O'Neill's that finally got them together on the last weekend of July in 1977. They were both 31 and were married three months later.

Most descriptions of Laura focus on how different she is in temperament and background to George W. Bush. 'George is always bouncing off the wall,' observed Anne Johnson, whose husband Clay had gone to school with him, 'and Laura is so quiet.'[6] An only child, she was very close to her parents and always focused. She admired her funny outgoing dad, Harold Welch, and in 1977 found the same boisterous character in Bush. The quiet girl was traumatized by the accidental death of one of her friends, Mike Douglas, when she ran a stop sign in November 1963 and hit his car. It was not till 1998 that she shared this accident with her daughters, fearing they may hear it in the media during Bush's upcoming campaign for president. Much has been written about Laura's calming influence on her husband, but her presence also served to deepen Bush's attachment to Midland and its values as they shared a hometown and childhood experience. Their twin daughters Barbara and Jenna, who were born on November 25, 1981, spent their early years in Midland, not leaving until 1986 when Harken Oil bought out Bush's third oil company, Spectrum 7. As a director on Harken's Board, George worked out of its Dallas office. Like his earlier transition to Houston when he was 13, Bush moved to a well-to-do area in the North part of the city. He was not to remain there long as Bush joined his father's 1988 presidential campaign and moved the family to Washington, D.C., for a few years.

Bush's final return to Texas also was his most significant. He had played a key role in his father's presidential campaign and could have been tempted to stay in Washington, perhaps as a 'loyalty enforcer' in the White House. Instead, after this important piece of 'family business,' George W. returned to make Dallas his home. As one of the managing partners in the Arlington-based Texas Rangers, he sealed his Texas identity once and for all.

The difference between the father and son is crucial. His father was and is a Bush who drew upon the opportunities offered by Texas as he pursued his life career in business and politics. But George W. Bush was and is a Texan who draws upon the opportunities offered from being a Bush.

Both Fun and Drive

There is a common theory in the Bush biographies that George became the family clown in order to cheer up his mother after the death of his three-year old sister Robin in 1953 when he was only seven.[7] Robin died after a short illness with leukemia and though the young George was at first shocked his parents had not told him, the theory goes, he soon turned to comfort his mother as his father was often gone on business. The whole thing is an exaggeration: Robin's death did not form Bush's character, nor did he become more serious after the family got over mourning Robin. George W. Bush was born with a very sunny outlook on life, a propensity for frivolity, a healthy dose of sarcasm, and a big mouth. The string of nicknames given to him in his lifetime such as 'The Lip, Bushman, and Bombastic Bushkin,' tell the tale.

A few Bush family habits have acted as fuel for Bush's outgoing and outspoken temperament. The family is fiercely competitive and social, always interacting in games or sports, kidding around with each other, and invariably making new friends and maintaining old contacts. These friends and contacts, of course, are also part of the extended network of business partners and political supporters. So Bush's outgoing people-friendly personality was given unprecedented practice by the large number of people he encountered; he learned as a youngster to shake everyone's hand in the room as he came in and again when he left. He was taught by his father to keep little notes on people, to remember their names and the things discussed. For the young Bush it was a natural outlet as he had honed his memory skills on baseball names and statistics. He wrote to the baseball 'stars' for signatures, including cheery notes, return envelopes and stamps.

Bush became cheerleader and chief prankster at Andover, 'lifting the spirits of his school.'[8] He took the informal pick-up stickball game and fashioned it into a league with himself as Commissioner. He made legions of friends and acquaintances, and showed an early tendency to be inclusive even bringing 'nerd' kids into the stickball game. Later at Yale, he would include non-Whites with no trace of effort. It is no surprise that he became one of the most liked persons in the academy making life-long friends such as Clay Johnson who accompanied him to the White House. Alongside the fun, there was strict discipline at the school and the days were filled with activities from early morning until lights out. Bush did have to work on his academics, especially his English, in order to keep second or third class standing. A discipline he had always struggled with, his mother helped him with it during the years he attended Kinkaid private school. Math was less of a problem and history was George's favorite. The history of leaders and of military affairs was especially dear to him. He would later share this interest with his close political adviser, Karl Rove, with Vice President Dick Cheney and with other influential advisers such as Paul Wolfowitz, the Deputy Secretary of Defense.

At Yale, the combination of Bush's outgoing personality and his sophisticated people skills began to take on a professional quality. At his induction to the Delta Kappa Epsilon, he alone could name all fifty people in the room. He had come to campus and started at once meeting and entertaining people. By the time he graduated, Clay Johnson estimated Bush knew a thousand people.[9] It was no surprise that Bush was invited to join the Skulls and Bones society, an old elitist club that sought lifelong loyalty and friendship among the selected few who were sworn to secrecy.

With the discipline of Andover gone, Bush's marks at Yale did not improve and his social life began to take up a large amount of his time and energy. Bush was certainly smart enough, though not a bookworm, and his Scholastic Aptitude Test scores were more than respectable. When Bush's intelligence became an issue in the 2000 campaign, these scores were released and showed him trailing Albert Gore by a small margin, but beating Bill Bradley. His marks at Yale were better than John McCain's at West Point military academy. Keeping a C-plus average at Yale required work, but he never failed a course. The larger point is that Bush was not interested enough to work harder on his academics, writing his papers at the last minute. During this period, he showed no interest in issue politics and certainly felt no sympathy for the rising tide against the traditional values that Bush had grown up with. He had a strong dislike for anti-Vietnam rallies which began at Yale in the last two years he was there. George hated the mentality that blamed the elite for all social ills and the social 'heaviness' that started to flourish on campuses.[10] Bush's personal experience with that part of the Sixties Generation would have a major impact on his thinking later in life as he rediscovered the basic values of individual responsibility and faith, which in turn helped him embrace the concept of compassionate conservatism.

George W. Bush moved from the undisciplined party life of Yale into two years of officer training and combat crew training with the Texas Air National Guard. When he wrote the admissions test in the spring of 1968, he scored high on leadership but very low on pilot aptitude. Bush got into the National Guard because of his last name, just as the sons of Lloyd Bentsen, Jim Tower, and several greats of the Dallas Cowboys. Some biographers have tried to delve into whether the elder Bush pulled specific strings to get his son in.[11] It is not obvious that his father even had to do so as the admitting officer, Colonel Walter Staudt was eager to have the son on board and saw to it that he was promoted early.

The interesting angle of this story is that Bush turned out to be a very good pilot, impressing his officers and peers alike. He liked the discipline and training and although he looked like another spoiled son of a famous father coming in on his last name, he won over the people he worked with. They saw him as a real person, unpretentious and a lot of fun to be with, and that he could compete with them in flying fighter jets. One of his performance reports stated that Bush was 'a top notch fighter interceptor pilot.'[12] In the National Guard one can see the beginnings of George W. Bush being underestimated the rest of his life. People jump to conclusions upon seeing his name, but then as he begins to perform, they realize he can beat them at their own game, a situation that rival politicians often found out too late.

Having a good time and being ambitious have never been opposites to Bush, but in the late 1960s and early 1970s he experienced some disappointments. His partying took a lot of his time and energy. Stephen Mansfield believes George suffered from 'boredom, aimlessness, and lack of purpose.'[13] That may be too stark a view as he continued to enjoy the party life, yet, the fun side lost some of its checks and balances and the disappointments followed each other.

Bush had been dating Cathryn Wolfman in his last year at Yale and they became engaged during the Christmas break in 1966, when George was only twenty years old. The relationship drifted apart and in 1968, Wolfman broke it off and it clearly hurt him. Some inferred that Bush's parents did not want him to marry a stepdaughter of a Jewish man, but the charge simply does not reflect the family.[14] If so, his parents would have intervened before he was engaged but the Bush family has no record of racial or religious intolerance. Quite the opposite is true, for while still a child in Midland, he was chided by his mother for using racial slurs. Even partisan detractors such as Paul Begala and Molly Ivins admit that there is no racist bone in Bush's body.[15] Moreover, his parents had no problem with Jeb, their second son, marrying a Roman Catholic girl from Mexico. Christopher Andersen interviewed Cathryn Wolfman and she plainly told him, 'Our relationship gradually died.'[16]

Bush later dated Christina Cassini, daughter of Jackie Kennedy's designer and film star Gene Tierney, but he was not serious about building a relationship. In fact, George never turned serious about a relationship until he met Laura in 1977. He remained unsettled, experiencing yet another disappointment in 1970 when the University of Texas turned down his application to enter law school. It is doubtful Bush would have made a good lawyer and the decision to apply was made quickly, but it was another closed door.

When George finished his basic training at the Texas Air National Guard, he spent two months assisting Edward Gurney's 1968 election campaign in Florida. This was Bush's fifth experience in a political campaign, after volunteering in all four of his father's campaigns. Bush also alternated between Guard duties and helping his father in his second bid to get a Senate seat in 1970, taking his father's loss pretty hard. After the race, Bush took a job offer his father had arranged with Stratford, an agricultural company based in Houston, and began as a management trainee. Again, he entered as the son of a friend of the boss, but once on the job, he became well liked and very good at his work. Had he stayed, he would have undoubtedly risen to the top fast, but he disliked the 'coat-and-tie' job and quit after nine months. After Stratford, George took on a full-time paid position as political director for Winton M. Blount's US Senate campaign in Alabama. Blount also lost.

Shortly after the November 1972 election, the now infamous incident took place when a half-drunk George returned after some partying with his younger brother Marvin with a garbage can stuck under the car, to his parents place in Washington,

D.C. As wise parents, they never aired dirty laundry, but they were concerned about their elder son's lack of direction. Yet, even during that difficult time, Bush was not completely adrift. He had applied to Harvard's MBA program and was accepted. His parent's concern about his lifestyle now prompted his father to find him a different type of job till he could start at Harvard. Former Houston Oilers' player John White had set up an inner-city program called 'Project PULL' (Professionals United for Leadership League) where famous players helped youths escape from poverty and crime. Bush became dearly liked by the kids and the other participants, and for the first time, he saw the urban ghetto up close as he participated in a community-based initiative to fight poverty and helplessness. Community and faith-based initiatives later featured prominently on George's list of social programs to promote.

In an effort to boost his upcoming biography of George W. Bush, which in essence was a 'bland, nice clip job' of the much better volume produced by Bill Minutaglio a year earlier, James Hatfield penned an afterword in which he accused Bush of being arrested for possessing cocaine.[17] Then, according to Hatfield, George's father personally intervened to sway the judge in the case to give his son community duty instead.[18] In 2003, Mark Schone conclusively showed that Hatfield was a con artist whose unnamed sources for his cocaine allegation turned out to be the fantastically implausible Karl Rove and Clay Johnson. Schone also proved that Hatfield could not have met with Rove in East Texas on the dates stated, as Rove was with Bush in California and Florida. St. Martin's press wisely dropped the book. Despite Hatfield and his second publisher, Sander Hicks' best attempts at peddling a Bush conspiracy against them, Hatfield took his own life in 2001 as the law was once again closing in on the 'scam artist,' this time for massive credit card fraud.[19]

Most biographers believe the issue that brought George W. Bush to PULL was alcohol use and that his father wanted him to see the other side of life as a warning.[20] None of Bush's party friends have corroborated the accusation of drug use. Bush openly joked with reporters in the 1990s about the cocaine use allegations, not a sign of someone trying to hide things.[21] There have been no other references to drug use before or after PULL while alcohol remained a sensitive issue until he quit cold turkey in 1986. His arrest and fine for driving under the influence in 1976 in Maine was made public just days before the November 2000 election.

When Bush ran for governor of Texas in 1994 he devised a strategy of dealing with his nomadic years. The first step was to admit that when he was young he at times acted irresponsibly. The second point was that he had learned from those mistakes and that he had matured (coinciding roughly with his marriage in 1977) and that he had since acted responsibly. The third part was that he would not 'inventory' all he had done nor answer the allegations or rumors that would inevitably be raised.[22] Given that Bush's campaign of values would obviously contrast with some of the choices of his nomadic years, this was a sensible strategy. Though it is better to have a 'clean youth,' the next best thing is to have learned from these errors and to lead a clean adult life. The downside of saying 'maybe I did, maybe I didn't' is that people keep wondering what he is trying to hide.

Both Failure and Success

With Harvard's MBA in his pocket, Bush's future direction was now set in business. The next decade in Midland was much more trying than Bush could have imagined. That he would go back to Texas was a given, that he went into oil in Midland rather than into business in Houston was largely driven by his connecting with old friends, the fact that oil prices were over $30 a barrel, and his adventurous, risk-taking personality streak. He spent about two years learning the ropes as a landman, finding and negotiating leases.

It is a Bush-Walker family tradition to invest in a member's business venture, but there is no custom to pay for anyone's keep. George had no money whatsoever and lived in an apartment above a garage, which his friend Charlie Younger called a 'disaster area, a toxic waste dump.'[23] He was notorious for bumming clothes, his cars were old and battered, and his friend's wife, Susie Evans, often did his laundry. He was cheap and lived cheap. Money for its own sake has never held a grip on Bush and he never lived like a rich young man. When he became a millionaire later on, he stayed with simple tastes.

Bush's first oil company, called Arbusto, began operations in 1979. George's outgoing personality, the family connections and his own network of Yale friends brought in the start-up investment. Given the price of oil, Bush had about five good years to make money but only about half of his wells produced oil, and none were gushers. Returns ranged from average to poor. Bush structured his company so that his share of cash returns combined with various fees slowly built him a net worth, but his investors were lucky to get 20 cents on the dollar. Most of them benefited, of course, from very high rates of tax write offs to cushion the blow. Just before George went public with his reshaped company in early 1982, now called Bush Exploration, a close associate of James Baker, then the Chief of Staff in the White House where George W.'s father was Vice President, made a one million dollar investment in the company. Bush raised more money from private investors than when Bush Exploration went public.

The mid 1980s saw oil fall below $10 dollars per barrel. Some, like Don Evan's Tom Brown Co. made it, but many companies went under. In 1982, Bill DeWitt and Paul Rea's company, Spectrum 7, bought out Bush Exploration because George needed the cash badly and DeWitt, son of the owner of the Cincinnati Reds and a friend of the Bush family, wanted a local manager and just as importantly, a company representative who could drum up investment. Thus DeWitt and Rea were helping themselves as much as they were helping Bush. Bush became CEO, Rea became the President. For Bush's net worth and the oil leases his company had, he received stock in Spectrum 7. Rea had the experience in the geology of oil drilling, and Bush brought in the investment. The Bush name opened the doors and Bush's attractive personality and people skills won over investors. Cheerleading, sales, and campaigning for political office are all a function of selling yourself. This was George W. Bush's real specialty, but meager wells and low prices doomed Spectrum 7.

Harken Oil took over the company in 1986. Between the original Spectrum 7 and Bush Exploration there were assets that would be profitable if the oil price rose again. Many biographers concluded Harken came to rescue the son of the Vice President.

Harken traded one of its shares for five Spectrum 7 shares. Bush Exploration, of which George was 80 per cent owner, had accumulated some $600,000 in cash distributions and fees in 1984 when Spectrum 7 took over. At that time, Bush received a little over 16 per cent of the Spectrum stock which in 1986 he exchanged for $312,000 worth of Harken stock and a salary as a board member. Bush had slipped from owner to CEO to board member and his oil days were effectively over.

It was DeWitt who informed Bush just before the November 1988 elections that Eddie Chiles wanted to sell the Texas Rangers, for Chiles also was hurting from the oil slump. Would George be interested in putting together an investor group to buy the team? The baseball team had lost consistently since it moved from Washington decades earlier and it needed a new stadium to have any chance at all. It was arguably as risky an investment as drilling for oil, but Bush borrowed $500,000 against the collateral of his Harken stock to invest a little over $600,000 (1.8 per cent share) in the new team. Bush became the linchpin of the entire deal, putting together a group of investors that raised most of the funds to buy the $75 million team. His Yale friend, Roland Betts, was a big player in this group. Betts – a wealthy movie producer – risked his money to invest in his friend's business. When the Rangers sold for $250 million in 1998, it turned out that Bush had made Betts a fortune. What Bush lacked were enough investors from Texas. Baseball Commissioner Peter Ueberroth convinced the Texas millionaire Richard Rainmaker to join the group, an agreement that included the condition that Rainmaker's partner, Rusty Rose, would co-manage the team with Bush.

Naturally, the question has been raised whether supporters of Bush's father were making investments in his son's companies to curry favor, or even to help the son avert the embarrassment of bankruptcy. Some allege that his father's friends kept Bush afloat in the 1980s, but Bush's business dealings were significantly more complex. Clearly he drew on his father's and his own network of friends to get investors: Harken bailed out Spectrum 7 partially because it had some $4 million dollars in assets should the oil price recover and partially because it would not hurt to have the Vice President's son on its board. Soon after, the government of Bahrain awarded Harken the rights to drill for oil off its coast. It was unusual for such a small company to win such a bid. Bush knew the 'bad political fallout' that would follow and spoke to the *Dallas Morning News* indicating he had counseled Harken not to proceed, but Harken did anyways, and years later the wells turned out to be dry.[24]

In 1989, Bush borrowed $500,000 against his Harken stock to buy into the Texas Rangers. He sold his stock in June 1990 for some $800,000, only to see Harken's stock prices fall by nearly 50 per cent a few months later. In the 1994 campaign, reporters questioned whether Bush had filed that transaction with the Securities and Exchange Commission. Bush said he had, but that the SEC lost his papers. In his defense he proved that he did file his intent to sell stock in June 1990. A subsequent SEC investigation concluded that there was no case for wrongdoing. Indeed, it seemed more a case of sloppiness than wrongdoing: George's other stock transactions also showed signs of late filing. His acquisition of Harken stock in 1986 was not reported until half a year later, and again, some extra stock he bought in June 1989, was not reported until September of that year.[25] Bush, who was on the finance committee of Harken, was also accused of insider trading. Although he has said he did not know the company would report such a great loss ($25 million), those who accuse Bush of pulling out of a sinking ship should keep in mind that by June 1991 Harken stock recovered above its June 1990 value. When corporate scandals shook the nation in the spring of 2002, opposition researchers in the Democratic National Committee tried to give the Harken story new legs, but there were no new facts. George W. Bush had a letter from the Securities and Exchange Commission stating that after preliminary examination, they found no cause to launch an investigation.

Bush's business career shows that while he did not succeed at first as an oilman, he did prosper in the baseball business. Throughout, he showed that he knew how to wheel and deal to increase his own net worth. He also showed great talent in developing a management team. Rusty Rose led the financial side of the company, while Tom Schriever ran the baseball side. George concentrated on representing the team to the public and the players to the owners. He played both the inside game of setting a vision for the team and creating a team spirit, and the outside game of selling the team and the new ballpark to the public.

With the Texas Rangers, Bush made his own name as a successful Texas businessman. Not only was he pivotal in turning the team around (from $28 million in yearly revenues to over $100 million in the mid-1990s), but he also led the project to build the widely praised Ballpark in Arlington. He made some $15 million when the team was sold in 1998. During his years at the Texas Rangers, Bush was gathering both business and political capital at the same time. When his father retired from politics in 1992, the lights for George W. Bush to pursue his first love, politics, turned green.

Both Politics and Values

Bush learned his politics, that is the strategy and the nuts and bolts of the campaign long before he was interested in values and issues. Many biographers stress that in his personal and business life, George was a late bloomer.[26] He was no late bloomer in politics as the political side of Bush's skills and experience has developed consistently since he was a young man. Bush gathered his early political experience almost entirely through the prism of the political campaign. As most early campaigns Bush worked for lost, they became his school of hard knocks. In this part of his life there was no room for complacency nor the idea that his last name would do the trick.

During the 1964 campaign for the US Senate, Bush's father asked his 18-year-old son to write briefing books on some of Texas's 254 counties. The young Bush also joined many campaign events, often organizing the cheerleading that accompanied his father's appearances. He was there to hang up posters, hand out leaflets, and speak to the media. In the 1970 campaign, George was stumping effectively as his father's surrogate. When working for Gurney in 1968, he started at the bottom again, driving the candidate and planning the mundane logistics of the campaign. In 1972, when Bush became the political director of Blount's race, he was part of all the major decisions of that race, which included analyzing polling data, and planning lines of attack and defense.

When his father served as Republican National Committee Chair in the mid-1970s, George W. Bush met Karl Rove who was then working with the RNC as president of the College Republicans, and later as personal assistant to his father. Lee Atwater, who in the 1980s would become the most famous Republican strategist, had helped Rove win that elected position. Bush bonded with both Atwater and Rove, watching them up close and in doing so, he learned the art of the campaign from the very best.

Just when Bush was ready to get his company, Arbusto, into drilling in 1977, his father's old friend, Jimmy Allison, the owner of the *Midland Reporter-Telegram,* suggested that he run in the Congressional seat vacated by a long-term Democrat in the area. If ever there was a test of what George really was in his heart of hearts, a politician or a businessman, it was then. An old Bush family rule has it that you need to be financially secure before you run for political office. Prescott Bush and George Herbert Walker Bush had both followed the rule.

George W. Bush broke the family tradition and ran for the US House seat. His father had waited till Prescott retired, but Bush ran when his own father was still in his political prime. It was a case of strong ambition and a case of Bush thinking he had enough campaign experience to try it on his own. Karl Rove, who had started a direct mailing business in Houston and was working on the elder Bush's presidential political action committee, became also an adviser to the younger Bush's campaign. George asked Don Evans to be his campaign finance chair, and Bush's brother Neil came to join the campaign full time. George, Rove and Evans worked the family network and the GOP client list developed by Rove to raise some $400,000 for Bush's campaign, a substantial amount in the 1970s. Except for a short honeymoon, Bush and Laura campaigned the entire first year of their marriage. The interesting thing is how well Bush did. He beat Jim Reece in the Republican primary who was supported by Ronald Reagan's organization, and he lost to the Democratic Texas State Senator, Kent Hance, by only seven points. As his cousin John Ellis put it, he learned by painful experience the family lesson of needing 'a fire wall.'[27] He had no seat and no money. Without establishing his own name and reputation, it would be hard to get elected in Texas.

George W. Bush, only 32 years old, had now worked in six political races and ran in one himself. That record alone shows how fascinated he was with the political campaign. He learned three things in the race against Hance. Many biographers stress only one side of Bush's heritage, namely the side by which George profits from his name and connection, but at several times in Bush's Texas life, the name actually made things more difficult. Hance had defined him as an East Coast Yankee from elite schools who could not possibly understand Texas. It was one thing for Ralph Yarborough and Lloyd Bentsen to do this to George's father who came to Texas in his twenties and who kept his Yankee accent, it was a stretch to do it to Bush. But Hance did just that, and Bush failed to define himself or to put Hance on the defensive. In 1999, Bush wrote that he learned from that instance that 'when someone attacks your integrity, you have to respond.'[28] Second, incredible as it sounds today, Bush concentrated on policy issues. Hance spoke in folksy simple language while George actually sounded more like a policy wonk. Third, when Hance pulled a dirty trick, notifying church members that the Bush campaign was planning to serve free beer at a rally on a local campus, George did not counter attack though he was given the opposition research to do so. Hance, he was told, owned the land on which a well-know pub operated.

George W. Bush played an active role in helping his father win the Iowa Caucuses in 1980, but this was also the take-off time for Arbusto. He was really squeezed for time and when Reagan took the lead, he backed off. His top political strategy experience came in 1988. The story goes that George and some of his brothers challenged Lee Atwater in 1987 to prove he was going to work for their father without divided loyalties.[29] Atwater's response to Bush was that he should come and watch him. What the anecdote hides is that both men knew and respected each other's political instincts. Soon they complemented each other in the campaign.

Those who did not know Bush soon learned the now familiar lesson – this was not a spoiled son who was there only because of his last name. Mary Matalin, a political aide to Bush's father and who would later serve under George W. Bush as communication's director for Vice President Cheney, described George as 'a wickedly confident authority figure, bold about internal and external strategy.'[30] At the start of the race, Massachusetts's governor Michael Dukakis was twenty points ahead. Bush was involved in all aspects of the race, and with Atwater, methodically destroyed Michael Dukakis. George kept close contact with the Christian conservative wing of the Republican Party, often substituting directly for his father. A few years earlier, he had renounced his drinking and confessed that he had renewed his Christian commitment. Bush's personal faith and his more conservative instincts made him a much better interlocutor with the Evangelical branch of the party than his father. George W. played very tough with the media. The lesson of defending yourself when under attack was now a part of his fiber. He aggressively counterattacked an attempt by *Newsweek* to label his father as a 'wimp' and put an end to the false rumor that his father had had an affair with one of his secretaries.

After his father won the election, George stayed on briefly to head the so-called 'Scrub team,' which evaluated key appointments to the new Bush administration on the basis of their loyalty to his father. Bush pleaded with his father to appoint Atwater as Republican National Chair. It may be that he simply pleaded for his loyal friend, but he also knew about Atwater's next mission. Atwater wanted to make the GOP 'the dominant political party of 2000.'[31] If most State Capitals became Republican, a future GOP presidential candidate would have a solid foundation to mount a race.

Bush's role in his father's last campaign in 1992 was limited by the fact that he could not leave the Texas Rangers for more than a few days at a time. It was an experience filled with frustration as Bush tried to fire up a lackluster political team that did not get traction until James Baker belatedly took control. Bush, who was among the first to see the threat of Ross Perot, ended up doing most of his campaigning in Texas as a surrogate for his father.

While Bush honed his political campaign skills all his life, his attachment to core values emerged only in the mid 1980s. His values and how they underlay his vision for a compassionate conservative culture are still a controversial part of his politics and personality. Some biographical accounts picture Bush as a prodigal son who was driven by his failing oil companies and excessive drinking to the brink of marital breakup, and who at the last moment was rescued by a religious conversion.[32] Others argue that Bush never personally connected to deep Christian beliefs, but that he uses these for pure political exploitation.[33] In the latter argument, George married Laura just before his Congressional race in order to be a 'family-man' candidate.[34] Then he turned religious in order to manipulate the Christian Right during his father's presidential race in 1988.

The notion that his religious values are only political is baseless, and frankly ridiculous. If so, he would have tripped up on his hypocrisy long ago. He did change in the mid-1980s and became a more conservative Christian than his parents, but he did not change as much as the evangelical doctrine of 'being born' again implies. Rather, the key to understanding George W. Bush's values and his vision is to know the traditional values in which he grew up, for he never rejected those, *and* how he rededicated himself to them in the mid-1980s, but now as a Texan in a more conservative Christian surrounding.

Bush grew up in Midland and Houston in the midst of the traditional, 1950s-like values of 'God, family and country.' Coming from Episcopalian roots, his parents joined the next closest thing in Midland, the Presbyterian Church. Bush grew up in mainline Protestant teaching and practice, with a doctrine that was orthodox, but not fundamentalist or Evangelical. The necessity of 'being born again' was not part of the life of the church. The family would go to church almost every Sunday, but not twice. Active in church and social affairs, the Bush family would practice charity and support various social causes, but it was not part of the movement that opposed abortion, sought to restore public prayer in schools, or maintain the King James Version of the Bible.

Even in his so-called nomadic years, George did not rebel against any of these values. His party life ostensibly contradicted them, but it was not a result of rejection. Even in his first years of marriage when his language could be rough, Bush would still somehow teach Sunday school. Gradually, through marriage, parenthood, failures in business, and finding emptiness in social binging, Bush became more serious and more searching.

Whenever interviewers try to get Bush to say that he is a born-again Christian, he dodges the question.[35] He tells them he is a sinner and that he has needed redemption, explaining that faith is a walk, not just a decision. There are two explanations for his caution with the term 'born again.' The first answer is that Bush avoids the label 'Evangelical' and the implication of 'being born again' for obvious political reasons. Though conservative and fundamentalist Christians are far from a monolithic bloc, the term 'Evangelical' has taken on the meaning of a political label. To be identified with this segment of the population means inviting the scorn of secular people, especially in the media, and the suspicion of other religious people. Mainstream American culture has made the term 'born again' a political liability. Bush knows he can appeal to the Evangelical movement in other ways and therefore can advance some of their values, which are also his values without the political baggage.

The second reason is that despite his fateful meeting with Billy Graham in July 1985 in which Graham asked him 'if he was right with God,'[36] and Bush's subsequent attendance at Community Bible Study in Midland with his friends such as Don Evans, Bush has not turned from his mainline protestant views, but has rather rediscovered them in a personal and powerful way. So Bush is not a born-again Christian who can be easily slotted into the Evangelical camp, but he shares enough Biblical doctrine, socially conservative values, and personal witness with them to fade in and out with the fundamentalist way of life. This explains why Evangelical leaders are sometimes enthralled with him, while at other times they are appalled. Pat Robertson supported Bush in the 2000 campaign, but was offended by Bush's warm embrace of Islam after September 11. James Dobson, the founder of Focus on the Family, has been very reluctant about Bush, pushing him to be more outspoken against abortion, while Gary Bauer, the Christian family activist, ran against Bush in the 1999 primaries. If Bush were a fundamentalist, he could not have cemented such close ties with religiously active Roman Catholics. He would have been badly torn to reach out with religious equanimity to the Muslim faith after the attacks of September 11, 2001 and he would have frowned upon Karen Hughes, his close confidante, being an elder in her church.

Nevertheless, Bush is a conservative Christian. His faith is not merely a label or a nominal identity and certainly not a political ploy. Likely, his faith influenced his decision to stop drinking. Alcohol was crowding his energy and the deliverance from it in 1986 – when he quit cold turkey – meant a powerful liberation. A new inner fire gave him clarity and purpose as never before and family fidelity, already a strong value, took on new meaning. To Bush, adultery is sin. Personal prayer and God's grace are real. He found the power of prayer in the 1980s and still lives by it today. There is prayer before meals and cabinet meetings and he asks people to pray for him. The Bible is not just some ceremonial book to be opened at special occasions but rather his first reading in the morning. At times, he quotes Bible verses to his staff. He asks Mike Gerson, his speechwriter, and a graduate of Wheaton College, to sprinkle Biblical and hymnal fragments in his speeches. They are not simply political crumbs to the Evangelicals; they are pieces of Bush's own identity. Every Sunday, he begins the day by worshipping at the small chapel in Camp David. Bush's church in Dallas was active in faith-based help to prisoners, the homeless and drug abusers. As governor, he helped out Teen Challenge when regulators tried to shut it down.

There is one more layer of complexity to Bush's Christianity. As a private individual, he holds close to the belief that salvation is only in Christ, but as a public person, as a politician, Bush believes that all faiths should receive equal status and treatment. Every serious Christian in public life struggles with this tension, but Bush is not a 'Christian' president in the sense of putting his personal witness role ahead of his political role. He believes all faiths should be permitted to act freely alongside secular viewpoints. As a political man of faith he shares public policy goals with other faiths because he shares their basic values. His personal Christianity makes no separation and does not favor one religious persuasion over another or one Christian denomination over another. His faith-based value perspective never clashes with other religions, but does clash at times with secular Liberalism. Even then, the fight is waged positively, showing a better way or leading by example. Bush is not anti-secular, but wants faith to enjoy equal rights. John Ashcroft, a more conservative Christian than Bush, has just as much right to be Attorney General as an agnostic. Bush's religious values do not war with his optimistic, inclusive and people-friendly approach. He believes in the power of positive examples and avoids sounding like a scold.

Both New and Prepared

When George W. Bush ran for Governor of Texas in 1994, he looked like a novice, but he was in fact well prepared. He had the people skills, the political campaign expertise and a handful of basic values all in place. Bush was now ready to combine the strength of all his Bush family experience with his own Texan identity and Texas Rangers accomplishment, and a fine-tuned campaign machine.

Bush integrated the lessons of his own defeat of 1978 and his father's defeat in 1992 to Bill Clinton with the lesson of victory he and Atwater had eked out in 1988. Seeing that Ann Richards was personally popular but weak on basic public values, Bush and Rove, who was now in charge of political strategy, concocted a rigid issue-discipline with equally rigid message control. First came a series of tutoring sessions where Bush was given the information to apply his basic values to the issues. Then, with laser-like focus he challenged Richards' approach to education, juvenile justice, tort reform, and welfare reform. The Bush team called them the 'four food groups.'[37] When Richards insulted Bush by calling him a 'shrub'[38] and referred to him before a large teachers' rally as 'some jerk,' Bush and Rove understood that Richards was not engaged in a calculated offensive, but was losing her discipline. So Bush kept the high road, referring to Richards as 'governor,' while relentlessly hammering on her record.

The Richards' campaign found out that belittling Bush as a person or his accomplishments in life was not an effective counter strategy because he connects so well with people. When people see and hear him, they like what they see and do not buy the negative picture about him. Bush combined his popular appeal with a disciplined repetition of a handful of basic public policy issues defined in terms of values. Bush is best in what is called retail politics. He can meet and greet, charm and joke with large numbers of people day after day. The attractive force of his personality coupled with what Lee Atwater called 'wedge issues' enforced the message. Bush beat Richards by 10 points.

After his surprise victory, it came as a second surprise to most political observers that Bush had a governing strategy ready to implement. He came to the Governor's Mansion far better prepared than was generally understood. In office, Bush turned his retail-politics charm into an inside game of personal relations and legislative compromise. He was able to take the 'big-vision' issues of the campaign and push them at lowest-common denominator level through the legislature. To lubricate this process, Bush practiced personal friendship, trust, and loyalty that crossed party lines. Bush's patient investment in establishing a personal friendship with the Democratic Lieutenant Governor and Leader of the Texas Senate, Bob Bullock, enabled him to turn a lot of his values into Texas law.

Bush was very successful in the 1995 legislative session, advancing on all his four core areas, but in 1997, he tried his hand at tax reform and achieved a stalemate. He could not get a new tax on professional businesses past the legislators. 'Getting things done' became the basis for Bush's second run for Texas Governor in 1998. In that campaign, he linked his personal likeability to his legislative achievements in education, justice and tort reform. Bush beat Democratic contender Gary Mauro by a 2-1 margin, including large victories among the female and Hispanic vote. By 1997 it was clear to many that he would be the front runner candidate for the White House.

His Own Man

By the time George W. Bush ran for governor in 1994, he was a complicated and independent political person with three invaluable leadership traits that explain his meteoric rise in Texas and in national politics. First, Bush emerged as a man with 'energetic charm and a common touch,' which gives him a tremendous capacity to relate to people.[39] Bush holds little appeal for the intelligentsia and the chattering class as his connection is with the common people. Bush has taken his people skills and developed them simultaneously at two levels: he uses them to sell himself to the outside – as he did with oil investors and Texas Ranger fans – and to build a team around him on the inside. Bush's father was able to set up a collegial White House team that served him well, but he could not sell himself to the people. Reagan had a strong rapport with the people, but did not have the inside skills to build a loyal and highly competent team around him after James Baker, Edwin Meese and Mike Deaver disbanded the original troika.[40] Bush combined both skills in Texas and would later be successful in bringing them with him to Washington.

George W. Bush's inner peace and character stability on the one hand, and his experience of having seen 'glory and riches' as a member of the Bush clan left him without pretense. He did not have to try to be smarter or smoother or more interesting than he was. Being at peace with himself, he lets his public and private personae be the same. His amazing ease and lack of self-consciousness means he can joke and banter without any fear of embarrassment and without losing his concentration. Bush can be light-hearted while working on serious moral issues. It baffled many observers; how can a man who looks frivolous be so dedicated? Bush's inner peace and lack of pretense allow him to be immensely self-confident. His ability with people also makes him a good reader of people. His informality, genuine lack of pretense or airs, and his sincerity invite people to integrate quickly into his advisory process and become loyal to him.

Second, like a 'cobbler's son,' George W. Bush watched how to make political shoes all his life.[41] As is common to many sons, he developed an early fascination with the family business. From grassroots campaign work to co-chair of the 1988 campaign, to persuading his father's Chief of Staff John Sununu to step aside, Bush has had a unique insider's experience. From his own life-long experience, he has learned to concentrate on how to win the next political race, and, he always keeps a watchful eye on his stock of political capital. Much is made of Karl Rove as Bush's master strategist, but given Bush's hands-on experience and personal fascination with political campaigns, it is simply implausible that he would delegate to Rove on strategy anymore than he would to Dick Cheney, Condoleezza Rice, or Chief of Staff Andy Card on domestic and foreign affairs.

Third, Bush who seemed to lack discipline as a student was now one of the most disciplined politicians in recent memory. George W. Bush partied as a young man, but is now a tee-totaler, devoted to his wife and family. He is as personally devout as Jimmy Carter and as happy to be simply clearing brush on his ranch as Ronald Reagan. Bush draws on his core moral values for all his decisions while his genuine beliefs and frank talk match his own walk. He can appeal to the people on the basic values he holds because he holds them sincerely.

Notes

1   The main accounts of Bush's background are found in: Bill Minutaglio, *First Son: George W. Bush and the Bush Family Dynasty* (New York: Times Books, 1999); Elizabeth Mitchell, *W: Revenge of the Bush Dynasty* (New York: Hyperion, 2000); Bush's own campaign biography, co-written with Karen Hughes: George W. Bush, *A Charge To Keep* (New York: William Morrow and Co., 1999); James H. Hatfield, *Fortunate Son: George W. Bush and the Making of an American President* (Brooklyn, New York: Soft Skull Press, 2002); Christopher Anderson, *George and Laura: Portrait of an American Marriage* (New York: William Morrow, 2002); Molly Ivins and Lou Dubose, *Shrub: The Short but Happy Political Life of George W. Bush* (New York: Random House, 2000); Sam Howe Verhovek, "Is There Room on a Republican Ticket for Another Bush," *New York Times Magazine* September 13, 1998; Seven articles written by Lois Romano and George Lardner, Jr. for the *Washington Post* in July 1999, including, 'Bush's Life Changing Year' (July 25), 'A Texas Childhood' (July 26), 'Following His Father's Path' (July 27), 'At Height of Vietnam, Graduate Picks Guard' (28 July), 'A Run for the House; Courting a Wife, Then the Voters' (July, 29), 'Life of George W. Bush: The Turning Point; After Coming Up Dry' (July 30), 'Moving up the Major Leagues' (July 31); A special feature edition of *Texas Monthly*, entitled, 'Who is George W. Bush', June 1999; A four-part series written by Hanna Rosin, Dana Milbank and Lois Romano for the *Washington Post* in July 2000, including, 'Bush's Resentment of Elites Informs Bid' (July 23), 'Applying Personal Faith to Public Policy' (July 24), 'Dispelling Doubts with the Rangers' (July 25), 'A Fierce Loyalty Marks Bush's Inner Circle' (July 26); A nine-part series written by Nicholas D. Kristof for the *New York Times* in 2000, including, 'A Philosophy With Roots in Conservative Texas Soil' (May 21), 'Earning A's in People Skills at Andover' (10 June), 'Bush's Choice in War: Devoid of Passion or Anxiety' (July 11), 'Learning How to Run: A West Texas Stumble' (July 27), 'How Bush Came to Tame His Inner Scamp' (July 29), 'A Father's Footsteps Ego Throughout a Son's Career' (September 11), 'Road to Politics Ran Through a Texas Ballpark' (September 24), 'A Master of Bipartisanship With No Taste for Details' (October 16), 'For Bush, His Toughest Call Was the Choice to Run at All' (October 29); Nicholas Lemann, 'The Redemption', *The New Yorker* (January 31, 2002, pp. 48-63); Gail Sheehy, 'The Accidental Candidate', *Vanity Fair* October 2000, pp. 164-195 ; Eric Pooley with S.C. Gwynne, 'How George Got His Groove', *Time* June 21, 1999; Richard Brookhiser, 'The Mind of George W. Bush', *Atlantic Monthly* April 2003, pp. 56-69); A set of interviews with Doug Hannah, Randall Roden, Clay Johnson, John Ellis, Doug Wead, and Tom Grieve   (www.pbs.org/wgbh/pages/frontline/shows/choice2000/bush.html),   *PBS Frontline: The Choice 2000* . Accessed on March 20, 2001.

2   An account of the family's background can be found in Herbert S. Parmet, *George Bush: The Life of a Lone Star Yankee* (New York: Scribner, 1997); and in Elizabeth Mitchell, *W: Revenge of the Bush Dynasty* (New York: Hyperion, 2000).

3   Evan Thomas and Martha Brant, 'A Son's Restless Journey', *Newsweek*, August 7, 2000, p. 35.

4   Bush, 'A Charge To Keep', p. 19.

5   Hanna Rosin, 'Bush's Resentment of "Elites" Informs Bid', *Washington Post*, July 23, 2000.

6   Frank Bruni, 'For Laura Bush, a Direction She Never Wished to Go In', *New York Times*, July 31, 2000.

7   See Aaron Latham, 'How George W. Found God', *George*, September 2000, pp. 79-102. See also, George Lardner Jr. and Lois Romano, 'A Texas Childhood: A Sister Dies, a Family Moves On; Loss Creates Strong Bond Between Mother and Son', *Washington Post*, July 26, 1999.

8   Nicholas D. Kristof, 'Earning A's in People Skills at Andover', *The New York Times*, June 10, 2000.

9   Interview with Clay Johnson, 'Frontline: The Choice 2000', (www.pbs.org/wgbh/pages/frontline/shows/choice2000/bush.html).

10   Minutaglio, 'First Son', p. 97.

11   For example see Ivins and Dubose, 'Shrub', p. 7; Minutaglio, 'First Son', p. 121; Mitchell, 'W: Revenge of the Bush Dynasty', pp. 106-109.

12   Hatfield, 'Fortunate Son', p. 46.

13   Stephen Mansfield, *The Faith of George W. Bush* (New York: Jeremy P. Tarcher/Penguin, 2003), pp. 60-61.

14   Hatfield, 'Fortunate Son', p. 37.

15   Ivins and Dubose; Paul Begala, *'Is Our Children Learning' The Case Against George W. Bush* (New York: Simon & Schuster, 2000), p. 105.

16   Andersen, 'George and Laura', p. 73.

17   Mark Schone, 'Unfortunate Con', *The Oxford American*, July/August, 2003, p. 40.

18   Hatfield, 'Fortunate Son', seems to suggest a link to alcohol on page 49, but then makes the cocaine accusation based on anonymous sources in his Afterword, pp. 306-318.

19   Schone, 'Unfortunate Con', pp. 39-51.

20   See for example Lois Romano and George Lardner Jr., 'Bush's Life-Changing Year', *Washington Post*, July 25, 1999.

21   Paul Burka, 'The W. Nobody Knows', (http://www.texasmonthly.com/mag/1999/jun/knows.1.php), *Texas Monthly*, June 1999.

22   Lois Romano, 'George Walker Bush, Driving on the Right', *Washington Post*, September 24, 1998.

23   Andersen, 'George and Laura', p. 114.

24   Ibid., p. 165.

25   Hatfield, 'Fortunate Son', pp. 104-105.

26   Verhovek, 'Is There Room', p. 57; Nicholas Kristof, 'How Bush Came to Tame His Inner Scamp', *New York Times*, July 29, 2000, p. 1.

27   'Interview with John Ellis', *Frontline: The Choice 2000* (www.pbs.org/wgbh/pages/frontline/shows/choice2000/bush.html).

28   Bush, 'A Charge To Keep', p. 174.

29   See Mitchell, 'W: Revenge of the Bush Dynasty', p. 213.

30   Minutaglio, 'First Son', p. 260.

31   John Brady, *Bad Boy: The Life and Politics of Lee Atwater* (Reading, Massachusetts: Addison Wesley, 1997), pp. 194-195.

32   For example, Aaron Latham, 'How George W. Found God', *George*, September 2000, pp. 79-102.

33   For example, Sheehy, 'The Accidental Candidate', pp. 187-188.

34   Ivins and Dubose, 'Shrub', p. 14.

35   Steve Waldman's Interview with George Bush, October 2000, (http://www.beliefnet.com/frameset.asp?pageLoc=/story/47/story_4706_1.html&storyID=4706&boardID=6339).

36   Sheehy, 'The Accidental Candidate', p. 186.

37   Minutaglio, 'First Son', p. 276.

38   Mitchell, 'W: Revenge of the Bush Dynasty', p. 307.

39   Lois Romano and George Lardner Jr., 'Bush's Life-Changing Year', *Washington Post*, July 25, 1999.

40   Bill Keller, 'Reagan's Son', *New York Times Magazine*, January 26, 2003, makes a series of comparisons between Reagan and George W. Bush.

41   Texas State Senator Teel Bivins used this expression at a roundtable titled 'How Would George W. Bush Govern?', American Enterprise Institute, July 31, 2000.

Chapter 2

Running for President

As early as 1997, polls showed Bush would top the list of Republican candidates for the 2000 presidential race.[1] There was little doubt about Bush's ambition, but Laura and their daughters were not as keen. Shortly after his father's victory in 1988, Bush had secretly commissioned a study, called 'All the President's Children', that revealed serious risks to political offspring, and Bush's twin daughters were not at all enthusiastic about the run.[2] They had one year left before graduating from high school and did not like the idea of going to college with Secret Service escorts. Laura Bush would be happy to move out of the limelight of the Governor's mansion and tend to the life of her family. While campaigning is in Bush's blood, campaign travel is not. He is a man of dearly held routines: First thing in the morning, he brings his wife coffee in bed and enjoys a fast run at noon in the hot Texas sun.[3] He likes to read a bit at night and goes to bed around 10:00 pm. He has no burning desire for the unknown and the untried.[4] He made his money on the Texas Rangers and was actually in the process of buying his 1600 acre ranch about 90 miles north of Austin near the hamlet of Crawford.

Of course Bush would run and soon after the 1998 Texas election his circle of loyal advisers headed by Karen Hughes, Karl Rove, Don Evans and Joe Allbaugh moved into campaign mode. Soon thereafter, Condoleezza Rice joined to be Bush's foreign policy adviser. She assembled a group of eight defense and foreign policy experts, the so-called 'Vulcans.' Still, Bush's message was largely domestic politics, including big tax cuts, education reform, and faith-based compassion to overhaul the nation's social welfare system and to promote a culture of life. Foreign and defense issues played second fiddle. Bush only announced two concrete action plans: missile defense and military transformation.

The Bush Team

Born in Paris into a military family, Karen Hughes spent a good deal of her childhood moving with her parents from one place to another. She settled in Texas while her father, Major-General H.R. Parfitt, was serving as the last American governor of the Panama Canal Zone.[5] She completed a degree in Journalism and English at Southern Methodist University and then went to work for a TV station in Dallas/Fort Worth. In 1980, as a TV reporter, she covered the elder Bush's bid for the White House. She loved politics even more than journalism and by 1984 she was working for the Reagan-Bush team in Texas. Hughes first met George W. Bush at the 1990 Texas GOP convention where he had been appointed chairman and Bush was impressed from the start. A straight shooter, unafraid, a strong woman with a square jaw and a booming voice, she radiated dedication and persistence. She became executive director of the Texas Republican Party in 1992, but left that position shortly thereafter together with Fred Meyer, the Chairman, as the grassroots of the Texas GOP came into the hands of very conservative activists. Bush then hired her as his communications director in his 1994 run against Ann Richards. Hughes had already made her mark early in that race, as she had been the hardest-hitting critic of Richards from the executive director's spot.

Hughes was among Bush's first full time assistants. She gradually took control over every word that went out of the Governor's office and became part of every major meeting. Her first specialty was message control as she wrote in her memoir, 'I learned message discipline early. I talked so much that my sister couldn't get a word in edgewise. So my parents began putting an alarm clock on the dinner table to limit the amount of time I could speak.'[6] Hughes was fair to the Press, not taking their criticism too personally, but she also was unambiguous. She worked for George W. Bush and never let her guard down. She could not be intimidated. At nearly six feet, she was tall enough to stare down any reporter. 'You absolutely cannot bully Hughes,' noted CNN's Charles Zewe, nor would you get inside scoops or any self-promotion from Karen Hughes.[7] Taking his cue from her maiden name Parfitt, Bush called her his 'High Prophet', though many in the Press called her the 'Enforcer'.[8]

Hughes was as much a peer to Bush as an assistant. Like Karl Rove, she could tell the candidate exactly what she thought. Later in the White House, she would keep a piece of unvarnished wood on her desk to remind her that Bush wanted her unvarnished opinion. She could argue with him and oppose his ideas and yet be totally loyal. Her second specialty was to make sure that Bush's conservative compassionate values came across in plain, everyday language. She helped him sound like a conservative with a heart. She coined most of the key phrases for which Bush has become known, including 'I am a uniter and not a divider.' As Rove helped Bush sharpen his strategy, Hughes helped him soften his language. When she left the White House as communications director in the summer of 2002, she still stayed in close contact, working on Bush's speeches and traveling with him on the campaign trail. In August 2004, she returned to work full time in the presidential campaign.

Karl Rove, who will be ranked with Lee Atwater and James Carville as the greatest campaign strategists in our time, came from a broken home and spent most of his younger years in the West. Like Lee Atwater, politics is a contact sport for Rove. Largely self-taught, he declared himself a Republican at age nine, and was a high school debater without rival. Extremely shrewd and with a born instinct for political strategy, Rove is anything but a 'nerd', as he once described himself.[9] When Rove, who never finished college because he was too busy in politics, ran for national College Chair of the Republican Party, Atwater campaigned for him, and upon being elected, he appointed Lee as his chief assistant. At the Republican National Committee, Karl worked for Bush's father who was then the Chair. In the 1960s, Atwater and Rove traveled the country, recruiting students for the Republican Party. Rove eventually settled in Texas where he founded a direct-mail agency.

When Bush ran for Congress in 1978, Rove was his chief political adviser. They have stayed in touch since that time, regularly comparing notes and statistics on political races all over the country. Bush and Rove talked about campaigns the way serious fans discuss sports. When Bush was still with the Texas Rangers, Rove's agency ran early polls for him on whether Arlington citizens would support a tax hike to build a new baseball stadium. Rove became campaign adviser and marketer in dozens of Texas races. He played a key role in turning Texas from a largely Democratic to a Republican stronghold and he helped Bill Clements become the first Republican governor of Texas in modern history. He had also gained a reputation as someone capable of 'dirty tricks' while covering his tracks carefully.

In 1994, Rove created a strict 'message discipline' campaign for George's race as governor. Rove and others coached Bush into keeping his temper under control as Ann Richards poked at Bush's privileged background and lack of experience. Bush and Rove are almost a single wired political antennae. Rove, whom he once nicknamed 'Turd Blossom' (a flower that grows out of a cowpie) and 'Boy Genius', has a knack for bringing out Bush's values while at the same time advancing his political capital.[10] Like Hughes', Rove's advice to Bush is leak proof and Rove can relate to him as a peer. Atwater had a bad reputation for womanizing which got him in trouble with Bush's parents on several occasions, and in one case, George W. actually pleaded with his father not to fire him.[11] Rove, though divorced and remarried, fits the stricter family values of the younger Bush. Darby Rove, Karl's wife, calls him 'a committed father to their 11-year old son.'[12]

Bush and Rove were not only comrades in political strategy, but they also developed a common philosophical bond. Both resented the arrogant liberalism of the 1960s and both looked for a revival in the Republican Party to set in motion a counter to the culture that says, 'if it feels good, just do it, and if you have a problem in society, blame someone else.'[13]

When Bush won the 1998 gubernatorial race by a landslide, he decided to concentrate on two things. Given that the Texas legislature sits only once every two years for a brief period in the Spring, he would work on his Texas agenda in 1999 in a very public way, while during lunch each day in the Mansion, Rove would organize a fundraising, policy or political strategy session for the presidential race. Karl Rove staked his career on George W. Bush in 1999 as the latter told him to sell his political marketing agency; they would swim or sink together. For a political strategist like Rove, Bush was the kind of candidate he had waited for a lifetime.

It came as no surprise that Bush turned to his close friend Don Evans for help with fundraising. When he finished his MBA at the University of Texas in 1975, Evans moved to Midland to work in the oil industry. He worked himself up to CEO of the Tom Brown Oil Company. Bush came back to Midland in the same year and they socialized from the beginning. Evans married Susie Marinis who had been George W.'s classmate in elementary school, and before he was married himself, George would come over for dinner to talk oil or sports with Don. Their friendship grew very deep: they would run together, golf together and, after Bush turned more serious, go to 'Community Bible Study' together. Evans was the quieter and more cautious of the two – his severely handicapped daughter had given him another perspective on life. In Bush's 1978 race for Congress, Evans acted as the main fundraiser, tapping into both the Bush family's connections and their oil friends. Again, in 1994 and 1998, Evans ran the fundraising part of Bush's campaigns.

Charlie Younger, George W. Bush's medical doctor friend in Midland, thinks Evans is the closest confidant Bush has after Laura. 'They are almost like brothers,' Karen Hughes said during the 2000 primaries.[14] Evans has seen all sides of Bush. One day Bush came up with the idea of flying a Cessna around Midland. After all, he had been a fighter pilot in the Texas National Guard. The Cessna was not an F-102 and Bush had not flown a plane for some time. He took off too fast, the lights went on red, and the landing was rough. It was the last Bush flight and a nerve-wracking test of friendship for Evans.

Rove and Evans set up a fundraising scheme where volunteers would commit to raising $100,000 each by clustering $1000 donations. These 'pioneers' proved hugely successful. In the first month, $6 million was raised from Texas friends and the large Bush network. By the end of 1999, $63 million had been gathered, and 'eighty-five per cent of the total had come in the form of five-hundred-dollar and thousand-dollar contributions.'[15]

The money and media bandwagon effect happened early for Bush. The network of Republican governors created by Atwater formed a crucial part in Bush's early momentum. Seeing $60 million raised in the fall of 1999, donors swarmed to the perceived front-runner and the Press began to write about 'a coronation'. The fundraising proved so successful, that Bush decided not to request federal matching grants for the primary races.

Don Evans played a bigger role than fundraising but preferred to work behind the scenes. He would not step in front of any of the other top aides unless, as happened once in the 1994 race, he saw his friend worn out by too many engagements. At that time, he shut down all activities for a while, and no one questioned his authority or judgment to do so.[16]

Not counting Don Evans, some reporters described Bush's inner circle as an 'Iron Triangle', in which Joe Allbaugh was the third player.[17] The big Oklahoman had earned his stripes by working as a political strategist for Bush's friend, Henry Bellmon, the governor of Oklahoma. Allbaugh is a man of few words, imposing in figure, with a marine haircut and a muscular 6-foot-4 frame.[18] 'I admit,' Bush joked during the campaign, 'he is not pretty to look at.' Self-effacing, loyal and completely trustworthy, Bush came to rely on him in Austin as his chief-of-staff. A 'take-charge guy', Allbaugh managed the flow of advice in a low-key manner, avoiding a rigid hierarchy and not shutting out advisers from direct access to Bush.[19] Unlike Hughes and Rove, Allbaugh never played the role of policy adviser. He was more of an enforcer. Allbaugh had a similar task in the campaign. Sometimes he would march through the campaign offices with a megaphone telling everyone to watch their pennies. It made an impression. Allbaugh called Rove, himself and Hughes, 'the brain, brawn, and bite' of the campaign.[20]

Compassionate Conservatism

This 'Bush team' produced a platform called 'Compassionate Conservatism'. It was not a 'phantom framework',[21] but a set of principles that could gradually be worked into substantial policy proposals. Marvin Olasky's 1992 book *The Tragedy of American Compassion* argued that the secular welfare state of the mid-twentieth century had replaced a culture of private charity and personal responsibility and had left the urban poor more destitute and with fewer values. Bush met with Olasky and was impressed that Olasky practiced what he preached, personally helping ex-convicts find their way back into society.[22]

The candidate also liked David Horowitz's point that Republicans needed 'to compete with Democrats on the caring issues.'[23] Rove brought Steve Goldsmith, the former mayor of Indianapolis, to Austin who impressed Bush with his record of lifting so many poor people out of the poverty trap. Bush met with Princeton criminologist, John DiIulio, a Democrat, and liked his idea of 'subsidiarity,' in which government should be limited to a few things and do them well. Faith-based and community groups could deal with many social problems better than the federal government. Bush hired Michael Gerson who had worked for Indiana Senator, Dan Coats, (another advocate of 'faith-based' charity) as his speechwriter. Gerson's task was to give Bush 'a distinctive voice' around this theme.[24] Gerson would show a tremendous ability to put the candidate's values into almost spiritual language.

Bush hired a former legislative assistant to his father, Joshua Bolten, to coordinate domestic policy sessions. Larry Lindsey, an economic adviser to Reagan and George H.W. Bush, and Glenn Hubbard, a Columbia University professor, joined to advice Bush on economic policy. Lindsey had experience as a former member of the Board of Governors of the Federal Reserve System. Lindsey and Hubbard are advocates for supply-side economics. They became the mastermind behind Bush's tax cuts proposal. Bush offered a larger tax cut than Bob Dole had done in 1996 or than the Republican House had proposed in 1999. His plan was to provide tax relief to all income brackets to the tune of $1.6 trillion spread over ten years. He called for easing the tax burden by doubling the child tax credit and reducing the so-called marriage penalty. To this peculiar mix of Christian charity, practical urban welfare reform, and steep tax cuts was added Bush's most successful Texas initiative: school reform and student testing. It took some journalists until early 2001 to figure out whether George W. Bush was actually a conservative or a moderate.

Bush does not fit either label because his values cross conventional lines. In Bush's view, traditional family values are key to curing societal ills, the market is usually right, and government should be limited to a few specific areas. In his campaign memoir, which Karen Hughes helped to write, Bush put his feelings on government this way: 'We must correct it and limit it, not disdain it. I differ with those who want to dismantle government down to the last paperclip. Government is neither the enemy nor the answer.'[25] Clearly, Bush is not simply a fiscal conservative, but neither is he a welfare Liberal. His compassionate conservatism is about helping the poor and fighting social ills, but not on the terms of Franklin Roosevelt's New Deal. In some ways, Bush began a social revolution that sought to overturn the liberal welfare state in which big government administers and dictates all solutions.

Bush's values are upbeat, as are his policies. His media consultants learned that the voters 'respond to his energy and optimism'[26] and this helped him figure out a way for Republicans 'to actually be *for* something.'[27] His solution to abortion is not to reverse Roe v. Wade (a president can't do that anyway) but to emphasize 'strong adoption laws', abstinence, and to change the cultural mentality that demands abortions.[28] The idea is to influence American culture so that it will gradually turn pro-life on its own. Bush will generally appoint anti-abortion aides and judges, but he will not make it a political battle point or a litmus test. Bush's positive approach to pro-life values tied into his political strategy. Bush and Rove knew that 'church going Catholics would be this year's soccer moms.'[29] They would be the swing votes. By pointing in the right direction without fighting a culture war, Bush could get support from both the center and fundamentalist vote.

The Firewall

The combination of good organization, intense advertising and a national wave of 'inevitability' secured Bush's victory in the Iowa Caucuses.[30] But Arizona Senator John McCain, who had ignored Iowa, put all his chips on New Hampshire, where the GOP voters are notoriously independent. Bush thought he could win them over by his tax cuts scheme, but New Hampshire voters balked at his very successful pre-primary fundraising campaign and the national media perception of him as 'crown prince.' Bush did not campaign as intensely in New Hampshire as McCain and avoided almost all debates because he and Rove figured that message control was critical and frontrunners could only lose in debates. McCain ran as the anti-establishment reformer, allowing reporters complete access to him on his 'Straight Talk Express' bus.

As early as New Hampshire, the primary race was essentially between Bush and McCain. In 1996, Steve Forbes had lambasted Bob Dole, a situation that many felt had harmed the Republican ticket in the general campaign. Now Forbes switched strategies and failed to attack Bush until it was too late. Elizabeth Dole never connected with the voters and she had to share the Conservative Christian base with Gary Bauer and Dan Quayle. The majority of the conservative Christian vote stayed with Bush. They knew he was a man of faith, Pat Robertson backed George, and above all, they wanted a winner after eight years of Clinton.

The day after the New Hampshire primary, Bush no longer looked like much of a winner. He had spent $40 million and lost the granite state by almost 20 points. Reporters wrote beautiful stories about McCain's heroism in Vietnam, his rapport with the voters, and his claim to be a fresh, new style of politician. The free media coverage from the 'McCain swoon' more than made up for his smaller budget to buy TV ads.[31] McCain's call for election reform single handedly redefined the agenda, rivaling Bush's tax cuts message. The Bush team seemed to have noticed the impending disaster too late. John Weaver, McCain's chief strategist and a rival of Rove, had concocted this 'crusade', and gladly admitted that they had 'just pulled off the biggest caper in history.'[32]

The Bush campaign was too late to rescue New Hampshire, or Michigan even though Rove thought the three days between New Hampshire and Michigan (February 19 and 22) could not undo all the groundwork and media blitzing Bush had done. The two losses showed that Bush was not invincible. Pundits asked for heads to roll, Rove's in particular, or for 'Washington professionals' to take over the campaign. But for Bush loyalty works in both directions, and he is not 'a second guesser or scapegoater.'[33] 'We're a team,' Governor Bush told Evans, Hughes, Rove and Allbaugh late on election day in New Hampshire, 'I don't want anyone pointing the finger of blame at anyone else.'[34]

Rove and Bush did have a 'firewall' in place. Again, it is remarkable to see how Lee Atwater's and Bush's fortunes intersect at this crucial juncture. After his College Republican days, and after working for Senator Strom Thurmond, Atwater went on to help elect South Carolina Governor Caroll Campbell. With Campell in the seat, Atwater, himself a native of South Carolina, devised a strategy for GOP primaries that would provide a 'firewall' against moderate or liberal Republican candidates in the South. The winning combination was Christian conservatism and a strong military. If the candidate could not pass this litmus test, he or she could not win South Carolina. Ronald Reagan was Atwater's first test. In 1980, George Herbert Walker Bush won the Iowa Caucuses. While Reagan had won the New Hampshire primary, the elder Bush was not 'finished off' until the South Carolina primary. Following in the footsteps of Atwater, who had died from brain cancer in 1991, Rove had made preparations to stop any contender in South Carolina.

Virginia was a write-off for McCain, but if he could take South Carolina, he might be able to swing enough GOP voters in the south to hold his own in the Super Tuesday primaries of March 7. McCain potentially had another advantage. For the first time in any presidential primary campaign, both California and New York voted early with many of the southern states on March 7. These states had many swing voters attracted to McCain. Still, it would be a long shot, for how could he expect to win the primaries by running against its core GOP voters? But none of that could have offered much comfort to Rove and Bush for McCain's polls shot up immediately after New Hampshire and his positives overtook Bush's. In South Carolina, veterans would determine a third of the total primary vote. McCain's campaign sent out thousands of 9-minute videos to this targeted voter list, presenting the heroic prisoner of the infamous 'Hanoi Hilton.'

Bush will go negative in a political campaign if there is the slightest need for it. Both he and his father had learned their lessons in Texas and practiced what Lee Atwater called 'comparative campaigning', during the elder Bush's race against Michael Dukakis.[35] At first, both Bush and Rove were cautious about negative ads against McCain. Bush had made a public pledge not to be first to do so and McCain's 'gateway' issue of electoral campaign reform had heightened the public's scrutiny of the candidates' conduct.

Clumsily, McCain's team gave candidate Bush the opportunity just a few days after his win in New Hampshire. In a TV ad, McCain compared Bush's record to Clinton's record, suggesting that like Clinton, Bush was a liar.[36] Bush's advertising group, called 'Maverick Media' was ready, showing ads that depicted McCain as an inconsistent and ineffective reformer, beholden to the special interests he was now fighting. Bush hammered on the theme that McCain 'was not conservative enough, but was Ted Kennedy in a flight suit.'[37] It was 'negative, but it was not dirty.'[38] Bush began to compare McCain's record aggressively to his own record in Texas. Karen Hughes coined the term 'Reformer with Results' (implying that McCain was without results).[39]

Bush went to Bob Jones University to appeal to the conservative Baptist community. McCain, who is conservative on many social issues, happens also to be highly critical of the Christian lobbies in the GOP. He really got nailed on that position in South Carolina and tripped the first lever of Atwater's firewall strategy. McCain and Weaver retaliated by launching a phone campaign in Michigan, calling

Bush anti-Catholic because he had not criticized Bob Jones' doctrinal opposition to Roman Catholicism.

Then, so-called 'push-polls' appeared in South Carolina.[40] These phone interviews venture a few lines of personal attacks camouflaged as opinion polls. For example: 'Did you know that Shirley McCain had been on such and such drugs …' The Bush campaign denied being involved and no one has proven a connection.[41] It was rumored two anonymous Texans were behind all this and though Bush benefited from them, he could have won without them. Enough veterans stayed with Bush to give him a decisive victory in South Carolina, thereby keeping him in the race. If it had not been for that South Carolina firewall, Bush might have gone the way of future Democratic contender Howard Dean in 2004.

By Super Tuesday the GOP race was effectively over. Bush then did to Vice-President Al Gore what Clinton had done to Bob Dole in 1996: He used the spell in the campaign to make the contrast between himself and Gore. Bush's early fundraising proved essential as he now had money left over to define the coming policy debate. While Gore was engaged in the final and most negative part of his campaign to defeat Bill Bradley, Bush produced well-timed and substantive ads, giving the public lots of upbeat policy substance. He accompanied these ads with visits to schools to underscore his education policy, and clips of families that would benefit from his tax cuts, switching to a positive tone to get back some of the independents who had supported McCain.

The campaign team enlisted the help of six Washington-based operatives, including as Mary Matalin and Ed Gillespie, a former aid to House Majority Leader Dick Armey, to "help chart the course" for the team in Austin.[42] While it showed the Bush team was opening up to outside advice, the six soon found out who was in control as the Austin gang kept firm control over all key decisions.

Dick Cheney, Andy Card, and Philadelphia

Bush's Vice Presidential selection process defied all expectations. He asked Richard (Dick) Cheney to head his search committee in April. Bush was interested in Colin Powell and Cheney right from the start, but Powell made crystal clear 'in a private moment' with Bush on May 25 that he was not interested in elected office.[43] Cheney reluctantly took on the position of searching for a vice president for Bush with the understanding that he would not be a candidate himself.

While he looks a lot older, Cheney is only 5 years senior to George W. Bush. There are interesting parallels between the two: Born and raised in rural Wyoming, Cheney grew up in an oil town called Jasper where a respectable Easterner, Thomas Stroock, used his influence to get him admitted to Yale University on a special scholarship. Cheney dropped out of Yale twice, and went to work constructing power lines. For a while he drank a little too much, mirroring Bush's own nomadic years, and avoided military service by enrolling at a community college. Like Bush, he eventually smartened up, married and began to build a career, first in academia and then in politics.

That is where the similarities end: Cheney wrote prize-winning essays as a political science student and became a 'quiet, hardworking technician' in the art of making government work efficiently.[44] Picked up by Donald Rumsfeld, who in 1969 headed Richard Nixon's Office of Economic Opportunity, and who saw in him a smart but tight-lipped assistant, Cheney later served as Deputy and then Chief of Staff in the Gerald Ford White House. In 1976, when Carter took over the White House, Cheney did an unusual thing, switching from his top-level executive experience to run for a seat in the House of Representatives, representing his native Wyoming. He served five terms and rose to become the deputy to GOP House Leader Robert Michel. He voted very conservatively and acted very pragmatically, building a reputation as a problem solver who can work the bureaucratic and legislative levers of the government. The elder Bush selected Cheney as his Defense Secretary in 1989 after Congress blocked the nomination of John Tower. Cheney ran the Department of Defense ably, growing very close to George W.'s father during the Gulf War. With Colin Powell and Norman Schwartzkopf, Cheney gained a national reputation from that famous war which one commentator described as Normandy with camels.

While Cheney searched for a vice presidential candidate, Bush would poke at him: 'You know,' he would say, only half in jest, 'you could make my problem go away.' When Cheney prepared the lists of finalist, Bush insisted he add himself. Cheney listed all his negatives, 'Add to that three heart attacks,' Cheney said, 'and zero electoral votes – you're going to carry Wyoming.'[45] Cheney's loyalty, lack of pretense, and selfless devotion endeared him all the more to Bush. Moreover, Bush knew that with several heart attacks behind him, Cheney would never run for the top office. He would be a seasoned inside adviser with unmatched experience and no political ambition of his own.

Cheney offered something Bush lacked: an intimate knowledge of how the executive and legislative branches in Washington work. His secret service code name at one point was 'backseat'.[46] He was loyal beyond a doubt and he would tie himself to the mast of Bush's ship. Bush valued Cheney's style: quiet, and without pretense, underplaying his tremendous experience and wisdom.

Bush was confident enough to appoint people like Cheney who knew a lot more than he did, but that did not mean he would let them make his decisions. During their first press conference, as Cheney was about to answer a question concerning their 'partnership', Bush cut him off – message: 'I am in charge, not Cheney.'[47] The Gore campaign pounced on Cheney's Congressional record, which was pro-life, anti-gun registration, and anti-South African sanctions. Bush circled the wagons around a loyal aide: "'This is a conservative man," Bush said, "so am I.'"[48]

Al Gore made a shrewd selection in Senator Joseph (Joe) Lieberman as his Vice Presidential candidate. Lieberman, a conservative Jewish politician could appeal to the social issues that small 'c' conservative Americans cared about, but who were hostile to Pat Robertson's Christian Coalition. The choice of Lieberman also helped Gore distance himself another notch from Clinton's aura of scandal.

The Bush team set one overall goal for the GOP convention in Philadelphia: to keep it positive and on message. In 1996, Pat Buchanan had used the convention to declare a war of values, providing an opportunity for the Democratic Party to brandish the GOP as radical. Clinton had used the fallout to appeal to centrist Republicans and independent voters. After a strategy session in May, Bush had delegated the plan for a 'smooth-as-silk' convention to Andrew Card, Jr.[49] Andy

Card had served as deputy chief-of-staff in the elder Bush's administration and as General Motors's top Washington lobbyist. Candidate Bush saw in him a 'hands on' manager like Allbaugh, and he used the convention to test Card. Card proved completely competent and trustworthy and without 'pyrotechnics',[50] and with the assistance of Ed Gillespie, delivered exactly on target. Each night showcased a positive policy theme, accompanied by images of racial, social and economic diversity. Compassionate Conservatism was in the center of the message. Bush went through 18 drafts of his speech, pushing Mike Gerson and Karen Hughes to the limit.[51] Ari Fleischer, who had been hired by Hughes from the Elizabeth Dole camp as one of the campaign's spokesmen, summed up the Bush team's satisfaction with the convention: 'We've changed the tone.'[52] Yet, Al Gore also received a strong positive bounce from the Democratic Convention. When both events were done, the polls showed the two candidates neck and neck in the race.

Low-Flying Vulcans

Like most governors, George W. Bush cut his teeth on domestic politics. As governor of Texas, Bush had built what he called 'bridges of personal diplomacy'[53] with the Mexican president Ernesto Zedillo and rejected all notions of 'Mexico bashing.'[54] Bush was a free trader and lobbied the Clinton administration to boost the Peso in the 1995 Mexican currency crisis. During a fact-finding tour in Israel, he met Ariel Sharon, and struck a friendship. Bush's personal friendships with Zedillo and Sharon were harbingers of how he would conduct his foreign relations as president. As a young man, Bush had visited his parents in China and while working for Stratford he had made a few trips into Central America. Yet, Bush was not primed for the broad spectrum of international issues. He thought there would be plenty of help and time to get ready.

Spotting a younger version of Ronald Reagan, George Schultz was one of the first 'old hands' in the Republican party to come out and help Bush on foreign policy. It was after one of Schultz's gatherings at his home in Palo Alto in April 1998 that Bush decided to bring Condoleezza Rice, a previous staff aide to his father, on board his emerging team.[55] He especially liked her ability to put international complexities into plain talk that matched his style. She was eager to serve, and became Bush's chief mentor on foreign issues, heading a loose group of defense and foreign advisers to the campaign team, nicknamed the 'Vulcans', after the Roman god of iron for which a statue was built in Rice's native Birmingham, Alabama.[56]

Brent Scowcroft, the elder Bush's national security adviser had brought Rice into the first Bush administration. Scowcroft met Rice in 1984 at a seminar on Soviet policy during a time when the standoff with Moscow was still sharp. Rice, then in her thirties, and a professor in Soviet Studies at Stanford University, immediately got his attention. Scowcroft was impressed how this 'little slip of a girl', stood her ground.[57] She was a young Black American realist who could take on the majority of her more dovish colleagues in a very articulate way, yet 'leave no personal animosity.'[58] In 1988, Scowcroft did not hesitate to bring Rice on his staff as a Russian expert. On his trip to Washington in 1989, while Mikhail Gorbachev was still in charge in Moscow, Boris Yeltsin insisted on seeing then President Bush in the

Oval Office. Rice literally stood in front of the door and told him he could only see Scowcroft. He tried to browbeat her and after she had let him rant for a few minutes, she turned around to call off the meeting. 'You can go back to your hotel,' she told him,[59] which changed his tune quickly and he followed her to meet Scowcroft.

Rice, whose first name 'Condoleezza' comes from a classical music annotation meaning 'with sweetness,' spent the first thirteen years of her life in Birmingham, Alabama. Her father, a Presbyterian minister, and her mother tried to give this only child the best education and at the same time maximum protection from the Civil Rights clashes breaking out around her. Two of her childhood acquaintances were killed in a church bombing during the height of the civil rights crisis in the American South. While her parents sheltered her, she learned to perform like a prodigy. Her father would drive circles through the city so she would not see 'whites only' events she might like to go to. From this grew 'Condi's' rugged individualism and her staunch defense of individual merit. The Rices would not march in protest rallies, but Condi was coached to compete and beat the dominant culture at its own game. Her father's 'little star' excelled in figure skating, classical piano, and academics.[60] She entered the University of Denver at a very young age when her father took up an administrative post there, and graduated at age 19. A fellow student remembered her as 'scary smart'.[61] Her father eventually became Vice-Chancellor of the university while she went on to study at Notre Dame University, and then came back to earn her Ph.D at the University of Denver.

She was fascinated by the study of power as described by Hans Morgenthau, the famous American 'Realist.' Generations of American students of international politics have been weaned on Morgenthau's six principles of Realism. Many memorize his famous dictum, that 'statesmen think and act in terms of interest defined as power.'[62] Professor Joseph Korbel, a Jewish refugee from communist Czechoslovakia and the father of Madeline Albright, was her mentor at the University of Denver. Morgenthau's focus on power combined with Korbel's insight into Soviet machinations turned Condi into a Soviet specialist. She became fluent in Russian as well as French.

Rice soon earned the elder Bush's confidence as a young NSC staffer. He told Mikhail Gorbachev at their Yalta meeting 'she tells me everything I know about the Soviet Union.' 'I hope she knows much,' Gorbachev responded.[63] She became an occasional visitor to the Bush compound in Kennebunkport. In 1993, she left the Bush administration to become Provost at Stanford University, but stayed in touch with the Bush family. When George W. Bush became governor of Texas, he and Condoleezza occasionally shared perspectives on education and trade issues. Rice was involved with a community-based project to help kids after school, which also appealed to Bush. As Stanford's Provost, she steered the prestigious university through difficult financial times and developed a decision-making style characterized by open discussion. Even the least agreeable opinions would get a chance to be heard, yet, she did not rule by committee or consensus. After all angles were aired, she would make the decision, often briskly, and move on. People interested in affirmative action or political correctness were soon disappointed in Rice. She would set preferences for hiring minorities, but when it came to the real threshold; whether or not an assistant professor merited tenure, she insisted on academic competence alone.

Rice became to Bush what Zbigniew Brzezinski was to Jimmy Carter in the 1976 campaign. She helped put form and shape on his foreign policy perspective. Rice has said that Bush has all the right instincts and that she helps him put these into an overall framework. What she did not say was that at the beginning of the campaign, Bush above all needed basic information about foreign affairs and America's foreign policy. He knew where he wanted to go and how to lead to that point, but he needed 'raw data' to deal with the various foreign policy issues that would be tossed at him during campaign stops and interviews. Likely, neither Bush nor Rice realized how quickly the candidate's uncertain command of foreign issues would be put to the test.

In November 1999, a Boston reporter tripped Bush up on a 'pop quiz,' asking him for the names of foreign leaders in five countries. Few Americans could have named the new president of Pakistan or the leader of Chechnya, but the impression was created that Bush was dumb. Hughes tracked down Rice and told her, 'We've got a problem.'[64] Another reporter mixed up a favorite Quebec fast food (poutine) with the name of Canada's then Prime Minister (Jean Chrétien) and Bush went along without correcting the journalist. Bush's lack of international fluency provided an opening for the Democratic campaign, so Rice increased the pace of briefings by the Vulcans.

Richard Perle remembers how Rice would lead the meetings in Austin at the governor's mansion. Bush would come in and tell the advisers or guests that he would become President and that he would take care of that part, but that he needed their best analysis on the issues to be 'a good president'.[65] Perle, who is officially still a Democrat, served many years as assistant to Washington Senator Scoop Jackson before joining the Reagan team. Jackson co-sponsored the Jackson-Vanik amendment tying the policy of détente with Moscow to the demand of letting Russian Jewish emigrants leave that country more freely. To Perle, Bush was 'the new Scoop Jackson'. He could cut through the murk.[66] Perle and other advisers, mainly from the Reagan and earlier Bush administration came away impressed by the candidate's tough questioning in these discussions. Bush was unselfconscious about admitting what he did not know. Rice led a team of eight 'Vulcans.' Paul Wolfowitz technically co-chaired the loose group, but he had less face time with Bush than Rice. Wolfowitz, like Perle, was an early Democrat who had turned more ardently conservative than realists such as Condi Rice. Wolfowitz was trained a scientist, but turned to political science in the conservative climate at the University of Chicago. Albert Wohlstetter, a famous American military strategist, was one of his mentors.

Watching Nixon and Ford deal too cautiously with Soviet governments while people all over Eastern Europe and in the Soviet Union were living under deep oppression turned Wolfowitz and Perle into activists.[67] Wolfowitz and Perle were critical of arms control policies pursued in the Nixon and Ford years. They sought to use American power in the service of freedom. Both served under Reagan: Perle as senior policy adviser to Defense Secretary Cap Weinberger and Wolfowitz as Assistant Secretary for Asian Affairs in the State Department, and later as Ambassador to Indonesia. During the Reagan years, Perle was called the 'Prince of Darkness', by his critics for his unfailing pessimistic assessment of Soviet policy.

Unlike Perle, Wolfowitz also served under Bush's father. As Under Secretary on defense for policy, he worked closely with Secretary of Defense Dick Cheney, and played a key role in the strategy and planning of the war to oust Saddam Hussein from Kuwait. Wolfowitz crafted the strategy to go around Iraqi forces to the West in Desert Storm rather than merely meeting them head on. Wolfowitz was among the few to make the case for not letting Saddam Hussein reestablish control in the South of Iraq after the victory in Kuwait. As the chief architect of the Defense Planning Guidance of the early 1990s, Wolfowitz began work on a 'strategic transformation of the whole region', a radical plan to revamp the political map of the Middle East.[68] In his thinking, the Middle East needed its own buffer against radical Islam and an alternative to dictatorship. Democracy in the Middle East is one of the keys that can unlock the Israeli-Palestinian crisis. Wolfowitz's ideas are bold, risky and full of optimism and activism.

Robert Zoellick became James Baker's chief assistant when Baker was appointed Secretary of the Treasury in the early 1980s. Later, Zoellick moved with Baker to the Department of State. There, Zoellick crafted the so-called 'Two-Plus-Four' strategy to guide the peaceful reunification of Germany. He later helped put together the Asia Pacific Economic Forum. After serving at Fannie Mae, Zoellick joined Bush's 'Vulcans' to advice on trade policy. Zoellick helped Bush write the policy plank that called for free trade in the Americas. Perhaps to lure Powell early, Bush also asked a close friend of Colin Powell to join his foreign policy brain trust. An ex-Navy Seal, Richard Armitage is an experienced Asia hand and diplomatic troubleshooter. He negotiated the transfer of ownership of American military bases in the Philippines. Robert Blackwill and Stephen Hadley, national security and defense policy advisers in the elder Bush's administration were also part of the Vulcans. Dov Zakheim was the last member. His career was in pushing reform at the Pentagon.

Of the eight 'Vulcans,' only Wolfowitz and Perle were passionate spokesmen of the Reagan tradition, and members of the so-called neoconservative wing of the Republican Party. They advocated the primacy of 'American values' in foreign affairs. The others were more representative of the elder Bush tradition: cautious realists and pragmatists.

The mixture of realists, pragmatist and idealist shows that Bush sought to benefit from diverse advice though he is most attracted to a values-based approach. He can relate to Reagan's quest for the freedom of the peoples of Central and Eastern Europe back in the 1980s when they were under Soviet rule. During the campaign, Bush spoke of the need to free the peoples repressed by the remaining dictators worldwide. Reagan felt strongly that to defend was better than to avenge. He cherished a great dream of a missile shield that would make nuclear weapons impotent. Bush likewise cannot see why, as Henry Kissinger put it, he would make 'a virtue out of our vulnerability' by keeping an outdated Anti-Ballistic Missiles Treaty in place with a Russia that is now our friend, while rogue states gather missile technology and weapons of mass terror to come in through the gaping hole.[69] Wolfowitz, Perle, and Armitage helped Bush formulate his theme of missile defense in the campaign.

At the same time, Bush has a pragmatic streak and is politically knowledgeable about how to obtain values. Bush also has an ear for strategic pragmatism of a centrist Republican adviser such as Bob Zoellick. Bush knows he may only get a portion of the value he seeks and only a little bit at the time. He knows he may need some 'diplobabble', as he jokingly calls it, at the right time to advance his values.[70] Bush embodies the two sides: he is a hardliner on his values, but he is a moderate pragmatist on how to get them. In addition, he is keenly aware how the politics of a certain approach will advance or reduce his political capital.

Candidate George W. Bush positioned himself in the autumn of 1999 as a president who would lead the country with 'Compassionate Conservatism' at home and with strong American values abroad. Bush and Rove knew that the election would not be won or lost on foreign policy. The only part of Bush's campaign on defense that was dead earnest was his plan to build missile defenses and his determination to bring about 'military transformation'.[71] 'Rebuilding' the military and missile defense were the only two themes that made it on to Bush's short list of campaign issues, the so-called 'food groups.' Given the large number of military folk and veterans in South Carolina and its importance in the primaries, Bush laid out his vision for 'the military of the next century' at the Citadel, a military college in Charleston.[72] A few months later, in a speech at the Ronald Reagan Library in California, Bush spoke about his 'American Internationalism'.[73] He explained in that speech and throughout the 2000 campaign how his vision of 'realism in the service of American ideals' would rest on three pillars: freedom for people from repression, free trade, and, as he later put it in his inaugural speech, 'defenses beyond challenge'.[74]

The Republican party traditionally has an advantage in military security issues, as voters tend to trust Republicans more on this issue. Bill Clinton's defense and foreign policy had made this advantage even bigger. Clinton started out very badly with the American military leadership in early 1993 and never fully recovered. His attempt to move the military brass away from a 'don't ask, don't tell' policy on gays in the military appeared to them as a fleeting political interest. Les Aspin, Clinton's first Secretary of Defense, managed the Pentagon in an uninspiring manner. Only when the Balkans could no longer be ignored did Clinton try a strategy of 'Lift and Strike.' The idea was to lift the arms embargo on Bosnia while bombing the Serbs. When Secretary of State Warren Christopher met with strong opposition to the plan from European leaders who had thousands of UN troops on the ground, Clinton dropped the idea. Soon thereafter, the Clinton administration ordered American military action to capture one of the chief warlords blocking progress in the peaceful reconstruction of Somalia. The US Rangers suffered a smarting defeat in Mogadishu as their operation failed and CNN showed captured US soldiers being dragged through the streets. These American casualties resulted in an abrupt decision by Clinton to withdraw from Somalia. In the eyes of the Bush election campaign, the principles America had sought in Somalia were suddenly cancelled because lives were lost. Ergo, there were no worthwhile values there. As far as most of the military establishment was concerned, the Clinton years had been bad years and the Bush team was eager to tap into that discontent.

Clinton's defense budgets were another issue picked up by the Bush campaign. In the early 1990s, Bush's father had devised a Two Major Theater War posture for the US Military. With the Cold War over, the new plan was to be able to fight in the two most threatening spots, Korea and Iraq, simultaneously. The younger Bush now criticized Clinton for letting this defense posture and the budget drift away from each other. Given budget restraints and the higher operational tempo in Bosnia and

Kosovo, troops had less time to train for combat. Most of Clinton's defense budgets were 'plussed up' by the Republicans in Congress.[75] Even so, with only six new ships being built each year, the navy would go down from 310 to 220 ships in the next ten years.[76] The Congressionally mandated Quadrennial Defense Review of 1997 re-affirmed the Two Major Theater posture but failed to fund it.[77] Unwilling to make hard choices, Clinton approved the procurement process of all major new platforms, including the Crusader, the Army's plan for a new short-range artillery rocket system, while cutting back on current procurement allocations. Clinton was simply pushing the 'defense crunch' into the future. By the late 1990s, the Congressional Budget Office estimated that the Pentagon needed an extra $50 billion a year simply to maintain its current position.

Candidate Bush stepped right into the middle of this growing military unease. Bush and his Vulcans sensed the drift in strategy and funding and made defense reforms a policy plank. Bush's goal was to articulate a totally different vision while building immediate bridges to shore up electoral support. First, seeing low morale, low recruitment numbers, and a growing trend of mid-level officers leaving the forces, Bush promised immediate pay raises, help with low-cost housing, and a boost to the military health plan. As Cheney put it in one of his speeches, 'help is on the way.'[78]

Second, Bush lamented the drop in readiness and combat training due to too many nation-building operations. He said, 'There may be some moments when we use our troops as peacekeepers, but not often.'[79] In his speech at the Citadel in September 1999, Bush said he would work hard to 'allow an orderly and timely withdrawal from places like Kosovo and Bosnia.' 'We will not be permanent peacekeepers,' he said, but he also added, 'we will not be hasty.'[80] He played into the public and military weariness about open-ended commitments to peacekeeping and Clinton's 'uncertainty on when and how to use American power.'[81]

When Condi Rice announced in October 2000 that the 101st Airborne division had no business escorting kids to school in Kosovo, the impression was created that Bush would immediately begin a withdrawal from the Balkans upon entering the White House.[82] European governments were especially apprehensive about this campaign 'position.' However, Bush carefully hedged his standpoint. He had no specific plans to bring American peacekeepers home. He intervened when some Republican Senators got ready to cut off funding for US forces in the Balkans in 1999. Working behind the scenes in Congress, Bush assured lawmakers that he would support their continued funding for peacekeeping.[83] During the 1999 War against Serbia, Bush was careful to refrain from any critique of Clinton the Commander-in-Chief. Unlike most realists, Wolfowitz, and perhaps even Bush himself, supported Clinton's military action over the skies of Kosovo to protect a suppressed minority against the strong-arm tactics of a regional dictator.

Bush vs. Gore

Despite Gore's policy expertise and Bush's laser-like focus on a handful of issues, the campaign was essentially fought and won on image and personality. The Bush team emphasized that their candidate had instinctive smarts, sound judgment, management skills, and a strong Texas record, but the Gore team kept raising questions about Bush's abilities; does he have enough expertise, gravitas, and stamina to be President? Like his father, Bush is not good at speaking fluently off the cuff on policy issues. Some of the 'Bushisms' have become famous thanks to Slate.com and ABC's 'English Patient', who zealously collected every gaffe. In one flub, Bush said he wanted to put 'food on your family'. He mangled tariffs and barriers into 'bariffs and terriers'. Perhaps because of his reading the King James Version of the Bible, he called Greeks 'Grecians'. [84] Former Clinton strategist Paul Begala used one alleged blooper 'Is our children learning?' as the title of his partisan attack book. Andrew Sullivan, however, alleges Bush was starting a sentence and said 'Is ...', then he stopped and went on to say: '*are* (not our) children learning?'[85] Given the Texas twang, it is certainly possible.

Frank Bruni from the *New York Times* came to realize that 'Bushisms' were interesting to the media, which otherwise faced rigid message control, but were lost on the wider audience. Bush's gaffes did not disconnect him from the people, likewise, the candidate's lack of book smarts did not alienate him from average Americans. Bruni also learned that the verbal Bush did not reflect the thinking Bush. One time Bruni was desperate to get an interview with Bush and tried an end-run around Karen Hughes, but she caught him. Bush wondered what was going on. In the heat of the moment Bruni mangled his own words: 'I had to seize the window,' he told Bush and Hughes. 'Seize the window?' Bush said, a grin consuming the entire lower half of his face. 'You're talking like me!'[86]

Bush's new press scrutiny made Hughes' role even bigger. She would always sit in his line of vision and move off to the side or use some other signal to have him close down an interview when he got in deep water. Hughes would cut off reporters or bar them from interviews if they wrote too negatively about her boss.

Rove and Hughes knew that Bush's likeability and upbeat personality had to be retailed. His speeches would be short, at most fifteen minutes, but his time with the average voter would be much longer, wise cracking here, manhandling there. Bush knew from experience that campaigning was like 'courtship', you have to make friends with the voter.[87] The speech changed little from place to place, boring the national media, but he would mix among the people, charm scores of them, and leave a very positive impression.

Yet, Bush never campaigned as intensely as Gore did. He kept his appearances to two or at most three a day. He tried to get back to Austin as often as he could. Most Sundays he was at home. He brought his own pillow along and kept his bedtime close to 10:00 pm. He used a lot of time on the campaign plane to banter with reporters as a form of uncoiling. Alexandra Pelosi's home-made video 'Journeys with George', which aired on HBO in 2002, captured the spirit of Bush's playful interaction with reporters. He gave suspicious scribes lots of ammunition to see him as a lightweight, snapping one reporter's suspenders, pulling faces, and smart-mouthing everyone. Late-night comedy picked up on the 'Bush as buffoon' theme.[88] Bush was not worried. He told reporters: 'Go ahead, underestimate me, you'll learn, you'll be sorry.'[89]

By Labor Day, political scientists and pundits alike predicted an inevitable Gore victory.[90] With a strong economy, widespread prosperity, no crime wave or foreign crisis, it was the incumbent's race to lose. Bush aide, Mark McKinnon put it this way, 'On paper, Gore ought to be beating us by 10 points.'[91] In September, Gore built a slight lead as Bush suffered several setbacks. The Bush campaign went for a while into the doldrums. Bush badmouthed a reporter, who had written negatively about Cheney, in front of a live microphone. A Gore campaign official divined that one frame in a Bush ad spelled 'RATS' inside the word 'bureaucrats.' The naked eye could not catch it, but Bush got bad press and pulled the ad off the air.[92] The Gore campaign, now led by the politically savvy son of the former mayor of Chicago, Richard Daley, found another way to push Bush off message. Bill Daley's people claimed that Bush's light campaigning schedule was proof that he was either not serious or felt he could not win.

James Carville, who masterminded Clinton's victory in 1992, had a dictum for running a presidential campaign: 'As long as you have your fist in the other guy's face, he can't hit you.'[93] Gore was keeping Bush from attacking him by keeping Bush on the defensive about his lackluster image. Don Evans got Laura to join Bush for a while to boost his spirit on the campaign trail and slightly expand his schedule.

Against all expectations, the event that should have put Al Gore over the top in fact turned things around for Bush. Presidential debates are subjective measures of people, but similar to the prognosis of who is ahead after the Iowa caucuses or the New Hampshire primary, the media's verdict after the debates is one of the turning points in the presidential campaign.

Bush obviously dislikes debates, but he and Rove concocted a strategy to make them work in his favor. Everybody in the Bush team expressed some form of hesitation about Bush's debating skills. Obviously, they were lowering expectations, but it had the added advantage of being plausible. After all, Bush was the candidate that could not speak well and did not seem to know much. At first the Bush team wanted to negotiate a radically different debating format away from the stand up confrontation. Gore used that opportunity to call his opponent 'intimidated'.[94] In the end, three presidential debates were scheduled, each with a different set up. While campaign spokesmen played scared, Bush started to practice for the debates months in advance under Hughes' tutelage.

The verdict after the first debate was essentially that Bush had been surprisingly coherent though a bit vague and repetitive, while Gore had sighed too often and had spoken too condescendingly. Gore's negative image as an overbearing policy wonk was then picked up by the Bush campaign and reinforced. The momentum shifted back to the Bush camp. By constantly reminding reporters that Gore had a nasty habit of exaggerating his stories, the Bush campaign was able to keep many people focused on Gore's communication and personality factors. When Gore seemed too friendly in the second debate, he was immediately perceived by many as being artificially sweet in order to erase his image of being overbearing and arrogant. In the middle of the debate Bush quipped, 'It seems like we're having a love fest tonight.'[95] From that point on, Gore was not able to shake off his opponent's main line of fire: that Gore was not comfortable in his own skin.

After the third debate, polls showed that Gore had lost his small lead.[96] Both the Gore and Bush team's poll trackers realized the race was very close and unlikely to budge either way. Gore ratcheted up his already frantic schedule and began calling all of Bush's policy proposals 'risky schemes'.[97] Bush kept campaigning in his Reaganesque manner: 'a genial Sun Belt governor not overly burdened by the details of governance' and with inclusive, optimistic themes.[98] The Bush campaign appeared too confident, having the candidate campaign in California even though the numbers in Florida were slipping and Bush had no chance whatsoever in California. It seemed that they had not learned from their over confidence in New Hampshire. Older voters preferred Gore's cautious, status quo approach; younger voters were slightly leaning towards Bush.

Just days before the election, a Democratic party official unearthed a 1976 charge against Bush for driving under the influence of alcohol. It appeared not to affect the race too much as Gore did not pursue it, and Bush repeated his line that when he was young and irresponsible he sometimes acted that way, but when he got married, and had a family, he had changed (unlike Clinton). With Hughes' iron discipline Bush would never get into answering any specific allegations. On the day of the election, Bush's early figures looked poor, but he was well rested and he was mentally prepared for defeat. Gore on the contrary had been going for 3 days without any sleep.

The Florida Finish

The Florida outcome was 'a long shot wrapped in a longer shot.'[99] The race was down to one final decisive state as neither Bush or Gore could get over the 270 Electoral College mark with all the other states counted. Had Gore not lost his home state Tennessee, the dead even vote in Florida would have been an important footnote, nothing more. If Clinton had not decided to take the young Cuban refugee boy Elian Gonzales back to his father in Cuba, Gore would likely have had larger margins of victory in counties such as Miami-Dade where Clinton in 1996 got 90,000 more votes than Gore did in 2000. If the Bush-McCain fight had not produced a Catholic backlash against Bush, he might have carried one extra state in the moderate and Catholic rust belt to get him over the top, but that was all hindsight.

Jeb Bush, George's brother and governor of Florida, and Karl Rove, as well as Al Gore's top man in Florida, Michael Whouley, knew that the networks had called Florida too early for Gore. Almost all networks rely on one number cruncher, Voter News Service, which operates out of New York and runs a national exit poll system that has a proven track record. TV networks rely on VNS to give them the best and earliest call. Likely, the early call for Gore in the Eastern time zone kept some voters in the more conservative Florida panhandle (Central Time Zone) at home, and thus cost Bush votes. Why bother to vote if the race is lost?

The networks reversed themselves and put Florida back in 'undecided' in mid-evening. Later that night, just before most viewers went to bed, Florida was declared for Bush. Whouley was still not convinced, but had not answered Gore's phone call quickly enough and Daley and Gore made up their minds to concede.[100] Perhaps Gore acted in too much haste, feeling exhausted by his 3-day marathon. When Whouley found out, Gore had already made his concession phone call to Bush and was en route to give his concession speech. With minutes to spare, Whouley ordered David Morehouse, Gore's trip director, to physically block Gore from getting to the podium.[101] Once in a holding room, Gore got the update and called Bush back saying that the results were too close to call. The Bush team already knew that the vote count would come in under 0.5 per cent and would thus by Florida law go to an automatic recount. Bush pressed Gore on the phone, 'You are calling back to retract your concession?' 'You don't have to get snippy about it,' Gore responded. 'Do what you have to do,' Bush said, ending the conversation.[102] That turned out to be a prophetic statement as Gore set out to do everything he could to get Florida, feeling vindicated because he carried the popular vote in the overall election.

The 37-day standoff in Florida had more inside games than a Russian nesting doll. One participant called it 'a roller-coast ride with pause buttons.'[103] It was new terrain for the tired campaign teams who were hurled into an unknown challenge. Gore was at a disadvantage. Most Americans went to bed believing Bush had won, so when they woke up and found out the election was on hold they automatically thought of Gore as the challenger.

The Gore team was quick to assemble a planeload of volunteers to go to the polling stations and raise any opportunity to get recounts. Steven Kirsch, a Silicon Valley billionaire, put up $1 million to get the team off the ground. The new political action committee set up for Gore in Florida would eventually raise $7 million. Their cover was blown as they landed at the same time as Jeb Bush's plane touched down from Austin.[104] The folks on Jeb's plane recognized the Gore ringleaders. If the Gore team was ahead in sending volunteers to the polling stations, the Bush team was ahead in contracting every major law firm in Florida. 'More lawyers' was the constant refrain in Florida. In the ensuing weeks, both the Bush and Gore teams organized public protests while their lawyers maneuvered behind the scenes and in various court cases. The Bush team brought in a planeload of Congressional staffers and other GOP workers to protest recount efforts for Gore in Miami-Dade County.

The basic positions of the two campaigns followed a historical pattern. The candidate who is behind demands recounts and looks for any possible irregularity. The Gore team made it sound as if the recount would produce thousands of additional votes, a claim without any historical foundation. On the other side, the candidate who is ahead insists on the validity of the status quo and tries to hurry up certification of the vote. If Bush had carried the popular (nation wide) vote, Gore's legitimacy in challenging the Florida count would have been almost zero, but Gore's popular victory helped him enormously and more Americans (58 per cent) were watching the Florida aftermath than had paid attention to the election itself.[105]

The Bush position was that machines count the vote as agreed by both sides. In the first count, Bush won by only 1800 votes, triggering a law-induced machine recount. The recount tally announced on November 10 was 300. While giving credence to Gore's claim that more recounts could change the outcome, Bush was ahead in both counts and thus the victor. Thus, Bush argued the votes have been counted, and recounted and now the findings should stand unless there is probable cause for fraud or other irregularities as stipulated by Florida law. Gore's argument that more recounting would produce different results sounded reasonable, but Bush's point that the rules had been applied and the game was over also made good sense.

What fiction writer could have matched the next complication? A well-meaning election official in Palm Beach County, Theresa LePore, had invented a so-called butterfly ballot to help make a crowded page more accessible without making the print smaller. Many witnesses came forward complaining that they accidentally voted for the Reform candidate Pat Buchanan (rather than Gore) as a result of the butterfly layout. The Gore team in Florida, led by former Secretary of State Warren Christopher, argued that this was sufficient cause for an investigation. The Bush team, also led by a former Secretary of State, James Baker, countered that both parties had agreed on the butterfly ballot before Election Day and thus there was no case for fraud. The atmosphere was heating up with one group of protestors holding up placards that read, 'butterfly confuses Gorons', and 'Gore Plan: Recount till I Win.'[106] Jesse Jackson led a protest march claiming that Jeb Bush and the Republican establishment were out to disenfranchise African Americans. In some counties, the machine counts were run three and even four times, but now there was hardly any difference in final outcome, still leaving Bush with a tiny lead.

If he was to have any hope of winning, Gore had to move away from the machines to manual recounts. A call for a recount in all 67 Florida counties would be most fair, but would take too long. The machines seemed to have done a sloppy job and Florida law mentioned 'voter intent' as a key factor. With the December 20th deadline looming when Congress would officially tally the electoral college votes, Gore chose for a manual recount in four counties. The Bush side saw this as political move. The four counties chosen by Gore were all alleged to have been selected on the basis of finding 'voter intent', but they had also voted predominantly Democratic in past elections. Now the argument shifted to what constituted the right criteria for a manual count. How much of the perforated area in the ballot had to be gone or pierced or hanging for it to count as a vote? When Broward county officials (prodded by Gore's lawyers) changed the rules from hanging to pierced, and then to dimpled chads, and then started to recount 500,000 votes which had already been hand counted, the Bush team declared it a 'crime scene'.[107] Bush moved to stop Gore's manual counts in court and from then on, it was total political and legal warfare between the camps.

Bush delegated most tactical decisions to James Baker and retreated to his ranch, trying to look presidential as he met with potential cabinet secretaries. Gore suffered a setback when his team challenged late absentee ballots, most of which were military votes, which likely would go Republican. It is not unimaginable that some were cast past the due date to help spread Bush's lead in Florida. The problem is that an aspiring Commander-in-Chief looks awful denying military personnel serving abroad their vote. Bush's friend and assistant in Florida, the former Montana governor Marc Racicot, claimed that Gore and Lieberman 'have gone to war against the men and women who serve in our armed forces.'[108] Lieberman went on TV to announce that the Gore team was dropping its challenge to these votes.

There is no way of knowing how all the political and legal knots could have been untied. Katherine Harris, the Florida Secretary of State, whose mandate it was to certify the vote, was also a strong supporter of Bush. Florida Attorney General, Robert Butterworth, a Democratic appointee, intervened at crucial points to advance Gore's legal process. There was something inherently slippery in the manual recounts. Was a dimple evidence of voter's intent? Thanks to the military absentee vote, Bush never lost his lead. In a crucial appeal decision that suspended Harris's right to enforce a deadline and certify the vote, the Florida Supreme Court, voted along what seemed politicized lines. In his minority opinion, the chief justice, 'an older pragmatist', wrote that the majority had re-written Florida election law by their verdict.[109] That smacked like blatant judicial activism. The Florida legislature threatened to choose its own slate of electors with or without the backing of Florida's highest court. This was no empty threat as Article 2 (Section 1) of the Constitution gives the legislature, not the court, the final say.

In its first ruling, the US Supreme Court had only ordered a temporary stay and had tried to get Florida actors to resolve the problem. Its final verdict on December 12 came down along partisan lines, but now it was a Republican line. The Supreme Court did not act out of political opportunism. Short of a judicial resolution, the Republican dominated Congress could have declared the presidential winner, perhaps leaving far more rancor in the system. In his analysis of the Supreme Court's decision, former US Appeal Court Justice, Richard Posner, argued that 'inconsistent chad-counting standards' was not really a violation of equal protection or due process under the constitution as the Supreme Court had argued. The key point, according to Posner, was that Florida's Supreme Court had 'flouted the letter and intent of Florida's election laws' and had thus violated the constitutional provision that the legislature 'determines the manner of choosing presidential electors.'[110] The Florida court had usurped the constitutional authority given to the Florida legislature and the Supreme Court set it straight.

The last chapter in the Florida saga vindicated Bush despite the vicious conspiracy theories floating around that the Supreme Court engaged in 'legal gimmickry' to give Bush the White House.[111] Ultimately, the Supreme Court's decision proved prescient. A study commissioned by the *Washington Post* and other news organizations, and conducted by a scientific team from the University of Michigan, which was released in November 2001, proved wrong all the commentators who predicted that Gore would be the legitimate winner.[112] The team concluded that if every ballot had been counted under the strictest guidelines in all four counties, Bush would have won, but with a slightly smaller margin than he was given in the official certification (537 on November 26). If the limited recounts requested by Gore and ordered by the Florida Supreme Court had proceeded, 'Bush would have held his lead over Gore, with margins ranging from 225 to 493 votes.'[113] The study also found that under every possible scenario, even if all 67 counties were hand counted, the winning margin would have been for Bush and remained under 500. Only in one scenario, the study concluded, might Gore have won. If the most liberal interpretation of voter intent (hanging and dimpled chads) in all 67 counties would be used, Gore might have won 'by 60 to 171 votes', but there were too many variations to ever know for sure. Concluded Kirk Wolter, a senior researcher in the project: 'it may be that we'll never know the exact vote total'.[114] One analyst noted, if the six-million Florida voters had all 'flipped fair coins', the winning lead would have been no greater than 600.[115]

Conclusion

While Gore made mistakes and Ralph Nader siphoned off Democratic votes, the Bush campaign did not win by accident. Bush beat the long odds and successfully challenged a sitting vice president. Bush, Rove, Hughes and Evans did so by putting into action what they had learned over a political lifetime. Bush capitalized on the grassroots' construction of the Republican Party started by Lee Atwater and Karl Rove. Having the early support of the majority of Republican governors, helped Bush raise funds and build early momentum. The Bush campaign pursued a set of public policy issues held together by the values of 'Compassionate Conservatism.' Bush believed sincerely in these values and his confidence and sincerity came across as real. In the exit polls, Bush scored high on 'honesty,' likeability, and 'strong leadership.'

When John McCain came very close to upsetting Bush's strategy during the early primaries, Bush did not panic, change course, or fire his loyal aides. They had pledged themselves to the candidate. The inner circle could be frank with him, and he shared his thoughts and feelings with them. His decisions sealed a team effort. Bush stayed with his people through thick and thin.

Given the Florida handicap, Bush would have to win the November 2002 midterm elections to settle the score and earn governing credibility. To do so, he needed domestic policy victories more urgently than foreign policy achievements. Many pundits advised him to move to the political center and to govern cautiously. Bush would do the opposite. He would take a big risk and invest all his capital on early tax cuts. In foreign affairs, he would stand for stronger defense, but would not let it clutter the agenda.

Notes

1   Nicholas D. Kristof, 'For Bush, His Toughest Call Was the Choice to Run at All', *New York Times*, October 29, 2000.
2   Nicholas Kristof, 'A Father's Footsteps Echo Throughout a Son's Career', *New York Times*, September 11, 2000.
3   Carl M. Cannon, 'For the Love of the Game', *National Journal*, March 24, 2001.
4   Frank Bruni, *Ambling into History: The Unlikely Odyssey of George W. Bush* (New York: HarperCollins, 2002), p. 62.
5   Michelle Cottle, 'The Enforcer', *The New Republic*, November 29, 1999.
6   Karen Hughes, *Ten Minutes From Normal* (New York: Viking, 2004), pp. 18-19.
7   Cottle, November 29, 1999, p. 21.
8   As quoted in Laura Flanders, *Bushwomen: Tales of a Cynical Species* (London: Verso, 2004), p. 105.
9   Melinda Henneberger, 'Driving W.', *The New York Times Magazine*, May 14, 2000, p. 54.
10   Lou Dubose et al., *Boy Genius: Karl Rove, the Brains Behind the Remarkable Political Triumph of George W. Bush* (New York: Public Affairs, 2003), p. xii.
11   John Brady, *Bad Boy: The Life and Politics of Lee Atwater* (Reading, Massachusetts: Addison Wesley, 1997).
12   Henneberger, May 14, 2000, p. 54.
13   Bush as quoted in 'God and the Governor', *Charisma Magazine*, August 29, 2000.
14   Frank Bruni, 'Donald L. Evans: Bush's New Campaign Chief Has Been a Steadfast Friend', *New York Times*, April 30, 2000.
15   Nicholas Lemann, 'The Redemption', *The New Yorker*, January 31, 2000, pp. 60-61.
16   Stuart Stevens, *The Big Enchilada: Campaign Adventures with the Cockeyed Optimists from Texas Who Won the Biggest Price in Politics* (New York: The Free Press, 2000), p. 132.

17   Frank Bruni, 'Bush Names A Texas Friend as Chairman of Campaign', *New York Times*, April 29, 2000,

18   Christopher Marquis, 'A Tough-Talking, but Self-Effacing, Loyalist: Joe Marvin Allbaugh', *New York Times,* June 5, 2001.

19   James A. Barnes, 'George W. Bush's Inner Circle', *National Journal*, June 6, 1998.

20   Hughes, p. 123.

21   Richard Brookhiser, 'The Mind of George W. Bush', *Atlantic Monthly* April 2003, p. 65.

22   David Grann, 'Where W. Got Compassion', *The New York Times Magazine*, September 12, 1999.

23   Julie Kosterlitz, 'Bush's Left Right-Hand Men', *National Journal*, May 5, 2001.

24   Stevens, 2000, p. 270

25   George W. Bush, *A Charge to Keep* (New York: William Morrow and Company, Inc, 1999), p. 235.

26   James A. Barnes, 'Bush's Hour', *National Journal*, July 29, 2000.

27   Dana Milbank, 'What W. Stands For', *The New Republic*, April 26 and May 3, 1999.

28   Sam Howe Verhovek, 'Is There Room on a Republican Ticket for Another Bush?', *New York Times Magazine*, September 13, 1998, p. 56.

29   Franklin Foer, 'Spin Doctrine', *The New Republic*, June 5, 2000.

30   Christopher Caldwell, 'Is W. Inevitable?', *Atlantic Monthly Online*, November 17, 1999.

31   Roger Simon, *Divided We Stand: How Al Gore Beat George Bush and Lost the Presidency* (New York: Crown Publishers, 2001), pp. 74-75.

32   Dana Milbank, *Smashmouth: Two Years in the Gutter with Al Gore and George W. Bush – Notes from the 2000 Campaign Trail* (New York: Basic Books, 2001), pp. 69 and 103.

33   Stevens, p. 126.

34   Hughes, p. 128.

35   Brady, 316.

36   Simon, p. 115

37   Milbank, 2001, p.192.

38   Fred Barnes, 'The Case for Bush', *The New Republic*, March 6, 2000.

39   Dana Milbank, April 26 and May 3, 2000, p. 70 writes that Steve Goldsmith coined the term.

40   David Grann, 'Ghosts: Can Lee Atwater's Legacy Save George W.?', *The New Republic*, February 21, 2000.

41   Nicholas Lemann, 'The McCain Code', *The New Yorker*, February 4, 2002.

42   Frank Bruni, 'Addressing Concerns, Bush is Said to Assemble Team of Washington Insiders', *New York Times*, April 21, 2000.

43   Adam Nagourney and Frank Bruni, 'Gatekeeper to Running Mate: Cheney's Road to Candidacy', *New York Times*, July 28, 2000.

44   Nicholas Lemann, 'The Quiet Man', *The New Yorker*, May 7, 2001, p. 63.

45   Carl M. Cannon, 'The Point Man', *National Journal*, October 12, 2002, 2002, p. 2964.

46   Bill Turque and Mark Hosenball, 'Backseat Driver', *Newsweek*, August , 2000.

47   Howard Fineman, 'The Ticket', *Newsweek*, August 7, 2000.

48   Bill Turque and Mark Hosenball, p. 28.

49   Barnes, July 29, 2000.

50   Stevens, p. 168.

51   Bruni, 2002 p. 185.

52   Milbank, 2001, p. 294.

53   George W. Bush, *A Charge to Keep* (New York: William Morrow and Co., 1999), p. 239.

54   Carla Anne Robbins, 'How Would Bush Fare With Foreign Policy?', *Wall Street Journal*, February 29, 2000, p. 1.

55   Bruce Cummings, 'The Emperor's Old Clothes', *The Nation*, February 2001, p. 18.
56   Nicholas Lemann, 'Without a Doubt', *The New Yorker*, October 14 & 21, 2002, p. 166.
57   Jacob Heilbrunn, 'Condoleezza Rice: George W.'s Realist', *World Policy Journal* (Winter 1999/2000), p. 52.
58   Heilbrunn, p. 49.
59   Ann Reilly Dowd, 'Is There Anything This Woman Can't Do?', *George*, June 2000, p. 102.
60   Idem, p. 88.
61   As quoted in Flanders, *Bushwomen*, p. 39.
62   Hans J. Morgenthau, *Politics Among Nations*, (New York: Alfred A. Knopf, 1973, Fifth Edition), p. 5.
63   Reilly-Dowd, p. 102.
64   Hughes, p. 116.
65   American Enterprise Institute, 'How Would George Bush Govern in Foreign Policy?', June 22, 2000
66   Sam Tanenhaus, 'Bush's Brain Trust', *Vanity Fair*, July 2003, p. 168.
67   James Mann, 'The Bush Team Shares a Vision But Not How to Reach It', *The Washington Post*, September 30, 2001, B-1.
68   Keller, 2002, p. 50.
69   Senator James Inhofe as quoted in 'Paul Wolfowitz, Testimony Before the Armed Services Committee', US Senate, July 12, 2001.
70   Evan Thomas and Roy Gutman, 'See George. See George Learn Foreign Policy', *Newsweek*, June 18, 2001, p. 24.
71   As quoted in an interview with Sam Donaldson on *ABC This Week*, (Transcript) July 16, 2000.
72   'A Period of Consequences', The Citadel, South Carolina, September 23, 1999.
73   'A Distinctly American Internationalism', Ronald Reagan Presidential Library, Simi Valley, California, November 19, 1999.
74   'Inaugural Address', Office of the Press Secretary, The White House, January 20, 2001.
75   Paul Wolfowitz, Testimony Before the Armed Services Committee, US Senate, July 19, 2001.
76   Donald Rumsfeld in testimony before the Senate Armed Services Committee, June 28, 2001.
77   James Kitfield, 'A Small Study Carries a Heavy Burden', *National Journal*, March 3, 2001, p. 646.
78   As quoted by John T. Correll, 'Struggling for Transformation', *Air Force Magazine*, Vol. 84, No. 5, May 2001.
79   James Kitfield, 'Peacekeepers' Progress', *National Journal*, December 23, 2000, p. 3948.
80   Citadel, 1999.
81   Robert B. Zoellick, 'A Republican Foreign Policy', *Foreign Affairs*, Vol. 79, No. 1, January/February 2000, p. 67.
82   'The World in Their Hands', *The Economist*, December 23, 2000, p.30.
83   'How Would Bush Govern'.
84   Bruni, 2002, pp. 38-39.
85   Andrew Sullivan, 'The Reluctant President: Frank Bruni's Insight into Bush', *Sunday Times of London*, March 17, 2002.
86   Bruni, 2002, p. 196.
87   Simon, p. 58.
88   Dick Schaap, 'Why We Are Laughing at Bush and Gore', *George*, July 2000.
89   Bruni, 2002, p. 57
90   Robert S. Erikson, 'The 2000 Presidential Election in Historical Perspective', *Political Science Quarterly* (Vol. 116, No. 1, 2001), p. 35.

91   Barnes, July 29, 2000.
92   Simon, p. 224.
93   James Carville and Mary Matalin, *All's Fair: Love, War, and Running for President* (New York: Random House, 1994).
94   Jack W. Germond and Jules Witcover, 'Like Father, Like Son', September 9, 2000.
95   Simon, p. 242.
96   Erikson, p. 40.
97   Carl M. Cannon, 'How Low Will Gore Go?', *George*, July 2000.
98   Jonathan Chait, 'Still His Party', *The New Republic*, August 7, 2000.
99   Political Staff of the Washington Post, *Deadlock: The Inside Story of America's Closest Election* (New York: PublicAffairs, 2001, p. 21.
100 Simon, p. 22.
101 Simon, pp. 7-8.
102 Simon, p. 43.
103 Simon, p. 273.
104 Political Staff of the Washington Post, pp. 53-55.
105 Milbank, 2001, p. 388.
106 Milbank, 2001, p. 384.
107 The Political Staff of the Washington Post, p. 136
108 Idem, p. 129
109 Idem, p. 202.
110 Stuart Taylor, 'Bush vs. Gore and the Partisanship of the Professors', *National Journal*, June 16, 2001.
111 Michael Moore, *Stupid White Men* (New York: Regan Books, 2001), p. 2; See also Vincent Bugliosi, *The Betrayal of America* (New York: Thunder Mouth's Press, 2001).
112 Hendrick Hertzberg, 'The Talk of the Town', *The New Yorker*, February 19 and 26, 2001, stated that the vote count was 'almost certainly wrong in its outcome'. Jonathan Cohn, 'Loser Take All?', *The New Republic*, January 29, 2001, noted 'it seems increasingly likely that those counts will show that Gore had enough votes to win the state.'
113 Dan Keating and Dan Baltz, 'Florida Recounts Would Have Favoured Bush', *Washington Post*, November 12, 2001.
114 Keating and Balz, November 12, 2001.
115 Erikson, p. 29.

Chapter 3

The Bush White House, the Decision-Making Process, and the Priority of Domestic Policy

The media's overall assessment of President Bush in mid-December 2000 was pretty low. *Newsweek* called him 'all name and no mandate', and 'a prisoner of his party and not the master of it'. Twenty-nine per cent of those polled by *Newsweek* regarded Bush as 'illegitimate'.[1] As the British magazine, *The Economist,* put it, Bush, 'the accidental president', was elected by the 'skin of his chad'.[2] Many assumed that Bush would 'bungle' his transition, but as had happened many times in his political life, the 'commentariat' in the media and academia underestimated him.[3] He benefited again from low expectations – this time from the still pervasive notion that somehow this President was not really in charge, and that he would not be 'adept at inside Washington politics'.[4]

Instead, the Bush transition to the White House was one of the quickest and most efficient in recent memory. The reasons were a disciplined management style by the president-elect, experienced and loyal advisers, an early game plan, and a very orderly decision-making process. Bush created an inner circle around Karl Rove, Karen Hughes, Andy Card, Dick Cheney and Condoleezza (Condi) Rice. With the help of Bush's friend and personnel director, Clay Johnson, this team helped select and organize the rest of the executive and assured that decision-making would be centered in the White House. A group of Cabinet secretaries were quickly nominated and put in the role of selling and executing Bush's priorities.

If the seriously handicapped Bush were to have any governing credibility, he would have to show firm control, a strict set of priorities, and above all score an early victory in Congress. With only half the normal amount of time to complete the transition due to the drawn-out legal competition in Florida, the Bush administration nevertheless pulled off 'a solid and close-to-seamless start'.[5] The start was focused on domestic politics.

Transition

Bush and fellow Texan Clay Johnson met at Phillips Academy in Andover when they were fifteen years old. They became friends and went on to Yale University where they shared a room. They stayed in touch when George left for Midland. When he became governor in Austin, Bush asked Johnson to help him make numerous statewide appointments. As with Hughes, Rove and Evans, there is complete trust between Bush and Johnson – the latter knew what the former wanted in people.

Bush told Johnson, 'I would like you to figure out what we need to do starting the day after the election. Come up with a plan – talk to people that have done this before, read what you can get your hands on, confer with people, pick their brains, and come up with a plan.'[6] Johnson went around the country researching and talking to people from previous administrations. He was able to operate, Karl Rove remembered, in 'stealth mode' for many months.[7] He had finished a lot of crucial work before the media and the Gore campaign found out about him. Reporting back to the campaign team, Johnson, Rove and Hughes formulated a set of priorities and strategies complete with deadlines. Bush approved this game plan in June 2000. Key principles included: the campaign leaders would not be in charge of the transition; by mid-December, the White House senior staff and an organizational structure should be in place; by Christmas all cabinet nominees should be announced. They would be briefed and ready to begin confirmation hearings in the first week of January. By the time of inauguration, January 20, Bush agreed the administration should have in place a 20-day, 100-day, and 180-day schedule to launch his presidency. Also agreed was that the White House would be ready shortly after the inaugural to nominate about 160 people for sub-cabinet and senior department positions before April 30. At the same time, Bush and his advisers agreed that they would reach out proactively to Congress, review the executive orders that would come to his desk, and prepare a budget for mid-February.

George W. Bush's instructions to Johnson revealed his general management style. From his own experience and instinct, Bush knew the transition needed to be done early and orderly; he therefore set a clear goal for Johnson. He trusted Johnson to propose the details and tactics, and to come back and brief him on these. When Clay Johnson brought the plans back, Bush went over them carefully, questioning Johnson and the other advisers, then making a clear decision so that everyone knew the way ahead.

In August, Bush put Cheney in charge of the transition, while Johnson continued the search for future appointments. Dick Cheney had been involved in five presidential transitions from Gerald Ford to the elder Bush administration. George W. Bush did not become president-elect until December 13. His transition time had been cut in half from 76 days to just 37. In early December, Cheney had to rent commercial office space in McLean, Virginia to work on the transition; the executive branch, still in the hands of President Bill Clinton, was not going to give the Bush transition team the funds and office space with the outcome still in the courts.

Having made the Philadelphia convention the testing ground for Andy Card, Bush made him his designate chief of staff in mid-October. Card's own experience was invaluable, having joined the elder Bush's White House as a legislative liaison to Congress. He later became deputy chief of staff under John Sununu, and when the elder Bush moved his administration out of town in 1993, Card was in charge of the transition. George W. Bush resisted the common temptation to put campaign staff or loyalists without Washington experience in charge of the decision-making process. Jimmy Carter had belatedly appointed Hamilton Jordan, but Jordan had no experience in dealing with Congress or the lobbies. Clinton appointed his Arkansas friend Mac McLarty on December 12, 1992 (two months behind Bush's similar appointment), but McLarty had no Washington experience and left, quite frustrated, a short time later. Wisely, Bush kept Allbaugh or Evans from falling into this trap.

White House Team

There is strong continuity between the campaign, transition, and governing team George W. Bush put in place with two exceptions; Don Evans and Joe Allbaugh were kept out of the top layer of White House management. Evans plays an important informal role. At Evans's swearing-in ceremony as Secretary of Commerce, Bush showed his feelings, saying, 'you're going to love him like I do.'[8] The President regularly has Don and Susie Evans over for dinner at the White House residence or brings them to Camp David to run ideas by him or just to have a 'friend in town to lean on';[9] Bush did not call on Evans to chair the fundraising campaign for his 2004 presidential race, but instead appointed Mercer Reynolds, an old business friend from the days of Spectrum 7 and the Texas Rangers. Joe Allbaugh was put in charge of the Federal Emergency Management Agency. He left government in March 2003 when FEMA merged into the Department of Homeland Security to work in the private sector.

Bush made Rove Senior Adviser to the President, and put him in charge of a new White House office called 'Strategic Initiatives'. Rove is also in control of the traditional Political Affairs Office where his protégé Ken Mehlman works on grassroots Republican issues. In late 2003, Bush made Mehlman campaign chairman for the 2004 election. Bush appointed Ruben Barrales, an Hispanic from California, to head the Intergovernmental Affairs Office which is the third pillar of Rove's White House office, coordinating regional strategy with party officials at the state level. More than Lee Atwater or James Carville before him, Karl Rove contributes both to the political mechanics of the White House and its policy pursuits.

After the 2000 campaign, Bush retained Jan van Lohuizen as his principal pollster and Fred Steeper remained in charge of focus groups. They feed their findings to Matthew Dowd in the Republican National Committee, who in turn reports directly to Karl Rove. Bush's aides insist that they do not poll on policy 'positions', but only on 'presentation'. Van Lohuizen commissions frequent national polls on 'Bush attributes'.[10] Poll data is very tightly held, with only a handful of advisers who see it and discuss it. Bush spent about half the amount of money on polling as Bill Clinton did in his first year.

Aside from attending virtually all meetings with Bush, Rove has organized a way in which the major White House offices are integrated into Bush's political strategy. The meetings are nicknamed 'Strategery Meetings' after a 'Saturday Night Live' play on Bush's mispronunciation of the word 'strategy.'[11] Senior White House staff from Domestic Policy, the National Security Council, Legislative Office and other offices get together once every two weeks to plan a horizon of three weeks in terms of political strategy. The 'Strategery Group' also meets at deputy level, with Mehlman in charge to prepare ideas for the Principal's group.

Until the summer of 2002, when she moved her family back to Texas, Karen Hughes was much more than a Communications Director. Bush also made her 'Counsellor to the President.' He told Card in December that he wanted Hughes present for every major decision. She and Karl Rove are unique among his top staff; she could and often did disagree with Bush, right to his face, and in front of other staff. Bush did not mind her 'unvarnished advice', in fact he encouraged it.[12] Bush said in a *Time* interview: 'The definition of loyalty is also somebody like Karen Hughes or Karl Rove, who walks in and says "you're wrong."'[13] Besides a very close personal adviser and sounding board to Bush, Hughes was in charge of the Bush Administration's message like Rove is still in charge of its strategy. She controled the Communications, the Press Secretary, the Speech Writing, and the Media Affairs Offices. She held daily meetings with key public affairs appointments in the departments and agencies, some in person and some by teleconference to set the message for the day. Everything that is planned to be said that day had to be cleared with Karen. If you have 'an idea', one staff aide commented, 'or a proposal, Karen better like it or it won't have a chance in any event'.[14]

While Hughes' foremost task was political messaging and Rove's is political strategy, both were also substantial policy advisers to Bush. They would give him their view on anything. In an interview in the Summer of 2002, Card depicted Rove and Hughes as the 'beauty and the beast'.[15] They formed a balance for Bush. Rove can be expected to come at it more from the right-wing side of the Republican Party, while Hughes is much more moderate, even populist. Her specialty is to keep Bush 'real'.[16] Card said his role often amounted to keeping the balance between the two.

Card is the type of manager who is expected to keep his own views from interfering with the process. 'I try to manage the issues and personnel', Card stated in an interview in September 2001, 'to accommodate the time that is available for the president to make decisions'.[17] Clay Johnson knew this was important to Bush. 'I knew,' Johnson said, 'that Bush did not want someone to be chief of staff who was over-territorial, or a control freak, or felt like they had to control the content or the recommendations that flowed to the president.'[18] Bush wrote in his campaign memoir that he had seen a heavy-handed gatekeeper and 'filter' in his dad's administration (meaning John Sununu) and vowed never to repeat that problem.[19] In Austin, Bush had made sure that his chief of staff, Joe Allbaugh, kept a 'much flatter organizational chart'. Bush had stated, 'I have direct access from more than one person.'[20] The chief of staff would facilitate all aspects of the decision-making process, but he would not hamper access to the governor for his major advisers. 'If they cannot communicate with me directly,' Bush had said, 'they will become dispirited': Bush wanted the same from Card.[21]

Even the best custodian of the process from time to time slips into personal advocacy. In that light, it is interesting to note that Bush did not choose a chief of staff with conservative instincts similar to his own. Card is a moderate Republican from Michigan, who often voted with Democrats when he was a Massachusetts legislator. Just as the personally conservative Cheney functioned without policy conflicts under moderate Republican Gerald Ford, so the more centrist Card, Bush felt, could work without problems for him. Well into the second year of the Bush administration, *National Journal* reporters Carl Cannon and Alexis Simendinger found that Card still was not 'Bush's main policy adviser or his message crafter or his political eyes and ears.' Rather, those roles are covered, 'sometimes in overlapping fashion, by Rove and Hughes.'[22]

The fourth player with unlimited access to Bush and a wide-ranging portfolio is Dick Cheney. Every president since Carter has claimed that he is giving unprecedented new powers to his Vice President. However, no one can dispute that Cheney's role is unique. Cheney will never run for president as his 'chronic artery disease' and history of heart attacks disqualify him.[23] Skeptics about Bush's command over his own decisions or his real interest in governing dubbed Cheney the 'Prime Minister' or the 'co-president'.[24] However, this view relies on the popular but inaccurate characterization of Bush as a hands-off decision maker.

Cheney is a 'super' senior adviser on almost everything and his office is fully integrated with Card's and the Oval Office, involving him in both domestic and foreign policy. Bush relies on him as Congressional liaison alongside Nick Calio who heads the Congressional Office. Bush told Congressional leaders early on, 'When you're talking to Cheney, you are talking to me. When Dick Cheney's talking, it is me talking.'[25] Often, Calio will lead the visible side of White House relations with Congress, while Cheney works 'quietly' behind the scenes.[26] Besides his office in the Senate, Cheney asked Dennis Hastert, the Speaker of the House, for a small office in the House where he can confer with House Representatives. Cheney brought with him his long-time friend and aide Lewis 'Scooter' Libby. Libby works closely with Card to keep the Vice Presidential operation in tune with Bush's staff. In addition, Cheney appointed Mary Matalin as his communications' director. Having worked in the elder Bush's campaigns, Matalin was trusted by George W. Bush, and soon established a close working relationship Karen Hughes.

Comparisons of Bush's inner circle to Reagan's troika of Edwin Meese, James Baker and Michael Deaver leave much to be desired.[27] First of all, as long as Hughes was there, and with Cheney's direct involvement, it was not a troika but a quartet. Baker had come into office with Vice President Bush, not Ronald Reagan, but all four in Bush's circle are solely loyal to him. All four enjoy open access to Bush and are tightly interconnected through a series of staff meetings and committee structures. Joshua Bolten, Card's deputy, and Michael Gerson, Bush's speechwriter, do not have the same seniority and peer status as this foursome, but they grew close to Bush over time and have become an integral part of the White House structure; they are the heads of the second tier in the White House.

During the campaign, Bush bonded with Joshua Bolten, the experienced policy guru recommended to him by Robert Zoellick. Bolten helped Rove to keep the candidate within his policy 'foodgroups.' This bonding does not come as a surprise because Bolten works in the style so valued by Bush. Always low-profile, Bolten is not worried about others taking credit for the work he does – he gives no interviews and is free of any pretense. Bolten is the son of a CIA official and grew up in Washington, D.C. and after obtaining his law degree, he served as a staffer on the Senate Finance Committee. Card picked him from that committee to serve in the elder Bush's Trade Representative Office under Carla Hills. Soon after, he joined Nick Calio in the legislative affairs office. In the 1990s, Bolten spent six years working for Goldman Sachs in London; Bush made Bolten Card's deputy in charge of policy. This allowed Card to stay focused on the decision process while Bolten pulled together the various policy proposals in the White House. Bolten had an office on the ground floor of the West Wing only two doors away from Bush. In addition to Card, Rove, Cheney, and Hughes, he spent a lot of 'face time with Bush'.[28] Bolten moved to the Office of Management and Budget in 2003, perhaps as a sign of Bush wanting to tighten spending as budget deficits continued to rise. Clay Johnson moved with Bolton to OMB as deputy director of management. One of the key staffers in Bolten's office was Margaret Spellings who heads the

Domestic Policy Council. She is Bush's 'longtime adviser on education policy', and came with Sandy Kress and Rod Paige from Texas to put together Bush's education bill.[29]

Bush gave his chief speechwriter Michael Gerson an office in the West Wing and access to key meetings. In July 2002, he added 'policy adviser' to Gerson's title. While Gerson's office was technically under Karen Hughes – and then under Dan Bartlett's who took over Hughes' position in 2002 – Gerson enjoys a good relationship with Bush. Gerson is a compassionate conservative by conviction and a conservative Christian like Bush. Gerson can pick the words that blend Rove's strategy and Hughes' populism with Bush's faith values. He can let Bush speak to religious conservatives and soccer moms in his own words without alienating one or the other. When Bush was preparing for his address to Congress in late February 2001, so many offices in the White House tried to get their lines into the speech that Hughes told him, 'This is unacceptable.'[30] Bush then asked her and Gerson to come to Camp David to rewrite the whole thing over the weekend. The speech was praised widely for its coherence and genuine voice.

Bush appointed a close Texan aide, Alberto Gonzales, as his White House legal Counsel. The second oldest in a poor family with eight kids, Gonzales worked himself into one of Houston's most respected law firms. Bush was impressed when Gonzales turned down an offer from his father to work for him. Gonzales wanted to become a partner in the law firm first. Bush appointed him as his general counsel in Austin in 1995 and later as his Secretary of State. In 1999, Bush appointed Gonzales to the Texas Supreme Court. Some speculate that the moderate Latino may be Bush's first in line for nominee to the Supreme Court.[31] In a politically savvy move, Bush, Rove and Gonzales agreed that all legal counsel to the major departments should form a loose team under Gonzales's umbrella.

None of Bush's economic advisers were part of his inner core although Larry Lindsey and Glenn Hubbard had the president's ear on tax reforms. Larry Lindsey was put in charge of the National Economic Council. However, Bush did not use this council actively and later put it under the Office of Policy Development. Glen Hubbard, Bush's campaign adviser on tax cuts, was given the chair of the Council of Economic Advisers in 2001. Hubbard left the administration in February 2003 as he had taken only a two-year leave from Columbia University. Like Lindsey, Mitchell Daniels had been on Reagan's economic team. Bush made Daniels his Director of Office, Management and Budget. From the start, Daniels fought an uphill battle to keep the administration from overspending its own declared targets.

Bush's economic team was the weakest part of his White House structure – the group did not jell. In his management survey of the Bush White House, Donald Kettl noted that, 'The economic team seemed missing in action.'[32] The addition of Secretary of the Treasury, Paul O'Neill, to this fledgling team did nothing to prolong its life. Cheney had recommended O'Neill, but it did not work out as O'Neill came in underestimating Bush and contemptuous of political advisers such as Rove. Unlike Rumsfeld who knew both what he wanted *and* who was in charge, O'Neill came in with an attitude of telling Bush what to do, including reversing his tax cut pledges.[33] O'Neill felt that Bush was disengaged in their weekly meetings, but it is far more likely that Bush's sharp political eye immediately noticed that O'Neill spelled trouble. Rove and Hughes realized early that O'Neill could not be managed and was 'armed and dangerous'.[34] As a result, Bush kept him out of the real loop of decision making. O'Neill often mispoke on prospects for the American economy, the merits of alleviating the financial woes of such countries as Argentina, and against aspects of Bush's own tax cuts. O'Neill doubted the wisdom of prolonged tax cuts in the face of rising deficits. If he had tried to become a loyal player, he could have made a difference. However, his disloyal and arrogant approach made it more difficult for his arguments to be taken seriously inside the White House. Bush showed remarkable patience in not firing O'Neill earlier.

By early 2003, John Snow had replaced O'Neill, Stephen Friedman had taken over from Lindsey, Gregory Mankiw took Hubbard's place and Josh Bolton replaced Mitch Daniels at the Office of Management and Budget. It was hoped that Friedman who had worked for years at Goldman & Sachs would be able to regain some of Wall Street's confidence in Bush's economic policy. The economic policy 'shop' was the only sector in the White House to undergo such a dramatic new beginning halfway during Bush's first term.

Every morning at seven sharp in the Roosevelt Room, Card begins the senior staff meeting – Bush's punctuality reverberates throughout the White House. 'Try coming late for a meeting and you will find out how laid back this president is,' commented one senior aide, 'Every meeting starts and ends on time.'[35] Each of the major policy shops are represented at the meeting which is also attended by the Press Secretary (Ari Fleischer, succeeded in 2003 by his deputy Scott McClellan), Michael Gerson and someone from Cheney's office. At one point, Ari Fleischer received some pointed questions from White House reporters about Bush closing Clinton's Office of Women's Initiatives. At the senior staff meeting the next day, Fleischer aired his concern, but Karen Hughes took a look at the eight women attending the 18 person meeting and gave him the answer: 'In this White House, the women's office is the senior-staff meeting!'[36] Hughes was the highest ranking woman ever in any White House and Condi Rice is the first female National Security Adviser. Margaret Spellings is the leading domestic policy adviser; working for Spellings, Anne Phelps was the senior White House staffer on Health policy and Mary Matalin commanded Cheney's communications office.

The agenda for the day is briefly reviewed and just before 8:00am, Card breaks the meeting to walk with Condi Rice to the Oval Office where they are joined by CIA Director George Tenet and Dick Cheney to attend Bush's morning intelligence briefing. Bush usually gets to the Oval Office around seven o' clock and checks in on some of the news and scheduling for the day prior to the briefing. At 9:05, Card, Rove and Hughes join Bush to go over the 'ready-set-go' launch of activities and messages for the day.[37] On regular days, Bush and Cheney sitting 'in the wing chairs' in the Oval Office get two more briefings in the afternoon, one on domestic policy, usually by Margaret Spellings, and one on economic policy by Larry Lindsey.[38] On a typical day, Card, Rove, Hughes and Bolten may pop in a dozen times to follow up on a piece of action. Many White House offices also hold morning meetings with their counterparts in the departments and agencies. Albert Hawkins, Bush's close Texas aide who was appointed as his Cabinet Secretary, checks in every morning with the chiefs of staff in the departments. Karen Hughes holds a communications teleconference. Alberto Gonzales does the same with the legal counsels.[39] The culture is, 'get your work done during the day and get out', according to Mary Matalin, 'You don't get bonus points for hanging around at night.'[40]

On a weekly schedule, the White House is organized into three focus groups. With Card in the chair they each meet once a week. The Strategery Group often meets in the Cordell Hull Room in the Eisenhower Executive Office Building to plan the political strategy for the administration for the next two to three weeks. The two other weekly meetings are the Legislative Group with Nick Calio's office taking the lead, and the Communications Group with Karen Hughes in the chair.[41]

When Hughes announced in April 2002 that she would return to Texas at the end of the summer, it sent shockwaves through the White House. It hit Bush hard as well. The first thing he said to her when she told him that she felt she needed to take her family back to Texas was, 'Will you still be involved?'[42] Of course, speculation was rife for a week or so whether Hughes' departure meant that Rove had outmaneuvered her. Others thought that the importance of the war on terror after September 2001 had rendered Hughes' job less salient because she felt uncomfortable in foreign affairs, but most commentators came to accept Hughes' simple explanation as 'the painful truth about ... balancing family and work.'[43] She had given all her time to Bush since joining his campaign for Governor in Texas. She had 'homeschooled' her son on the campaign plane in 1999 and 2000. Her husband, Jerry, about 20 years older than she, and her son felt lost in Washington. Jerry also had a daughter and granddaughter back in Austin. Hughes had to make a decision in May whether to enrol her son another year in the prestigious St. Albans High School where Gore had once been a student. She felt her family could not go on in Washington and said she would continue to be an adviser to the President from Texas and fly in as often as needed. Bush did not put anyone else in her 'counselor' job, signalling that she was irreplacable, but Dan Bartlett, another Texan whom Hughes had chosen as her assistant began to fill her communications duties in the summer of 2002. Bush said, 'She may be changing addresses, but she's not leaving my inner circle.'[44]

Hughes remained involved in speech writing, including the 2003 and 2004 State of the Union addresses, travelled frequently with Bush on the campaign trail and stayed in touch by phone on a daily basis. It will take time to know how much difference Hughes' daily absence made, but for the first eighteen months of the administration when she was there in the thick of it, her role was invaluable. Many speculated Hughes would have handled the criticisms better that were levelled at the White House for failing to find weapons of mass destruction in Iraq and failing to detect the terrorist plot before September 11.

Cabinet

Bush had all his cabinet picks nominated by January 2, 2001 and had them confirmed by the Senate in rapid fashion. You could not call Bush's cabinet simply conservative or liberal; there were moderate Republicans, such as Colin Powell at State and Christine Todd Whitman at the Environmental Protection Agency, whom Bush gave cabinet status. On the other side, there was Attorney-General John Ashcroft, son and grandson of Assemblies-of-God ministers, and a very strong pro-life politician, and there was Gale Norton, at the Department of the Interior, a right-wing conservation lawyer who had battled traditional environmentalist groups most of her professional life.

After Linda Chavez failed to disclose the status of an illegal immigrant who had lived in her residence some years back, the Bush team quickly dropped her – avoiding the drawn out controversy experienced by Bill Clinton over Zoe Baird and Kimba Wood – and nominated Elaine Chao as Secretary of Labor instead. Thanks to Clay Johnson's appointment process, the Bush team had already done some pre-clearing of Chao. She faced little opposition even though she was nearly as conservative as Chavez. The four women, Chao, Norton, Whitman, and Anne Veneman, a Californian headed for Agriculture, were joined by African Americans Colin Powell and Roderick Paige at Education. Mel Martinez at Housing and Urban Development was the only Hispanic-American appointment to the cabinet, and Norm Mineta for transportation was the only Democrat.

The Senate confirmed Powell and Whitman early and unanimously, while the toughest nominations were Gale Norton and John Ashcroft. Bush and the Senate leadership made sure Ashcroft went ahead of Norton to catch the front of the storm. The White House had good reason to be confident about Ashcroft all along, as he had been a Senator and the bond of that collegial body is not easily broken. Cheney made the case that Ashcroft 'is being hounded only because of his political views.'[45] In historical context that has never been enough reason to deny a former Senator a major post in government. Serving two terms as Attorney-General and twice as Governor of Missouri, Ashcroft had a solid record as a law enforcer. Some tried to tar him as a racist because he once waged a campaign in the Senate to deny Clinton nominee Judge Ronnie White a position on the Federal Court, however, he has also worked all his professional life with (conservative) African Americans such as Clarence Thomas and had voted for the other 26 black judicial nominations that Clinton made when Ashcroft was a senator.[46] Ashcroft was confirmed by a narrow vote of 58 to 42, only one vote ahead of Ted Olson, his Solicitor-General and famous advocate for Candidate Bush in the Florida court struggle.

Some made the point that Bush's cabinet had no overall vision, calling Bush's choices, 'horses for courses',[47] while others praised Bush's cabinet for its executive experience. It was called a 'cabinet of grown ups', and 'competent conservatives',[48] and a good number of the nominees were former Chief Executive Officers of large corporations. The cabinet certainly reflected Bush's outlook that businessmen are better managers than lawyers and intellectuals. Bush received mainly favorable spin out of his cabinet selection, and praise for not being afraid to surround himself with people more experienced than himself.

The cabinet also reflected Bush's appetite for non-traditional Republican solutions. Tommy Thompson at Health and Human Services is the former governor of Wisconsin who has put in practice Bush's new welfare vision. Like Bush, he rejects the 1960s worldview of 'Liberal Welfarism' whereby ever growing amounts of funds are spent on people who are unable to escape chronic poverty. Forcing welfare recipients into a path of re-training and work and then rewarding them with real wages, Thompson had been able to cut the welfare rolls sharply in Wisconsin and put many people back into the workforce.[49] He did so often with bipartisan cooperation and has in the process increased the state's spending. Rather than abolishing the Department of Education as some Republicans proposed, Bush has no problem with increasing the role of the federal government in education as long as the results are there. Paige, a former school disctrict superintendent, created a system in Houston where schools were held accountable, where minority performance was monitored and where successful schools were rewarded. Paige is the symbol and salesman of Bush's vision 'to leave no child behind.' Treasury Secretary Paul O'Neill was a 'maverick' from the start.[50] Yet, on the idea of partially privatizing Social Security, O'Neill is a fellow conservative revolutionary, for like Bush, he wanted to change the culture from an 'income transfer mentality to a wealth accumulations mentality'.[51]

Clay Johnson had also prepared the deputy secretary and key policy positions for each department. The Bush White House had a firm strategy for staffing the departments in cooperation with the secretary or department head. The motto was 'do it with them, not to them'.[52] If a Cabinet Secretary was not on board for a nomination, Clay Johnson would not take it forward. Johnson would also run every nomination by Rove and if Rove and Johnson disagreed, Card would break the tie. Card also had the power to veto any name on his own. If Johnson and Card agreed, the briefing paper would go to Bush the night before a meeting with the president. Bush personally approved every appointment that required Senate confirmation. The meeting with Bush would include Johnson, Card, Cheney and other White House staff depending on the nature of the appointment. Bush would often run people by Cheney beforehand, asking, 'he worked in my father's administration, do you know him, or do you know her?'[53] As such, Cheney wielded an informal veto and Johnson included Cheney for every national security nomination.

Bush's White House pursued a communications, Congressional liaison and legal strategy for the entire executive branch. That meant the Bush team took a particular interest in those appointments which would amount to being White House's 'lieutenants in the field'.[54] In practice, Karen Hughes excercised a veto over all public affairs nominations, Nick Calio over all Departmental persons in charge of legislative affairs, and Gonzales over legal counsel. The goal was 160 nominations by the end of April. In fact, the Bush White House was only able to have 60 nominations ready by that time. However, given the complicated and slow vetting process, and the 'holds' some senators put on candidates, Bush did better than average; he had 29 positions confirmed by April 20, 109 by August 7, and 341 by year's end.[55]

The White House was especially keen on having direct involvement in selecting the deputy position in each department and agency. Bush filled the Environmental Protection Agency's No. 2 slot with Linda Fisher, a conservative businesswoman with experience in Reagan's administration. Likewise, William Hansen, who had worked on Bush's education team in the campaign was placed as Rod Paige's deputy. Kenneth Dam, Deputy Secretary of the Treasury, has been a close associate of George Schultz who was an early mentor to Bush in the campaign.

Bush stated in January that he would work with each cabinet member 'to set a series of goals for each area of government',[56] but what he did *not* promise was policy made in Cabinet. In politically fragmented Washington, the need for centralized decision making is high and for that purpose the White House is irreplaceable. In the Bush team, cabinet secretaries are the administration's chief representatives to the nation and the implementers of presidential policy. In the first year, the Cabinet has on average met once per month. The first meeting on January 31 reviewed treasury and energy briefs. On February 26, the cabinet reviewed the budget and the plans Bush was going to send to Congress for tax relief. The April meeting reviewed the budget in detail while the May 16 gathering received Cheney's energy proposals.

As in previous adminstrations, the cabinet acts more as a review panel and a sounding board than a real dynamo for decisions. While the White House is in charge, it is not completely 'hogging the ball.' Bush created specific task groups that combine White House staffers and Cabinet members. For example, the 'budget review board' included Paul O'Neill, Mitchell Daniels, the Director of OMB, and the President's economic advisers Larry Lindsey and Glen Hubbard.[57] Likewise, Cheney chaired an energy group in which Secretary of Energy Spencer Abraham participated. Ashcroft and Gonzales lead a group of fifteen White House and executive officials to guide a slate of federal court nominees through the Senate.

Bush's Style and the Decision Making Process

When he was completing his MBA degree at Harvard, Bush preferred to sit in the so-called 'sky decker' seat.[58] High up in the center back of the amphitheater, Bush 'sat back and listened,' monitoring the debate before jumping in. The President's decision-making process still features this role, but Bush's listening does not mean he is uninterested or simply delegates. He is not detached from the decision-making process and his alleged aloofness from the process has been exaggerated, just as initial observers had done with Dwight Eisenhower.[59] Many have questioned whether Bush has enough 'intellectual curiosity' for decision making, in other words enough 'oomph' to ask questions that go beyond the briefing books.[60] Those who have participated with him in the decision-making process portray him as active and involved. He is quite open to how his aides argue the case for this or that approach to get the desired results. Bush has a great capacity to sit back and listen to his advisers, knowing he has given them his 'vision' and that they understand his objectives.[61]

In the 1980s, Stanford University professor Alexander George described a decision strategy in which he pictured the role of president as that of a 'magistrate' who would listen to the arguments before making up his mind.[62] Some of Bush's early decision-making features resemble George's prescriptions. Those who have been in decision-making sessions with Bush have commented how he likes to draw in people with different perspectives, and how he likes to question and push people to defend their point. 'He is not one that gets locked in,' according to Clay Johnson. 'The thing all people who work for him learn he does best,' Karen Hughes wrote, is 'ask questions that bore straight to the heart of the matter.'[63] In his deliberations with staff, he 'encourages people to push back. He is interested in good ideas and in giving people confidence to have a dialogue with him, to have that exchange of ideas and difference of opinion.'[64] Texas State Representative Steven Wolens (a Democrat) commented that Bush will 'bring in four or five aides on oppposite sides to argue the dickens out of an issue.' Often he will ask them to close their briefing book and tell him what they think in their own words. Bush can be a bit of a 'buzzard chewing at an issue' before ultimately making up his mind.[65]

Bush's open approach to decision making is directly related to his sense of self-confidence, his absolute inner calm. Andrew Sullivan observed an 'uncanny composure' in the man and directly connects it to Bush's 'calm sustaining' faith.[66] Presidential scholar Fred Greenstein defined emotional intelligence as the 'capacity to control one's emotions and channel them to constructive purposes.'[67] Bush's self confidence allows him to banter one moment and concentrate the next. Bush can be dead serious one moment, then 'walking past a staffer standing strictly at attention, Bush will suddenly embrace him with a bear hug. "Amigo," the president will cry. It's totally discombobulating,' according to Karl Rove.[68] Bush insists that all cell phones and beepers are off during meetings. The Oval Office is treated with awe and respect. If you do not wear formal attire, you are not welcome at the meeting. At the same time, Bush will tell the steward of the White House mess when ordering a hamburger, 'I am from West Texas, we don't need these fancy [onion] buns around here. It probably costs more.'[69] At Camp David, Bush makes his guests play lots of tennis, horseshoes and other games, but back at the White House, everyone returns to decorum and order.

He reads more than he lets on. He takes a briefing binder with him most nights to study the agenda and issues for the next day. His pointed questions are evidence to his staff that he has carefully read the briefing book. Still, Bush prefers a good oral presentation and an open discussion to paper work. He certainly is not a speed-reader as Jimmy Carter was, who often read several hundred pages before the days' meetings started. Bush is not afraid to tell people what he does not know and to bring experts in and bombard them with questions. The downside to this preference is that Bush may depend too much on the willingness of his advisers to confront him with divergent views. If Andy Card in domestic issues, and Condi Rice in foreign policy would assure that there are always multiple points of view, this dependency can be lessened, but often the Chief of Staff or National Security Advisor are themselves part of an argument, making it difficult to add that extra advocacy which may weaken their own position.

Many have observed Bush's instinctive ability to know when a decision must be made. This instinct combined with a very orderly schedule, punctual meetings, and a habit of being decisive and not looking back, gives Bush the tools to be a highly efficient decision maker. Hundreds of decisions come his way every week, and while he may give twenty or so to a trusted aide like Karen Hughes, the others he will process speedily. His whole being dislikes procrastination.

Bush's National Security Team and Process

With Cheney joining Rice as a close adviser on foreign policy in the summer of 2000, Bush added both a sounding board and, in Karen Hughes's words, a 'wise counselor' on foreign and defense policy.[70] As different as the styles of Bush and Cheney are – Bush often emotional and bashful, Cheney cool and unrevealing of his emotions – they share a deep, instinctive conservative outlook not based on rigid dogma but on the experience of traditional values.

Cheney became an important adviser to Bush in selecting other national security appointments. Several of the Vulcans such as Stephen Hadley and Paul Wolfowitz had worked for Cheney in previous capacities. Wolfowitz became Rumsfeld's deputy, and Hadley joined as Rice's right hand. It was rumored in January 2001 that Cheney would co-chair National Security Meetings and that his office would dominate the interagency process on national security policy. This flies in the face of Bush's desire for an orderly process and clear demarcation of the roles of his advisers; Cheney had too much on his plate to run the bureaucratic wheels of the National Security Council beside his other advisory duties.

Condi Rice was given the position of National Security Adviser and she was put in charge of the interagency process, but as in domestic policy, speechwriting and communications, Cheney's office was fully integrated into the deliberations among the Departments of State and Defense and others on national security. Libby, Cheney's Chief of Staff, was also given the title Assistant to the President and he became Cheney's deputy on national security issues. Cheney participated in the 'Principal' level meetings of the NSC alongside Colin Powell and Donald Rumsfeld. Both Hadley and Libby attended Principal meetings as assistants to Rice and Cheney, respectively. Libby attended the so-called 'Deputies' meetings of the NSC in which the second in command in each department and agency clear as much of the decision process as possible before their bosses make the final recommendation to Bush. Libby's right hand man, Eric Edelman and his staff participated in the lower levels of the interagency process.

Though Colin Powell declined elective office, he never ruled out an 'appointive' position.[71] The most prestigious appointive office is that of Secretary of State and Bush was visibly moved when Powell joined him at his Crawford ranch in December 2000 to announce his nomination for this post. At his swearing-in ceremony in January, Bush called Powell 'an American hero' and repeated the words Harry Truman had used when he chose General George Marshall, saying that Powell was a 'tower of strength and common sense'.[72]

Powell had risen from a humble childhood through the ranks of the army; he had seen combat in Vietnam and been wounded. When he rose to be National Security Adviser under Ronald Reagan, Powell worked with Cap Weinberger to create a new doctrine for military engagement. Their point was that the United States should not 'commit military forces until we had a clear political objective'.[73] When such an objective was spelled out, Washington should employ overwhelming force to reach it quickly, having an exit strategy ready to move forces out as quickly as they went in. Beyond the doctrine, Powell had proven to be very reluctant about the use of military force, for as Chairman of the Joint Chiefs of Staff under Bush's father, he was the most hesitant among Bush's top advisers to use force in Panama in 1989 and against Saddam Hussein in 1990-91. Powell agreed to stay at his post when Clinton took over in 1993, were he again cautioned against using overwhelming force in Somalia and Bosnia, because American objectives were not clear.

Newsweek reported early in the Bush administration that Powell had put conditions on his job and that he had an agreement that he would 'run Bush's foreign policy'.[74] Some thought Powell's position would become 'a first among equals'.[75] These stories proved groundless, however, as the President would not delegate his foreign policy. Bush and Powell did agree that the balance of power in foreign policy making had shifted too much towards Sandy Berger in Clinton's White House and that Powell would correct that imbalance. Powell has a lot of bureaucratic experience, but he is also a loyal soldier, willing to fight hard for his views, but circling the wagons once Bush has made a decision.

Richard Armitage, one of the Vulcans whom Powell called, 'A friend of the heart', became Powell's deputy.[76] Besides Armitage, Powell did not appoint many close confidants in policy positions. He brought in 'old army buddies' such as Colonel Paul Kelly to help him manage the department and its relationships in Washington, and he put Richard Haass, who shared Powell's internationalist views, in charge of policy planning. Powell wanted to 'elevate morale' among the career staff.[77] Neither Bush nor Powell insisted on putting a point man as Undersecretary for Political Affairs. Instead, the career civil servant Marc Grossman who had run European affairs for Clinton took that post, while another career bureaucrat, Elizabeth Jones moved into his place as the Assistant-Secretary for European Affairs. Most of her experience had been in Asia and the Middle East. James Kelly, like Armitage a Navy veteran with experience in the Reagan and elder Bush administrations and with interest in Japan, was appointed Assistant Secretary for Asian and Pacific Affairs.

The White House insisted on a few major appointments in the Department of State, including Paula Dobriansky at Global Affairs and John Bolton as Undersecretary for Arms Control and International Security Affairs. Senator Jesse Helms likely recommended the latter to Bush. Bolton, an international lawyer, had been an ardent advocate for a values-first approach to international treaties while at the American Enterprise Institute. In Bolton, Bush would have someone to keep 'bad' treaties at bay and who would insist that existing treaties on arms control and disarmament would either yield real verification or be mothballed. Bolton also made sure that Bush's plans to amend or abandon the Anti Ballistic Missile treaty was well defended at State. Bolton was confirmed on May 8 by a narrow partisan margin of 57-43. In the world of arms control (dominated by European diplomats), Bolton became Bush's version of what Perle had been under Reagan, a type of sequel to the 'Prince of Darkness.' So State had a mixture of Powell lieutenants, career officers, and a few people who shared the more conservative value-oriented foreign policy favored by the White House.

The last of the big foreign policy players to come on board was Secretary of Defense Donald Rumsfeld. A wrestling champion and Navy fighter jet pilot, Rumsfeld was a four-term Congressman from the Chicago area when Nixon picked him to run the Office of Economic Opportunity. Rumsfeld gained a reputation as someone who 'relished bureaucratic combat', and who had strong views.[78] Yet, Rumsfeld's views are not always predictable. He is not a flat-footed hawk, as his critics like to portray him; when working for Nixon, Rumsfeld was critical of the way the government was handling the Vietnam War. Rumsfeld was a military 'transformist' before many knew the army needed reform. He had a keen interest in the possibilities of space early on. Nixon appointed Rumsfeld as NATO ambassador just before the Watergate scandal broke out. In the early 1960s, the 'Rumsfeld's Raiders', a group of Republican Congressmen led by Rumsfeld, had been instrumental in making Gerald Ford House Minority Leader.[79] When Nixon resigned, one of the first things Ford did was call on Rumsfeld to put together a transition team. After serving as Gerald Ford's Chief of Staff, Rumsfeld became the youngest Secretary of Defense (at age 43) in American history, but his tour at the Pentagon was brief, as Carter won the 1976 campaign. Rumsfeld left government and made his next career in business where he went on to lead several large companies, including G.D. Searle in the 1980s and Gilead Sciences, a biotech firm, in the 1990s, where he gained a reputation as a reformer in business. James Mann noted, 'When Rumsfeld was brought in as a CEO at your company, you were in for a pretty wild ride. He really would shake things up.'[80]

Bush looked at a few candidates for Defense, including Governor Tom Ridge and Senator Dan Coats before picking Rumsfeld. Of course, Cheney's life-long close ties to Rumsfeld played a big role in Bush settling on 'Rummy, ' as he often calls him, but it is also true that Rumsfeld fitted the job Bush had in mind for the Secretary of Defense much better than Coats or Ridge. As early as January 2000, Bush had met with Rumsfeld to be briefed on missile defense, 'I met with him for hours just alone,' Rumsfeld later confided.[81] If Bush was serious about missile defense and thoroughly transforming the military, he needed a knowledgeable secretary and a tough-minded corporate manager, someone, in Newt Gingrich's words, who could 'redo the Pentagon'.[82] While being a corporate chief, Rumsfeld's passion for military affairs was never far from the surface.

He was appointed chairman of arguably the two most important Congressional commissions on defense issues in the late 1990s. In the late 1990s, Republican Congressmen were leery of the CIA's National Intelligence Estimate about the ballistic missile threat from rogue states such as North Korea, Iran, and Iraq. In 1997, the CIA put this threat at least 15 years away. Newt Gingrich asked Rumsfeld to head a new commission to look at the rogue missile threat. The so-called 'Rumsfeld Commission' concluded in 1998 that the threat from North Korea was as little as 'five years away'.[83] Iran's capability in intercontinental missiles was a close second. The ink was hardly dry on that report when Pyongyang tested its Taepo Dong I missile over Japan and to the consternation of US intelligence revealed a third stage launcher that came as a complete surprise.[84] Rumsfeld's much more pessimistic intelligence assessment combined with North Korea's surprise capability greatly strengthened the view that very soon, North Korea would be able to deliver a small warhead onto US territory.

A few years later, Rumsfeld headed another congressionally mandated commission to look at the role of space in the so-called (technological) revolution in military affairs.[85] Rumsfeld stepped down from this commission on December 28, 2000 when he was nominated Secretary of Defense, but its findings were already clear. The report urged the US government to 'develop the means to deter and defend against hostile acts directed at US space assets.'[86] Space, it concluded, is the new high frontier and the United States must act quickly to prevent a 'Pearl Harbor' in space.

Preoccupied with transformation, Rumsfeld was comfortable with Wolfowitz as his deputy, taking the lead role in policy. Almost all the top spots in the Department of Defense were filled with strong advocates for missile defense, military transformation and assertive American values. Douglas Feith became Undersecretary for Policy. A former assistant to Richard Perle and an outspoken international lawyer, Feith provided strong policy support for Wolfowitz. He would have no problems working with John Bolton on arms control issues. Stephen Cambone, Feith's Principal Deputy, also acted as a close assistant to Rumsfeld and had been Rumsfeld's chief of staff at the Rumsfeld Commission. Rumsfeld appointed him as Undersecretary for Intelligence in early 2003. Finally, with Jack Crouch as the Assistant Secretary for Policy and Peter Rodman from the Nixon Center as Assistant Secretary for International Security Affairs, Rumsfeld created a fireproof wall for missile defense that spanned the four senior civilian levels in the Pentagon. Rumsfeld made Dov Zakheim, another Vulcan, Comptroller, who, together with Undersecretary for Logistics Pete Aldridge, helped Rumsfeld put his transformation ideas into concrete plans for cost savings and acquisitions. As at the State Department, there was no one in the senior staff at the Pentagon brought in by Rumsfeld who had a special stake or experience in West European relations. Crouch would handle the file, but like Bolton, his priority was to correct Clinton's multilateral drift and to make clear to the Europeans that a new approach was in the offing.

Though a Clinton appointee, President Bush saw no reason to replace the 'passionate and personable' Central Intelligence Director, George Tenet.[87] Bush liked his 'outgoing personality and upbeat attitude'.[88] Tenet's style matches Bush's as he likes to present his intelligence material in an 'unpretentious way'.[89] Some presidents prefer their National Security Adviser to give the so-called Presidential Daily Brief, but this one enjoys Tenet's company and several days a week, Tenet would arrive sharply at 8:00 in the Oval Office. Bush, whose father had been CIA Director, had a great deal of respect for Tenet's work. Before September 11, Tenet joined Bush a couple of times at Camp David and the President regularly took a CIA briefer with him on his trips. After the terrorist attacks, Bush and Tenet's relationship grew even closer.

There never was any doubt that Bush would appoint his chief Vulcan and foreign policy mentor as his National Security Adviser. During the last years of the Clinton Administration, National Security Adviser Samuel (Sandy) Berger's staff included a separate speechwriting and communications shop, reflecting Berger's large role in Clinton's foreign policy apparatus. Rice trimmed the NSC staff from 120 back to about 90 and she also put communications, speechwriting and Congressional liaison under the overall direction of Karen Hughes, Mike Gerson, and Nick Calio.[90]

Bush appointed Senator Jesse Helms' right-hand man, Steve Biegun, as Rice's liaison to the Senate. After Trent Lott stepped down as Senate Majority Leader in December 2002, Beigun went back to the Hill to work for Bill Frist the new Senate majority leader, thus continuing the close connection. Rice appointed Stephen Hadley as her deputy. Hadley had most recently made the case for an accelerated program for sea-based missile defense.[91] Rice's early appointments of senior directors in the NSC staff shed some light on Bush and Rice's views on key policy areas. Franklin Miller was put in charge of defense strategy. Even more than Hadley, he was a strong advocate for missile defense. So was Miller's colleague, Robert Joseph. Rice put him in charge of counter proliferation strategy.

Daniel Fried was Rice's choice for European Affairs. Fried served on Clinton's NSC until 1997 when he was appointed ambassador to Poland. Fried, who has held several postings in Eastern Europe, is a strong advocate for the region's full status in NATO and the European Union. Bush's frequent visits to Poland are doubtless related to Fried's influence in the policy process. Daniel Fried's position confirmed the pattern in the Bush administration about Western Europe. When Europe is represented at the table, it is through the eyes of career civil servants at State, East Europeanists such as Fried at NSC or Russian experts of whom Rice herself is chief. Robert Blackwill, the Vulcan with the most European experience, was made ambassador to India. In 2003, Rice brought him back to help her run the efforts to reconstruct Iraq and Afghanistan. The Bush Administration could have benefited from more experienced European hands to better massage the West Europeans on the revolutionary changes Bush wanted to bring about. There was no reason to pander to the French and Germans or to compromise Bush's values, but on the other hand, there was little to be gained by sticking it to them. 'We like the Europeans,' one military adviser in the Pentagon said revealingly, 'especially the Central and East Europeans.'[92]

On February 13, 2001 Bush issued National Security Presidential Decision Memorandum-1, which laid out the organization and staffing of his National Security Council. The NSPD-1 memorandum set up an interagency process under the overall coordination of Condi Rice.[93] She chairs the 'Principals' composed of cabinet secretaries and agency directors with Steve Hadley as executive secretary; Hadley chairs the 'Deputies' meetings, which were held twice a week before the terrorist attack in September 2001 and more frequently thereafter. The 'Deputies Committee' in the Bush administration is as formidable a group as any in recent memory. Richard Armitage and Paul Wolfowitz are matched by Cheney's powerful chief of staff, 'Scooter' Libby.

Wolfowitz is a strategist and Armitage is a 'doer,' but when it comes to fundamental views, the two of them, alongside the other deputies Steve Hadley and Lewis Libby, have a good deal in common. Armitage and Wolfowitz worked side by side on Asia policy in the Reagan administration. Libby worked closely with Wolfowitz under then Defense Secretary Cheney. Some called Libby 'Wolfowitz's Wolfowitz.'[94] In Bush's national security structure, the dividing line cut across the principals and deputies. Rumsfeld and Armitage have a testy relationship and over time, Wolfowitz and Powell also came to represent opposite arguments. Naturally, Armitage moved away from some of the other Vulcans to protect Powell.

NSPD-1 created six regional Policy Coordination Committees in the interagency process. Various Department of State officials chair all of these. Rice also set up eleven functional ('cross-cutting issues') Policy Coordination Committees. Of these, the Department of State only chairs the group on Development and Humanitarian Assistance. Defense is in charge of the committee on Defense Strategy, but Rice and Hadley hold the reigns over all the others, including Arms Control, Counter-Terrorism, Intelligence, and Proliferation issues. In 1977, President Carter and Zbigniew Brzezinski set up several Policy Review Committees under the Department of State as well as some Policy Coordination Committees under the control of the national security adviser. Soon it became clear that the latter were more powerful vehicles in the decision-making process than the ones run by State.

Before September 11, Bush usually let the National Security Council meetings be chaired by Rice. She would then bring the recommendations to him in the Oval Office where Cheney and Card would join Bush and Rice. Rice does not usually engage in the substance of the debate when Bush is present at the NSC meeting, but will ask, 'Pointed questions'.[95] She knows not to shut down the debate too early. Bush is leery of precooked or papered over advice and demands 'clear choices and original thinking'.[96] At the end of the debate, Bush, not Rice, pulls the consensus recommendation together as he sees it. Albert Hawkins, Bush's cabinet secretary until 2003, said that Bush has a 'great sense of timing as to when a decision is necessary'.[97] Robert Zoellick said that Bush 'delegates' the options preparation, but is then 'quite hands-on when they come back', that he 'prods very hard' in those sessions and then 'makes his own decisions'.[98]

When Bush takes the recommendations back to the Oval Office, Rice is among the last to give her assessment. As such, Rice can have 'the last word' of advice, if she so chooses.[99] Rice is extremely cautious about this role and will not tell even her own staff about her personal conversations with Bush. By not showing off her real influence and keeping her counsel to Bush confidential, she keeps her post strong. Sometimes, Bush makes the decision when Cheney, Rice and Card have left and announces it the next day.

If Condi Rice did not scrupulously represent Powell's and Rumsfeld's views in those Oval Office meetings, she would never have survived thus far. Rice is very aware of her responsibility as 'honest broker'.[100] Her mentor, Brent Scowcroft was well known for his integrity in coordinating the advice of the secretaries. At the same time, however, Rice speaks up clearly during the Principals' Meetings when Bush is not there.[101] As Powell said, 'there is never a doubt in my mind where Condi stands'. It is unlikely that she is trying to 'upstage' either Rumsfeld or Powell, as some reporters suggested.[102] Colleagues have praised her for being 'a terrific team player'.[103]

In addition to the NSC meetings, the Bush foreign policy 'team' set up myriad communication points to keep the flow of information as open as possible. Rice, Powell and Rumsfeld start out with a conference call at 7:15 each morning. Besides formal NSC meetings, both Powell and Rumsfeld saw Bush two times per week before the terrorist attacks, and every day right after the disaster.[104] Rice, Powell, Rumsfeld, and Cheney join for lunch once a week. Cheney also has breakfast or lunch with Rumsfeld and Powell respectively once a week and Card invites a different Department Secretary for lunch each week.

In the first months of the Bush administration, some observers wondered how Rice could possibly manage the 'titans', or '800-pound gorillas' such as Colin Powell and Donald Rumsfeld.[105] They both have tremendous experience and could easily do each other's jobs.[106] While they are loyal to Bush, they are both known for offering their advice 'with the bark off'; neither would be easily persuaded against his will.[107] They often made strong statements making the president's counsel look divided, leading many analysts to suspect there was heavy bureaucratic fighting between the two. Some wrote 'good cop' Powell versus 'bad cop' Rumsfeld stories and labeled the dynamic as 'hawk versus dove'.[108]

Their relationship is more complex, and Bush is not afraid of their arguments; 'He does not mind the tensions in his administration,' noted a State Department Official.[109] Unlike his father who insisted on stricter collegiality, Bush may let a policy fight among his advisers hang out in the open quite long. Bush is secure in his own fundamental beliefs. Policy battles over how to reach his goals are not seen by him as threatening.

'I talk to him twice or three times a day,' Rumsfeld said in August 2001, referring to Powell. 'We must solve six or eight problems every two or three days just on the phone;'[110] 'It is nonsense to suggest that Powell is the odd man out.'[111] In an interview with Tim Russert in June 2001, Powell showed his strong sense of loyalty to Bush and good rapport with Rumsfeld. 'The only one I am worried about satisfying, and the only gap I want to make sure never exists,' said Powell, 'is between me and the president. There is no gap. I am carrying out his foreign policy, not Colin Powell's.' Powell added that he and Rumsfeld got along well: yes, they have 'differences' and yes, occasional disagreements as well, but as Powell put it, 'We know how to work them out. We have known each other for 25 years. These are all hyperventilated comments about gaps between me and my colleagues.'[112] Still, reports of bureaucratic infighting between Powell and Rumsfeld never fully went away and flared up during the late summer of 2002 when Bush was preparing his final options on Iraq and again in early 2003 over the reconstruction efforts in Iraq.

Cheney's political instincts are closer to Rumsfeld's than Powell's; even Rice's natural propensity would be to come out to the right of Powell. Still, Bush often chooses very pragmatic and politically cautious means to pursue his values. As such, he is often open to Powell's approach to move cautiously while siding with Cheney or Rumsfeld on final goals. Powell and Rumsfeld have reversed a decades-old trend in which the Secretary of State typically called for military options and the Secretary of Defense for diplomacy, but to call Powell a 'dove' is misleading. There was competitive advice, but Bush started with a 'joined-up administration'.[113]

There is more to Bush's foreign policy process than an argument between Powell and Rumsfeld. Cheney may see the president as often as seven times a day. John Newhouse believes that Cheney is 'the strongest, probably the dominant, member of Bush's national security apparatus.'[114] Newhouse and other critics allege that hard-liners eventually took control of Bush's foreign policy. That thesis is too easy: it underplays Bush's own role and omits other key players such as Card, Rove and Hughes and Rice. Andy Card plays a very quiet part in orchestrating all policy, and Karen Hughes and Karl Rove were increasingly involved in the communications and political dimension of foreign policy. Even after Hughes left for Austin in the late summer of 2002, she still returned every two weeks to Washington for a few days to work on some aspect of the President's policy. Rove and Hughes are not part of the formal NSC meetings; however, as the Bush administration struggled in its first six months of foreign policy, especially in public relations clashes with Western European allies, Rove and Hughes became more involved.[115] Rove also invited Rice to join the 'strategery meetings,' so she would have a chance to integrate foreign policy issues into the overall strategy of the White House.

Rice was not given cabinet rank; her real power was not in being a policy coordinator or in 'working the seams' of the interagency process, but in her proximity to Bush.[116] After September 11, people began to notice Rice's stature in the administration as opposed to earlier, when some thought of her as a 'super-briefer', nothing more.[117] It is now clear that Rice plays a much larger role than briefer and policy coordinator, for as one State Department official put it, Bush calls her all the time, asking 'why can't we do this or that?'[118] The President praised her in the first weeks of his administration not only for being 'brilliant' and a good manager, but added, 'I trust her judgment'.[119] Rice frequently joins the Sunday TV talk shows to explain Bush's positions; she gives background briefings to the media and is always present when Bush meets with foreign heads of state or ministers. After Bush's second meeting with Russian President Vladimir Putin in Genoa, Italy, Rice flew on to Moscow to continue high-level talks on the ABM treaty. Right after the war on Iraq, Rice went to Moscow to begin to repair the relationship between Bush and Putin.

Rice's real power lies in the fact that like Karen Hughes and Karl Rove, she has entered Bush's innermost circle. Condi Rice began to accompany George and Laura Bush to Camp David on the weekends and then to the Crawford Ranch. She shares many values with Bush beyond foreign policy, also disdaining the self-indulgent and protest culture of the 1960s. Maureen Dowd of the *New York Times* derisively called Bush 'Eisenhower with hair', but the 1950s values in the Bush household is a type of continuation for Rice of her own formative years.[120] Her widowed father passed away in December 2000, just before Rice joined the Bush administration; she has no close relatives, she is not on the Washington social circuit, and her job is her life. In some ways, Rice has become part of the family. Being at Camp David does not mean talking policy all the time. First there is a church service in the Chapel, followed by brunch, probably a fair bit of banter all day long, likely some tennis or running and then Rice and Bush may switch to watching their earlier aspirations which they both overshot by some length: being baseball commissioner for Bush, and National Football League commissioner for Rice.

Tax Cuts and the Launch of the Domestic Agenda

President Bush's foreign policy was not part of the early game plan as he was geared to score a few early victories with Congress on domestic politics. Of course the Bush administration could do both domestic and foreign policy at the same time, but his game plan and focus was at home. The President threw a lot more political capital into the game than he actually had. He leveraged his tiny amount of reputation and gambled for a total victory on his flagship issue; tax cuts. If he could show that he had the persuasive power to make the government produce results on his agenda and in his time frame, he could dispel the Florida fog, make a run at the November 2002 mid-term elections and eventually create the political conditions to pass most of his compassionate conservative policy agenda.

The domestic agenda of the elder Bush was washed out by a lack of vision; the younger Bush learned from this lesson. Rather than a 'thousand points of light', he had his five 'laser beams'; the White House would go after the tax cuts with all guns blazing. Bush's strategy for education reform and faith-based community initiatives was very different, using the 'persuasive power' gained from his tax cut victory, he would proceed on education in a very bipartisan mode.[121] Likewise on faith-based welfare plans and prescription drug assistance to seniors, Bush would try to build ad hoc coalitions between Democrats and Republicans who were result-oriented and willing to bury their ideological differences. He would try to build personal relationships and a sense of mutual loyalty with key Congressional leaders on these issues. Knowing that too many priorities would clutter the agenda, Bush set up a commission to study proposals for privatizing parts of Social Security, which would report back in late 2002. It turned out that Bush would have his hands full on education reform, faith-based welfare and a handful of other issues forced on him, as shown by the fact that prescription drugs did not make it on the agenda until after the midterm elections. Declining stock markets, a growing budget deficit, and corporate scandals poisoned the idea of turning a part of Social Security into private investment accounts and in 2003, Social Security reform was pushed down the road, possibly for a second term.

The White House applied a 'rolling announcement format' for Bush's agenda.[122] First the White House would announce when an initiative was to air, then it would make the announcement accompanied by key players and, finally, Bush would travel to various states to repeat the theme for several more local news cycles. The tremendous discipline in the president's public pronouncements was by design. Hinting at Clinton, Mark McKinnon, one of Bush's campaign assistants, said, 'When you speak out on everything, you don't stand for anything.'[123] Ari Fleischer soon gained respect as a Press Secretary with iron discipline: the Bush administration was not interested in 'a happy press', but rather in 'getting its message across'.[124]

Beginning with his address at the Republican Convention in Philadelphia, Bush showed determination to become a 'capable communicator'.[125] His short acceptance speech in Austin in December 'to heal a divided nation' had been well received.[126] His inaugural on January 20 was spiced with values. 'Responsibility, compassion, and character' showed up repeatedly. With two lines, he was able to highlight his education and community priorities: 'The ambition of some Americans are limited by failing schools,' he said, and 'compassion is the work of a nation, not just a government.'[127] He was going to fix the schools and unleash armies of compassion to address America's social ills.

Bush created a lot of goodwill inside the Washington beltway with superb performances at the Gridiron Club in March and the Correspondent's Dinner in April, 2001. The President knew exactly where the media determined his weak spots were and how to make self-deprecating fun with it: 'I hope one day I can clone another Dick Cheney,' Bush jested at the Gridiron dinner, 'Then I won't have to do anything.' Showing family slides at the correspondent's event, Bush showed himself as a young boy on horseback, 'I trusted that horse fully and here's the really weird part, his name was Dick Cheney.' Another slide shows young Georgie's first grade report card. It has 'A' after 'A' for every subject, 'So my advice is, don't peak too early,' Bush said. 'There have been stories about my intellectual capacity,' Bush intoned at the Gridiron. 'For a while I thought my staff believed it. There on my schedule first thing every morning it says "intelligence briefing".'[128]

While courting the media, the White House was fully engaged in establishing ties with Senators and Congressmen: the President met with over 90 Congressmen and women in the first few weeks, some in small groups, some individually. In an 'unprecedented' move, Bush addressed both the Democratic House and Senate retreats.[129] Bush does not use a 'one-size-fits-all' charm, rather he picks and chooses his targets and they are directly related to his specific legislative strategy. Nor does Bush think that mere charm will do the trick, for he knows that a few schmoozing sessions will not cause a Senator to drop his ideology and agenda and simply follow him. The idea, as Rove put it, is to create familiarity, to allow the legislator to see Bush without the media as 'intermediaries'. Based on familiarity, Bush then seeks to build a 'civil dialogue' between himself and the legislator in order to create an atmosphere of mutual dependence and trust.[130]

Speaker Dennis Hastert and conservative Republican House lieutenants Tom DeLay and Dick Armey were to rally the troops on tax cuts in the House, where Republicans enjoyed a tiny majority of six members. The Senate was evenly split after the 2000 elections and Republican and Democratic leaders had agreed on evenly divided committees, staff and budgets. While Cheney could break any tie for the Republicans, the Bush White House knew that a few moderate Republicans such as James Jeffords from Vermont were leery about the program: it would be risky to steamroll tax cuts through the Senate.

The Bush White House devised an inside and outside game on tax cuts. First, they kept the plans extremely simple and essentially beyond negotiation. There would be an across-the-board cut in income tax rates for every taxpayer and there would be no corporate tax cuts or any loopholes. The White House presented its blueprint to Congress so early that most lobbies on K Street had no chance to muddy the waters. Early in the 2000 campaign, the Bush team had rationalized the tax cuts in terms of the growing surplus, but now, the halting economy was used to justify tax cuts, as a much-needed economic stimulus. Often, White House officials would use either argument (or both) as it suited the circumstances.

Bush's first breakthrough came when Federal Reserve Chairman Alan Greenspan declared in Congress on January 25 that tax cuts were affordable, given the large budget surplus, and a 'real necessity'.[131] Even though Greenspan later lent quiet support to an amendment (it failed by one vote in the Senate) that would make the tax cuts conditional upon the level of public debt remaining, Greenspan's early support took the wind out of the sails of many Democrats ready to attack Bush's plan. Greenspan, a Reagan appointee whom Bush jokingly called 'El Taco Grande', was one of the first people Bush visited when coming to Washington.[132] Senators who came to the White House in anticipation of brokering a compromise on tax cuts, such as Johnny Breaux from Louisiana, found themselves in the wrong game. Bush would talk with 'Johnny-be-Good', as he nicknamed him, but then fly off to Louisiana to urge voters to put pressure on Breaux to support Bush's tax cuts: That was the essence of the outside game.

Back in 1981, Reagan had relied heavily on his communications skills and used TV and radio to rally his base throughout the country to pressure Congress to support his tax cuts. However, the Bush White House knew that this president could not rely on that tactic because he simply was not as effective a television communicator. One of Lee Atwater's dictums was that the first word in president is 'PR'.[133] Bush knew that his 'PR' was in local politics, and so he traveled to 22 states in the first two months of his presidency. He campaigned more than any president before him at this stage of his term; in fact, Bush never stopped campaigning. In the 1980s, Hedrick Smith wrote about 'the constant campaign', describing how House Representatives with their short two-year terms never stopped campaigning.[134] The same can be said of Bush and the presidency. More so than Reagan and Clinton, Bush worked the outside public in a type of 'permanent campaign'.[135] For his tax cuts, he campaigned intensely in states that were quite conservative but that had one or two Democratic senators such as Nebraska's Don Nelson. Lobbies such as

'Americans for Tax Reform' and the 'Club for Growth' put their own campaigns in full swing to create 'outside the Beltway passion' for the Bush plan. Grover Norquist, who heads Americans for Tax Reform, encouraged Republican legislatures in the various states to pass resolutions 'urging' their Democratic Senators to support Bush's plan.[136]

On February 8, The White House submitted the formal plans to the House. On February 27, Bush addressed a joint session of Congress. Using a type of 'goldilocks' strategy, Bush made the case that some (referring to fiscal conservatives in his own party) 'want less government regardless of the need', while others (the Democrats) 'want more government regardless of the cost'. Bush's plans for an overall budget increase of only four per cent (in contrast to the nine per cent increase of Clinton's last year) combined with his tax cuts was portrayed as getting it just right. Using a line given to him by Karen Hughes, Bush added: 'The people of America have been overcharged and, on their behalf, I am here asking for a refund.'[137] Bush excelled at laying out his plans as a shortlist of principles and then adding, 'In my plan, no one is targeted in or targeted out.'[138]

The Democratic leader in the Senate, Tom Daschle, commissioned a TV ad showing that the middle class American would gain a muffler from Bush's plans, while the rich guy could buy a Lexus.[139] Paul Krugman wrote column after column in the *New York Times*, hammering Bush for allowing more tax dollars to return to the rich then to the lower-middle class, but for Bush it was a classical case of equality of opportunity for all.[140] Daschle's disingenuous but effective visual only showed the obvious. The top two per cent of tax payers who would get their rate cut from 39.6 to 33 per cent also happen to pay about 50 per cent of the total volume of income taxes paid.[141] For a person paying $500,000 in taxes, a six per cent cut adds up to a lot more money than a 10 per cent cut for an income of $40,000 with a current tax rate of only 20 per cent. Bush said tax cuts should reward all brackets and he also called for doubling the child tax credit and reducing the so-called marriage penalty.

At first, Democrats seemed to think that Bush would compromise. After all, the President's plan, which called for a $1.6 trillion cut over ten years, was much bigger than the $800 billion the Republican Congress had sought in 1999. Bush also included the gradual abolition of the estate tax in his plan, and Democrats expected him to negotiate on that part of the package. What the Democrats found instead was stonewalling at the White House and growing pressure at the grass roots. Perhaps the deciding factor among the voting public about tax cuts was the surplus. Estimates in 2001 were for about $5 trillion in surplus by the end of the decade, but given the Social Security commitments, the actual surplus was 'only' around $3 trillion.

In early March, the House passed Bush's plans without major change, without a single dissenting Republican vote and with many Democrats voting alongside the Republicans. The ball was now in the Senate's court where such moderates as James Jeffords of Vermont, Lincoln Chafee of Rhode Island and Arlen Specter of Pennsylvania made it clear that they would not support Bush's plan as passed by the House. With most Republicans and a dozen conservative Democrats on side, Bush's tax plans could not be killed in the Senate and so on April 6, the Senate voted 65 to 35 for a $1.18 trillion tax cut. Senator Phil Gramm called it 'pretty good for the semifinals'.[142] Now the President was ready to compromise just enough to save the bill. The negotiations in the Conference Committee were intense and produced a final package of $1.35 trillion in tax cuts over eleven years. A lot of the big cuts, including the end of the so-called death tax, were stacked in the later years, presumably fair target for another round.

Bush had spent a tremendous amount of political capital to get his tax relief. Friendly legislators such as Senator Breaux grumbled, 'It's creating a legacy of bitterness.'[143] What mattered most to the White House was that Bush had scored an early victory. It had taken Ronald Reagan until August 1981 to get his tax cuts even though he had been shot two months into his first term and received massive public sympathy. Bush had his tax cuts before June. Journalists had called Bush's debut in January 'a smashing success', now they recognized his governing capacity.[144] Rove had said that the first 180 days were 'the critical horizon', yet Bush scored at the 120-day mark.[145] He had told the reluctant Paul O'Neill, 'I won't negotiate with myself.'[146] His approval rating rose to the solid mid-fifties and stayed there till summer. Bush was beginning to emerge as his own man away from the shadows of Florida.

Bush won on his tax cuts, but it came with a price. If Bush wanted to keep the deficit down during a declining economy, he had no practical plan to do so as he faced Senate Democrats determined to make him appear as a president who could get nothing done. In order to show results, Bush had to compromise on the costs of all the other legislative pieces; education policy was the first item to present itself on this list.

In May 2001, Senator Jeffords left the Republican Party and allowed the Democrats to take back the Committee chairs. There were various tension points between the White House and Jeffords, but what caused his defection was that Jeffords felt he had given Bush and Trent Lott a good deal. He had helped broker the $1.18 trillion Senate deal on tax cuts and he had expected some money to come his way on education in the final deal on tax cuts. Senator James Jeffords' personal mission for years had been to bring the Federal contribution to disability education to at least 40 per cent of the total bill (it has been stuck at 15 per cent for some time). Given that the federal share of all funding for elementary and secondary education is only seven per cent, this was a tough target. Jeffords saw the government budget surplus as a window of opportunity to invest some $180 billion into the educational disabilities fund, and so Bush and Jeffords tried to cut a deal. The President did have Jeffords over at the White House, but Jeffords was as adamant about his huge investment in special-needs education as Bush was on his tax cuts. Bush did not compromise with anyone to a serious extent on tax cuts and he was not going to do it with a moderate from his own party. When the House-Senate Conference committee on tax cuts came back 'without special-education funds', Jeffords said, 'That's it,' and left the GOP.[147]

Education Reform and Faith-Based Welfare

Bush had built his reputation in Texas on education reform; 'It is what he came here to do,' one close aide commented.[148] All who met with Bush on education admitted that he commanded the details of this file. It was Bush's 'strongest policy suit', and he came to Washington 'versed in the politics of education'.[149] In Washington, he represented the grass-roots movement for standards in education as the National Assessment of Education Progress tests continually showed failing 'report cards.' The 2000 test showed that 63 per cent of black students and 58 per cent of Hispanics performed at 'below basic level, meaning they were unable to get any sense of what they'd read.'[150]

The President's objectives remained unchanged since his days in Austin; his 'leave-no-child-behind' approach meant that all students should be able to read before entering Grade Four. There should be no 'soft bigotry' that allowed Black or Hispanic kids to perform at lower levels – they should be tested so that no schools could let minority or poor children slip through the cracks under the guise of not wanting to single anybody out. Such 'social promotion' was anathema to Bush for it meant discrimination by low expectations. He had fixed that problem in Texas by insisting on disaggregated data. Test results should not give only overall scores, but break them down by racial groups. In Bush's philosophy, there should be standards, tests, and disaggregated test results, and the schools should be held accountable. If schools failed systematically to meet statewide standards, they should first receive help, but if they did not improve in a set time frame, 'there should be strong consequences', including giving parents education vouchers to take their youngsters elsewhere.[151]

In 2000, Congress failed to find agreement on re-authorizing the Elementary and Secondary School Act. This provided Bush with an opportunity to attach his school reforms to a bill re-authorizing this Act and so he started early, using the opposite strategy from his push on tax cuts. In a policy session in Austin in December 2000, Bush impressed one of the House leaders on education, the California Democrat 'Big George' Miller, with both his knowledge and his charm, to create a working relationship with.[152] While Margaret Spellings and Sandy Kress worked with Miller, Secretary Rod Paige traveled the country explaining Bush's objectives and how he, as former school superintendent in Houston, had produced results with 'high-stakes testing'.[153]

In the Senate, Bush went directly to the point man, the liberal Democrat Ted Kennedy.[154] The President met with Kennedy four times in the first four weeks of the administration. During one visit at the White House, they watched the newly released movie 'Thirteen Days' about the Kennedy brothers and the Cuban missile crisis over hamburgers and hotdogs. Bush was able to convince Kennedy that they shared a common focus on the kid that gets left behind; left behind by many Republicans who wanted to abolish the Department of Education and by the National Teacher's Association, which opposes mandatory tests. They may not agree on *how* to help the inner-city Black or Hispanic children, but Bush, like Kennedy was sincere in wanting to help them.

The other shrewd move by Bush was to signal early in January that he would be willing to drop the voucher provision, 'realizing that Congress would not approve it.'[155] This was not popular with conservatives, but vouchers were firmly in the terrain of state governments and not something the federal government could easily control. The teachers unions were dead set against them, alleging that it would turn education into 'a culture of testing'.[156] By dropping them, Bush made it easier for

Kennedy to accept mandatory tests and parental choice for supplemental services. 'Tests-but-no-vouchers' was the necessary condition to give the 'No Child Left Behind Bill' serious reception in both Houses of Congress. There would be a great deal of detail to fine-tune, but at least Conservatives had their tests and Liberals had stood up against vouchers. The Bush-Kennedy compromise looked very much like the Bush-Bullock legislative strategy in Texas.

Where Bush and the Democrats were miles apart was on the funding that should go with the re-authorization. In his budget statement, Bush had targeted an eleven per cent increase in education spending, but the Senate, after the Democrats took control, proposed a 40 per cent increase.[157] By the end of April, the House and Senate were still ten billion dollars apart. Bush proposed that funding for failing schools should be diverted to the parents. Schools might lose their Title I funding (money to help children in the poverty bracket) if they continued to fail. Congressman Miller resisted this feature and also objected to Bush's idea of 'Straight A's', a program which would award states that have schools who persistently score well by giving them more freedom on how they spend federal funds.[158] Kennedy came on board on setting up a limited experiment program for 'Straight A's' but Miller killed it in the House.

In May, Bush ran into unexpected resistance from several states: State governors such as John Engler from Michigan were worried about the new tests, as Michigan voters might hold him responsible for failing schools. Sandy Kress re-jigged the average yearly progress requirements so that the law would label only a small percentage of schools 'non-performing'.[159] Further compromises were struck on how long schools should be given before they had to show progress – in the end, schools ended up with a twelve-year schedule. Thanks to Kennedy's influence and involvement, both the House and the Senate passed close versions of the Bill in late May and early June. Most of the hard work in the Conference Committee would be on funding levels.

The Conference Committee on education could not report before the August recess, but when the terrorist attacks struck on September 11, the Bill was pushed down the list of priorities. The final version of the Bill passed both the House and Senate on December 18, 2001. Jeffords voted against the Bill, as it did not provide enough for disability education. The Education Bill was a moderate victory for Bush's education principles and values and a massive victory for Democrats on education spending. In 2001, the Federal Government had spent $18.2 billion on education, which Bush had proposed to raise to $19.8 billion in 2002. Instead, Congress agreed to authorize $26.5 billion, with Title I funding rising from $8 billion in 2001 to $13.5 billion in the new Bill. According to a senior White House aide involved in getting the deal, 'The Democrats helped achieve bigger education spending increases than any time in history, including the Clinton years.'[160]

Bush has never been a 'debt hawk,' and if it was going to take funding to get the Democrats on board, he would go along provided he could advance his value of testing all kids. Having another legislative victory would show Bush could get things done. On January 8, 2002, he went to Hamilton, Ohio, in the home district of Jim Boehner, the Republican House Chair of the Education Committee, accompanied by Ted Kennedy and George Miller, to sign the Bill into law. Bush praised Kennedy and gave him wide credit for the Bill, yet, Bush was not able to transfer their joint success on education into a bigger working relationship on other issues. Soon Kennedy and Bush would spar over patients' rights legislation.

Bush unveiled the third plank in his compassionate conservative platform on January 29, when he announced that he would set up a White House Office for Faith-Based and Community Initiatives. Its function was threefold: to find ways to increase charitable giving, to expand public-private partnerships in delivering social services and to look at ways in which faith and community organizations could apply for federal grants and programs. Each of the major departments involved, such as Labor and Health and Human Services, would set up centers to realize the three goals. The new White House Office would be quite small (about ten staff) and would not have power or funds to disburse grants to any organization. Bush appointed Stephen Goldsmith to chair the board of the Corporation for National Service and to act as his adviser on faith and community based issues and appointed John DiIulio as the Director of the new White House Office. A conservative Catholic, and a Democrat, DiIulio's new job, it was hoped would fit with the President's and Rove's concentrated effort to get more political support from the so-called religiously active Catholics.

The idea of faith-based organizations delivering social services paid for by federal dollars is like setting the cat among the pigeons. The idea was so radical that many people simply reacted rather than tried to find out what Bush meant. Many accused the President of trying to hijack the so-called Establishment Clause in the American constitution on the separation of church and state to please his Christian conservative supporters.[161] Ferocious debates on religion and politics followed and in the end it was a complex mix of groups who argued for and against, with many religious organizations in the latter category.

It was Bush's experience in Texas that showed him that faith-based organizations such as Teen Challenge, Prison Fellowship, and the Salvation Army were performing social service functions for which they could not get any governmental support. Yet, their success rate at helping people out of crime, poverty and addiction was often better than the government's. As Bush has said consistently for years, he feels that this is a form of 'government discrimination against people of faith'.[162]

What Bush intends with faith-based initiatives is to supplement but not replace state-based endeavors to help people. Many social ills are caused by 'bad choices', such as dropping out of school, abuse of alcohol, and illegitimacy. 'It is a point that contradicts more than 30 years of received opinion among liberal policymakers, but Bush delivers it as if it were obvious.'[163] Researchers at New York's Manhattan Institute argued that decades of 'liberal welfarism' had made little difference.[164] More money from bland generic federal programs cannot fix these bad choices. Faith-based and community programs, however, can help people recognize those wrong choices and give them an opportunity to change their path. During the launch of his initiative at the White House Bush said, 'We will not fund the religious activities of any group, but when people of faith provide social services, we will not discriminate against them.'[165]

The 1996 Welfare Reform Act had a provision added to it called, 'Charitable Choice', proposed by then Senator John Ashcroft. It opened the way for large organizations such as Roman Catholic hospitals to apply for federal funding for some areas of their activities not related to 'worship, instruction or proselytizing'.[166]

Simply put, Bush wanted bureaucratic barriers lowered so that smaller alternate providers, including churches, mosques, and synagogues, could qualify for non-proselytizing services. The Welfare Reform Act also added a provision for non-itemized tax deductions for charitable donations. 'Despite the sound and fury,' the *Economist* concluded, 'the basic idea is modest and intriguing.'[167]

John DiIulio shared Al Gore's view that government funding for faith-based groups should rigidly enforce 'segmenting', meaning that faith-building activities and social programs should be separated.[168] Many church denominations in the Christian Coalition were actually leery about the whole idea, fearing they would not be allowed to teach the Gospel or would have to water it down. The denominations that were in favor wanted an integrated approach, where the government might pay for the beds and electricity, for example, while the religious organization would pay for the religious components. The budget would be segmented as it were, but not the program.

From the beginning, Bush had outlined his faith-based initiative in very wide terms, speaking about Christian, Jewish, Muslim and non-religious organizations all having access to this initiative. At the launch of his new job in the Bush administration, Steve Goldsmith stated that, 'those in need should never be required to go to faith-based service providers' and that, 'faith-based programs are not a panacea.'[169] Knowing that key players in Bush's initiative such as Goldsmith stood for empowering cities to shape local programs, the US Conference of Mayors quickly endorsed Bush's initiative. While the leadership of most African American organizations is overwhelmingly critical of Bush, more than 70 per cent of Black inner-city churches engage in community outreach programs and the local leadership of these churches by and large favored Bush's provision.

On the legislative aspect of faith-based initiatives, Bush had House Representatives J.C. Watts, a Republican, and Tony Hall, a Democrat, sponsor his 'Community Solutions Act'. It was a battle to get the Bill through the House Judiciary Committee. Karl Rove had from the beginning of the administration set up a weekly conference call with conservative Protestant leaders on Monday and a separate session with religiously active Catholics on Thursday, the latter directed by Tim Goeglin in the public liaison's office.[170] Later in the administration, Pete Weher joined Rove as special liaison to the Protestant conservatives as Rove tried hard to keep a majority coalition behind the Bill. By April it was clear that in any attempt to expand the granting program to child care, hunger relief, extra schooling or domestic violence assistance, the faith-based idea would have to include stringent segmenting and program review standards. The White House made sure to put them into the Bill. This was still not enough for vocal lobbies such as 'Americans United for the Separation of Church and State' who were against any expansion of the 'Charitable Choice' provision. During the all-day mark up session on the Bill on June 28, opponents of the idea were able to get not only segmenting but also a 'secondary opt-out provision' into the Bill.[171] In the latter measure, a faith-based organization is required to provide a secular alternative service for those who seek assistance, but want to be exempt from the religious aspects. Some conservative Christian groups got off the train at this point. Pat Robertson, the leader of the Christian Coalition spoke out against the Bill, as did Marvin Olasky, now a reporter for *World Magazine*.

While the 1964 Civil Rights Act contained important provisions allowing religious organizations exemptions in their hiring practices, opponents of the Bill now demanded that such exemptions should be rolled back if the faith-based organizations became involved in social services.[172] It became a messy scene: DiIulio wanted to work with Democratic Senators and was critical of the demands of the Evangelicals who resisted compromise. Rove did not want to alienate Protestant conservatives. The Bill not only became a battleground for the separation of church and state, but also for civil rights. At one point, the *Washington Post* published a story alleging that Karl Rove and the Salvation Army were negotiating a deal where Rove would try to get federal protection for the Sally Ann from municipalities that require it to hire gays and pay domestic benefits, in exchange for the Salvation Army's support for the Community Solutions Act.[173] Bush made a personal and strong emotional appeal at the Capitol to Republican members of the House on July 11 to advance his values in the Bill. He told them 'I want you to overlook some of the details and get it done.'[174]

The House Ways and Means Committee did as much financial harm to the Bill as the Judiciary Committee had done to its principles. Bush had asked for an $84 billion increase over ten years for non-itemized charitable income tax deductions: instead, he received $6 billion, or $25 dollars for individuals, at the start of the ten-year period. Many churches fearing that, 'with the shekels come the shackles', now had little financial incentive left to fight for the legislation.[175] At the end of July, the Community Solutions Act passed the House (233-198) with fifteen Democrats voting with the Republican majority. The compromise that made it possible was 'secondary opt-outs for vouchers,' but the Bill never found a sponsor in the Senate and died.

Seeing his influence diminished, DiIulio resigned from his White House post in August of 2001.[176] Bush replaced him with Jim Towey, also a Catholic but with more political experience and a lower profile. The President revamped the office, giving more power to the Community National Service. Having lost the first round with Congress on faith-based welfare, Bush did not abandon his values. He would advance the faith-based agenda within the executive government eliminating, as he put it, 'barriers that discriminate against community and faith-based organizations', and not fight another legislative battle until he had more political capital.[177] Throughout 2002 and 2003, Bush used a variety of executive orders to keep the policy alive.

The Rest of the Domestic Agenda

Bush also had to deal with issues Congress forced on him such as election reform and a patients' rights bill. On top of that, Bush added a comprehensive energy bill to his short list of priorities.

Bush decided to settle quickly with Senator John McCain, a 'definite burr in the Bush saddle', who proceeded to renew his fight for election reform the same day the President launched his tax cuts. Bush told Trent Lott, 'Let McCain have his moment.'[178] The Senate voted 59 to 41 on March 20, 2002 (the House had approved it on February 14) and Bush signed it, taking a tiny bit of the limelight for a measure he had opposed since the 2000 presidential campaign.

Senators Kennedy, McCain and John Edwards launched their Patients' Rights Bill just days after Bush's inauguration. As governor of Texas, one of Bush's first initiatives had been to introduce tort reform – fighting 'frivolous law suits' is a long-held value for Bush. Since the 1974 Employee Retirement Income Security Act, Health Management Organizations (HMOs) had become exempt from liability suits and most state regulations. Bush stated in early 2001 that he was in favor of a Patients' Rights provision as long as it did not lead to large increases in medical insurance rates and as long as it had real teeth to prevent frivolous lawsuits. To help prevent these, Bush proposed that such suits must be 'a last resort', preceded by an outside review panel looking at the malpractice case first, that suits should be filed in federal court (which are generally more cautious and less awarding than state courts) and that there should be 'reasonable caps' on the amounts people could sue for non-economic damage such as pain and punitive damages.[179] Bush proposed that each should be capped at five hundred thousand dollars.

The Kennedy-McCain-Edwards bill contained no limit on non-economic damages, a five million dollar cap on punitive damages, and allowed suits in both federal and state courts with no restrictions. Despite various efforts by the White House and by House Representative Charlie Norwood to find compromises, the two sides could not find a closing deal on the bill. When the House passed its version with a narrow majority on August 2, 2001, the White House offered to negotiate directly with the Senate. Kennedy compromised a little: He would allow federal law to curtail state court suits. It became a game of chicken, of who would veer first on the caps, now at $1.5 million. One of the major lobbyists on the issue commented in August 2001 that a compromise 'seemed in the province of the doable', but the terrorist attacks pushed the issue beyond the November 2002 midterm elections.[180]

The battle on patients' rights and limits on malpractice suits was rejoined in late 2003, after Bush and Congress had passed a Bill on prescription drug benefits. However, by early 2004, the bill was still tied up and now part of a strategy by several Senate Democrats to block both it and Bush's proposals for corporate tax reform. Senate Majority Leader Bill Frist cut a deal with Senator Daschle in early April 2004 to let the malpractice bill die in order to rescue the corporate tax bill.[181]

Neither energy policy nor the environment were major election themes for Bush, yet, they became a lightning rod early in his administration. Bush decided in January 2001 that there was a need for a new overall approach to energy and 'officially empowered Cheney' to handle it.[182] The rolling blackouts in California in 2001 (and later the massive blackouts in the Northeast in August 2003) showed the power grid needed reinvestment. It was also true that no nuclear power plants and no major oil refineries had been built for 20 years and that the United States was becoming more dependent on foreign oil. Cheney justly pointed out that conservation is 'not a sufficient basis for a sound comprehensive energy strategy', but Bush's proposal to drill for oil in an Alaskan wilderness preserve ignited the environmental lobbies.[183] Democratic Senators vowed to filibuster the measure.

The Democrats were able to tie the energy policy, a variety of executive orders, international decisions, and appointments into a coherent offensive proclaiming that Bush and Cheney were 'helping their oil friends' and were 'anti-environment'.[184] On January 5, 2001 in 'the dying days of his administration', Clinton banned building roads on 58 million acres of land run by the Forest Service.[185] Clearly this was an environmental booby trap that Bush could not get around, so he merely put it on hold, but was slammed in the press for it. For years Clinton had postponed stricter controls on arsenic in drinking water; when Bush postponed it again, he was severely criticized.

Apart from carbon dioxide, Bush has in fact made some important environmentally friendly decisions in his term. Most significantly, the President upheld 'a sweeping, expensive regulation that requires petroleum companies to remove most pollutants from diesel fuel'.[186] He added further controls on diesel emissions in 2004. Cheney, as head of the 'interagency, cabinet level-task force' on energy, became embroiled in a dispute with Congress, which ended up in court, about whom he consulted.[187] The Supreme Court eventually cleared Cheney, but it left a negative public image. David Gergen commented that the Bush administration had failed to craft a 'buy-in' strategy for 'mainstream' environmental groups.[188] When Enron, the large energy corporation that had contributed big sums of soft money to the Bush-Cheney campaign, was embroiled in corporate fraud in 2002, many environmental critics tried to convict the Bush White House by association.

After September 11, the White House cast the floundering Energy Bill in terms of national security, but that did not make its passage easier. The Energy Bill gradually turned into omnibus legislation, pork-laden with provisions for both the energy and conservation lobbies, such as subsidies for corn-derived ethanol to reduce gasoline emissions. The Senate finally passed its version on April 25, 2002, giving $14 billion in tax breaks and subsidies divided over fossil fuels, renewable sources and conservation. Like the House, it did not tighten fuel efficiency standards for cars or SUV's by much, but it defeated attempts by the White House and Senator Murkowski from Alaska, to include drilling in Alaska's National Wildlife Reserve. Like Patients' Rights, the Bill did not make it out of the Conference Committee before the 107th Congress closed its doors for the November 2002 election. Given the worsening deficit in 2003, the 'pork' in the Bill made its passage even less likely. Not willing to raise the environmental issue in the 2004 campaign, the Bill seemed without momentum in the spring of 2004.

Conclusion

If Bush had not come in with a loyal team, a rapid-fire transition machine, and a game plan for his priorities, he would have been a lame-duck president from the start. Passing any major piece of legislation in the Congressional system is a feat. During his first year, Bush scored a clear victory on tax cuts and on education reform. Put into comparative perspective with Reagan and Clinton, those were huge achievements. His faith-based initiatives as well as issues that had not been part of his 2000 campaign such as Patients' Rights and energy legislation got bogged down.

While Bush tried to build a relationship of trust, friendship and personal loyalty with Ted Kennedy, he did not succeed beyond the education bill. Perhaps if Kennedy had been majority leader, Bush could have been more successful, but Democratic Senate Majority Leader Thomas Daschle made sure not to be lured by

Bush's charm. He showed that he was 'a tough-as-nails political hardballer'.[189] Bush was indeed an effective lobbyist for his program, but Daschle was a powerful 'blocker'.[190] Yet, both Bush and Daschle avoided complete gridlock, knowing it would cause them both harm in 2002, if the Congress could get nothing done. The President was good at that line of attack on Congress, quipping in Pennsylvania in August 2001, 'Congress is on vacation; the country's never run better.'[191] Bush for his part never vetoed a single measure even though the Senate Democrats ratcheted up spending on all bills. He signed a six-year Farm Bill in 2002 that increased subsidies by $248 billion.

Bush's approach in tax cuts, education reform, and patient's rights showed that he adjusts his legislative strategy according to the circumstances. While he pursues his values, he does not use a one-size-fits-all strategy to advance them. Strong values, but flexible means best describe his legislative style. When he did not get all of his values, as in faith-based initiatives, he waited for the next round, in this case till after November 2002, to use the executive order route. Bush's biggest domestic decision was to push the deficit into the future, hoping that the consumer stimulus caused by tax relief would come early enough to produce the needed economic growth to offset overspending and make passage of the rest of his Compassionate Conservative agenda more palatable. But before he had a chance to act on this, his foreign policy agenda, which thus far had simmered in the background, presented itself front and center.

Notes

1   Howard Fineman and Martha Brant, 'The Test of His Life', *Newsweek*, December 25, 2000–January 1, 2001, p. 33.
2   'The Accidental President', *Economist*, December 16, 2000, p. 19.
3   Fineman and Brandt, December 25, 2000/January 1, 2001, p. 36.
4   Howard Fineman, 'What Bush Needs', *Newsweek*, June 4, 2001, p. 28.
5   Alexis Simendinger, 'Stepping Into Power', *National Journal*, January 27, 2001, p. 246.
6   James Bennett, 'C.E.O., U.S.A', *The New York Times Magazine*, January 14, 2001, pp. 27-28
7   'A Discussion with Karl Rove', American Enterprise Institute, December 11, 2001.
8   'Remarks by the President and Secretary of Commerce Donald Evans at Swearing-In Ceremony', Office of the Press Secretary, February 5, 2001.
9   'Election 2000', *Newsweek*, December 25, 2000–January 1, 2001, p. 41
10   Joshua Green, 'The Other War Room', *The Washington Monthly*, April 2002.
11   Dana Milbank, 'Serious "Strategery": as Rove Launches Elaborate Political Effort', *Washington Post*, April 22, 2001.
12   Ron Suskind, 'Mrs. Hughes Takes Her Leave', *Esquire*, July 2002, p. 103.
13   Walter Isaacson and Jim Kelly, 'Bush Speaks', *Time*, December 25, 2000–January 1, 2001, p. 76.
14   Suskind, p. 103.
15   Suskind, p. 110.
16   Martha Brant and Tamara Lipper, 'The Road Show', *Newsweek*, August 26, 2002, p. 34.
17   Martha Joynt Kumar, 'Recruiting and Organizing the White House Staff', *PS*, March 2002, pp. 35-36.

18 John P. Burke, 'The Bush Transition in Historical Context', *PS*, March 2002, p. 24.
19 George W. Bush, *A Charge to Keep* (New York: Willliam Morrow, 1999), p. 97.
20 As quoted by David Brooks, 'How Would George W. Bush Govern?', American Enterprise Institute, Transition to Governing Project, January 13, 2000.
21 Bennett, p. 49.
22 Carl M. Cannon and Alexis Simendinger, 'The Evolution of Karl Rove', *National Journal*, April 27, 2002, p. 1214.
23 Howard Fineman, 'The Heart of the Matter', *Newsweek*, March 19, 2001, p. 26.
24 Lexington, 'The Power Behind the Throne', *Economist*, December 23, 2000, p. 34.
25 Nicholas Lemann, 'The Quiet Man', *The New Yorker*, May 7, 2001, p. 68.
26 Richard E. Cohen, 'The White House's Top Lobbyist: an Interview with Nick Calio', *National Journal*, March 26, 2001.
27 See for example, Charles E. Walcott and Karen M. Hult, 'The Bush Staff and Cabinet System', in Gary L. Gregg II and Mark J. Rozell (eds) *Considering the Bush Presidency* (New York: Oxford University Press, 2004), pp. 54-55.
28 Ryan Lizza, 'Bolten the Door', *The New Republic*, August 20, 2001, p. 12.
29 Carl M. Cannon et al., 'The Decision Makers', *National Journal*, June 23, 2001.
30 Karen Hughes, *Ten Minutes From Normal* (New York: Viking, 2004), p. 205.
31 Ramesh Ponnuru, 'Speedy Gonzales', *National Review*, April 30, 2001, p. 19.
32 Donald Kettl, *Team Bush: Leadership Lessons from the Bush White House* (New York: McGraw-Hill, 2003), p. 151.
33 Ron Suskind, *The Price of Loyalty: George W. Bush, The White House, and the Education of Paul O'Neill* (New York: Simon & Schuster, 2004), p. 117.
34 Suskind, *The Price of Loyalty*, p. 172.
35 Lexington, 'George Bush, homme sérieux', *Economist*, February 10, 2001, p. 38.
36 Martha Brandt, 'Bush's "Power Buff Girls"', *Newsweek*, May 7, 2001, p. 36.
37 Suskind, 'Mrs. Hughes', p. 104.
38 Lemann, 2001, p. 67.
39 Simendinger, p. 247.
40 Dana Milbank, 'White House Distaff Make Family a Priority', *Washington Post*, February 15, 2001.
41 Dana Milbank, 'A Loyalist Calls White House to Order: Chief of Staff Card Streamlines Bush's Agenda, Staff, Schedule and Message', *Washington Post*, February 20, 2001.
42 Karen Hughes in interview with Barbara Walters, March 26, 2004, from excerpts on Answers in Action (http://answers.org/aia/20040326122731659.html).
43 Elisabeth Bumiller, 'An Influential Bush Adviser, Karen Hughes, Will Resign', *New York Times*, April 24, 2002.
44 Dan Balz and Mike Allen, 'Hughes to Leave White House', *Washington Post*, April 24, 2002, p. 1.
45 *Newsweek*, January 22, 2001, p. 27.
46 Ward Connerly, 'A Battle, and an Opportunity', *National Review*, February 5, 2001, p. 33.
47 'By George', *The Economist*, January 6, 2001, p. 26.
48 Andrew Sullivan, 'Sounds of Silence', *The New Republic*, January 15, 2001, p. 6; Mike Allen, 'A Team Built on Conservative Discipline', *Washington Post*, January 3, 2001.
49 Jonathan Cohn, 'Moral Minority', *The New Republic*, January 15, 2001.
50 Julie Kosterlitz, 'The O'Neill Enigma', *National Journal*, August 9, 2001.
51 Julie Kosterlitz, Insider Interview, 'Treasury Secretary Paul O'Neill: A Wealth of Opinions', *National Journal*, August 10, 2001.
52 Johnson, p. 53.
53 James A. Barnes, 'Bush's Insiders', *National Journal*, June 25, 2001.

54   Barnes, June 25, 2001.
55   Press Releases, 'The Presidential Appointee Initiative', Brookings Institution, April 20, August 7, and December 18, 2001.
56   Ryan Lizza, 'Spokesmen', *The New Republic*, January 29, 2001.
57   Glenn Kessler and Dana Milbank, '"Review Board" Rules the Funding Process', *Washington Post*, March 1, 2001.
58   Fineman and Brandt, December 25, 2000–January 1, 2001, p. 36.
59   See Fred Greenstein, *The Hidden-Hand Presidency: Eisenhower as Leader* (New York: Basic Books, 1982).
60   David Gergen, as quoted in 'How is Bush Governing', American Enterprise Institute, May 15, 2001.
61   Carolyn B. Thompson and James W. Ware, *The Leadership Genius of George W. Bush* (New York: John Wiley & Sons, Inc, 2003), pp. 3-5.
62   George called it 'Multiple Advocacy'. See: Alexander George, *Presidential Decision Making in Foreign Policy* (Boulder: Westview Press, 1980), Chapter 11.
63   Karen Hughes, *Ten Minutes From Normal*, p. 92.
64   Martha Joynt Kumar, 'Recruiting and Organizing the White House Staff', *PS*, March 2002, pp. 37-38.
65   As quoted in 'How Would George W. Bush Govern', American Enterprise Institute, January 13, 2001.
66   Andrew Sullivan, 'Destiny's Child: George W. Bush and His God', *The Sunday Times*, October 28, 2001.
67   Fred I. Greenstein, 'George W. Bush and the Ghosts of Presidents Past', *PS*, March 2001, p. 80.
68   Evan Thomas, 'First Brush with History', *Newsweek*, May 7, 2001, p. 34.
69   Thomas, p, 34.
70   As quoted in Howard Fineman, 'The Heart of the Matter', *Newsweek*, March 19, 2001, p. 26.
71   In an interview with Sam Donaldson, ABC News, *This Week*, May 21, 2000.
72   *US Foreign Policy Agenda*, US Department of State, Vol. 6, No. 1, March 21, 2001, p. 28.
73   Colin L. Powell, *My American Journey* (New York: Ballantine Books, 1995), p. 561.
74   Michael Hirsh, 'Leader of the Pack', *Newsweek*, December 25, 2000–January 1, 2001, p. 39.
75   James Kitfield, 'A Diplomat Handy with a Bayonet', *National Journal*, January 27, 2001, p. 250.
76   James Kitfield et al., 'State Department Profiles', *National Journal*, March 6, 2002.
77   Author interview with State Department Official, March 16, 2004.
78   James Mann, 'Young Rumsfeld', *Atlantic Monthly*, November 2003, p. 92.
79   Midge Decter, *Rumsfeld: A Personal Portrait* (New York: Regan Books, 2003), p. 41.
80   Interview with James Mann by Katie Bacon, 'Rumsfeld's Roots', *Atlantic Online*, October 8, 2003 (www.theatlantic.com/cgi-bin/send.cgi?page=http3a).
81   Rowan Scarborough, *Rumsfeld's War: The Untold Story of America's Anti-Terrorist Commander* (Washington, D.C., Regnery Publishing, 2004), p. 108.
82   Scarborough, p. 109.
83   *The Rumsfeld Commission Report*, US Senate, July 31, 1999, p. S9523.
84   Charles L. Glaser and Steve Fetter, 'National Missile Defense and the Future of US Nuclear Weapons Policy', *International Security*, (Summer 2001).
85   The official title is: Commission to Assess National Security Space Management and Organization.
86   Report of the Commission to Assess National Security Space Management and Organization, Executive Summary, January 11, 2001, p. 7.

87   Cannon, 2001.
88   Carl M. Cannon, 'Central Intelligence Agency Profiles', *National Journal*, June 23, 2001.
89   Walter Pincus and Vernon Loeb, 'CIA Resurfaces', *Washington Post*, July 29, 2001, p. 5.
90   Karen De Young and Steven Mufson, 'A Leaner and Less Visible NSC', *Washington Post*, February 10, 2001, p. 1.
91   Carla Anne Robbins, 'Among the Unknowns About Missile Defense Is Who the Enemy Is', *Wall Street Journal*, February 9, 2001.
92   Author interview with Department of Defense Official, March 15, 2004.
93   National Security Presidential Directive, The White House, February 13, 2001.
94   Lawrence F. Kaplan, 'Containment', *The New Republic*, February 5, 2001, p. 18.
95   Evan Thomas, 'The Quiet Power of Condi Rice', *Newsweek*, December 16, 2002, p. 29.
96   idem.
97   'How Would George Bush Govern', American Enterprise Institute, January 13, 2000.
98   'How Would George Bush Govern', 2000, p. 24.
99   Susan Baer, 'The Voice in Bush's Ear', *The Baltimore Sun*, October 1, 2001, p. 1.
100   Lemann, 2002, p. 167.
101   American Enterprise Institute, 'Assessing the Bush Transition', January 16, 2001.
102   Carla Anne Robbins, 'Powell's Caution Against Quick Strike Shapes Bush Plan', *The Wall Street Journal*, September 21, 2001, p. 24.
103   Baer, 2001.
104   Mike Allen and Alan Sipress, 'Who Meets When to Discuss What and Why?', *The Seattle Times*, September 28, 2001, p. 3.
105   'The Bush Merry-Go-Round', *New York Times*, Editorial, September 8, 2001, p. 12.
106   For example, see Jane Perlez, 'Bush Team's Counsel is Divided on Foreign Policy', *The New York Times*, March 27, 2001, p.1, and 'Working out the World', *The Economist*, March 31, 2001, p. 24.
107   Evan Thomas and John Barry, 'The Family Firm', *Newsweek*, January 8, 2001, p. 23.
108   Morton M. Kondracke, 'US Offer to Share Missile Defenses Could Quiet Critics', *Roll Call*, June 18, 2001.
109   Author interview, March 16, 2004.
110   Department of Defense, Press Conference, August, 23, 2001.
111   Quoted in Al Kamen, 'Donny We Hardly Knew You', *Washington Post*, September 7, 2001, p. 27.
112   Transcript: Powell June 3, 2001 Interview on NBC's 'Meet the Press'.
113   David Wastell quoting NATO's Lord Robertson, 'President's Men Vie for Control of Foreign Policy', *The Daily Telegraph*, March 11, 2001.
114   John Newhouse, *Imperial America: The Bush Assault on the World Order* (New York, Knopf, 2003), p. 22.
115   Allen and Sipress.
116   Ivo Daalder and I.M. Destler, 'How Operational and Visible an NSC?', Briefing Book, Brookings Institution, February 23, 2001.
117   Lemann, 2002, p. 173.
118   Author Interview, March 16, 2004.
119   *US Foreign Policy Agenda*, Department of State, Vol. 6, No. 1, March 2001, p. 30.
120   As quoted in Byron York, 'Bush to a "Tee"', *National Review*, September 3, 2001, p. 32.
121   Richard E. Neustadt, *Presidential Power: The Politics of Leadership* (New York: John Wiley & Sons, Inc., 1964), Chapter 3.
122   George C. Edwards, 'Strategic Choices and the Early Bush Legislative Agenda', *PS*, March 2002, p. 43.

123   Howard Kurz, 'The Quiet American. President Bush's Style: Keep Your Headlines Low', *Washington Post*, April 9, 2001.

124   Bob Schieffer as quoted in Kettl, *Team Bush*, p. 84.

125   Morton Kondracke, 'Bush Starts Well, But Should Be Open With the Press', *Roll Call*, January 25, 2001.

126   Benjamin Stokes, 'Man in the Mirror', *The New Republic*, January 1 and 8, 2001, p. 10.

127   Inaugural Address, January 20, 2001, Office of the Press Secretary (http://www.whitehouse.gov/news/inaugural-address.html).

128   Quotes are from Frank Bruni, 'President Plays It for Laughs at Dinner', *New York Times*, March 26, 2001; Godfrey Sperling, 'George W. Rolls a Strike', *Christian Science Monitor*, April 3, 2001; Office of the Press Secretary, 'Remarks by the President at White House Correspondents Dinner', The Hilton Hotel, Washington, D.C., April 28, 2001.

129   Anne E. Kornblut, 'Bush Outreach Runs on Persistence and Charm', *The Boston Globe*, February 3, 2001.

130   'A Discussion with Karl Rove', December 11, 2001.

131   Howard Fineman, 'Texas Two-Step', *Newsweek*, February 5, 2001, p. 24.

132   Bruni, March 26, 2001.

133   John Brady, *Bad Boy: The Life and Politics of Lee Atwater* (Reading, Massachusetts: Addison-Wesley Publishing Co., 1997), p. 79.

134   Hedrick Smith, *The Power Game: How Washington Works*, (New York: Ballentine Books, 1988), pp. 124-126.

135   Ryan Lizza, 'Root Cause', *The New Republic*, March 26, 2001, p. 12.

136   Glenn Kessler and Juliet Elperin, 'Tax Cuts Impetus Building', *Washington Post*, February 8, 2001.

137   Suskind, 'Mrs. Hughes', p. 103.

138   Address of the President to the Joint Session of Congress, February 27, 2001.

139   Jacob M. Schlesinger and Laura Heinauer, 'Well-to-Do Gain Most in Bush Tax Plan', *Wall Street Journal*, February 7, 2001.

140   See Paul Krugman, *Fuzzy Math: The Essential Guide to the Bush Tax Plan* (New York: W.W. Norton, 2001).

141   'Read His Lips', *The Economist*, January 20, 2001, p. 26.

142   Glenn Kessler and Helen Dewar, 'Senate Scales Back Bush's Tax Cuts', *Washington Post*, April 7, 2001.

143   As quoted by Morton Kondracke, 'Nice Talk Aside, Bush Team Wants to Win Above All', *Roll Call*, March 8, 2001.

144   Howard Kurz, p. C1.

145   Comment attributed to Norman Ornstein, 'How is Bush Governing?', American Enterprise Institute, May 15, 2001.

146   Suskind, *The Price of Loyalty*, p. 117.

147   Jonathan Alter, 'The Odyssey of Jeezum Jim', *Newsweek*, June 4, 2001, p. 24.

148   Nicholas Lemann, 'Testing Limits', *The New Yorker*, July 2, 2001, p. 34.

149   Sue Kirchhoff and Anne Kornblut, 'Bush Follows Legacy of School Priorities', *The Boston Globe*, February 8, 2001.

150   Morton Kondracke, 'If Fourth-Graders Can't Read, Congress is Failing to Lead', *Roll Call*, April 23, 2001.

151   Correspondence between author and White House aides involved in education policy, March 26, 2004.

152   Lemann, p. 31.

153   Stephen Metcalf, 'W. and the Uses of Testing', *The New Republic*, February 12, 2001, p. 21.

154   Anne E. Kornblut, 'Bush Tries to Build Ties with Kennedy', *The Boston Globe*, January 11, 2001.

155 Correspondence between author and White House aides involved in education policy, March 26, 2004.
156 Stephen Metcalf, 'Teaching Test-Taking?', *The Nation*, January 29, 2001.
157 Dana Milbank, 'Bush Says He'll Seek $4.6 Billion Boost in Education Spending', *Washington Post*, February 22, 2001.
158 Michael Crowley, 'Teddy Bear', *The New Republic*, August 13, 2001, p. 12.
159 Lemann, p. 32.
160 Correspondence between author and White House aides involved in education policy, March 26, 2004.
161 See Molly Ivins and Lou Dubose, *Bushwhacked: Life in George W. Bush's America* (New York: Random House, 2003), p. 219.
162 As quoted in 'Remarks by the President at Bush-Cheney 2004 Luncheon', Louisville, Kentucky, Office of the Press Secretary, February 26, 2004.
163 Tucker Carlson, 'The Politics of Virtue', *City Journal*, Volume 8, Number 3, Summer 1998.
164 For example see, Myron Magnet, 'Solving President Bush's Urban Problem', *City Journal*, Vol. 11, No. 1, Winter 2001.
165 Office of the Press Secretary, 'Remarks by the President, Announcing the Faith-Based Initiative', Dwight D. Eisenhower Executive Office Building, January 29, 2001.
166 Speech by John DiIulio, 'Compassion in Truth and Action', Delivered before the National Association of Evangelicals, Dallas, March 7, 2001.
167 'Compassionate Conservatism Takes a Bow', *Economist*, February 3, 2001, p. 29.
168 DiIulio, March 7, 2001.
169 Stephen Goldsmith, 'The Bush Agenda', Office of the Press Secretary, The White House, January 30, 2001.
170 Ryan Lizza, 'Salvation', *The New Republic*, April 23, 2001, p. 14.
171 Marvin Olasky, 'Rolling the Dice: How a Bill Becomes Law', *World Magazine*, August 4, 2001.
172 See for example, Eyal Press, 'Faith-Based Furor', *The New York Times Magazine*, April 1, 2001.
173 Dana Milbank, 'Charity Cites Bush Help in Fight Against Hiring Gays', *Washington Post*, July 10, 2001.
174 Olasky, August 4, 2001.
175 Abraham McLauglin, 'Few Recruits for the Armies of Compassion', *The Christian Science Monitor*, June 27, 2001, p. 2.
176 'The DiIulio Letter', *Esquire*, October 24, 2002 (http://www.esquire.com/features/articles/2002/021202_mfe_diiulio_1.html).
177 'President Names New Faith-Based & Community Initiatives Director', Office of the Press Secretary, February 1, 2002.
178 Fineman, 'Texas Two-Step', p. 24.
179 'Principles for a Bipartisan Patients' Bill of Rights', Office of the Press Secretary, February 7, 2001.
180 Edward Howard as quoted in Amy Goldstein, 'The Patients' Rights Fight, Round 2', *Washington Post*, August 5, 2001.
181 Andrew Mollison, 'Senators Block Tax, Malpractice Bills', *The Atlanta Journal Constitution*, April 7, 2004.
182 Suskind, *The Price of Loyalty*, p. 143.
183 Margaret Kriz, 'Energy: Still Hooked on Oil', *National Journal*, October 11, 2001.
184 'Alaska or Bust', *Economist*, February 10, 2001, p. 22.
185 'Monumental Struggle', *Economist*, January 27, 2001.
186 Gregg Easterbrook, 'W. The Environmentalist Health Nut', *The New Republic*, April 30, 2001, p. 16.

187   Dana Milbank and Ellen Nakashimas, 'Cheney Rebuffs GAO's Records Request', *Washington Post*, August 4, 2001. p. 11.
188   'How is Bush Governing?', *American Enterprise Institute*, May 15, 2001.
189   Kirk Victor, 'Deconstructing Daschle', *National Journal*, No. 22, June 1, 2002, p. 1609.
190   Michael Crowley, 'Tom Daschle's Struggle to Save the Dems', *The New Rep*ublic, March 26, p. 22.
191   Nicholas Lemann, 'William Jennings Bush', *The New Yorker*, September 10, 2001, p. 44.

Chapter 4

Foreign and Defense Policy before September 11

Candidate Bush positioned himself in the 2000 campaign as a president who would lead the country with 'Compassionate Conservatism' at home and with strong American values abroad. Bush identified the 'foundation of our peace – a strong and capable military.'[1] Not peace through treaties, not peace through loosely defined multilateralism, but 'peace through strength.' American strength first and foremost followed by the strength that flows from friendships and alliances based on commonly held values. Strength based on civilized coalitions that pursue the same needs together. None of this implies American isolationism, unilateralism or hegemony as a dogma. Rather, Bush sees the world from the vantage point of a type of conservative internationalism where cooperation is the logical result of the pursuit of common national interests and where national interests derive from deeper values.

Bush defined the new threat to American values well before September 11, 2001 as 'the contagious spread of missile technology and weapons of mass destruction.' He called it 'barbarism emboldened by technology', but it is not limited to missile defense. In his speech at the Citadel in North Carolina in August 1999, Bush said, 'These weapons can be delivered, not just by ballistic missiles, but by everything from airplanes to cruise missiles, from shipping containers to suitcases.' Bush listed his priorities to deal with these threats as missile defense, a new emphasis on 'defending the American homeland' and 'a high priority on detecting and responding to terrorism on our soil.'[2] To deal with these threats, he determined he not only needed more defense dollars, but also military transformation. As Bush stated on May 25, 2001 at Annapolis Naval College in his Commencement Day Address, 'to keep the peace', we must 'redefine war on our terms', and 'envision a new architecture', and 'skip a generation of technology'.[3]

When Bush spoke about new threats, new capabilities and strong American values, some observers worried that this President was aiming for a strategy of global dominance. These suspicions were fuelled by the fact that Paul Wolfowitz was one of Bush's campaign advisers. Wolfowitz was believed to be one of the authors of a draft of the Defense Planning Guidance of 1992 that was in part leaked to the *New York Times*.[4] The draft called for American military primacy across the globe. In an interview in 2003, Wolfowitz claimed that he had not written or seen that draft before it was leaked. It did not become official policy, but some critics now concluded that George W. Bush's defense policy was simply 'Wolfie's' first draft brought up to date and thus Bush's real agenda was American military global dominance. Some called it 'democratic imperialism'.[5]

Like Bush, Reagan was often accused of seeking power for its own sake. However, American dominance as a goal in itself has no appeal to either man. Bush believes there is evil that must be fought – with military means if nothing else works, but he is no militarist. 'Military power is not the final measure of our might,' Bush stated in the Reagan Library speech. He explained that great powers, such as Russia and China, need not fear his administration; what they can expect is friendship if they join together in the pursuit of individual freedom. The President went out of his way to explain that his missile defense plans would not diminish Russian security and that he strongly believed in open trade with China, but the Bush team also clarified that Russia's concerns about a 30-year old arms control treaty could not stop American plans to defend against new rogue states with aggressive arms programs. If China would threaten the stability of its region, and especially the fledgling Taiwanese democracy, it would find 'a competitor' in the United States.[6] Like Reagan, Bush believed that Russia and China would understand his underlying good will and that they would want to seek partnership with him. While Sino-American relations would have a bumpy start under Bush, the new administration went out of its way to forge a new 'strategic partnership' with President Vladimir Putin.

Free Trade, Missile Defense, and Military Transformation

As the focus of the Bush administration's first 180 days in office was on 'tax cuts, education reform, faith-based welfare, Medicare, and social security reform'[7] – there was no foreign policy revolution on the agenda. There were to be no foreign policy initiatives to compete with the domestic limelight except for missile defense and military transformation. The President would also work on his promise to bring free trade, especially in the Americas, but first of all that required a domestic strategy. Bush appointed his trade 'Vulcan,' Robert Zoellick as United States Trade Representative, a man most insiders considered 'a master strategist'.[8] The challenge was to develop a political plan whereby Bush could obtain fast-track authority in order to negotiate foreign trade deals while Congress would only have the power to approve or reject the entire deal. Bush and Zoellick took months to build a broad coalition in Congress, and during most of 2001 it seemed that Zoellick was Trade Representative to the US Congress. During his confirmation hearings, he coined the term 'trade promotion' to replace 'fast-track' – words matter, and trade promotion seemed more inclusive. He would need all the words he could get because Clinton had sought fast-track authority since 1994 with no success. He worked 'non-stop, visiting and consulting with Democrats', bringing the key players in Congress and the American Federation of Labor and Congress of Industrial Organizations together on a shared strategy.[9] While Bush made speeches on free trade, selling his vision for a whole hemisphere 'trading in freedom',[10] Zoellick worked with the key Washington insiders.

In order for Bush to fulfill his goal for a free trade agreement for the Americas, as launched at the Summit of the Americas in Quebec in April 2001 and also to begin a new so-called 'trade round' in the World Trade Organization, he needed to find common ground especially with leaders such as House Minority Leader, Dick

Gephardt and AFL-CIO President John Sweeney. Conscious of Congress's tendency to use labor or environmental ('blue and green') issues to limit trade or impose trade sanctions, Bush and Zoellick proposed an 'enforcement toolbox' of 'blue and green issues' that could be included in trade deals.[11] Bush made it clear that he believed poorer nations had neither the wealth nor the time to meet all Western demands and that incentives rather than trade sanctions were the means for them to close the gap on these issues. Zoellick then negotiated a toolbox with carrots and sticks that would include fines rather than sanctions or punitive tariffs if labor and environmental standards were not met.

Contradictory as it may sound, Bush needed to do one more thing to earn the trust of industry and labor, and Democrats in Congress, to negotiate trade deals; he needed to show that he would fight for them and not for mere ideals. In the summer of 2001 Bush hinted that he would be prepared to 'adopt protectionist measures' for the steel and farm industries, among others, to show that if given trade promotion authority, he would defend American interests.[12] America's steel industry suffered from a small amount of dumping by foreign firms, but more importantly, the Bush administration knew that the steel industry needed retooling to regain its competitive edge. By imposing steel tariffs, Bush and his closest advisers saw an opportunity to combine their point about 'trust me on trade deals' with investing political capital in key states such as West Virginia, which had voted for Bush in 2000 and were again needed in the mid-term elections. On March 5, 2002, Bush decided to put a 30 per cent tariff on imported steel; Vice President Cheney said, 'We'll do it for eighteen months', which is pretty much what happened.[13] Just before the European Union was to slap on counter duties in late 2003, Bush lifted the tariffs.

It still took a lot of negotiating in the summer of 2002 to get the 2002 Trade Act that contained the coveted trade promotion authority – it passed by the slimmest of margins. 'No longer,' President Bush suggested at the signing ceremony on August 6, 2002, would American trade policy be 'stuck in park'.[14] Yet, Bush did not make much progress and the domestic tactics on steel tariffs, followed by Bush's agreement to approve Congress's lavish extension of farm subsidies, made America's negotiating partners more reluctant. Agricultural subsidies became a major dividing point between developing and developed countries at the World Trade Organization's summit in Cancun, Mexico in September 2003. The war on terror and the subsequent war with Iraq slowed down progress in the so-called Doha Round of trade liberalization talks.

Meanwhile Bush and Zoellick negotiated several bilateral free trade deals, including one with Australia that eliminated tariffs on nearly all exports of American manufactured goods and, in a precedent-setting move, removed some of the protection for the agricultural sector.[15] Having invested so much political capital in trade promotion authority, Bush is likely to return to more broad-scale free trade efforts should he get a second term.

Bush's second priority was military transformation which was foremost a domestic issue. The plan was that Rumsfeld would begin a review process to create a vision for military transformation by the summer of 2001. First of all, Bush would make good on his campaign pledge to improve the quality of life of military personnel. He had promised immediate pay raises, help with low-cost housing, and a boost to the military health plan. As Cheney had put it in one of his campaign speeches, 'help is on the way'.[16] In his February 2001 Budget Brief ('A Blueprint for New Beginnings'), Bush proposed a defense budget increase of nearly $2 billion for housing, pay and health, seeking an average pay raise of five per cent.

Except for this quality of life issue and Bush's pledge to boost spending on missile defense research, his first military budget would be a 'placeholder budget'. It would contain 'a down payment on the research and development' for transformation, but would not be a transformation budget.[17] Bush, in his address to a Joint Session of Congress on February 27, said, 'Our defense vision will drive our budget, not the other way around.'[18] The idea was that Rumsfeld's rapid top-down review would merge into the congressionally mandated Quadrennial Defense Review (QDR), which was due September 30, 2001. This plan would allow Rumsfeld – though it turned out there was not enough time – to put the Bush stamp on the QDR review. Rumsfeld knew there would be a tremendous struggle ahead to get the military leadership and the close network of Congressmen and defense contractors to agree to radical changes in the budget. Bush quoted Abraham Lincoln, who likened the challenge of military change to emptying the Potomac with a teaspoon. Once the military transformation strategy was in place, the Bush administration intended to propose (sometime in early 2002) a five-year budget plan, starting with fiscal year 2003, that would begin to craft 'the military of the twenty-first century.' The plan was predicated on the administration using all its persuasive powers to slow down or halt existing procurement plans in order to free money to build the new.

At the same time as Rumsfeld was planning his opening move in military transformation, Bush was to begin an intensive diplomatic outreach effort to Russian President Vladimir Putin, who had been elected in March 2000, to persuade him to drop his opposition to American missile defense. The administration would try to court him out of the Anti-Ballistic Missile Treaty. In December 2000, Karl Rove was asked by a small gathering of Washington policy wonks whether Bush would make good on his pledge to protect the American people against missile attacks. Rove answered, 'People in this town are going to be surprised to discover that George W. Bush means what he says and does what he says he'll do.'[19]

Bush had high hopes that he could persuade Putin to begin a 'new strategic partnership,' in which Russia and America would become nuclear partners much like Britain and France – both have nuclear weapons, but it causes no threat or rivalry between them. Bush was determined to build missile defenses, but the 1972 ABM treaty and its subsequent protocols prevented most serious research and all but a speck of development. The treaty was signed by the two nuclear superpowers in the deep freeze of the Cold War as a result of a cold-blooded strategic calculation. Both felt that they could deter better if neither had defensive capabilities. It was called mutual assured destruction. Though the standoff ended when the Soviet Union crumbled, the strategic rationale seemed to linger, but it made no sense to Bush.

Rumsfeld, the White House knew, would have to 'break some china' to get military reform, but the idea was not to break any pottery with Putin.[20] Bush would pull out all stops to build a personal relationship with Putin to lead both countries beyond the ABM Treaty, which the White House called 'that Cold War relic'.[21] The idea was for Bush to create a sense of friendship and loyalty between Putin and himself, a relationship not unlike those he had fostered with Bob Bullock in Texas and would attempt with Ted Kennedy on education reforms. If need be, Bush would offer substantive amendments to the treaty. What he would not do, was water down or slow down his promise to build missile defenses at the earliest possible date.

True to form, Rumsfeld moved briskly into the reform process. He made Stephen Cambone his point man on the Quadrennial Defense Review. The QDR, which had always been guided by the Joint Chiefs, was put on ice while Rumsfeld appointed more than a dozen small panels to look at all the key issues from personnel to space technology. Rumsfeld's plan was to use the panels to bring him up to date on the defense portfolio and to make their conclusions the terms of reference for steering the quadrennial defense review closer to the target of military transformation. Rumsfeld picked a mix of civilian and retired military people to head panels on the whole gamut of issues from quality of life and conventional forces to the cutting edge of technological development. For the last panel, he chose a nearly eighty-year old maverick, Andy Marshall, who has made a career out of calling for radical reforms. Marshall heads the somewhat secretive Pentagon think tank, the Office of Net Assessment and his findings remained secret during the entire process.

Soon enough some of the Joint Chiefs of Staff started to worry out loud about being 'shut out' of the decision process.[22] They called Rumsfeld's transformation panels 'filters', because they stood between them and direct access to Rumsfeld.[23] Rumors spread on Capitol Hill about massive cuts coming down the pipeline, that Rumsfeld wanted to retire two more army divisions and reduce the Navy's aircraft carriers, the Air Force's short-range jet fighters, and eliminate some major military platforms such as the Army's Crusader artillery rocket system. The Pentagon's 'crown jewels', as some commentator called them, were in danger and Congress clamored for more consultation.[24]

Perhaps Rumsfeld kept too many people in the dark too long. His brusque style did nothing to smooth ruffled feathers in the Pentagon or on Capitol Hill, yet, it is difficult to imagine what else he could have done, given the ambitious mandate he received. He needed the panels to frame the debate, but there hardly was time for a debate – it did not help that Rumsfeld was also largely without help. Wolfowitz was confirmed in March, but Undersecretary and Comptroller Dov Zakheim, Rumsfeld's numbers man, did not get there until May 1. The Undersecretary for Acquisitions, Pete Aldridge was not confirmed until September.

Having delayed the budget to give the major tax cuts a head start, the White House had to move swiftly on the budget in June. It was up to Rumsfeld to calibrate his 'Terms of Reference', the Quadrennial Review and the various budget outlays before they would be looked at by the White House's Office of Management and Budget.[25] By the end of May, Rumsfeld brought the Chiefs of the Joint Staff into his process[26] – the Quadrennial Defense Review was now put on a 'forced march'.[27] Even though the substance of Rumsfeld's work would be well received in the fall, he did not have many friends at this point in time, but Bush was behind him and that was all that mattered. Bush took Rumsfeld's terms of reference and incorporated them into his address on defense at Annapolis on May 25. He called for, 'a future force defined less by size and more by mobility and swiftness ... and that relies more heavily on stealth, precision weaponry and information technologies.'[28]

In the early summer of 2001, Rumsfeld came out arguing for an end to the ten-year old defense posture characterized by the Two-Major-Theater War scenario – most people believed the likely theaters would be Korea and Iraq. Having underfunded operations and procurement for the last five years, after deep cuts in the early 1990s, the military simply did not have enough strategic airlift, according to Rumsfeld, to execute this strategy. Moreover, the posture was burdensome and impeded military reform as it called for large amounts of legacy forces (mainstream conventional forces) to sit on standby. Instead, Rumsfeld wanted more mobile and leaner forces. Just to bring this two-theater war force sufficiently up to date would cost $50 billion a year for at least five years, according to the Congressional Budget Office.[29] Rumsfeld's Quadrennial Defense Review changed the approach, but not dramatically (that would come later). The United States would be prepared to fight and achieve 'a decisive victory' in one theater, while holding or containing another conflict in a different theater.[30] Another change Rumsfeld introduced was the idea of threat assessment based on 'capabilities' rather than on a mixture of political and military factors.[31] The idea translates into a wide front of capabilities to deal with all the rogue states and their various capabilities regardless of whether they look more or less friendly on any given day.

Air Force General James McCarthy, who chaired Rumsfeld's Transformation Panel, concluded that transforming ten per cent of the force would be 'an achievable and sufficient goal'.[32] Wolfowitz and Rumsfeld explained during their Congressional testimony in the summer of 2001 that even a very aggressive transformation program would leave the military ten years from now with 80 per cent to 90 per cent of its current forces. Hitler's army, which so effectively executed the 'blitzkrieg', was 90 per cent traditional. Rumsfeld put the dilemma of where to spend money in terms of several risks: any decision had to weigh a variety of the risks such as not spending enough on people, not investing enough to modernize and not starting early enough to begin the transformation process. Smart risk management means finding the right mix, while a blind ideological approach that would charge madly in the direction of only new things would risk losing the systems that work before having reliable substitutes.[33] One of Rumsfeld's close aides quoted Arleigh Burke, a famous naval commander during World War II, 'You stop building aircraft carriers when they fail in war.'[34] Rumsfeld and Bush wanted to take as much risk as possible to modernize quickly, but short of losing proven weapons systems.

To put all these expectations and processes into a 'placeholder' budget proved exceedingly difficult. Military transformation with fiscal prudence would mean making some difficult trade-offs; it would require a political fight in Congress in which the Bush administration would have to spend a lot of political capital. As in the tax cuts and educational programs, the White House was consistent in pushing for its principles, but at the same time unwilling to incur political cost to stop the budget from rising sharply. To get its objectives, the White House kept enlarging the pie. Rumsfeld realized that he had to try and get some 'bridge funding' for operations and most needed modernization plans to even have a chance at transformation the next year.[35] He told Congress that every time he turned over a rock in the building, a voice would cry out, 'I need $3 billion', or 'give me $5 billion'.[36]

The Office of Budget and Management (OMB), under the direction of Mitch Daniels, set tight spending goals early in 2001. The overall increase in discretionary funds for domestic programs would have to stay below four per cent. Cheney's former defense assistant Sean O'Keefe, was now the chief military budgeter at OMB. He initially put quite a bit of pressure on the Pentagon. The Joint Chiefs of Staff were not going to get a budget with only increases and no cost savings. Rumsfeld set up a Senior Executive Council in the Pentagon, chaired by Wolfowitz, which included Pete Aldridge, the Undersecretary for Acquisitions, 'a known champion of space programs', and the Service Secretaries for the army, navy and air force.[37] This panel was not meant to exclude the Joint Chiefs from major decisions, but to offer a balancing voice. Rumsfeld wanted this committee to do a corporate makeover of the Pentagon's budget and accounting practices, to find savings and efficiencies. Rumsfeld was fond of saying that there was no organization that could not squeeze five per cent out of its budget by more efficiency.[38] For the Pentagon that would mean $15 billion. The problem was he could not accomplish this reduction before the 2002 budget, unless the White House was willing to take on a bruising appropriations fight with Republicans and Democrats alike. The White House was not going to do so, as it would jeopardize its domestic priorities.

Rumsfeld was also working on other savings – the Chiefs agreed that there was a 23 per cent surplus in military bases and infrastructure. To find these bases and shut them down is a politically driven process hard enough in itself, but the savings of some $3 billion a year would not show up until five years down the road.[39] Rumsfeld announced he was going to shut down the entire MX 'Peacekeeper' nuclear force. The problem with dismantling these missiles and their nuclear warheads was that it actually costs money up front and savings accrue only later. Another very sensible idea was put in the budget – Rumsfeld began refitting Trident submarines by replacing their nuclear-tipped intercontinental ballistic missiles with conventional cruise missiles. The Gulf War and the conflict with Serbia had shown the urgent need for more of these guided missiles.

At the last minute, Rumsfeld squeezed a little bit of savings out of the Air Force: its B-1 bomber force would be reduced from 93 to 60 and all of them would be housed at two bases, instead of their current spread around five facilities. The remaining two bases would be in Texas and South Dakota. A 'political impact' paper leaked out of the Pentagon, or 'Fort Fumble' as some army officers endearingly call the building, which noted that the two bases happened to be in the home states of the President and the Senate Majority Leader.[40] Two prominent figures on the Senate Armed Services Committee were seriously upset: Senator Max Cleland from Georgia called the whole affair a 'mackerel in the moonlight. It both shines and stinks at the same time'.[41] The Republican Senator Pat Roberts from Kansas was furious, for 'his' Kansas B-1 base would be shut down and he was not even consulted. Rumsfeld apologized before the committee, but did not change the decision.

There was a lot of speculation about the final budget crunch. Some Congressmen suggested that Rumsfeld had 'tried strenuously' to get some $30 billion extra dollars for Defense in late May and early June, but the story was that OMB had offered 'only' $15 billion.[42] In the end, OMB and the Pentagon settled on $18.4 billion with most of the money earmarked for operations and readiness.[43] In this version,

Rumsfeld battled valiantly, but had to settle for so little that it amounted to a defeat. The editors of the conservative *Weekly Standard* called on Rumsfeld and Wolfowitz to resign in the face of this 'impending evisceration of the American military'.[44] The perception was created that Rumsfeld had become 'Rums fled.'

The controversy between OMB and Rumsfeld appears exaggerated. Rumsfeld was deeply involved in the Bush game plan and he knew that the President did not want a lot of new money for defense in fiscal year 2002. He also knew that while Bush was committed to military transformation, he was not in a hurry – he had said that future presidents, not he, would reap the fruits of this endeavor. Of course, at the end of the day, Rumsfeld sought more money. No responsible secretary lets a budget cycle go by without trying for more money, but the so-called 'defeat' of Rumsfeld at the hands of OMB was actually an $18.4 billion increase above the $4.4 billion Bush had announced in February. Thus, the total increase over Clinton's last defense budget would be some $22.8 billion that added up to the single largest defense budget increase since 1986. Despite OMB's call for restraint, Bush's defense increase over fiscal year 2001 was 11 per cent.[45] If corrected for inflation, that amounted to a hefty increase of seven per cent in 'real money.' Given that Bush's overall budget target was four per cent, Rumsfeld's budget can hardly be called a defeat, yet Rumsfeld put people on notice, warning that cuts would come. One of Rumsfeld's review panels on conventional forces had tagged various big items for major savings in the future, including the navy's DD-21 destroyer, the army's Crusader self-propelled artillery and the Comanche helicopter program.

Some of Bush's critics from the right claimed that the President had simply talked about military transformation during the election to score political points. Now that he was in office, they claimed he fell in line with traditional across-the-board spending.[46] However, they overlook the fact that to Bush, military transformation is a value. There is a big difference between the general statements Bush made about peacekeeping and nation building, and the goal of military transformation; the latter is a matter of principle. Bush commented at Rumsfeld's swearing in ceremony, 'We will promote the peace by redefining the way wars will be fought.'[47] Bush instinctively shares the views of defense strategists such as Wolfowitz and Richard Perle, that unless the US military remains at the cutting edge of technology and innovation it will cease to become the military that is 'second to none.' Bush believes the military is still carrying too much of its Cold War baggage and must shed this in order to rejuvenate, but as with his compassionate conservative values at home, when Bush is in pursuit of a value he appears not to be in a hurry. The real question is not whether Bush believes in military transformation, but what price he is willing to pay to get it? When he entered office, the defense budget was roughly three per cent of Gross Domestic Product ($310 billion), yet the President's inner circle calculated it could go up to 3.5 per cent without much hardship. If no hard choices are made it will drift to half a trillion dollars a year without much new capacity and before September 11, no one could imagine the additional pressures that would soon be added to the defense budget.

The only new money in Bush's 2001 defense budget (apart from pay, housing and health care) was $3 billion in research and development for missile defense. It meant a 57 per cent increase over the $5 billion Clinton had spent in his last year. This part of the budget was absolutely non-negotiable – it connected seamlessly with the

Bush administration's priority on missile defense and neither the President nor Rumsfeld needed a defense review on this issue. For Bush, missile defense is a 'moral imperative'.[48] He wanted more spending to start immediately for two reasons: first and foremost, the Bush team believed (with good cause) that Clinton had never been serious about robust R&D for missile defense. The Congress passed the National Missile Defense Act in 1999 with veto-proof majorities in both chambers; in the Senate, the vote was 97-3. The act committed Clinton to missile defense 'as soon as is technologically possible',[49] but at the signing ceremony, Clinton added that he did not intend to jeopardize the ABM Treaty. What followed was research on a single, land-based option – the only opening the ABM treaty afforded. Inadvertently, this meant that the US was really testing for a system that would only protect the US mainland and thus decouple the defense of America from its allies and leave Europe and Asia more vulnerable to nuclear blackmail than before.[50]

The Bush administration set out to change the terms and objective of the research. Like Reagan, he was intuitively attracted to the 'simplicity' of defense and the strategic calculation of mutual assured destruction was to Bush a thing of the past. He also embodied Reagan's optimism that American research and technology could overcome the most difficult obstacle of 'shooting down a bullet with a bullet.' Unlike Reagan, Bush was closely involved in the decision-making and diplomatic process, because for him it was not only a vision, but also a deliberate shift in strategy. Any means to defend against rogue states should be explored to the fullest. Bush wanted missile defenses that could provide a degree of added protection for American forces abroad, allies and friends, and the American homeland. He wanted a 'layered' system that included shooting down missiles as they were lifting off, in mid-course, and as they were making their final approach to earth. He wanted to test land-based (even mobile ones) as well as sea-based and air-based methods to kill these missiles. Preliminary research on space-based capabilities was also not excluded. His view was to let the R&D have a free rein and let it determine where defense investment should go; treaty and political considerations would take second place.

The scientific debate about missile defense has raged for some time, but the United States has never pulled out all the stops on the research. It has not had a 'crash program' on missile defense the way it had on putting a man on the moon in the 1960s. Reputable scientists disagree on the chances of getting a robust system of layered defenses, but failures in tests are not a standard to go by as most weapon tests have a failure rate of 50 per cent during a long period of their development. It is possible that the Clinton team set the requirements so high and the parameters of research so narrow that test failures would create a political climate to be able to walk away from a missile defense program. Many military leaders such as Clinton's last Chairman of the Joint Chiefs, Henry Shelton, feared that missile defense would only bring a small amount of added security and at a high price.[51] Some think of it is 'pie-in-the-sky', but what they worry about most is that missile defense will 'siphon off' funds from other military priorities.[52]

In August, Bush replaced Chairman Shelton with Air Force General Richard Meyers, a strong advocate of missile defense, who had recently finished a tour as commander of North America's Aerospace Defense Command and US Space

Command. The successful intercept of a missile launched in the South Pacific by a missile fired from California on July 14, 2001 was offered by the Bush administration as proof that its plans were on solid ground. Critics argued that the missile's 'straightforward' task bore little comparison to the complexity of dealing with multiple launchers, sub munitions and decoys. The Bush team argued that missile defense is no longer 'a problem of invention but rather a challenge of engineering'.[53]

If theater missile defense is any example, the ambitions of the Bush administration are not simply pie-in-the-sky. Theater missile defense simply means intercepting missiles that have not had time to get up to really fantastic speeds. There has been a mini-crash program in this area in the 1990s, after more than twenty American soldiers lost their lives to Scud missile attacks in the Gulf War. The current PAC-3 Patriot system and its cleverly adapted Israeli counterpart are now having good results. The Navy argued that its Aegis system would have equal results, but that it is stuck behind the ABM Treaty, which prohibits sea-based anti-ballistic missile activity.

Bush revealed his diplomatic plans in a major speech on May 1 at the National Defense University. He went out of his way to explain that he intended not to get an advantage over Russia, but to remove a treaty that 'enshrines the past',[54] or as Wolfowitz had put it, that was an 'Achilles Heel' in America's defense against rogue states.[55] This initiative was carefully situated inside a strategic, military and diplomatic plan: At the strategic level, Bush explained, he wanted a system to catch rogue missiles as well as accidental launches. In the best scenario, this defense would only be able to deal with a small number of incoming missiles and Bush officials went out of their way in 2001 to assure Moscow that their plans were not intended to erode Russia's nuclear effectiveness. Perhaps the most important objective of the entire missile defense contingency is to avoid being held hostage by some dictator bent on aggression or regional domination. For sure, if Slobodan Milosevic or Saddam Hussein had possessed nuclear missiles, America's military options would have been severely restricted. Bush and Rumsfeld wanted to dissuade rogue regimes from going into the direction of building missiles in the first place. Wolfowitz explained in Congress that the US Navy was an example of an US capability that was in fact dissuading other states from 'investing in competing navies'.[56]

Bush's missile defense plans were not meant to replace nuclear deterrence, counter terrorism, homeland security or, for that matter, even modern conventional forces. Missile defense would not replace any existing system but would be yet another arrow in a quiver full of military measures. In fact, the US spent approximately $11 billion on counter-terrorism in 2001, more than twice the amount it spent on missile defense research. After September 11, counter terrorism funding leaped even further ahead of missile defense. The Bush administration also countered the argument of critics that rogue states would use far less sophisticated means than missiles to attack the United States. With good reason, some argued that missile defense would be a waste of time and resources because terrorists are more likely to smuggle weapons of mass terror in suitcases, or rented trucks, or launch them from the hull of a nearby cargo ship. That may be so, but as Wolfowitz said in Congressional testimony, just because thieves may break through your window does not mean you leave the door unlocked – missile defense is about plugging one hole in a range of vulnerabilities.

Other critics fear that Bush's missile defense program is about containing China. They contend that such a program will cause China to speed up and beef up its own missile development in order to assure that it can overwhelm a future American defense. Bush mentioned the Chinese missile threat in several of his campaign speeches but has kept mum about China and missiles since coming to the White House. Theater defenses are key to protecting Taiwan, to which Bush is unequivocally committed. Administration officials pointed out that the Chinese have been aggressively expanding their defense budget and missile program for the last ten years and have done so regardless of what the United States is doing on missile defense. In 2001, China had some 20 nuclear warheads that could reach US territory – a 'robust' missile defense system that could intercept a dozen or more warheads would thus offer a serious counter measure. However, missile defense will take a long time and few suggest it will form a future defense against China. In Powell's words, 'they are planning to increase no matter what we do'.[57] Keeping in mind Rumsfeld's switch from a threat-based to a capabilities-based defense posture, it is unlikely that the Bush administration is pitting its defense program against any one state. The issue is not defenses against whom, but against what; in this case it is defense against all potential forms of ballistic missile proliferation.

The ABM treaty prohibited research on sea and air-based missile defense systems as well as mobile ground-based systems. Given its robust R&D plans, there was no way the Bush administration could keep within those limits for long, thus the diplomatic plan was to fully engage the Russians and consult with the European NATO partners. The ideal diplomatic outcome would be if Russia and America could agree to put the ABM Treaty to sleep. The White House was serious about consulting with its NATO allies, for as Rumsfeld put it, the administration did not want missile defense 'to separate us from our allies and friends'.[58] Peter Rodman, who joined Rumsfeld's policy team in the fall of 2001, had recently concluded that allied opposition (to missile defense) had 'essentially peaked', but the administration's approach also looked predetermined.[59] The allies were consulted and briefed, but they were also given the unmistakable impression that the United States would not slow down or alter its plans significantly as a result of their concerns. This did not endear Bush and his emissaries to the Europeans, but then that was not really their major concern in early 2001.

The administration was off to a rocky start in terms of defense consultations with Europe. Rumsfeld was the first senior official to travel to Europe to meet informally with his counterparts at the Munich *Wehrkunde* Conference, which was held in early February. In his typical forthright manner, he told his colleagues that the United States would develop and deploy a missile defense system 'with or without its NATO allies'.[60] The Europeans were 'unnerved' by what they felt was the new administration's disregard for classic arms control treaties.[61] Europe's reluctance emboldened Putin to start the consultation game with his toughest stance: rumbling about how Russia would use 'national means' (meaning more nuclear weapons) to counter the threat and how it might withdraw from other arms control agreements. Russia's reaction further set the Europeans on edge, as they feared another arms race with Europe again sandwiched in the middle. Yet, the Bush administration knew that the Russians 'were not serious about blocking' American efforts at missile defense. Unlike the Europeans who were mainly fixed on preserving treaties for their own sake, the Russians 'were thinking strategically about missile defense'.[62] At the end of February, Colin Powell met with his NATO colleagues in Brussels, not to deliver a different message, but to paint another end of the canvas. Powell had said during his nomination hearing 'we hope to persuade the Russians to move beyond that treaty'.[63] He went on to brief them on Bush's rationale and promised consultations along the way. The NATO meeting had a more positive tone with NATO allies declaring they had no interest in opposing American attempts to improve its own defense: the NATO ministers had been prepared also by an earlier briefing between Britain's Prime Minister, Tony Blair, and some of his European colleagues.

Blair's comments were based on his meeting with Bush at Camp David in mid-February. That early meeting, which was simply pitched at the two getting acquainted, has turned out to be pivotal for both. At Camp David, Bush and Blair struck up a strong relationship right from the start. There was more to it than Britain's traditional quest to have a special relationship with America as Blair apparently trusted and liked the president. It was a remarkable shift for a British Prime Minister from the Labour Party who had been close ideologically to Bill Clinton to reach out so quickly to a conservative antidote of Clinton. Though Blair is intensely private about his Christian faith – his inspired Bible reading at Princess Diana's funeral of First Corinthians Chapter 13 provided a rare public insight – Bush and Blair established a connection on this point that neither has with any other statesman. Shared Christian values cemented their mutual respect and trust.[64]

At Camp David, Bush and Blair got rid of a few early misperceptions. Bush assured him that Britain and the others would not be left hanging in the Balkans, in terms of peacekeeping. During the campaign, Bush had exploited Clinton's vague commitments to nation building and peacekeeping. In his Citadel speech, Bush had said, 'We will not be permanent peacekeepers.' Many European governments had been concerned that Bush would withdraw from NATO's peacekeeping mission in Bosnia and Kosovo as soon as he came to office. It haunted the Bush administration for some time until they convinced their European friends that they had no immediate plans to withdraw.

At Camp David, Bush assured Blair that he would continue the informal agreement among NATO members' troop commitments to the Balkans, as once coined by a retiring British Officer, 'In together, and out together.'[65] The US would do nothing unilaterally that would ill affect its allies while at the same time, Bush did not change his basic view on such 'open-ended peacekeeping missions' which in his view did not result from America's vital national interest. When NATO approved a mission in Macedonia in the summer of 2001, to collect arms from Albanian nationalists, Bush did not offer any new troops. When Bush met with his European colleagues in June of 2001, he reaffirmed the mantra of 'in together-and-out-together', but then added 'and our goal must be to hasten the arrival of that day'.[66]

Also during this first meeting, Blair made clear to Bush that the recent European Union's push for its own defense ambition, the so-called European Security and Defense Policy, with plans for a 60,000 strong military force, would not be a spoke in the wheel for NATO. Blair also got a feel for Bush's devotion to missile defense and upon his return to Europe, he urged his colleagues to adopt his own position, which most of them did in due course. Blair's point was that Europe should not stand in the way of an obviously deeply felt American conviction to defend themselves against rogue missiles; there was nothing to be gained by such rhetoric. In fact, Blair argued, there was no real need to take a strong stand because missile defense would take a long time and they should wait for a specific request or offer that might emerge over time. The Canadians were pursuing a similar tactic: we'll cross that bridge when we get there. At the same time, almost all West European governments and Canada were keen to protect the multilateral structure of arms control treaties; they would put diplomatic pressure on Bush to find a compromise solution with Putin to stay inside the ABM Treaty.

In his keynote speech on missile defense on May 1, Bush said, 'We are not presenting our friends and allies with unilateral decisions already made', yet that impression was gaining ground fast, especially in Western Europe.[67] Just before the speech, Bush had telephoned Putin to spring no surprises on him.[68] Immediately after the speech, Bush dispatched Paul Wolfowitz and Stephen Hadley to start consultations in Moscow and Europe; Richard Armitage flew to Asia to brief Japan and India and Assistant Secretary of State, James Kelly, briefed the Chinese government.

The carrot in Bush's missile defense diplomacy vis-à-vis Moscow was deep cuts in existing nuclear missiles. 'We must not be strategic adversaries,' he said in his May speech. At the time the United States had a little over 7,000 such weapons and Russia nearly 6,500. In the Strategic Arms Reduction Talks II both sides had made a political commitment to bring their number down to 3,500, but so far the Russian Parliament, or Duma, refused to ratify the accord. Bush made clear he meant to go lower than the START II levels. Earlier, Rumsfeld had set in motion a Nuclear Force Posture review to determine exactly how low the US could go, without compromising its deterrence capacity. Putin liked the idea, as Russia needed to downsize its nuclear inventory due to financial pressures and safety concerns with an aging nuclear fleet.

The first big moment in the missile talks would be Bush's initial encounter with Putin in Slovenia in June 2001. It would also be a chance for Putin to get a sense of the President's personable and rather informal negotiation style. Like his father, Bush spends a lot of time on the phone with other leaders, but in their meetings, he is more direct, more personable, more like Reagan. He emphasizes the personal ties and commonalities and thus tries to create another dimension alongside state interests. 'I looked him in the eye,' Bush said after meeting Putin, 'and got a sense of his soul.' He also said he felt 'he could trust him.'[69] 'Look,' Bush told Putin, 'We're young. Why do you want to stay stuck? This isn't the Nixon-Brezhnev conversations. We both love history. We have a chance to make good history.'[70] Bush went on, 'Vladimir, we're out of the ABM Treaty – that's no longer an issue. But ... you need to be comfortable with that because you're not our enemy.'[71]

Some journalists scoffed at Bush's sudden 'discovery' of Putin's soul. They were reminded of what Harry Truman said of Stalin at Potsdam that he 'liked the little guy' and thought he could work with him. Indeed, Bush would find out that the relationship was tougher and more complex than their new camaraderie would suggest, but it was not naiveté on Bush's part; he had a lot at stake in winning Putin's trust. He was not about to air any concerns the administration had about, for example, Russia's sale of nuclear technology to Iran as that was being done at lower levels in the relationship. Bush had set his sights on creating a bond of trust and loyalty and he explained to Peggy Noonan that Putin had shared the story about a small Christian cross he had received from his mother as a young man and how it was miraculously saved in a house fire. 'Putin told Bush, "It was as if something meant for me to have the cross."' Bush felt Putin was hinting at a higher power and so he answered, 'Mr Putin, President Putin, that's what it's all about – that *is* the story of the cross.'[72] Maybe Putin made it up to charm Bush, but as lawmakers in Austin and in Washington can attest, once the President has set his sights on building such a relationship, he can be relentless. It would require patience because Moscow was not going to give up the ABM Treaty easily. Perhaps just as important to the final outcome was the fact that Putin was interested in close relations with Washington to help it join the World Trade Organization.

In July 2001, Bush and Putin met again during the G-8 meetings in Genoa, Italy. They advanced their mutual friendship while making little progress on the ABM treaty. Putin wanted the ABM talks directly linked to cuts in nuclear weapons. Bush wanted to convince Putin of an entirely bigger and new strategic partnership, not based on the mutual suspicion of counting warheads, but on a joint vision. He was not asking for a Russian counterproposal, he just wanted to volunteer his own cuts and trusted Russia would respond. Bush invited Putin to visit him at his ranch in Crawford and Condi Rice went to Moscow to follow up on the negotiations. She admitted the nuclear weapon cuts were 'inter-related', but not a package deal.[73] On August 13, Rumsfeld traveled to Moscow to convince his counterpart, Sergei Ivanov, that the limited nature of US missile defense testing and much lower nuclear weapons would preserve the existing balance of forces between the two powers.

Bush's efforts to find a way beyond the ABM Treaty were received with mixed sentiment in the US Congress. Most opposition to plans came from the Senate. In the first few months of the Bush administration, when Jesse Helms was still chairman of the Senate Foreign Relations Committee, Bush had strong wind in his sails. During Clinton's last year, Helms vowed to oppose any amendment to the ABM treaty that did not virtually kill the whole thing. After Vermont Senator James Jeffords left the GOP caucus in May of 2001, the Democrats took over the chairs of the committees with Joseph Biden at the Committee on Foreign Relations and Carl Levin as chair of the Senate Armed Services Committee. Both were cautious about missile defense and believed that the end of the ABM treaty could provoke another arms race. Levin periodically sparred with Rumsfeld and with Lieutenant-General Ron Kadish, the director of the Ballistic Missile Defense Organization, about the Bush administration's proposals for increased funding on missile defense R&D. Levin took the strongest stand and eventually tried to kill Bush's whopping 57 per cent increase in missile defense research and development.

It was not 'whopping' to Rumsfeld or Wolfowitz. They argued that the eight billion dollars amounted to 2.5 per cent of the total defense budget and that half of the new money would go to theater missile defense research. Rumsfeld, it was reported, was looking at seventeen different testing plans, including preliminary work on laser interceptors. Indeed, the budget included $165 million for space-based laser research.[74] The plans also included construction of a test bed facility at

Fort Greeley, near Fairbanks, Alaska. The Pentagon felt this would be the best location to intercept missiles from North Korea, in midcourse. Skeptical senators believed the so-called test bed facility at Fort Greeley was a form of stealth deployment; there were rumors that the administration wanted to have a rudimentary capability there by 2005.[75]

Most Democrats in the US Congress were in favor of missile defense, especially theater defense, indeed, upward from 80 per cent of Americans supported a defense system in 2001. In polls in January 2001, as many as 57 per cent of those asked approved of missile defense even if it would cost $100 billion,[76] but some Democratic lawmakers worried that an ambitious ballistic missile defense program such as proposed by Bush would lead to a build up of nuclear weapons by Russia and China in an attempt to overwhelm the new American capability. In this argument, America would be left less, not more secure.

In the summer of 2001, Bush's budget request for missile defense and his diplomatic efforts on the ABM treaty began to overlap, causing a good deal of friction between Rumsfeld and Carl Levin's committee. Would the budget plan cause the US to violate the ABM treaty? Would it run 'up against the restraints of the treaty' this fiscal year?[77] It was a fairly nuanced affair: the Bush administration wanted the Russians to know how serious it was about moving beyond the ABM treaty. It spoke of tests 'bumping into' the treaty 'in a matter of months, not years'.[78] Meanwhile, during Senate hearings, Rumsfeld and Wolfowitz had to downplay that language because Senate Democrats did not want to authorize a budget that would make them party to those pressure tactics on Moscow, let alone to treaty violations. Rumsfeld put the administration's position in four points: first, it was hard to tell when tests would run into the treaty because plans changed and the ABM treaty spoke of 'intent'. Second, the US would not violate the Treaty; the Soviets had actually cheated persistently, but that was not the way the United States would operate. Third, Washington would do its utmost to move the Russians to drop the whole thing for a new strategic partnership. Finally, if the administration failed to change Moscow's mind, Bush would give notice according to Article 16 of the treaty and withdraw six months later. When confronted with the argument that his missile plans might worsen nuclear proliferation, Rumsfeld indicated that it was rogue proliferation of weapons of mass destruction and missile technology, in many cases spurred by Chinese and Russian arms and technology sales, that necessitated American missile defense. Rumsfeld's testy relationship with Senate Democrats on this issue was to continue right until September 11.

Like the education budget, the defense budget was stuck in the Democrat-controlled Senate in the summer of 2001. In the first week of September, the entire defense package was held up by its missile defense component. Senator Levin introduced an amendment to take $1.3 billion from the missile defense budget, to allocate all of that money to other military needs; Rumsfeld said he needed 'every nickel' of the defense budget.[79] There was no flexibility in the White House to move money away from the missile defense category.

There is no doubt that the calamitous events of September 11 unlocked the missile defense and budget battle with Congress. Only a week later, Levin withdrew his amendment and Bush got his increase in missile defense inside his $328.9 billion defense budget.[80] Putin grasped the strategic earthquake caused by the terrorist attacks more quickly than some European leaders – he was the first to call Bush and it elevated the relationship another step. Putin told him Russian forces would cancel exercises for that day and not respond to the heightened US military alert. Bush and Putin found a common mission in fighting militant Islamic terrorists. None of this meant that Putin simply buckled on ABM. During their meeting in Shanghai at the Asia Pacific Economic Cooperation Forum, on October 21, there still was no resolution and Bush told Putin missile defense was 'a matter of some urgency'.[81]

On November 13, the two leaders met at the White House. Bush now had the specific numbers produced by the Nuclear Posture Review and told Putin he would go down to between 1,700 and 2,200 nuclear warheads. Putin wanted to go down to 1,500, but Bush's defense advisers were against going to a lower number. Putin also sought a formal treaty on the nuclear warheads so that he could claim a victory of sorts at home – with a treaty in hand, it would be easier for Putin to deal with his domestic critics. In this argument, America's withdrawal did not worsen Russia's overall security status, given the deep cuts in offensive weapons. 'If we need to write it down on a piece of paper, I'll be glad to do that,' Bush reportedly said.[82] That 'piece of paper' turned into the Treaty of Moscow, which the two partners signed in May 2002.[83] It committed them to go down to the American numbers by 2012. It was a treaty based on clear intent and trust, yet, as critics pointed out, the Moscow or Strategic Offensive Reductions Treaty provided only for the dismantling of nuclear warheads, not their destruction. The treaty would also expire exactly at the time when the new targets would be reached, and finally, it did not contain any provisions for verification. Bush felt that as long as Russia and the United States acted out of a sense of common strategic understanding, the legal details did not matter. In Slovenia, Bush had said 'trust', and had not bothered to add 'and verify'. He felt the last part was obvious. 'Sophisticates surely understand that once you lie, you know, trust isn't forever ...'[84]

The White House did push for a final deal on ABM during the preparations for the November meeting. If the Russians would let Bush do research without any treaty constraints, the Americans would be willing to stay in the treaty for the time being – it was meant as a face-saving device for Putin. The Russians in turn wanted the power to vet every test beforehand; that killed the deal from Bush's side. The US would brief them and indeed is still keeping the Russian side up to date on its research work, but it would not submit its tests for approval by another state. Putin and Bush spent the next couple of days at the ranch, giving Putin a chance to see that Bush was the same person in public as he was in private, and that he had no hidden agenda. During their joint question and answer session with the school kids of Crawford, Bush answered a question on the ABM Treaty in this way: '[it] was signed during a time when we really hated each other, and we no longer hate each other.'[85] Putin confirmed that he could not agree to the cancellation of the ABM treaty, but that he was prepared to make Russia's criticism of the president's imminent withdrawal muted. Bush and Putin reviewed the whole relationship in a relaxed atmosphere. Bush was prepared to make Russia as equal a partner in NATO as possible and he proposed joint defense planning sessions between the two states to put flesh on the strategic partnership. Moreover, he would lobby strongly for Russia's entrance into the World Trade Organization. Bush had sent his close friend Don Evans, now the Commerce Secretary, to Moscow in October to give strong assurances. Step by step Putin was being prepared for the imminent American notice on the ABM treaty. 'One day I am going to call you,' Bush reportedly told Putin in Crawford, 'and say it is time.'[86]

At Crawford, Putin and Bush agreed that the ABM treaty would not contaminate their relationship. When Bush announced on December 13 that the United States was giving formal notice for its withdrawal from the treaty, the Russian side merely called it 'a mistake', a very mild term in international politics, and added that it would 'not threaten Russian security'.[87] In the months after, Russia did not build up its nuclear weapons stockpile and did not withdraw from other treaties such as the Conventional Forces in Europe agreement. The Bush-Putin relationship continued to improve slowly, especially in their common fight against terrorism, yet, the next two years would prove that Bush had plenty of work left to finish his 'new strategic relationship' with Putin, especially in the area of joint counter-proliferation of weapons of mass destruction. The crisis over Iraq would bring a new low.

Values Without a Strategy

Besides defense modernization and moving beyond the ABM Treaty, the Bush administration did not really have an overall foreign policy blueprint before the attacks of September 11, 2001. Of course, Bush had laid out his vision for American values and his advisers had strong views, but that is not the same as a governing strategy. His foreign policy was cast in the broadest of terms: he was for freedom, free trade and a strong defense. This level of generality is not atypical of new American administrations, but it often causes a new president problems that take a long time to correct.

Contrary to the domestic scene, Rove did not have an unfolding foreign game plan on the table right after the inauguration; there was no strategy on where to spend and invest political capital in foreign affairs. Would Bush be willing to compromise on key issues as he did on education reform and patients' rights? Where would he make his stand beside missile defense? Often the Bush White House was clear about what it did not want (business as usual with North Korea and in the Middle East) but then failed to provide a good alternative, creating a policy vacuum and attacks from all sides. It looked like a '"Just-Say-No" foreign policy.'[88] Karen Hughes, Bush's communications guru had her hands full on domestic communications and felt she lacked the expertise to foray into the foreign realm. As a result, the messages in Bush's foreign policy at times sounded too harsh, different parts of his foreign policy were not well connected, and his advisers were sometimes out of sync with each other.

The administration was vulnerable on style and tone. Bush had pitched his foreign and defense principles in strong values, but he had also called for a humble tone and attitude. In the Inaugural Address, he said, 'we will seek defenses beyond challenge, we will confront weapons of mass destruction,' ... and 'shape a balance of power that favors freedom,' but then he added, 'We will show purpose without arrogance.'[89] The latter theme had often come up in campaign speeches, where Bush spoke of 'power exercised without swagger and influence displayed without bluster.'[90] He referred to 'the modesty of true strength' and the 'humility of real greatness.'[91] He meant this sincerely and practiced these virtues at a personal level, yet for an unrivalled world power with a very hard-nosed crew of national security advisers, such an approach would require the most careful governing and communications strategy imaginable. Plain and blunt talk is helpful, but has to be balanced with the appearance of understanding and at times soothing words, for the other side.

Aside from the tone, there has to be a calculation of political capital towards friends and allies, such as the Europeans, just as there was a plan to construct a new relationship with Putin. Instead, the administration 'got off on the wrong foot' with the Europeans and offered no areas of compromise for Europe to engage the new administration.[92] As a result, some of the allies felt 'bullied'.[93] The Bush White House clashed on a broad score of themes with Europe, yet it never seemed to re-invest in the relationship until mid-summer. By the spring, European critics put the Bush administration on the defensive; Democrats picked up on this refrain, calling Bush 'unilateralist' and 'unsmooth'.[94] Democratic campaign literature smearing Bush as 'dumb', inarticulate, and 'the Toxic Texan' and 'a trigger-happy cowboy' was peddled in Europe as the truth about Bush. The public relations battle in foreign affairs detracted from Bush's achievements, such as his push for seven East European states to enter NATO almost immediately.

Hainan: Passing the First Test

Bush's early foreign policy problems did not stem from inability or inexperience. When the administration encountered its first foreign policy crisis on Saturday March 31, 2001, the team pulled together under the President and showed a good deal of coherence. Bush was relaxing with his Yale friend Roland Betts at Camp David on that Saturday night when Condi Rice briefed him on an apparent accident in the South China Sea: an American electronic surveillance aircraft had collided with a Chinese jetfighter. The fighter and Chinese pilot were lost, but the 24 American crewmembers were all alive after a harrowing emergency landing on the Chinese Island called Hainan. In order to avoid any overreaction, Bush stayed at Camp David till the next day.

Back at the White House Sunday afternoon, Bush and his advisers identified two principal values: the crew should be returned speedily, and the accident should not 'escalate' into an international incident.[95] Meanwhile there was no response from the Chinese government. The White House demanded that the US Military Attaché, Brigadier-General Neal Sealock, be allowed to visit the crew at once. Bush's national security team decided that the Chinese would be given only a little more time to answer urgent American calls. Bush made sure that only Colin Powell and he would speak publicly on the crisis. Donald Rumsfeld would be in touch with key members in Congress, but would not speak out to avoid any suggestion that the accident could escalate into a military crisis. Rumsfeld ended up 'soothing angry voices in Congress'.[96] Bush rejected the demand from some hardliners that the downed EP-3 surveillance plane was 'sovereign territory' and could thus not be boarded by Chinese officials. The fact of the matter was that the plane was already on Chinese territory and that Chinese officials were already in the plane – such a stance would only enrage the already agitated Chinese.

By Sunday night, Vice Premier Qian Qichen was still not answering Powell's phone calls. Qichen had visited Bush in Washington on March 21 and 22, but the visit had been a polite exchange of differences. Consistent with his campaign speeches, Bush had emphasized the need for more political and religious freedom in China. Bush and Powell told Qichen that while the new administration believed in open trade with China and would support its status in the WTO, it would not hesitate to be a 'strategic competitor' to China in regional security matters and would defend Taiwan.

The Chinese began making extravagant claims, asserting that the much larger and slower, propeller-driven American EP-3 had suddenly veered into the agile jetfighter and thus 'caused' the accident.[97] They treated the unauthorized emergency landing as a gross violation of Chinese sovereignty, but the American ambassador in Beijing, Admiral Joseph Prueher, a former navy pilot, immediately disputed the accident theory advanced by the Chinese. In an earlier encounter, this 'hot-dogging' Chinese pilot, had moved his F-8 fighter so close that the Americans could read the email address he was holding up.[98]

The second meeting on the crisis on Monday morning was the most difficult and turned out the most decisive.[99] The question was how to engage the Chinese on substantive negotiations to resolve the crisis peacefully and quickly. Powell proposed that the administration formulate a statement of regret over the incident, but others calculated the administration had to begin with a strong stand as a weaker opening might tempt the government in Beijing to ask for even more concessions. The decision was to start with a strong but non-provocative demand, to be followed immediately by serious negotiations if the Chinese responded and gave access to the crew. It was not a game of chicken for there is no evidence that either side wanted a confrontation. While Jiang Zemin continued his travels in South America and the government in Beijing made strong claims, the Chinese media was held firmly in check. This was an important sign for Washington because they wanted no replay of the unbridled Chinese rage after the US accidentally bombed the Chinese embassy in Belgrade in 1999.

Bush stepped out of the meeting and announced: 'Our priorities are the prompt and safe return of the crew, and the return of the aircraft.' He added, 'I am troubled by the lack of a timely Chinese response to our request for access.'[100] Some American commentators thought that George W. Bush overreacted and showed 'pique', making the crisis worse, but these early reports overlooked the fact that Bush's first public statement on the incident was part of a deliberate strategy to put pressure on Beijing.[101] The tactic worked. While Jiang Zemin responded with an equally stern demand for 'an apology', General Sealock was allowed to see the crew. Sealock spoke with Bush personally by phone on Monday night and reported that the crew was safe and in good spirits. On Tuesday, Bush's tone was milder, indicating that his approach was to 'keep this accident from becoming an international incident'. And he spoke of his hope for 'a fruitful and productive relationship' with China.[102] It was not a case of 'backpedaling', as others have suggested, but having made his point about the crew, Bush was signaling his intent to find a mutually agreeable outcome and by Tuesday night, Beijing started to respond.[103]

What followed was a carefully calibrated diplomatic dance between two major powers. The allegedly 'inexperienced foreign policy president' turned out to be a very shrewd diplomatic player. Bush let Powell be the interlocutor, but he remained 'a closet engager', staying on the issue till the end.[104] First Powell offered 'regret' over the loss of the Chinese pilot. Beijing demanded an apology, but Bush would not 'apologize' for something the Chinese had most likely caused. On that word, Richard Armitage said, Bush 'drew a line in the sand'.[105] In the weeks prior to the collision, Chinese fighters had become more and more daring in their tailing of US reconnaissance planes and Beijing demanded an end to the flights. The White House never considered this seriously, as the flights were over international waters. Powell used the word 'sorry', and then 'very sorry'.[106] Sending another signal, Bush inserted his own 'regret' in a speech he gave to newspaper editors on April 5. Meanwhile, Henry Kissinger was asked to play a quiet role, indicating to the Chinese that if they held the detainees too long, the American public would begin to see them as 'hostages', and implied that escalation would then be inevitable.[107]

Having heard from both Bush and Powell, the Chinese settled for the 'letter of the two sorries'.[108] The American side was 'very sorry' about the loss of the pilot and 'very sorry' about the EP-3 'entering Chinese airspace' to make its emergency landing, but the letter was signed off by the American ambassador, not Undersecretary Armitage nor Secretary Powell. The crew was released on April 11 and other items, including the return of the plane, would be dealt with by a bilateral commission, which would look into various Chinese assertions without any preconditions. The plane returned in crates on July 3 and soon thereafter, the Pentagon resumed low-level contacts with China.[109]

Kissinger praised Bush for his 'deft handling'[110] of the crisis while most media accounts agreed that he had shown 'patient diplomacy'.[111] Indeed, Sino-American relations did not seem harmed by the Hainan incident. In January, Bush had written a letter to Jiang, but on April 13 he spoke with Jiang by phone for the first time. On April 23, the President did re-affirm his pledge to defend Taiwan, yet, despite Congressional pressure, Bush did not sell Taiwan the Aegis battle-management system. Putting the onus on Beijing, he indicated that should China increase its offensive missile capacity, he might sell the Aegis system in the future. On June 1, the Bush administration requested Congress to extend China's normal trade relations, which it did on July 19. Just before Powell's visit to Beijing in early August, China released two US scholars who had been arrested on trumped up espionage charges. Beijing then placed a $2 billion order with Boeing for 737s. Bush had passed his first international crisis.

Overall, the relationship was unharmed. Bush had made clear from the start that he would not continue Clinton's idea of 'strategic ambiguity', but would be straightforward with China.[112] Bush would defend Taiwan, but not let it unilaterally change the status quo of the nuanced China–Taiwan–US triangle. Bush slapped sanctions on the Chinese state-owned arms producer Norinco in the fall of 2001 for proliferating missile technology to Pakistan, but also granted China permanent 'most favored nation treatment' in trade in December 2001. China's own concerns about militant Islam in Asia after September 11, and the deepening tension over North Korea have gradually brought the two powers closer together.

Israel and the Middle East

The Bush administration inherited two policy hot spots (Iraq and the Palestinian-Israeli crisis) in the Middle East. The sanctions regime against Iraq had been unraveling since Saddam Hussein expelled the United Nations (UNSCOM) inspectors in 1998. Increasingly, Britain and the United States were the only ones left that wanted Saddam to live up to the strict interpretation of various UN resolutions, but those sanctions had not shown results. Saddam's hold on power was stronger than when the sanctions began and the Clinton administration had been very hesitant about supporting a dissident-led uprising or an invasion to overthrow Hussein. The existing policy appeared to be failing while there were no good alternatives on the horizon.

Anyone looking at the line up of Bush senior officials, including Cheney, Rumsfeld and Wolfowitz, could predict that Saddam Hussein was in for a real challenge, but the removal of Hussein was not a foregone conclusion. The Bush team did not come in with a plan to oust him, in fact, the Bush administration started very cautiously.[113] The State Department allocated funds to the Iraqi opposition groups located in London and Powell started a policy review on the sanctions policy on February 14. Rice explained that the administration sought to 'regain the initiative', as Powell began an intense effort to get the permanent five members of the United Nations Security Council to support a new 'smart sanctions' approach.[114] The idea was to deflect some of the criticism that the sanctions were hurting the Iraqi population while at the same time enhancing monitoring on oil, weapons, and dual-use technology. Thus, sanctions on food and consumer items would be eased. In early July, Powell was unable to tie his smart sanctions to the oil-for-food program extension – Russia made it clear that it would veto such a move and France was also hesitant. By September 11, the negotiations were nowhere near a solution. If anything, Saddam Hussein was hardening his position, threatening to boycott all oil exports if smart sanctions were approved.

Bush also inherited a second Palestinian uprising and a 'peace process' in tatters. Clinton had coached Israel's Ehud Barak into an unprecedented set of concessions vis-à-vis Yasser Arafat, giving back most of the West Bank and joint control of Jerusalem. When Arafat declined the final offer, the peace process literally came apart and Palestinian violence broke out afresh in September 2000. On February 6, 2001, Israeli voters gave Ariel Sharon an overwhelming mandate (Likud received 62 per cent of the vote) as he had campaigned on restoring security first, peace negotiations second. On March 7, he formed a unity coalition government with the help of the Labor Party.

The Bush administration started an internal policy review process on the Israeli-Palestinian crisis, but the White House refused to give the Palestinian issue the same profile as Clinton had done in his last few years. As a result Bush was accused of being disengaged. Though he was clearly preoccupied with other issues, he also had a reason for his 'standoff' approach. To Bush's national security team the lesson learned was that they could not better Clinton's job and there was no use starting open-ended negotiations with Arafat if they had no confidence in either his interest or governing ability to settle on a final deal. The White House avoided the term 'the Middle East Peace Process'.[115] Bush also had a good relationship with Sharon, stemming from when he had visited Israel when still governor of Texas in 1998. Sharon had given him a guided helicopter tour of the land and the 'two men hit it off immediately', with Bush joking that the average driveway in Texas was longer than most stretches of land between Israel's borders.[116] The Israeli voters had given Sharon a clear mandate and Bush wanted to respect that verdict. What could Sharon offer Arafat that Barak had not?

Though there were fewer pronouncements on the crisis, Bush met personally in early 2001 with the key leaders in the conflict, with Sharon in March, and Egypt's Mubarak and Jordan's King Abdullah in April. Powell made his first major trip to the region in the last week of February. Before the House Foreign Affairs Committee, Powell testified on April 26 that quiet negotiations were taking place, 'not with a billboard announcement everyday'.[117]

Bush's basic philosophy was that the two parties had to want negotiations themselves. If the United States were to force one or the other into a set of talks against its will, the whole thing would simply backfire. For Bush, the prime responsibility to stop the so-called 'cycle of violence' lay on the Palestinian side and both he and Powell grew more and more convinced by early 2001 that Arafat could exercise more operational and moral authority to quell the violence, but chose not to do so. Bush refused to meet with him. Powell with the help of his head of policy planning, Richard Haass, tried hard to coordinate pressure on Arafat with the UN's Kofi Annan, the European foreign policy point man, Javier Solana, and with his Russian counterpart, Igor Ivanov. Powell called negotiations 'down the end of a long locked hallway'.[118]

In May, Bush endorsed the George Mitchell Report, the end product of a commission that had been launched during the Clinton years. It called for an end to the violence, followed immediately by Israeli concessions on settlements in the West Bank, but neither of the Middle East parties paid much attention to the report. In June, Bush sent CIA Director George Tenet to exploit an apparent window of opportunity in which the American could walk the parties toward a cessation of hostilities. Again, the Palestinians shot down the opportunity with more suicide bombings, and by late June 'Bush had enough' of Arafat and was ready to call for his ouster.[119]

Bush revealed his so-called 'Road Map' to peace between Israel and the Palestinians in June 2002. This three-year plan promised a state for the Palestinian people if they renounced terror and if they reformed their corrupt government, headed by Yasser Arafat. American support for Palestinian statehood showed that Bush was not simply backing Ariel Sharon in the conflict – it was the first time an American president had made such a concrete promise. The condition of reform confronted the Palestinians with a choice. In Bush's view, Arafat had failed to deliver most conditions of the Oslo Accords of the early 1990s and was no longer a partner in future negotiations as he would not condemn or stop ongoing suicide bombings by Palestinians in Israel. The ball was in the Palestinian court as Bush would not pressure Sharon to make concessions without any reasonable prospect of gain in the midst of a sustained campaign of terror by Palestinian militants against Israeli citizens.

Bush's 'Road Map' brought the European Union and others back to the table and forced Arafat to appoint Mahmoud Abbas, a moderate Prime Minister. Bush's Road

Map was not rhetoric. At the summit meeting in Aqaba, Jordan, in June 2003, he showed willingness to move quickly with Abbas and Sharon to work out a three-year deal, culminating in a Palestinian state. While Israeli defence forces were redeploying, as agreed at Aqaba, massive suicide attacks launched by the terrorist group called Hamas killed scores of Israeli citizens and the talks appeared stillborn. Abbas resigned and the Road Map seemed destroyed.

Bush does not easily abandon a goal he has publicly set. He wrote to Saudi's Crown Prince Abdullah, after the latter had sent him a harsh letter in August 2002, 'I am troubled and feel deeply the suffering of ordinary Palestinians in their day to day life and I want such tragedies to end.' He continued: 'I firmly believe that the Palestinian people have a right to self-determination and to live peacefully and securely in their own state in their own homeland.'[120] But Bush would not push Sharon if Palestinian leaders had only one response to all American and Israeli proposals (more suicide bombings) and thus could do nothing good for the Palestinian people. He would not condemn unilateral Israeli moves to protect their own people, including the construction of the new security fence and unilateral dismantlement of Jewish settlements in the Gaza and Westbank.

North Korea

Bush received more early criticism for his handling of North Korea than for his 'disengagement' in the Israeli-Palestinian issue. It was a case of Bush saying bluntly what he did not want, before presenting an alternative plan – he threw away the old policy before he could spell out the new. Clearly, if there was a communications strategy on this issue, it flopped badly. Even if Bush was on the right path – which became clear when North Korea admitted in the fall of 2002 that it had been cheating on its nuclear program before Bush became president – he did not get any credit for challenging the existing policy. Bush's values and political skill seemed out of kilter.

Clinton had tried very hard during the last months of his presidency to secure a missile deal with North Korea. Like the 1994 Agreed Framework on nuclear material negotiated between North Korea and the United States, with the help and backing of South Korea and Japan, the missile deal contained rewards up front in return for North Korean promises to abandon its missile technology program later. It was a philosophy with which Bush and most of his advisers were terribly uncomfortable. American presidents, both Democrat and Republican, have been concerned about North Korea's nuclear and missile programs for some time. In 1993 American intelligence revealed preparations at North Korea's Yongbyong nuclear facility to reprocess fuel rods to produce plutonium for weapons grade material. President Clinton made serious preparations for a surprise military strike, just as the Israelis had destroyed Iraq's Ochirak facility in 1981.

It was former President Carter who 'saved' the day, when in Pyongyang, he claimed he had received assurances that the North Korean government would 'freeze' its nuclear program and was willing to start serious negotiations. Those negotiations led to an agreement where North Korea promised to halt all nuclear operations in its graphite-moderated reactors and the United States would lead 'an international consortium' to build two light-water reactors.[121] In the interim, the consortium would supply the Democratic People's Republic of Korea with 500,000 ton of heavy oil per year. After construction on the two reactors was in process, North Korea would permit international inspections into its nuclear facility, at least so it said. The framework also set the two countries on the path to full normalization of relations.

To Bush officials and Congressional Republicans, the policy smacked of bribery, even blackmail. It looked like rewarding the North for stopping things it ought not to have been doing in the first place. South Korea, led by Kim Dae-Jung called its overall approach towards North Korea the 'sunshine policy'. To many Republicans, Kim seemed willing to give away everything to appease the despotic and wildly unpredictable leadership of the North. Most of the Vulcans on Bush's 2000 campaign team were deeply suspicious of North Korea – in 2000, Condi Rice called the government of Kim Jong Il, the 'evil twin' of the South.[122] In her view, the regime's days were numbered. The Clinton administration felt engagement and even some appeasement would be better than confrontation given the erratic nature of the regime in the 'Hermit Kingdom,' and the many weapons it had aimed at North Korea's capital Seoul. Japan was nervous about North Korea's Taepo Dong II missile program and thus enthusiastically backed any buy-out attempts to halt North Korea's capability. Meanwhile, North Korea was still selling missile technology to Iran.

The new Bush administration duly started a policy review on the North Korean relationship with Rice's assistant, Robert Joseph, chairing the Policy Review Committee. President Kim Dae Jung wanted to visit Bush early with the hope of influencing this policy review, as he had only two years left in office and hoped that Bush would pick up the Agreed Framework and the missile talks where Clinton had left off. Clinton had not simply run out of time on the missile deal, rather, there were great obstacles. In order to freeze its missile program, North Korea wanted the United States to provide it with launchers for its satellite program. The CIA advised Clinton against the idea, warning that North Korea could convert the technology used in the launchers into building more missiles. Moreover, the North wanted Washington to pay $1 billion for all the missile exports it would forego as a result of the deal and it threatened with more missile tests if no progress was made.

Except for Wolfowitz, none of the deputy or assistant secretary positions in either State or Defense were filled on March 7 when Kim arrived in Washington. Quite literally, the administration had no policy on North Korea. With the benefit of hindsight, the visit by Kim should have been postponed. A State Department Official admitted that, 'the timing was not good. Nobody came out looking good.'[123] If Kim thought to advance his cause, he took a terrible risk and came ill prepared. To make matters worse, a week prior to his coming, Kim and Putin signed a communiqué to 'strengthen' the 1972 Anti-Ballistic Missile Treaty when Putin visited Seoul.[124] This slight against Bush's top priority did not go unnoticed by the White House.

Being a plain talker, and having only a few general principles to go by, Bush told Kim that he did not trust the North and that the 1994 framework and the recent missile talks lacked 'transparency'. Bush told Kim that in the future there would have to be a better way to verify compliance on the nuclear question. He did not quite give Kim a verbal 'slap in the face' as one German newspaper put it nor did he use 'harsh words' as a Korean paper reported, unless saying that the North could not be trusted constitutes 'harsh' language.[125] Kim also did not get a sense of what the Bush administration would do other than apparently confront North Korea – he knew better than Bush that the regime in the North would likely escalate its own aggressive behavior as a result.

Because the administration did not have a policy in place, it also created the impression of internal division. Powell, speaking on the day prior to Kim's visit, said, 'We do plan to engage with North Korea to pick up where President Clinton and his administration left off.' He added, 'Some promising elements were left on the table ... and so in due course you'll hear about our plans.'[126] There was nothing wrong with the last two comments, but to say that Bush would pick up where Clinton left off was too much. Powell was 'pulled back' by the White House.[127] The next day (March 7) Powell expressed the same overall caution about the North as Bush and Rice. Obviously the impression was created that Powell thought differently from Rice, Cheney or Bush on the subject, but it was more a matter of emphasis and Powell filling in the blanks without White House direction, than a fundamental disagreement on policy.

The President's position was not that far from Powell's. After the meeting with Kim, Bush said that he had, 'no immediate plans to resume missile talks', but also that he supported Kim's 'sunshine policy' of rapprochement with the North, and that the US would continue to honor the terms of the 1994 Agreed Framework, just as Powell had said during his confirmation hearing.[128] Rice knew that the 1994 agreement could not 'easily be set aside'.[129] All along, Bush kept the food aid and oil flowing to North Korea. Bush wanted time to coordinate his Asia policy closely with Japan as well as South Korea. He had appointed several Japan experts, such as Richard Armitage and James Kelly, both with experience in the Reagan administration. Powell said on March 8 in Congress, 'We have no illusions about the nature of the gentleman who runs North Korea ... We are going to put together a comprehensive policy and in due course, and at a time and place of our choosing we will decide how best to engage with the North Korean regime.'[130] Unfortunately for Bush, his controversial start with Kim muddied the waters and many in Europe and Asia now thought of Bush's approach to North Korea as simply bellicose.

On June 6, the administration revealed the result of its policy review. Bush would start 'serious discussions' with the North Koreans, but the parameters would be turned upside down. Instead of rewards first and inspections later, the Bush team insisted on early inspections including, 'improved implementation' of the 1994 framework.[131] Bush wanted International Atomic Energy Agency inspections to come to the forefront. North Korea reacted angrily to the fact that Bush did not continue on Clinton's terms and some in Europe accused Bush incorrectly of 'abandoning talks with North Korea'.[132] The European Union, with strong German backing, sent a hasty mission to Seoul to supposedly fill the diplomatic gap, but it was the North Koreans who blocked progress now, apparently determined to avoid inspections.

Bush added North Korea to the 'axis of evil' in early 2002 because of the threat it posed to the proliferation of weapons of mass destruction. Pyongyang responded angrily and demanded a non-aggression pact. Powell was 'stunned' when he learned in the summer of 2002 that while North Korea had allowed seals on its plutonium rods and cameras to monitor the reactor site, it had secretly opened another plant to produce enriched uranium.[133] The standoff was now complete with Bush demanding that the regime of Kim Jong Il first comply with its treaty obligations and dismantle its nuclear program before formal talks could begin. Bush stopped oil shipments under the Agreed Framework and demanded complete, verifiable and irreversible elimination of North Korea's nuclear weapon's programs. Instead, North Korea began to produce nuclear weapons and a stalemate ensued.

Europe

European governments are usually apprehensive about the arrival of a new American president. They thought Jimmy Carter was too moralistic and naïve in his approach toward Brezhnev and human rights; Reagan was seen as a simpleton and a dangerous 'cowboy.' They even grew impatient with George H. W. Bush, who took a whole year to consider whether or not he wanted to engage Mikhail Gorbachev in bringing down the Soviet system. They resented Clinton's single-minded focus on the American economy as they struggled with a civil war in the Balkans.

In George W. Bush they encountered at first near total neglect. Rumsfeld was busy with his defense review and Colin Powell was at first pre-occupied with breathing new life into the State Department. Powell lobbied hard with the White House for a five per cent increase in State's budget. He announced new embassy building projects as well as computer and security upgrades.[134] He went out of his way to empower the career staff, having the Mexico desk officer, for example, brief Bush personally before his February 16 visit to Vincente Fox's ranch. Powell and Rice also started work on a new aid initiative for Africa. No high level Europe hands were appointed – Daniel Fried at the National Security Council was the first on board and his focus was Eastern Europe. Bush and Rice were focused on Vladimir Putin. Blair, of course, took matters in his own hands and after his Camp David meeting with the new president, Bush joked, 'he put the charm offensive on me, and it worked'.[135]

There were no major problems or threats in Europe and logically the administration could not be faulted for being more concerned about hot spots in Asia and the Middle East, but Bush took Europe for granted. Early misgivings about what Bush would do in the Balkans caused in part by Bush's ambiguous campaign talk had to be straightened out. There were about 11,000 US troops in Bosnia and Kosovo and 700 personnel in Macedonia, the latest flashpoint. When NATO led a small operation there in August named 'Amber Fox' to supervise a weapon's collection program for the Albanian rebels, the US supported the diplomacy behind the mission and provided logistical and intelligence support.

In the summer and fall of 2000 there had been a lot of wrangling between the Clinton administration and the Europeans about ensuring that a rapid reaction force under the auspices of the new Common European Security and Defense Policy agreed to in Helsinki in 1999 would remain compatible with NATO. Rumsfeld sounded a little suspicious at Munich in early February 2001 and top policy advisers inside the Pentagon took a more dire view of European designs than their colleagues in the State Department. There was a sense, as one Defense Department official put it, that 'France was organizing Europe against us'.[136] Cheney, Rumsfeld and the other experienced players had watched European contortions about common foreign policy for decades so they had no illusions. As long as the Europeans were not going to add real military capability – and the German defense budget was still going down at the height of the European defense euphoria – Bush was not going to waste any diplomatic energy on European defense. The administration simply declared Europe's defense policy compatible with NATO and moved on. Plenty of people in Washington believed the European Union's defense policy was going to be another 'belly flop' and were ready to call 'humbug'.[137] Bush officials did not wish for that, but so long as there was no concrete military investment, they were going to wait and see – the Bush administration conveyed a sense of 'show us the capabilities and we will talk.' The topic was not on the table when Bush traveled to Europe in June and July and Rice said that Bush wanted to do away with 'years of mixed signals and ambivalent body language' and to be sure to 'welcome' a European security and defense identity.[138]

Bush and Europe collided head on when it came to international treaties. The administration was not as politically savvy on this score as it was on domestic policy, or in its relations with Congress. While the Europeans were not simply the innocent party, often lecturing the Americans with smugness about the virtues of their new-found internationalism, the question still remains: Could the Bush team not have made their point and created less ill feeling? Surely, there was room for smoother diplomacy, but on substance the Bush administration and such conventional multilateralists as France and Germany were very far apart. The President's new team was determined to change the tone in almost all arms control agreements, arguing with good cause that these regimes were stuck in the strategic rationale of the Cold War and were doing little to stop rogue states from developing dangerous weapons. Rice said that Bush was not elected 'to sign treaties that are not in America's interest'.[139]

In the White House, in Rice's staff, and at the highest levels at State and the Defense Department, there was a solid block of people who believed that the entire arms control treaty regime started in the early 1970s had failed miserably. They included Douglas Feith and Jack Crouch at the Pentagon, and John Bolton at the State Department. Lewis Libby, Cheney's adviser was also among them. Bolton, the feisty and outspoken point man on international arms control at the State Department, tore into the sleepy status quo consensus with a vengeance. It was Europe and Canada that had the most to lose from throwing out the existing multilateral arms control fora. At the Biological Weapons Convention, Bolton named six violators (North Korea, Iraq, Iran, Syria, Libya, Sudan) and blocked any further movement toward a verification and monitoring regime. Bolton and his counterpart at the Pentagon, Douglas Feith, believed the convention to be another example of treaties 'that bind only the honest but give cover to the cheat'.[140]

The Europeans had already been notified that the ABM Treaty was dead in the water and in 1999, the Senate had overwhelmingly rejected ratification of the Comprehensive Test Ban Treaty. Bolton wanted Bush to un-sign America from the treaty, but while he said he had no plans to submit it for ratification, at the same time Bush would continue the existing moratorium on nuclear testing. Rather than being bound by a treaty which some of the rogue states openly flogged, Bush wanted to have 'flexibility' should future testing be necessary.[141]

In the eyes of the Bush team, the West Europeans and Canada had outmaneuvered Clinton on three recent treaties that were not in American national interest: anti-personnel landmines, the international criminal court, and the Kyoto Protocol. The new administration was loaded for bear and Bolton made sure to water down a pending accord on small arms trafficking. There was nothing the Bush administration could do anymore on the landmines, but it was going to let Europe know there was a new player in town on the criminal court. Clinton had signed on to the International Criminal Court (the 1998 Rome Statute) on December 31, 2000, lamely suggesting the US had a better chance to influence the deal from the inside than from outside, but the treaty never had any chance in the Senate. When he was still Chairman of the Joint Chiefs of Staff, Powell had already been opposed to the idea of an international body with little control by the UN Security Council, prosecuting American soldiers and possibly even former statesmen. Bolton called the treaty 'a stealth approach to eroding US constitutionalism'.[142] One Bush official likened the court without Security Council control to 'Kenneth Starr to the Nth degree'.[143] Bush made a point of unsigning the United States from the pending treaty – Bolton was given the honor and he said it was 'the happiest moment of my government service'.[144]

Later in 2001, the Bush administration tied its continued participation in the Balkans to its demand for bilateral deals that would exempt Americans from the terms of the treaty. Both sides dug in and agreed on a one-year respite on the Balkans, meanwhile, the administration continued negotiating bilateral deals with Eastern European countries about to join the European Union to exempt US personnel in those countries from the Rome Statute.

Bush's 'abrupt' rejection of the Kyoto Protocol on carbon dioxide emissions 'stunned' the Europeans and created a veritable uproar on the continent.[145] He did little to stop a public and governmental backlash against him in Europe. Of course, it would not be European voters who would vote in November 2002, but Bush's lack of diplomatic capital in early 2001 cost him needless amounts of public capital in Europe in the years to come. If the Europeans had paid closer attention they would not have been surprised, for during the campaign, Bush said that he did not believe the Kyoto Protocol 'addressed the problem of climate change in a way that the United States could support'.[146] During his years as Texas governor, Bush had always resisted a 'spend and sue' approach to environmental goals. Bush did not deny the need for carbon dioxide reductions, but believed it should be done through incentives and new technology.

Once in the White House, Bush's views of Kyoto dimmed even more. He found himself in the midst of an electricity-supply crisis in California and a rapidly slowing economy. Cheney had started his Energy Task Force consultations and he leaned towards increased supply, yet, apparently, Christine Todd Whitman had not been fully included in the emerging White House direction. As with North Korea, the administration did not start out with a clear policy and did not have a communications strategy to deal with it. At a G-8 meeting of environmental ministers in Trieste, Italy in early March, she left the door open for a role by the Bush administration in rescuing the stalled Kyoto negotiations. Like Powell on policy toward North Korea, Whitman had to be pulled back by the White House. Cheney shortly thereafter suggested Kyoto was in fact 'seriously flawed'.[147] At a luncheon with European Union Ambassadors in Washington, on March 22, Condi Rice delivered the final blow. She told them outright 'Kyoto is dead'.[148] She 'was surprised that they were surprised', but the fact of the matter was that the Europeans had clung to some hope that at least the Bush administration would continue the talks.[149] Rice's message came as a cold shower, nor did the White House offer any alternatives.

The Kyoto debacle overshadowed the first meeting between Bush and German Chancellor Gerhard Schroeder on March 29. Schroeder wanted Bush to know the depth of European concern, but Bush told him that the Kyoto Protocol with its harsh emission rollback targets would hit the American economy too hard and was not the right way to deal with the problem. 'I have to take care of the people who fear they will lose their jobs,' Bush said to Schroeder.[150] It was a bad deal for America and it probably was a bad treaty, exempting large and upcoming economies such as China and India and favoring states such as France, which derives a lot of its energy from clean nuclear power. Many people in the Clinton administration feared the same and it had taken a personal intervention by Vice President Gore to push the American negotiating team along, yet the talks were stalled in November 2000. In 1997, the Senate voted 95-0 against the Kyoto Protocol. Instead of being hypocritical about it, Bush decided the best thing he could do was to kill the initiative quickly. To the Europeans it looked like Kyoto is dead, you 'deal with it'.[151]

By April, the 'prevailing impression' in Europe of Bush was 'overwhelmingly negative'.[152] It did not help that the European media uncritically copied the US media stories that Bush was 'too inexperienced', delegated too much, was beholden to right wing lobbies and had stolen the Florida election.[153] On his first working day, Bush reinstated Reagan's approach to aid organizations that sponsor abortions. He cut off all federal funds to those groups. Bush said, 'Those are organizations I don't want to support.'[154] It was reported that he was 'mollifying' the Christian Right,[155] but Bush is solidly pro-life and where he can, he will try to promote a culture of life. In Bush, many Europeans found a fresh face for the 'Ugly American.' The combination of Texas oilman, Christian Right, pro-death penalty, and anti-Kyoto became a crusade against Bush among many politicians and intellectuals in Europe. In Germany, it would soon boil over and create serious hard feelings in the bilateral relationship. On May 3, West European diplomats worked with many developing countries in the General Assembly of the United Nations to vote the United States out of the UN Human Rights Commission. It was meant to show their spite, for as Powell noted, there was a 'diminished solidarity between the United States and its democratic partners.'[156]

Finally the White House realized it had to fight back against the growing negative perception of Bush in Europe. It appears that Bush added a quick European tour to the planned Bush-Putin meeting in June in order to dispel some of the negative stereotypes of himself as a heartless unilateralist and show that he did value his European allies and wanted to consult with them personally. It meant that Bush would go to Europe in June and again in July for the G-8 meetings in Italy. For the first time in its dealings with Europe, the Bush White House showed a coherent and effective strategy and message plan. The message was that Bush was a friend to a

'Europe whole, free and at peace.'[157] He would listen to their concerns and consult with them – he also cared about their institutions. Bush instructed Karen Hughes in early June to 'focus' on the Europe speech.[158] Rove and Hughes had come together with Rice and Daniel Fried to get this right, as the entire trip, including its schedule and messages, showed Bush's values and his objectives.

He started in Spain on June 12, visiting a conservative 'new voice' in Europe. Prime Minister José Maria Aznar received Bush at his ranch for a warm meeting of friends. Aznar strongly supported Bush's missile defense plans. Then Bush went to NATO and affirmed America's confidence and participation in the Alliance. He also left no doubt that his administration was determined to add seven aspiring members from Eastern Europe, and wanted NATO to make this decision at its planned 2002 Prague Summit. From here, Bush went to his toughest meeting with the fifteen European Union heads of state and government in the Swedish city of Göteborg. Later in the Oval Office, he told Peggy Noonan that he sat patiently (practicing his modesty) as all fifteen told him how wrong he was, especially on Kyoto. He told Noonan that he listened and at the end told them, 'I appreciate your point of view, but this is the American position because it is right for America.'[159] Bush felt he had shown openness, telling them, 'I hope the unilateral theory is dead', but many Europeans where disappointed that he offered no compromises, no real dialogue or engagement on the issue.[160] European doubts were not removed.

After the European Union meeting, which Powell described as 'frank discussions', Bush went to visit another friend: Poland. At Warsaw University he delivered the most important speech of his trip, a values speech, similar to the ones his trusted speechwriter Mike Gerson had written for him at home. Bush emphasized the 'unity of values' between Poland and America and that these included 'spiritual values'. He spoke of freedom in Europe as 'a house of many mansions'. He rallied them to 'lift up their hearts'.[161] Quite obviously, Bush found a warmer home in the 'new Europe' in the East than in the critical West. The trip's finale was with Putin in Slovenia, which White House officials called 'warm and straightforward'.[162]

Conclusion

The Bush administration defined the threat of rogue states such as North Korea firing missiles at the United States and its allies, or blackmailing their freedom of action, as an immediate priority. Two obstacles stood in the way of addressing this danger: a thirty-year old arms control treaty and the absence of a full-blown R&D project on missile defense. When Bush spent time on foreign policy, it was to bring the ABM Treaty to a speedy end while constructing a new partnership with Russia. If one defines success as achieving one's own stated objectives, Bush scored a victory on this issue. Putin allowed the ABM Treaty to fade away with relatively little opposition and by mid-2004, Bush had the first interceptor missile in place in Fort Greely, Alaska. The Pentagon is developing sea-based radar platforms to be stationed in the Pacific and North Atlantic and by 2006, Bush will have the beginnings of a layered missile defense in place as promised. Allies who dragged their feet in 2001, such as Japan and Canada, 'are now lining up to join the effort'.[163]

On military transformation, Bush did not make as much progress as he had hoped. The first modest proposals became mired in a Congressional-Presidential tug-of-war on the budget. Like Bush's domestic initiative on education, the two sides were still dug in when the terrorist attacks took place. The new political environment after the attacks unlocked the transformation funds that Bush had requested, but now without the political pressure to adjoin them to cost savings in other areas.

Despite the strong words directed at China during the campaign, Bush proved in the Hainan 'Spy Plane' incident that he had the right instincts to deal calmly with a foreign crisis. After the rough start, both sides went out of their way to solidify a working relationship.

Bush hired outspoken and experienced foreign policy advisers who at times added a sharp edge to the President's own outspoken values about America's role in the world. Bush changed the tone of American foreign policy, but did not invest enough capital in diplomacy or communications to bring allies alongside. Except for Britain, Western Europe was especially vulnerable to a radical shift in American policy, as it had little hard military power and relied heavily on a set of international treaties to advance its soft interests around the world.

From arms control talks to the Kyoto Protocol, and from North Korea to the Palestinian issue, the Bush administration emphasized a set of values that flew in the face of conventional multilateralism. Bush put the assertion of fundamental American values up front while his policy proposals where still making their way through the policy-making process. Clinton's handling of North Korea looked to this President like a lack of leadership, if not a sell out. Chiding the Israelis for a crisis caused by a lack of leadership on the part of Arafat just did not seem fair or make sense. Too quickly, many critics called Bush's policy a case of raw unilateralism, but it was not that. He had no desire to be alone or to create some American empire, yet what he did want to do was lead in a new direction.

Notes

1   'A Period of Consequences', The Citadel, South Carolina, September 23, 1999.
2   'A Period of Consequences'.
3   As quoted in 'In an Age Without Heroes', *Economist*, June 2, 2001, p. 24.
4   Frances Fitzgerald, 'George Bush and the World', *The New York Review of Books*, September 26, 2002.
5   Ivo H. Daalder and James M. Lindsay, *America Unbound: The Bush Revolution in Foreign Policy* (Washington, D.C.: Brookings Institution Press, 2003), pp. 15, 41-49.
6   Excerpts from Colin Powell's Confirmation Hearing, US Senate, January 17, 2001 (www.clw.org/bush/powellconfirmation.html).
7   In Karl Rove's own words, 'Transcript of a Discussion with Karl Rove', American Enterprise Institute, Washington, D.C., December 11, 2001.
8   Paul Blustein, 'Getting Out in Front on Trade', *Washington Post*, March 13, 2001, p.E 1.
9   Morton Kondracke, 'Coming Soon: A Battle Royal Over Free Trade', *Roll Call*, March 29, 2001.
10   'Remarks by the President to Agriculture Leaders', Office of the Press Secretary, June 18, 2001.

11   'Will Bush Fight for Free Trade?', *Economist*, June 23, 2001, p. 25

12   Ryan Lizza, 'The Insider', *The New Republic*, July 30, 2001, p. 27.

13   Ron Suskind, *The Price of Loyalty: George W. Bush, The White House, and the Education of Paul O'Neill* (New York: Simon & Schuster, 2004), p. 221.

14   'Remarks by the President At the Signing Ceremony of the 2002 Trade Act', Office of the Press Secretary, August 6, 2002.

15   Robert Zoellick, 'Don't Go Bitter About Sugar', *Wall Street Journal*, February 25, 2004.

16   As quoted by John T. Correll, 'Struggling for Transformation', *Air Force Magazine*, Vol. 84, No. 5, May 2001.

17   News Briefing on Amended Budget for Fiscal Year 2002, Department of Defense, Washington, D.C., June 27, 2001.

18   Address of the President to the Joint Session of Congress, Office of the Press Secretary, February 27, 2001.

19   Frank J. Gaffney, Jr., 'A Milestone for Missile Defense', *The Wall Street Journal*, December 13, 2000, p. 16.

20   Thomas E. Ricks, 'For Rumsfeld, Many Roadblocks', *Washington Post*, August 7, 2001, p. 1.

21   Barry Schweid, 'Bush Pulls out of 1972 Missile Treaty', *Associated Press*, December 13, 2001.

22   Lexington, 'Rumsfeld's Defence', *Economist*, May 26, 2001, p. 34.

23   Rowan Scarborough, *Rumsfeld's War: The Untold Story of America's Anti-Terrorist Commander* (Washington, D.C., Regnery Publishing, 2004), p. 112.

24   Ivan Eland, 'Rumsfeld vs the Pentagon', Cato Institute, April 11, 2001 (http://www.cato.org/dailys/04-11-01.html).

25   John T. Correll, 'In Pursuit of a Strategy', *Air Force Magazine*, Vol. 84, No. 8, August 2001.

26   Ricks, 2001, p. 7.

27   Correll, August 2001.

28   Remarks by the President at US Naval Academy Commencement, Annapolis, Office of the Press Secretary, May 25, 2001.

29   Frederick Barnes, 'Can Bush Turn Around US Defenses?', *Defense and Foreign Affairs Strategic Report*, December 11, 2000, p. 14.

30   'Quadrennial Defense Review Report', *Department of Defense*, Washington, D.C., September 30, 2001, p. 17.

31   'Quadrennial Defense Review Report', 2001, p. 13.

32   Correll, August, 2001.

33   Secretary of Defense, Donald Rumsfeld, 'Testimony Before the House Appropriations Committee', US Congress, July 16, 2001.

34   As quoted in Nicholas Lemann, 'Dreaming about War', *The New Yorker*, July 16, 2001, p. 38.

35   Paul Wolfowitz, 'Testimony to the House Budget Committee', US Congress, July 11, 2001.

36   Rumsfeld, testimony, July 16, 2001.

37   Sydney Freedberg et al., 'Defense Department Profiles', *National Journal*, June 23, 2001.

38   In interview with Neil Cavuto, *Fox News*, August 13, 2001.

39   Rumsfeld testimony, June 28, 2001.

40   Jackson Diehl, 'B-1 Blundering', *Washington Post*, July 9, 2001, p. 17.

41   Testimony before the Senate Armed Services Committee, June 28, 2001.

42   Senator John Warner as quoted in Rumsfeld Testimony before the Senate Armed Services Committee, June 28, 2001.

43   News Briefing on Amended Budget for Fiscal Year 2002, 2001.
44   As quoted in Helen DeWar, 'Aide Softens Daschle's Hints at Retirement', *Washington Post*, July 22, 2001, p. 4.
45   Prepared Statement by Donald Rumsfeld, '2002 Defense Department Amended Budget', Senate Armed Services Committee, US Congress, June 28, 2001.
46   Michael O'Hanlon, 'Rumsfeld's Defense Vision', *Survival*, Vol. 44, No. 2, Summer 2002, pp. 103-117.
47   US Foreign Policy Agenda, 2001, p. 29.
48   Editorial, 'The Missile Offensive', *Washington Post*, February 7, 2001.
49   Section 2 of the 'NMD Act of 1999', Center for Defense Information (www.cdi.org).
50   Joseph Fitchett, 'Washington's Pursuit of Missile Defense Drives Wedge in NATO', *International Herald Tribune*, February 24, 2000.
51   George C. Wilson, 'Guns Aplenty, Butter Be Damned!', *National Journal*, January 27, 2001, p. 252.
52   Thomas E. Ricks, 'War College Details new Taiwan Attack Scenario', *Washington Post*, August 31, 2001, p. 2.
53   Paul Wolfowitz, Testimony, Armed Services Committee, US Senate, July 12, 2001.
54   Remarks by the President at National Defense University, May 1, 2001, Office of the Press Secretary (http://www.whitehouse.gov/news/releases/2001/05/print/20010501-10.html).
55   Wolfowitz, July 12, 2001.
56   Wolfowitz, July 12, 2001.
57   Powell, June 20, 2001.
58   Comments made by Defense Secretary Donald Rumsfeld at the Munich Conference on European Security Policy, February 3, 2001.
59   Peter W. Rodman, 'Shield Embattled: Missile Defense as a Policy Problem', (Washington, D.C., The Nixon Centre, October 21, 2001), p. 63.
60   John D. Morrocco, 'UK Seeks to Bridge US–Europe Divide', *Aviation Week & Space Technology*, February 12, 2001, p. 29.
61   'George Bush's Revolution', *Economist*, May 5, 2001, p. 19.
62   Author interview with Department of Defense official, March 15, 2004.
63   Stephen Seplow, 'Trying Situations Both Home and Abroad Await Eager New President', *Philadelphia Inquirer*, January 20, 2001.
64   Peter Stothard, *Thirty Days: Tony Blair and the Test of History* (New York: HarperCollins, 2003), p. 107.
65   Joint Press Conference with Colin Powell and Lord Robertson, Brussels, March 1, 2001.
66   As quoted in testimony by Colin Powell, 'Hearing Before the Committee on Foreign Relations', US Senate, June 20, 2001.
67   'Remarks by the President at National Defense University', White House, Office of the Press Secretary, May 1, 2001.
68   Stephen Fidler, 'Bush Consults Putin on Missile Defense', *Financial Times*, May 2, 2001. p. 6.
69   Condi Rice as quoted in 'Readout to the Press Pool on the Bilateral Meeting of President Bush with President Putin', Office of the Press Secretary, White House, July 22, 2001.
70   As quoted in Peggy Noonan, 'A Chat in the Oval Office', *Wall Street Journal*, June 25, 2001.
71   Bill Sammon, *Fighting Back: The War on Terrorism from Inside the Bush White House* (Washington, D.C.: Regnery Publishing, Inc, 2002), p. 365.
72   Peggy Noonan, *When Character Was King: A Story of Ronald Reagan* (New York: Viking, 2001), p. 307. (emphasis added).

73   'Dr. No', *Wall Street Journal*, August 24, 2001, p. 17.
74   Jack Hitt, 'Battlefield: Space', *New York Times Magazine*, August 5, 2001, p. 35.
75   Vernon Loeb and Thomas E. Ricks, 'Bush Speeds Missile Defense Plans', *Washington Post*, July 12, 2001, p. 1.
76   Karlyn Bowman, 'Americans High on Missile Defense System', *Roll Call*, May 3, 2001.
77   Rumsfeld Testimony, July 16, 2001.
78   Senator Carl Levin as quoted in 'Wolfowitz Testimony', July 12, 2001.
79   Secretary Rumsfeld at Pentagon Briefing, August 23, 2001.
80   Vernon Loeb, 'Levin Agrees to Cut Missile Test Curbs from Defense Bill', *Washington Post*, September 19, 2001, p. 3.
81   Condoleeza Rice 'Briefing on Bush-Putin Meeting in Shanghai', October 22, 2001. (http://usembassy-australia.state.gov/hyper/2001/1022/epf103.htm)
82   Carla Anne Robbins, 'Bush, Putin Pledge to Cut Nuclear Arms', *Wall Street Journal*, November 14, 2001, p. 24.
83   'Strategic Offensive Reductions Treaty', Office of the Press Secretary, The White House, May 24, 2002.
84   Noonan, p. 305.
85   Carla Anne Robbins, 'US Russian Dance on ABM Pact', *Wall Street Journal*, December 13, 2001, p. 10.
86   Robbins, 'US Russian Dance on ABM Pact', p. 10.
87   'Russia Proposes Plan to Work On Missile Defense With US', *Associated Press*, January 9, 2001.
88   Daalder and Lindsay, 'America Unbound', p. 66.
89   Inaugural Address, January 20, 2001.
90   Bush, Speech at the Citadel, September 23, 1999.
91   Bush, Speech at Ronald Reagan Library, November 19, 1999.
92   Thomas and Gutman, 2001, p. 21.
93   Carla Anne Robbins, 'US Brinkmanship Worries Its Allies', *Wall Street Journal*, September 26, 2002, p. 1.
94   Roger Cohen, 'Arrogant or Humble? Bush Encounters European Hostility', *New York Times*, May 8, 2001.
95   John Barry, et al., 'Collision with China', *Newsweek*, April 16, 2001, p. 29.
96   Carla Anne Robbins, 'As Spy-Plane Impasse Ends, US and China Face Sensitive Issues', *Wall Street Journal*, April 12, 2001, p. 8.
97   Barry, 2001, p. 28.
98   Daalder and Lindsay, 'America Unbound', p. 68.
99   Alex Keto, 'Bush Meets with Rice, Powell, Rumsfeld over China', *Dow Jones Newswire*, April 2, 2001.
100   Bush's Statement, April 2, 2001 (www.pbs.org).
101   Evan Thomas and John Barry, 'The Conflict to Come', *Newsweek*, April 23, 2001, p. 22.
102   Bush's Statement, April 3, 2001 (www.pbs.org).
103   Daalder and Lindsay, 'America Unbound', p. 69.
104   Judy Keen and Barbara Slavin, 'Bush Relies on Powell and Rice in Crisis', *USA Today*, April 12, 2001.
105   Interview with Jim Lehrer, The News Hour, Washington, D.C., April 13, 2001.
106   'Beyond Hainan', *Economist*, April 14, 2001, p. 25.
107   Thomas and Barry, April 23, 2001, p. 22.
108   Idem.
109   Neil King Jr., 'Ties on 'Upswing' Despite Spy Cases, Powell Says as Visit Nears', *Wall Street Journal*, July 26, 2001. p. 16.

110   Henry A. Kissinger, 'Face to Face with China', *Newsweek*, April 16, 2001, p. 36.
111   Bill Gates, 'China Policy, Without Regrets', *The New York Times*, April 12, 2001.
112   Editorial, 'The End of Strategic Ambiguity', *Washington Times*, April 27, 2001.
113   Nicolas Lemann, 'How It Came to War', *New Yorker*, March 31, 2003, p. 37.
114   Suskind, *The Price of Loyalty,* p. 83.
115   Bruce W. Jentleson, *Special Update to American Foreign Policy*, (New York: W.W. Norton & Co, 2002), p. 17.
116   Robert S. Greenberger and Jeanne Cummings, 'Faith, Trust and War Keep Bush Firmly in Israel's Corner', *Wall Street Journal*, April 3, 2002, p. 24.
117   Powell as cited on (http://usinfo.state.gov).
118   Jane Perlez, 'Powell, Meeting Both Sides in Israeli-Palestinian Conflict, Makes Little Headway', *New York Times*, February 26, 2001, p. 8.
119   Robbins, September 26, p. 10.
120   As quoted in Elsa Walsh, 'The Prince', *The New Yorker*, March 24, 2003.
121   US-DPRK Agreed Framework, October 21, 1994.
122   Condoleezza Rice, 'Promoting the National Interest', *Foreign Affairs*, Vol. 79, No. 1, 2000, p. 60.
123   Author interview, March 16, 2004.
124   'Seoul on Thin Ice', *Wall Street Journal*, Editorial, March 6, 2001, p. 22.
125   *Frankfurter Rundschau* and *Hankook llbo* as quoted in 'South Korea's Hopes for North/South Accord Dimmed but not Dashed', March 27, 2001, (www.fas.org).
126   Excerpts from Powell Remarks, March 6, 2001 (http//:usembassy.state.gov).
127   Ivo Daalder as quoted in 'Assessing the Bush Foreign Policy Transition', American Enterprise Institute, April 8, 2001.
128   Jim Garamone, 'US Will Renew Dialogue With North Korea in Future', *American Forces Press Service*, March 8, 2001.
129   Rice, 2000, p. 61.
130   Colin Powell in Hearing Before the Committee on Foreign Relations, US Senate, March 8, 2001.
131   Carla Anne Robbins, 'US Offers New Talks on Koreas', *Wall Street Journal*, June 7, 2001, p. 17.
132   Peter Spiegel, 'Bush Tones Down His Language', *Financial Times*, March 1, 2003.
133   Daalder and Lindsay, p. 178.
134   Powell Hearing, March 8, 2001.
135   Thomas and Rutman, 2001, p. 24
136   Author interview with Department of Defense Official, March 15, 2004.
137   Senator Gordon Smith as quoted in Powell Hearing, June 20, 2001.
138   Rice in a speech to the National Press Club. As quoted in John O' Sullivan, 'The Curse of Euro-Nationalism', *National Review*, August 6, 200, p. 36.
139   As quoted in Robin Wright, 'Officials Deny the US is Going it Alone', *Los Angeles Times*, August 31, 2001, p. 4.
140   Tom Shanker, 'Bush's Way: A la Carte Approach to Treaties', *New York Times*, August 1, 2001.
141   Walter Pincus, 'Senate Bill Requires Study of New Nuclear Weapon', *Washington Post*, June 12, 2000.
142   John R. Bolton, 'What's Wrong With the International Criminal Court', *The National Interest*, Winter 1998/1999.
143   Author interview with Defense Official, March 15, 2004.
144   Carla Anne Robbins, 'Disarming America's Treaties', *Wall Street Journal*, July 19, 2002, p. 4.
145   Warren Strobel, 'Leading Foreign Policy, Rice Confounds Doubters', *Philadelphia Inquirer*, December 8, 2001, p. E3.

146   Press Briefing by National Security Adviser Condoleezza Rice on President's Travel to Europe, June 6, 2001.
147   Alan Sipress, 'Aggravated Allies Waiting for US to Change its Tunes', *Washington Post*, April 22, 2001, p. 8.
148   Jeffrey Kluger et al., 'A Climate of Despair', *Time Magazine*, April 9, 2001, p. 32.
149   Rice Press Briefing, June 6, 2001.
150   As quoted in Robert von Rimscha, *George W. Bush: Präsident in Krisenzeiten* (Munchen: Wilhelm Heyne Verlag, 2001, p. 134.
151   Peter Grier and Francine Kiefer, 'Nations Resist Bush's Harder Line', *Christian Science Monitor*, April 5, 2001.
152   'Insider Interview', *National Journal*, May 16, 2001.
153   Morton Kondracke, 'Europe's Disdain for Bush Echoes Error on Reagan', *Roll Call*, May 10, 2001.
154   Seplow, January 20, 2001.
155   Debra Rosenberg, 'A Pro-Life Foreign Policy', *Newsweek*, September 3, 2001, p. 24.
156   Powell in Testimony before Foreign Relations Committee, US Senate, May 23, 2001.
157   'A Bumpy Landing', *Economist*, June 16, 2001, p. 29.
158   Karen Hughes, *Ten Minutes From Normal* (New York: Viking, 2004), p. 214.
159   Noonan, 'A Chat in the Oval Office', June 25, 2001.
160   as quoted by Powell in Powell Hearing, June 20, 2001.
161   Remarks by the President in Address to Faculty and Students at Warsaw University, Office of the Press Secretary, June 15, 2001.
162   Condoleezza Rice in 'Briefing on President's Trip to Europe', Brdo Pri Kranju, Slovenia, June 16, 2001.
163   James T. Hackett, 'Missile Defense Milestone', *Washington Times*, March 23, 2004.

Chapter 5

The War President

The big photographs on the front page of the *New York Times* on January 14, 2001 show George W. Bush, the 43rd president-elect of the United States, on the top right and a gruffly-looking Osama Bin Laden on the left. Neither the newspaper nor Bush could have known how foreboding this page was. Bush, it turned out, was literally in a race for time with the radical Islamic terrorist. Shortly after the launch of his administration, he signed off on an interagency review that would search for a new strategy to counter terrorism – the final results of this review were in his reading package on September 10 – and this new policy would have been launched within days from the September 11 attacks. This is not to say that the policy could have prevented the attacks, as it called for a phased in approach of diplomatic, economic and military actions against Al Qaeda and the Taliban that would take years to execute.

From the beginning of his campaign for the White House, Bush was aware of terrorism as a threat to the United States. In his hallmark defense speech at the Citadel in the fall of 1999, he mentioned counter-terrorism, homeland defense and the need to prevent weapons of mass destruction from falling into the hands of terrorists. He even warned that those who tolerate or encourage terrorists would be held responsible. Once elected, the President focused on his domestic agenda. In foreign and defense policy, Bush put a robust missile defense program and Rumsfeld's plans for military transformation ahead of counter terrorism. It was not a case of neglect or wrongdoing, but a case of choices. A president needs priorities to keep his agenda from clogging up and fighting terrorism was on the list, but just not high enough to make it to the top before the summer of 2001.

Bin Laden had only one goal: to harm and kill as many Americans as possible, allegedly to chase them out of the Middle East. He had a safe haven in Afghanistan, where he wrapped his virulent anti-Americanism in an Islamic *Jihad* (holy war) to recruit a wide variety of Islamic extremists, which he called Al Qaeda or 'the base'. His 1998 *fatwa* (religious decree) called it the 'individual duty of every Muslim' to kill Americans and their allies.[1] While Bin Laden won the first round, his fateful rendezvous with Bush on September 11 changed the priorities and the intensity of the Bush presidency. In just a few weeks after the attacks on New York, the Pentagon, and over the skies of Pennsylvania, Bush fundamentally changed the definition and the perception of his presidency – he was now a 'war president'. Few people then realized that Bush would go on to write an entirely new script for world politics.

The record shows that it is not right to suggest that Bush could have known about the *specific* attacks and failed to act properly or in time. Indeed, the 9/11 Commission Report does not make this claim. Senator Hillary Clinton used a *New York Post* story in May 2002 to ask 'what did the president know and when did he know it?' It had a

Watergate ring to it, as if Bush was conspiring to hide something from the public. Ari Fleischer, Bush's spokesman, said in response 'anytime anybody suggests or implies to the American people that this president had specific information that could have prevented the attacks on our country on September 11, that crosses the line.'[2] Laura Bush, who was for the first time traveling abroad (in Europe) as First Lady without her husband, responded that she felt 'very sad' that some would try to make partisan politics out of the September tragedy.[3] Bush who had hit 92 per cent in approval ratings in October of 2001 was now highly regarded by US voters.[4] They were now rooting for him and trusted his leadership in the fight against terror.

It is also not true to suggest that the Al Qaeda attack against US civilians came as a complete surprise – there were intelligence warnings in general and a good deal of government activity in response. Bush's first defense budget (fiscal year 2002) which boosted funding on missile defenses to over $8 billion, kept the counter terrorist entry still higher at $13.6 billion. In fact there was 'stunning continuity', as Richard Armitage told the 'National Commission on Terrorist Attacks upon the United States' during its hearings in early 2004, between Clinton's and Bush's approach on counter-terrorism in the first eight months of the Bush administration.[5] Most of the senior positions in the agencies remained unchanged and Condi Rice instructed her counter-terrorist adviser, Richard Clarke, to continue the same measures against Al Qaeda, but it was not a total effort by any means. Neither the Bush administration nor the country as a whole had 'really felt the threat in their bones'.[6] Secretary of State Colin Powell explained before Congress in early 2001 that embassy protection against terrorist attacks, such as had occurred in East Africa in 1998, was one of his top budget priorities. In the pre 9/11 terminology, he still referred to terrorists as 'criminals who had to be brought to court'.[7] Despite the money, there were many problems on the homeland security front, not least that the funds and information gathering were dispersed across some 40 departments and agencies with overlapping authority.

To most of the public, Osama Bin Laden and Al Qaeda were unfamiliar names, but this was not true for the Bush administration or for key committees in Congress. Bin Laden inherited several hundred million dollars from his father, who was the largest building contractor for the Saudi royal family. Unlike his business-minded siblings, he turned radical in the fight of Afghan Muslims against their Soviet invaders. He even accepted American money in that fight, but he turned into America's fiercest enemy after Western troops were allowed into Saudi Arabia to fight against Saddam Hussein. He slipped out of his native land in 1991 and set out to build Al Qaeda infrastructure in Yemen, Somalia, Sudan and Afghanistan. In 1993, Western intelligence finally discovered his organization. After the Riyadh bombing, which took the lives of five Americans in late 1994, the Clinton administration pressured Sudan to expel him. In May 1996, he fled to Afghanistan, and a month later his group killed nineteen US service members at an American military residence in Dhahran.

A National Commission launched after the 1998 embassy bombings in Kenya and Tanzania, which killed over 200 people, had called for better human intelligence abroad and for looser wiretap authority at home so that the CIA and FBI could detect potential terrorists. A Congressional Commission, chaired by Senators Gary Hart and Warren Rudman, recommended in early 2001 that the government create a 'Department of Homeland Defense'.[8] It warned that a 'direct, catastrophic attack against American citizens on American soil is likely'.[9] During hearings before the House Budget Committee with Undersecretary of Defense Paul Wolfowitz in July 2001, one House Representative commented, '[I]t was 60 years ago this December that a terrible thing happened in Hawaii, and I pray to God that doesn't happen again, but if we are not careful it's going to. The *USS Cole* should have been a wakeup call for us.'[10]

The American navy ship *USS Cole* had been bombed in the Yemeni port of Aden on October 15, 2000 – seventeen sailors had died. This was the latest in a string of Al Qaeda attacks. On February 9, 2001, Vice President Dick Cheney briefed Bush on the final report into the incident. It concluded that without any doubt Al Qaeda had been responsible for the attack. Bush instructed Cheney to chair a broad review on homeland defense against terrorism. The President's former chief of staff, Joe Allbaugh, now at the Federal Emergency Management Agency (FEMA), was told to set up an Office for National Preparedness to respond to terrorist attacks. Nicholas Lemann, who interviewed Dick Cheney in the spring of 2001, found him concentrated, even preoccupied with US vulnerability to terror attacks. Cheney was especially worried about so-called asymmetrical attacks, in which terrorist might use a 'dirty bomb' (nuclear materials dispersed by conventional explosives) or a biological or chemical agent. Cheney, wrote Lemann, was fixed on 'the theme of peril to the United States'.[11]

Secretary of Defense, Donald Rumsfeld was fond of challenging everyone who thought they could predict the next threat to the United States. He wrote, 'It is unlikely that any of us know what is likely.' He spoke of 'known unknowns' and 'unknown unknowns'.[12] Like most experts, he was thinking about 'mass casualty terrorism' inflicted with biological or nuclear weapons. Most people believed such attacks were still more likely to occur abroad than at home. Preparations off shore and at home were in swing. A crisis response exercise for government officials, called 'TopOff', was conducted in early 2001 – the CIA had set up a tracking unit on Osama Bin Laden in 1995. In the summer of 2001, the CIA was testing armed Predator UAV's (unmanned aerial vehicles) in the Nevada desert. They built a mock up version of Osama Bin Laden's Kandahar villa and were practicing firing anti-personnel missiles into it. The CIA and the Pentagon were fine-tuning a plan in which they could fire the missile within minutes of confirming Bin Laden's presence.

Given all the concern and ongoing preparations, why did the Bush administration not receive better intelligence, or as it is called 'actionable intelligence,' and why did it not do more in its race against Al Qaeda? The first problem was a lack of human intelligence on the ground in Afghanistan. During the trial of the terrorists who attacked the World Trade Center in 1993, it was revealed that the CIA tracked Bin Laden by his satellite phones, 'whereupon he stopped using them'.[13] Some believe that the CIA had been defanged in the 1970s – its officers were so often chastised in Congress and in the public sphere for covert operations gone bad that the Agency became risk adverse. They thought the CIA was also too limited in the kinds of 'dirty tricks' it could execute.[14] That may be so, but the agency had not been without successes in its fight against Al Qaeda. It foiled a plot to bomb New York's Lincoln and Holland tunnels in 1993 and it staved off a plan to bring down 11 American airliners in Asia in 1995.[15]

The FBI's errors in the summer of 2001 may turn out to be more fateful than the CIA's weaknesses or the slowness of Bush's decision-making process. On July 5, Kenneth Williams, an FBI agent in Arizona warned the Bureau that there were suspicious Middle Eastern students at flight school who were interested in flying, but not in landing or take-off. The FBI gets a good number of alarming memos and it is admittedly difficult to know which one to put on top of the pile, but then on August 17, FBI agents arrested Zacarias Moussaoui on immigration charges. Not a big deal *per se*, but a flight school in Minnesota told the FBI they were suspicious of him for only wanting to know how to fly without landing and take-off. If the FBI had asked (or had the legal right to ask), the CIA could have told it that French intelligence had informed the CIA that Moussaoui belonged to Islamic terror groups. Moreover, the CIA knew of a 1994 plan by terrorists to fly a plane into CIA headquarters in Langley, Virginia – there was a similar item of intelligence about plans to fly into the Eiffel Tower in 1995. Not knowing more about Moussaoui, the FBI did not open a criminal investigation on him – he was to be one of the September 11 hijackers. If the agencies had been on top of him, they may have picked up information about the sleeper cells that would strike on September 11, or on the travel of some of the hijackers in and out of the country. During the Commission hearings into the attacks of September 11, Bush administration witnesses insisted that there were legal and bureaucratic impediments to CIA-FBI communications, which the Bush team could not erase with one stroke of the pen.

Obviously, there was a lack of creative compilation of evidence between the FBI and the CIA which led to a series of operational failures.[16] They were 'stovepiping' their own information[17] and not keeping Richard Clarke, Bush's director of counter-terrorism, fully up to date.[18] He warned Stephen Hadley, Rice's deputy, about 'sleeper cells' in a memo on January 25, 2001. Clarke, a longtime watchdog on terrorism, was the first one to urge Condi Rice to look at Al Qaeda in a systematic way. On January 3, Rice instructed him to prepare 'an organized strategy review', after she had received similar advice from Clinton's National Security Adviser, Sandy Berger.[19] The outgoing Secretary of Defense, William Cohen, left Rumsfeld an ominous hand-written memo with just the home phone numbers of the handful of top anti-terrorism people in his department. On January 10, the Bush team got briefings by the CIA and later by the Joint Chiefs of Staff in the Pentagon's secure room (the Tank as it is called), which included important segments on Al Qaeda and Osama Bin Laden. The CIA labeled Al Qaeda 'a tremendous threat' which was 'immediate'.[20]

Bush, Cheney, Powell, Rumsfeld and Rice discussed early parameters around the strategy review that was about to start. In 1998, Clinton had signed a measure (Presidential Decision Directive 62) to expedite terrorist arrests and the protection of military sites overseas, but it did not go far enough. Bush did not want to simply 'pound sand,' that is, to lob cruise missiles at a tent camp in Afghanistan. This explains why Bush did not order immediate strikes after Cheney briefed him on the USS Cole report. Clinton had launched 70 such missiles at three Al Qaeda camps in August 1998, 13 days after the bombings in Kenya and Tanzania, but by the time the missiles struck, Bin Laden and his lieutenants were long gone. Bush wanted to go after the entire global network of Al Qaeda, not just after Bin Laden – unlike Clinton, he wanted to speak softly on the subject, but carry a big stick. He wanted a bottom up review of what Al Qaeda was and how to get rid of it for good. The underlying assumption was that there was time to do all this.

Clarke started the counter terrorism strategy group's work early. On January 2 he presented Rice with a set of ideas he had failed to get passed in the last few years of the Clinton administration and hoped would be picked up quickly by Bush. He had a set of plans ready for Bush's interagency process called the 'Delenda Plan' and the 'Blue Sky' proposals.[21] It was essentially a three-prong approach to pressure the Taliban, assist the Northern Alliance in Afghanistan and pressure Al Qaeda to a point where it could no longer threaten the United States. The draft discussed plans for a 'rollback strategy' and called for help for the Northern Alliance in Afghanistan to fight the Taliban.[22] It also sought more assistance for Uzbekistan in its fight with Islamic terror groups. It recommended more financial resources for CIA operations inside Afghanistan and called for the Treasury Department to start an asset-tracking center on terrorist groups.

The Deputies Committee (Paul Wolfowitz, Richard Armitage, Stephen Hadley, and Lewis Libby, with their colleagues from the CIA, Treasury and Justice) looked at the draft on April 30, 2001. Richard Armitage was one of its strongest supporters, having labeled the fight against Al Qaeda as the highest priority for US foreign policy in South Asia. Bush, who likely received a briefing by Rice on the Deputies' discussion stated, 'I am tired of swatting flies. I am tired of playing defense. I want to play offense. I want to take the fight to the terrorists.'[23]

Yet, the interagency process on counter terrorism moved slowly. Clarke was frustrated because he was now asked to work with the Deputies Committee, rather than with the Principals, though, admittedly, having worked directly with the Principals in the Clinton years did not produce an overall policy with teeth against Al Qaeda either. Where Clarke wanted specific actions in response to the *USS Cole*, Bush wanted an overall policy first. Stephen Hadley was instructed not to break the effort into different pieces. One of the key points as Condi Rice testified in 2004 was to build a robust or strategic military option in which US military forces could do more than use cruise missiles and long-range bombers. Such a strategy, Bush's advisers felt, had to be built on renewed cooperation with Pakistan. Rice testified that, 'America's Al Qaeda policy wasn't working because our Afghanistan policy wasn't working, and our Afghanistan policy wasn't working because our Pakistan policy wasn't working.'[24] The Bush team only implemented pieces of Clarke's plans, such as more aid to Uzbekistan and more power for the Treasury Department to interrupt the financial flow to terrorists. Rice felt Clarke's plans relied too much on the Northern Alliance and needed a broader strategic footing. 'We decided to take a different track,' she said.[25]

Some wondered why Bush did not fire George Tenet, the CIA Director immediately after the attacks of September 11. The answer is not simply that Bush and Tenet got along famously, and that Bush enjoyed Tenet's personal morning intelligence briefings. In retrospect, if anyone appeared to be doing his job just prior to the attacks, it was Tenet. The summer of 2001 brought 'a storm of intelligence warnings', and Tenet was getting 'nearly frantic' with worry about an imminent attack.[26] On July 3, he asked twenty foreign intelligence services to arrest a list of chief Al Qaeda suspects. A few weeks later, the US ambassador in Pakistan was instructed to tell the Taliban that it would be held responsible for any Al Qaeda attacks. The CIA station chief in Italy urged Bush to change his venue for a meeting with the Pope on July 23. Bob Woodward writes that on the morning of September 11, Tenet was visibly worried while having breakfast with former senator David Boren. When his aides interrupted him in the middle of his meal, he knew immediately what it was about. '[T]his has Bin Laden all over it,' he told Boren as he hurried out of the restaurant.[27]

With the obvious benefit of hindsight, one wonders if Bush should have started a two-prong approach in mid summer. Rice met with Clarke and Andy Card on July 5 to discuss the large amount of threat reporting. Although Clarke instructed the various agencies such as the Federal Aviation Administration and FBI to 'take additional measures to increase security and surveillance', little of this urgency seemed to have filtered down the bureaucratic ladder.[28] While the strategy review was moving through the interagency system, should the administration have taken immediate emergency measures, for example, suspend some civil liberties to try and sweep up sleeper cells, boost airport security, and give the FBI immediate legal authority to extend their wiretapping? After the attacks, Attorney General John Ashcroft immediately arrested hundreds of people, yet in the months that followed, it turned out that few of the people arrested were directly linked to the attacks. None of these measures might have actually averted the attacks, which were planned with incredible competence. Nineteen people worked for as long as five years, mostly inside the United States, to command at least four airliners to different targets. Yes, it was an intelligence failure and communications failure, but even in retrospect it is not easy to pinpoint what specific measures could have averted the catastrophe. Who could have imagined systematic 'kamikaze hijackings?'[29] While Richard Clarke was frustrated enough with the slow decision process to ask for a reassignment and, like Tenet, urged the Bush team to do more and more quickly, he also admitted that his recommendations earlier in 2001 could not have prevented the attacks. Whether the Bush administration could have done more or not, the fact remains that it never had specific threat warnings in terms of time, place or manner of attack.

With few changes, the Deputies' Committee agreed to Clarke's recommendations in June. The Principals ran out of time in July and would pick it up first thing in September. Condi Rice briefed Bush on the preliminary outcome of the strategy review during their time at Bush's ranch near Crawford in August. On August 6, Tenet added to his daily intelligence briefing a warning that Al Qaeda may use hijackings in order to 'win concessions'.[30] That Presidential Brief entitled 'Bin Laden Determined to Strike in the United States', gave Bush a CIA assessment of Al Qaeda's previous attacks and an alert that OBL had not only designs to attack US facilities abroad, but also to attack the United States at home. Yet, According to Rice, the memo did not contain 'new threat information' or change the prevailing view that the most likely attack would be abroad.[31] It also informed Bush that the FBI was conducting 'approximately 70 full field investigations throughout the United States that it considers Bin Laden related.'[32]

On September 4, the Principals' Committee with Rumsfeld, Powell, and Tenet in attendance and with Rice in the chair examined the interagency report. The rollback strategy against Al Qaeda now received its final imprint. The NSC approved a plan in which diplomatic and economic pressure would be applied first, complemented by military force, if necessary. The objective was toughened – it would not be a rollback, but a complete elimination that was sought. As soon as Bush would sign the directive, the CIA and the Pentagon were instructed to prepare immediate options for action. Bush was reading this policy draft, later called National Security Presidential Directive-9, in Florida on September 10 as part of his reading package. There would be a special briefing on it on September 12, but first he would make another school appearance in a poor neighborhood in Sarasota to press his 'Leave No Child Behind' bill, which was still stuck in the Senate.

The Decisions after September 11 and the War on Terrorism

Bush had dinner on September 10 at the Colony Beach & Tennis Resort on Longboat Key with his brother Jeb and a small group of state GOP leaders. The conversation was mainly about strategy for the November 2002 midterm elections. After his morning run the next day, Bush left the seaside resort to head into Sarasota. When the motorcade came close to the school where he would join in a second-grade phonics lesson, Andy Card took a phone call from Condoleezza Rice who alerted him that a plane had crashed into one of the towers of the World Trade Center. Bush called Rice when he got to the secure area set up for him at the Emma E. Booker Elementary School – both thought it was 'a terrible accident', perhaps caused by the pilot suffering from a heart attack.[33]

Only several minutes into the reading of *The Very Hungry Caterpillar*, Card broke protocol – about which Bush is very strict – and interrupted the President with a short message whispered in his ear. For the first time in history, cameras captured a president at the exact moment he is told that his country has been attacked. 'A second plane hit the second tower. America is under attack,' was Card's crypt message.[34] Bush's eyes, wide open, show the consternation. Ari Fleischer soon moved in behind the cameras in the back of the class room with a hastily written message for the President on a piece of cardboard: 'Don't say anything yet.'[35] Bush did not panic or leave the room, but stayed put, going through the entire phonics lesson and even making some small talk with a few kids at the end. When he got back to the secure room, he phoned Dick Cheney and Rice again, then FBI Director Robert Mueller and New York Governor George Pataki. Bush was apprised of the early information: the planes had been commercial airliners and Osama Bin Laden's network was the chief suspect. Bush then huddled with Fleischer and Dan Bartlett, Karen Hughes' deputy, to write a brief statement that he would give before canceling his address on education for later that morning, to return to Washington.

He said to his aides, 'We're at war.'[36] Given the small fragments of information he had at this point, it was a big conclusion. He made his first key decision based more on instinct and moral clarity than on anything else. Later that day, as Bush finally made his way back to Washington and as Marine One was flying past the burning Pentagon, Bush said, 'That's the 21st century war you have just witnessed.'[37]

The president's first statement on the attacks in the school library did not yet show clarity. Bush's words also lacked Karen Hughes's touch for she had stayed behind in Washington, as September 10 was her wedding anniversary and she wanted to be with her husband and son. The strain was showing and Bush inadvertently called the terrorists 'those folks'.[38] On Air Force One, he spoke with Cheney every half-hour. Cheney had been whisked away to the Presidential Emergency Operations Center, the bunker underneath the White House. Bush told Cheney to brief the congressional leadership, and by this time the Pentagon had also been hit. Secretary of Transportation Norm Mineta had ordered all aircraft in US airspace to land within twenty minutes of the second jet hitting the World Trade Center, but several were still unaccounted for, and so fighter jets were scrambled to intercept more possible hijackings.[39] Cheney asked Bush for authority to order the shooting down of commercial airliners, if it had to come to that. The President weighed the dilemma briefly: if a hijacked airliner were doomed to crash, the lesser evil would be to shoot it down and save the people on the ground, and so he responded, 'You bet.'[40] Bush was strongly advised by the Secret Service and Cheney not to return to Washington. Obviously, Air Force One would land at Andrews Air Force base and would thus be an easy target. A decision was made to land at Barksdale Air Force Base in Louisiana to unload non-essential personnel and to fuel up. Fleischer and Bartlett were working another statement, this time with Karen Hughes working on the draft from Washington.

Bush's main advisers, George Tenet, Donald Rumsfeld, Colin Powell, Dick Cheney and Condi Rice each experienced the attacks with different emotional intensity. Tenet rushed from his breakfast back to Langley and was soon working with his top staff on options and plans to present to Bush at the earliest opportunity. Rumsfeld interrupted a breakfast meeting at the Pentagon after he heard a plane had struck the World Trade Center to get an immediate intelligence briefing. During the briefing, he felt the building shake, ran to the scene, started loading the wounded on stretchers and holding IV bags. When his aides finally convinced him to leave the scene, he ordered a special command and control plane airborne while he moved with his top staff into his command bunker under the Pentagon. Rumsfeld pushed the top military brass immediately for innovative ways to strike back – at the September 11 breakfast, he had spoken about the threat of a massive attack. The 'who, what, and how' of the attack were the only surprise to him. Now he wanted to be ready, as he knew Bush would get to the point immediately. He asked his staff to determine what targets to recommend, how soon they could be hit and what allies to have on board. He wanted to present the President with a list of decisions he would need to make in the coming days. Upon hearing about the existing military plans, Rumsfeld told the Chair of the Joint Chiefs of Staff, 'Your plans are neither imaginative nor creative.'[41]

Powell's native New York had been hit and like Paul O'Neill, who was in Tokyo, he was far away on the day of the attacks. After receiving word of the attacks, Powell had to wait a whole hour before his plane was ready to leave Lima, Peru, where he had been attending a meeting of the Organization of American States. He told his counterparts 'America will deal with this tragedy in a way that brings those responsible to justice.'[42] To add to his frustration, Powell did not have secure communications for the entire seven-hour flight. When he landed, Bush's decision that 'this was war' had become policy. It was not that Powell disagreed, but he did not have the same opportunity to speak with Bush during the day, as Rice and Rumsfeld had. Cheney's mindset on an imminent threat was close to that of Rumsfeld's, while Rice had lost one of her friends as a young girl in the (terrorist) bombing of a Black church by a White supremacist group in Birmingham. Rice later said that those bombings in Birmingham 'shaped her views on the war on terrorism.'[43]

On his way to Barksdale, Bush got word of a fourth plane crashing near Pittsburgh and confirmation from Tenet that the CIA was picking up evidence of Bin Laden's involvement. The White House reported that it had received a 'specific threat' to the presidential airplane.[44] Vladimir Putin was the first foreign leader to reach Bush by phone, and told him that for the first time in post World War II history, Russia would not reciprocate America's high military alert – the tit for tat of the Cold War was over. This was exactly how Bush had wanted Putin to think.

Bush received word that Laura and his daughters were all safe. Laura had been scheduled to appear before Senator Kennedy's education committee that morning. When the threat to the Capitol Building became clear, Kennedy made personally sure that she was well taken care of until the Secret Service took her away. Bush went out of his way in early 2002 to praise Kennedy for his work on Bush's education bill and in a revealing sign of the friendship Bush tried to cultivate, he thanked Kennedy for 'providing such comfort to Laura'. In the Bush vernacular, Kennedy was not only a good senator, but also more importantly, 'a good man'. Kennedy, in turn, called Bush 'a very skilled politician'.[45]

The President told the nation at Barksdale that, 'the resolve of our great nation is being tested and we will pass the test.'[46] It was a short statement that sounded better than his words in Florida. Still, he did not look reassuring: anger, grief and determination were still battling for the upper hand. He halted several times over different words. Airborne again, Bush talked individually with his advisers, for example, telling Rumsfeld that soon the ball would be in his court. Bush needed to hold a National Security Council Meeting to engage his top national security advisers as a team on the immediate decisions. Just as urgently, he wanted to go back to the White House, as he told Cheney, 'I think I need to come back.' Hughes advised him to come back 'as soon as possible.'[47] A certain frustration was beginning to build in Bush. 'I don't want some tinhorn terrorist keeping the President of the United States out of Washington. People want to see their President and they want to see him now!'[48] But both Cheney and Card counseled him to stay away; 'Let the dust settle,' as Card told him.[49]

Hughes appeared before reporters to tell the public that the federal government continued to function effectively. Bush accepted the military recommendation that he go to Offut Air Force Base in Nebraska where there was a secure communications facility for the President to hold a teleconference with his national security team. He chaired a short meeting, learning from Tenet that Al Qaeda members were on the passenger lists of the doomed airliners and that congratulatory phone calls from other Al Qaeda operatives had been intercepted. The NSC team decided to meet again that evening to discuss military options. Bush made one decision that proved impossible to implement. 'We will fly at noon tomorrow,' he said, referring to lifting the order that grounded all airliners, but it would take three days.[50]

With the meeting over, Bush's patience was exhausted. He overruled Cheney, Card and Secret Service Director Brian Stafford, saying, 'I'm coming back.'[51] He called Laura to tell her that he was on his way – that evening and the next day several media commentators criticized Bush for staying out of Washington too long. Laura told him to 'ignore it', but that criticism hurt.[52] He knew all along that it would play badly and would not make a similar mistake again. Later in the evening of September 11, the Secret Service moved the President and the First Lady into the bunker underneath the White House for what turned out to be a false alarm. Bush overruled his security people again by deciding not to stay in the bunker that night. He never went back there again, but became determined to remain visible and in his own quarters no matter the threat to himself. When his father and Cheney pressed Bush in the next days that the issue was not just his own safety but also the stability of the Office of the Presidency, Bush and Cheney decided that the latter would go to 'an undisclosed secure location' as often as necessary, but Bush would not hide again.[53] For example, when Bush gave his address to a joint session of Congress on September 20, Cheney was in hiding: the threat to the White House was real enough and would be repeated in the coming weeks, but Bush decided not to hide. If they cut off the head, Cheney would take over. It was a gutsy decision, but it was also politically smart.

Karen Hughes and Mike Gerson had been working all afternoon on the Oval Office Address that Bush would give on the evening of September 11. Every time Bush spoke that day, his comments and demeanor improved. Many analysts have argued in the wake of the September 11 attacks that Bush found his voice that day, but in fact it took several tries and several days. Anger and raw grief slowly gave way to a sense of patience in suffering, determination in the long road ahead, and moral clarity about the outcome. Gerson and Hughes brought out the President's values amidst the vastly changed circumstances. Bush said that evening, 'These acts of mass murder were intended to frighten our nation into chaos and retreat. But they have failed,' (notice: not they will fail, but they have already failed); 'our country is strong. A great people has been moved to defend a great nation. Terrorists can shake the foundations of our biggest buildings, but they cannot touch the foundation of America.'[54]

Bush wanted to tell the American people what was ahead. He discussed with Hughes and Rice how to word his determination to take the war to the places that gave free haven to Al Qaeda. In many conversations during that day with his advisers Bush said and heard that this was bigger than a group of terrorists. It was clear to Cheney, Tenet and Rumsfeld that the US would go after more than just the immediate perpetrators: the whole network would be in the cross hairs, including the state sponsors. In fact, Bush had come close to this view in a general way in his 1999 defense speech at the Citadel. In one paragraph he described the threat of 'biological, chemical and nuclear terrorism.' He followed that description with a succinct two-sentence statement: 'Let me be clear. Our first line of defense is a simple message: Every group or *nation* must know, if they sponsor such attacks, our response will be devastating.'[55] In his Oval Office address on September 11, he said, 'We will make no distinction between the terrorists who committed these acts and those who harbor them.'

Bob Woodward wrote that Bush composed this most crucial part of his speech with only Hughes, Gerson and Rice, but that should not be construed to mean that Bush's other advisers did not know what Bush had in mind.[56] Not yet decided was what concrete action to take and which countries to tackle first. On this there was a divergence of opinion among Bush's advisers as would become clear in the next days. Meeting with his principal national security advisers just after the speech, Tenet told them, the administration had a 60-country problem. 'Let's pick them off one at a time,' was Bush's response.[57] He instructed Powell to tell Pakistan that it 'would have to choose sides'.[58]

September 11 prompted some changes in the President's daily schedule and in his decision-making process. He came a little earlier to the Oval Office (now between 6:50 and 7:00 AM) to read his briefing papers for the next forty minutes and then make a few phone calls. At 8:30, a FBI brief would now follow his eight o'clock intelligence update with Tenet, Rice and Cheney. Right after, Hughes and Rove joined Bush for the 'daily message' meeting. Rove and Hughes 'co-chaired' these meetings before September 11 in which Bartlett, Hughes' deputy and Ari Fleischer joined as well.[59] Bush continued to keep Hughes and Rove out of formal NSC meetings as he felt their presence would signal that he made foreign policy with political overtones. Of course, that did not mean Rove was not involved in strategic aspects of foreign policy decisions, or Hughes in the communication of those issues, but Bush wanted to avoid the appearance of a conflict of interest. Fleischer, whom Bush had nicknamed 'Ari-Bob' was kept out of NSC meetings so that he did not have to worry about inadvertently divulging who said what, but he was assured 'direct access to the President',[60] and saw him 'very often'.[61]

Bush set up a 'Domestic Consequences Group' under Josh Bolten that would meet each day to manage the economic response to the attacks.[62] This group devised the bailout package for the airlines and the economic stimulus package. Together with the National Security Council and the message meetings, this group formed the engine of the Bush White House in the War on Terror. The President also beefed up his briefings and meetings with the Congressional leadership: every Tuesday or Wednesday, House and Senate leaders joined Bush for breakfast in the family dining room of the White House. This close contact helped Bush and the Congress to capitalize on their bipartisan resolve in the wake of the attacks. House Speaker Dennis Hastert recommended to the President on September 13 to bring his requests for emergency spending and for the authorization of the use of force to the Congress. Bush did so, and the next day, the House and Senate authorized him to use 'all necessary and appropriate force against those nations, organizations and persons he determines ...'[63] Congress also authorized $20 billion for homeland security and the military and another $20 billion for emergency aid to New York.

The biggest change in Bush's decision-making scheme was that he now took the helm of the key National Security Council meetings. Almost every day, between the attacks and the launch of Operation Enduring Freedom on October 7, the NSC met at 9:30 in the morning. When matters were unresolved, Rice often called another meeting in the afternoon with only the Principals in order to be better prepared for the next morning. Meanwhile, the regular interaction among the Deputies increased. Powell's deputy, Richard Armitage, estimated that he was in touch with Hadley and Wolfowitz '20 times a day'.[64] In between NSC meetings, Powell, Rice, Rumsfeld and Cheney often talked without their deputies.

The NSC met every day that week after September 11 and often twice a day. On September 12 Attorney General John Ashcroft laid out a plan to shift his department's focus from prosecution to prevention in the fight against terrorists.

After Tenet found Al Qaeda's involvement conclusive, it was decided to put maximum pressure on Pakistan and to put an ultimatum to the Taliban to hand over Osama Bin Laden and dismantle his network in that country. The head of Pakistan's intelligence service happened to be in Washington and Armitage told him later that day that Musharraf would be 'with us or against us'. When General Mahmoud Ahmad demurred, Armitage 'leapt up from his desk', and 'growled that history starts today'.[65] 'We gave them a black and white choice,' Armitage later recalled, and 'one day to think about it.'[66] That same day, Bush agreed with Rove and Hughes to deliver an address to a joint session of Congress, once he had a clear view of what his policy would be. Tenet briefed Bush the next day on what the CIA could do – the Taliban and Al Qaeda were 'joined at the hip' in Tenet's view, and a coalition of CIA agents, Special Forces and the Northern Alliance could bring decisive pressure on the Taliban.[67] Rumsfeld, to his chagrin, had no concrete military plans ready to present, but Bush was not in a hurry. He had decided to have a memorial service in the National Cathedral on September 14 and had asked Hughes and Laura to organize it. Afterward he wanted to visit Ground Zero and spend time with the grieving families who had huddled in the Jacob K. Javits Convention Center. He decided that the NSC would meet all day on Saturday, September 15 at Camp David.

The President's speech in the National Cathedral again surprised many people for its eloquent determination – it did not become an emotional puddle or a war cry. Powell had worried about the former and had advised his boss to take out every word that might cause him to break down, but Bush assured him he would be okay. He wanted it to be a day of prayer and remembrance. He spoke with personal humility. Many people had interpreted Bush's plain talk and folksy manner before the attacks as swagger and brashness and they would do so again in 2002 and after, but at this time the President received a warm audience. Neither Bush nor Laura ever saw his manner in that way, to them it was more their Midland, Texas, style of directness. Laura said that her husband's true image had never 'resonated' before September 11.[68] Bush spoke with profound admiration and almost personal loss about the people who had been killed. Of the rescuers he said, 'the ones whom death found running up the stairs and into the fires to help others.'[69]

Bush spoke after a string of 'faith leaders'. He invited several religious speakers to the National Cathedral service, including his Methodist preacher from Austin, a Roman Catholic Cardinal, a Jewish Rabbi, an Islamic cleric, and finally Billy Graham. It was a deliberate decision to have Islam present alongside Christianity and Judaism. Because Bush had a clear value system in place before the attacks, he was never tempted to lash out at Muslims in general or cast a suspicious eye toward that religion.

Bush's outreach to the Islamic faith in the wake of September 11 came as a result of an instinctive decision he made. Just as he did not need any 'legal briefings' to tell him that this was 'war', he needed no advice on how to deal with the fact that these terrorists had all been radical militant Muslims.[70] On September 17, Bush visited the Islamic Center in Washington and exclaimed that the terrorists had 'hijacked the Muslim religion'.[71] In his September 20 speech to the Congress, Bush underlined that this would not be a 'war of civilizations' and that Islam was one of the great religions of peace. At the United Nations on November 10 he spoke of the

'God of Isaac and Ishmael'.[72] On September 26, Bush met with Muslim leaders from around the country at the White House. The President assured Muslims in America that his war was not against them.

Some questioned whether Islam was a religion of peace. David Frum, a Jewish-Canadian speechwriter on the President's staff, noted in his memoir that Islamic leaders in America had indeed been reluctant and sporadic in their condemnation of the terrorists. None of this wavered Bush's determination as President to tighten the solidarity among the 'great faiths' in the aftermath of the attacks. Some conservative Christians were shocked at the extent to which he treated Islam as a moral equal. Some Liberals were amazed at Bush's 'Islamophilia'.[73] They had assumed Bush would disdain Muslims and had been ready to pounce on him, but his inclusiveness was pretty watertight. It also did not escape Bush's attention that *not* to separate between a few radicals and the entire Muslim religion would guarantee a 'clash of civilizations.'

The President also used his National Cathedral Address to frame the War on Terror in a larger moral context. Again, his personal faith provided a clear reference. He said, 'Just three days removed from these events, Americans do not yet have the distance of history. But our responsibility to history is already clear: to answer these attacks and rid the world of *evil*.'[74] Just before his first cabinet meeting after the attacks, Bush had said, 'In the monumental struggle between good and evil, good will prevail,' placing the conflict squarely as a contest between good and evil. Frum writes that Bush would often quote Romans 12:21 to staff members in the days after the attack, saying, 'Be not overcome of evil, but overcome evil with good.'

Bush made several early decisions rather spontaneously. On the morning of September 11, he knew he was at war. He then made the crucial move to embrace Islam, rather than implicate it. Now he framed the fight not as a conflict between competing interests or perspectives, but as a struggle between absolutes – He would end up calling Osama Bin Laden, the 'Evildoer'. He overstated it once, when on his return from Camp David on September 16, he called the war 'a crusade'.[75] He did not mean a religious war, but he understood it was the wrong term and never repeated it.

Ronald Reagan had called the Soviet Union the 'Evil Empire' and had been ridiculed for it, but he believed this and held onto it until the evil empire was no more. Early in the 2000 primary campaign, George Schultz had said that this young man (Bush) would become another Ronald Reagan. Rice explained later that by framing the conflict in these moral and absolute terms, Bush early on resolved the question of what would be the objectives of US policy. He set the big vision for his team, as Reagan had done in his first term – now what remained was how to go about winning the war against evil.

Before turning to the final round in his string of NSC meetings, Bush wanted to see Ground Zero for himself and to spend about a half-hour with the bereaved families. On September 13, he had conducted a public conference call with Governor Pataki and Mayor Rudolph Giuliani. He told them he would visit with them the next day, after the Cathedral ceremony. Bush's eyes filled with tears when he talked with reporters at the end of that phone call, telling them 'he was a loving guy'.[76]

The President's visit to the smoking rubble was as unusual an event in the Bush administration as imaginable. Unusual in the sense that it was completely unstaged and unscripted – there was no preparation as Bush told Pataki and Giuliani that he was coming the next day, and there was minimal advance preparation. Besides walking around a little with Pataki and Giuliani, there was nothing planned for him. There was no speech, no notes, no special visuals and no pre-planned people to meet. Nothing. Yet, Rove and Hughes knew the cameras would be all around Bush. It is a puzzle why they left this event so open-ended, but most likely Bush did not want the attention to be on him.

So here was Bush walking around Ground Zero and some of the rescue workers, firefighters and ironworkers yelling at him, 'Go get them George'. A retired firefighter, named Bob Beckwith, who scammed his way into Ground Zero to help, was watching from a crushed fire engine. Bush was handed a bullhorn and climbed on the wreck beside Beckwith. Rove called Beckwith to come down but Bush told him to stay and then the President put his arm around him. There was a lot of shouting around him ('USA! USA! ...') and when Bush tried to say something he was easily drowned out. He tried again. 'Can't hear you,' the crowd shouted. Pumped by now, Bush responded with what will probably be his most memorable lines as President: 'I can hear you. The rest of the world hears you, and the people who knocked these buildings down will hear all of us soon!'[77] The roar of approval, *Washington Times* reporter Bill Sammon wrote, was like a 'thunderous primal scream'.[78]

Whatever communication problem Bush had before September 11 was now completely wiped out. He had connected with the people in a spontaneous event and had gotten through to their hearts. His eloquent moral clarity in the Cathedral speech was now matched by this 'baring' of Bush, the human being, as angry as the common man. Since his Oval Office address, the President had shown full control in his formal speeches, he had cried in public, and now he had shouted in anger. American voters already liked Bush as a person before September 11, but now they flocked behind him with approval ratings unprecedented in history. Unplanned and unanticipated, he had set the stage for a national audience for his September 20 speech in Congress – they would listen to him as never before. Bush spent two hours with some 200 family members of the victims and felt 'whipped' when he helicoptered to Camp David.[79]

The next day, Bush was most impressed with Tenet's presentation in the morning session. Tenet wanted the gloves off, he was going to 'rent' every warlord necessary in Afghanistan. Back in 1999, while he was still working for Clinton, Tenet had already begun building up human intelligence in Afghanistan and now he wanted the freedom to conduct covert lethal action. His plan was to strengthen the Northern Alliance (of Uzbeks and Tajiks) who had kept a toehold in Northern Afghanistan against the Taliban regime; his CIA teams would prepare the ground for US Special Operations Forces to join in later. Bush said, 'great job'.[80] As Senator Richard Shelby commented later, the 'CIA has been given the go-ahead to untie their hands and take the shackles off.'[81] Tenet's triad – CIA, Northern Alliance and Special Forces – would become the backbone of Operation Enduring Freedom. Tenet took the initiative as Rumsfeld was still working on better, 'conventional' military plans with the Special Operations Forces. Some Green Berets and SEALs put on CIA hats to become 'covert warriors'.[82] Robert Mueller, the new FBI Director had comparatively little to add to the discussion – the CIA became the lead agency in the first phase of the war. In a few days, Bush had turned the Agency upside down.

There was broad agreement that Powell would present an ultimatum to the Taliban to deliver Osama Bin Laden and dismantle his network. President Musharraf of Pakistan had agreed to begin a new relationship with America, but he also had conditions. Powell would negotiate with him, general-to-general. Bush was prepared to lift the economic sanctions from both Pakistan and India – in place since their recent nuclear weapons' tests – and to reschedule part of Pakistan's debt. He put tremendous pressure on Pakistan not only to use its airspace and ground facilities, but to break off ties with the Taliban, close the border and to start unraveling the fundamentalist leaning Intelligence Service. He further demanded that restrictions be put on the Madrasses, the religious schools in Pakistan that were a breeding ground for militant extremists.

Musharraf tried to bring the Taliban to their senses, but his missions to Kabul and Kandahar were rebuffed by Mullah Omar and the council of Islamic clerics who went no further than 'recommending' Bin Laden leave the country. In short order, Musharraf wrought one of the biggest turnarounds in Pakistan's history, taking a big domestic risk by moving aggressively to cooperate with the Bush administration. Repeated assassinations attempts on him in 2003 and 2004 revealed how big a risk he took. On November 10, Musharraf met with Bush just prior to his address to the United Nations. Bush told him, 'You have made the right choice,' but Musharraf was worried; would the United States 'abandon' Pakistan after the war was over? Bush turned his 'eye contact theory of diplomacy' on himself.[83] 'Tell the people I looked you in the eye and told you we wouldn't do that.'[84] The President kept his word and when British and American intelligence exposed the nuclear export industry coming out of Pakistan in 2004, Bush did not drop his friend.

A big question before Bush and his advisers that day at Camp David was whether to confine the immediate military activities to the Taliban or whether to open a second front in the War on Terror. There was a powerful majority among the President's Principals and Deputies to take out Saddam Hussein's regime sooner or later. Paul Wolfowitz was one of the advocates for doing it now. On September 13, Wolfowitz had taken the Oval Office Address to mean, 'End states that sponsor terrorism.'[85] Bush overheard 'Wolfie' discussing Iraq with others during a break in the Camp David session and encouraged him to put it on the table, but Powell made a powerful counter argument. 'Focus on the provocation,' he said.[86] There was no evidence that Iraq was behind the attacks; there were possible links to Iraq in the 1993 World Trade Center bombing and plenty of suspicion, but nothing concrete. Our allies will see it as 'bait and switch,' Powell argued.[87] International support was rock solid behind Bush but would fall to pieces if he used September 11 as a *causus belli* for Iraq. Rumsfeld like Wolfowitz favored the overall strategy of removing Saddam, but did not press it as an urgent course of action. General Shelton had no concrete plans for taking out the Taliban, let alone the much stronger Iraqi regime. Cheney, another hawk on Iraq, also agreed the time was not right. Even Andy Card joined in, questioning the benefit of going after Iraq at this point.

The President had simply 'listened'.[88] 'I am going to think about it,' he said, 'and I will let you know what I have decided.'[89] After coming back to the White House, on September 16, Bush called Rice in to give her his decision.[90] He had written up a point-by-point 'War Plan'[91] and gave his full endorsement of Tenet's role for the CIA. He approved Ashcroft's plan to write a preemptive strategy for domestic surveillance and he wanted the Pentagon to come in behind the CIA to 'hit with all military options'. He ordered a specific ultimatum to the Taliban: Turn over Osama Bin Laden 'and his Al Qaeda or you will suffer the consequences.' He wanted a stabilization plan for Pakistan that included economic aid.[92] On Iraq, Bush concluded, now was not the time, 'We need to stay focused,' he said.[93]

On September 17, Bush reviewed his decision with the full NSC. Bush liked Wolfie's big strategy. He knew about his ideas of removing the threat of Saddam Hussein and lessening the American dependence on Saudi Arabia, followed by a change in the Palestinian leadership and a decisive peace between Israel and the Palestinians, but for now he took the Iraq option off the table. 'We have to be patient about Iraq,' he said.[94] This did not mean that Bush felt he could only do things that would keep a 'big coalition' behind him.[95] In a prophetic comment, Bush remarked on September 19, 'two years from now only the Brits may be with us.'[96] Before September 11 many critics at home and in Europe called Bush's foreign policy 'unnerving unilateralism',[97] while after the attacks, some thought he had suddenly converted to 'multilateralism'. In fact Bush is neither: His idea of international cooperation is a coalition of like-minded states in pursuit of specific values and interests – September 11 did not change that view. Rumsfeld turned the concept into one of his famous 'Rumsfeld Rules': 'The mission must determine the coalition, and the coalition must not determine the mission.'[98]

Despite the tightly loyal decision team, word leaked out that there was a policy conflict on whether or not to attack Iraq. It inevitably pitched Powell against Rumsfeld and Wolfowitz. Unnamed 'people' were quoted as saying that Powell was 'standing on the brakes'.[99] Word about the internal debate set off renewed speculation about Powell's 'isolation' within the administration. On September 15, Powell was asked what he made of Wolfowitz's comment about 'ending states'. He responded, 'we're ending terrorism, let's leave it at that,' but Powell did not appear isolated. In fact, his observation that 'we argue, but we almost always find the answer,' was borne out.[100] More intriguing than the 'Powell vs. the rest' story is the question whether Bush, Cheney, Rumsfeld and Powell implicitly understood that Iraq would be somewhere in phase two. About Iraq, Powell himself said 'not right away,' Cheney said 'at some point,' and Bush said 'first things first.'[101]

The President upgraded a low-key announcement planned by the Treasury Department that would freeze the financial assets of some 27 terrorist groups to a Rose Garden appearance by himself. 'Today we have launched a strike on the financial foundation of the global terror network,' Bush announced.[102] Treasury got the hint and created a 'war room', which by the end of November led to a total of nearly 150 entities whose assets were frozen.[103] He also told his National Security team that the United States must be dropping humanitarian aid packages to the displaced Afghans the same day bombing would begin. Bush initiated a lot of the early actions, pushing his staff into a new war mentality, calling and receiving foreign leaders at a good pace. French President Jacques Chirac paid a visit on September 18, the same day the Taliban rebuffed Bush's ultimatum. The French President expressed 'total solidarity' with the United States but doubted that 'war' was the right word.[104] Either he was not well briefed about the tremendous transition that had taken place in the White House since September 11 or he wanted simply to restrain American foreign policy from going in that direction.

Britain's Prime Minister Tony Blair, with whom Bush had forged a good relationship right from the start, took the opposite tack. He threw his full support behind the War on Terror. Bush told his advisers to make sure that the Brits would play a role. This was no problem for Tenet or Rumsfeld as British intelligence had worked closely with the Northern Alliance and the UK's Special Air Services were the type of Special Forces the US military could use. Blair and Bush talked often by phone, and the former found out that Bush would confide in him *and* listen to him if there was complete mutual trust and no daylight between them in public.

Bush singled out Blair as America's premier ally in his September 20 address to Congress. At Bush's direction, Gerson and Hughes had divided the speech into three simple questions: 'who attacked our country, why do they hate us, and how will we fight and win this war.' Bush made it 'a primer on terrorism'.[105] He exceeded even the high expectations with a speech that was well rounded, easy to understand and profoundly eloquent. Its most memorable line was, 'Whether we bring our enemies to justice or bring justice to our enemies, justice will be done.'[106] Bush neither stumbled nor swaggered. Newt Gingrich once said that this president was not a good 'practice athlete', but a 'great game athlete'.[107] He hit a home run that evening – Frum wrote that Bush's oratory in the ten days after September 11 'transformed his leadership'.[108] More accurately, his oratory transformed how the world perceived his leadership.

In plain words he laid out the atrocities of Al Qaeda and the Taliban, with a clear ultimatum for the Taliban. There was an admonition not to lash out against Muslims or American Arabs. 'Those who commit evil in the name of Allah, blaspheme the name of Allah,' Bush said. In the section 'why do they hate us,' he packed a spirited defense of the heart and soul of American democracy, and in the war that lies ahead, the President gave a frank assessment that it would be a lengthy campaign. The world sensed the newfound determination when he said, 'Every nation now has a decision to make. Either you are with us, or you are with the terrorists.' He did not have traditional allies in mind when he said this, as he assumed they were with him already; he meant such states as Pakistan and Saudi Arabia, which had been somewhere in the middle. Bush announced a new Office of Homeland Security. Only the day before had he asked his long-time friend Tom Ridge, the governor of Pennsylvania to be its first director. There was near consensus that the forty-odd agencies and departments involved in homeland defense needed to work better together and Bush wanted someone he could trust and that was close to him to start the process.

The President's personal mooring in faith and providence came out in the end of the speech without any sense of religious arrogance. 'Freedom and fear, justice and cruelty have always been at war,' Bush said, 'and we know that God is not neutral between them.' He would draw upon that serenity in talks to come. At the Pentagon on October 11 he said 'great resolve' had come from the 'great sorrow' experienced. In Atlanta on November 8, he noted, 'we have learned that out of evil can come great good.'[109]

In three weeks, the Bush presidency had been transformed from a domestic focus to a global war on terror. The early intuitive decisions and the immediate moral clarity of his vision earned him the reputation of a leader. He filled in the communication gap that many argued his presidency was lacking and his strong Secretaries were working in tandem on his policy. White House confidants such as Cheney, Card, Rove, Hughes and increasingly Condi Rice tried to make sure that the entire administration moved with the President's rhythm. His patience to get all the pieces in place before attacking the Taliban gained him wide respect, as the *Economist* exclaimed on September 24, 'A leader is born.'[110] The American analyst of the presidency, Fred Greenstein said, 'you really do see him growing.'[111] There was a large amount of writing how September 11 completely transformed Bush from a 'bumbling lightweight' into a statesman, but these 'growth in office' and 'sudden transformation' theories have little to back them up. Howard Fineman and Martha Brandt – by no means fans or supporters of Bush – got it right when they concluded that they had underestimated him. 'Bush,' they wrote, 'is who he was, essentially the same guy who organized the stickball league at Andover.'[112]

There is no evidence that September 11 'overwhelmed' Bush.[113] Unlike Jimmy Carter whose personal schedule was thrown off by the hostage-taking incident in 1979, and who seemed consumed by it, Bush did not markedly change his habits or his style. He kept jogging, going to bed early, and bantering with his aides. Close observers commented that he looked more assured and spoke with more crispness. 'You are just paying more attention,' Rove joked in response to press inquiries.[114]

In fact, Bush was more focused and more intense. He had shown before September 11 that he was a formidable player in domestic politics and he was respected in Congress because of his tax cut victory and his flexibility towards the education bill, but by August, the rest of his agenda had run thin. The President's premier proposals, such as prescription drug benefits for the elderly and social security reform, looked like they would be long drawn-out battles, while the energy bill was completely stuck. In January 2001, Bush had insisted on a clear eight-month plan; in December, Rove said that Bush had realized during the summer that his agenda was 'not adequate for 2002.'[115] Policymaking committees in the White House were busy cooking up new issues to launch in the fall and preparing a major foreign policy speech. He was widely criticized by the Democrats at home and the European Press for being too militaristic and unilateralist.

Thus, September 11 did not so much transform Bush as give him a new challenge and a new lease on the presidency. The thesis that 9/11 'transformed' Bush makes little sense, for if he had to accumulate all his skills and talents in the few days after September 11, he would have failed miserably. Instead, when faced with his first massive national security crisis, he drew on all the personal, managerial and political strengths and assets that he had accumulated over a long time. Presidential scholar, Hugh Heclo, recognized that Bush had a firm 'political ethos' in place before the crisis, which guided him through.[116] September 11 showed an internal fortitude and a managerial preparedness that partisan politics had shrouded. In the words of Peggy Noonan, September 11 'blew the blur away'.[117]

Laura's Role Revealed

September 11 also shed light on the critical role Laura Bush plays in providing Bush with emotional stability. Both Bush and his father have known for a long time that their wives are more popular than they, yet, Laura like Barbara before her, did not look for the limelight. Frank Bruni of the *New York Times* learned that Laura is 'guarded in the extreme';[118] in multiple interviews over the years, she indicated that she was not Bush's 'adviser' and that politics did not consume her.[119] After a quiet career as a teacher and librarian, she married into the intensely political family. Her teaching gave way to being a wife and mother and that in turn merged into the political demands of the Bush family. In her first year of teaching, she was 'shocked' to see that most students in her third grade class could not read – she later said that teaching in a minority school, 'opened my eyes'.[120] Early reading skills have been Laura's theme ever since, and inevitably, that rubbed off on her husband's education agenda. She launched various reading and literature initiatives from the Governor's Mansion and also from the White House, including 'Experience Corps', which brings retired teachers back to teach disadvantaged children.

Laura meant to champion such causes with the more traditional low profile of the First Lady. She has always been a traditional wife, but insisted that this goes alongside being a 'contemporary woman'.[121] Some immediately called her the 'anti-Hillary'.[122] She moved the First Lady's offices back from the policy-centered West Wing to the conventional East Wing. Still, Laura has a strong and loyal Texan staff that is in tune with the goings on of the administration.

Unlike Nancy Reagan and Hillary Clinton, Laura does not have a public relations problem. She appears completely genuine; strong, quiet, and thoughtful. If she has strong independent interests and views from her husband, as Ann Gerhart argues, she keeps them well hidden.[123] It is easy to see that her chief influence at home is to 'bring it down a notch'.[124] 'She keeps me humble,' Bush acknowledged.[125] Laura does look out for Bush's public perception, watching how the media depicts him. It obviously bothered her that the Gore campaign portrayed Bush as an intellectual lightweight, stumbling over every speech and that it had traction with the media, and became folklore around the world in 2001. 'He says the wrong words about the same amount of time that probably everybody says the wrong words,' Laura stated somewhat defensively in an interview in March 2001.[126] She also had her hands full in 2001 with her twin daughters, Jenna and Barbara. Between the two of them they were caught three times trying to buy alcohol while under age – a British newspaper jokingly called them 'Jenna & Tonic'.[127] Bush had issued a subtle threat to the media that unlike him and Laura, they could not treat the twins as 'fair game'. The vast majority of the media respected Bush's position, but the twins did make it tempting – these were two chips off the old block.

While consoling the mourning families near Ground Zero on September 14, Bush told one group that Laura was a great comfort to him. 'She's got a war mentality,' he told them.[128] She visited the injured and spoke at the memorial for the victims of the plane that went down in Pennsylvania and came to be seen as a type of 'First Comforter'.[129] In an interview a few months later, she realized that since September 11, 'I've had the opportunity, maybe I should say responsibility to be steady for our country and for my husband.'[130] 'Steady for her husband,' was a role the American public strongly endorsed – not only did Bush have a wise father to counsel him as well as brothers, a sister and friends to relax with, but he also had a strong wife to keep him even keeled.

Operation Enduring Freedom

The CIA was on the ground in Afghanistan within hours from Bush's announcement of his war plans to his national security team on September 17. The military plan that emerged would entail strategic bombing followed by precision-guided bombing supporting the Special Operation Forces who worked directly with the Northern Alliance. There would be no heavy contingent of regular troops entering Afghanistan for fear of 'Americanizing' the war, with the exception of troops from the 10th Mountain Division in the north and a few thousand Marines in the south. Rumsfeld assured Bush that a large number of US regular troops would not be needed. Besides Pakistan, Rumsfeld needed basing facilities and logistical help from Uzbekistan and Tajikistan. Getting permission and then building the facilities took time. While Bush worked the phone, Powell and Armitage traveled from capital to capital. Putin's assistance proved essential as he gave the two 'Stans' the nod of approval to allow American troops on their soil. Putin also began supplying the Northern Alliance with equipment.

The President kept prodding when the military would be ready, as he was committed to not start unless they were fully ready. It required patience. This MBA president with a special liking for human organization had set up his White House in accord with the best principles of CEO management. He set a clear vision, ran a disciplined White House, delegated responsibility and saw results, but when it came to preparing for Operation Enduring Freedom and at times during the war, Bush was tempted to micro-manage a few things. Card had to slow him down, 'You have to let the generals win,' he said. Rice likewise told Bush on October 16 that he was not the 'quarterback' in this operation – that was General Tommy Franks. 'The President,' she said, 'is the coach.'[131] On October 2, Rumsfeld left for Saudi Arabia, Qatar, Oman, the United Arab Emirates and Uzbekistan to speed up basing decisions. On October 5, Bush asked the new Chairman of the Joint Chiefs, Richard Meyers, 'is Tommy Franks ready to go?' On the 6th, Bush questioned every member of his National Security Council, 'are you confident with the plan you developed?'[132] 'We are ready,' Rumsfeld responded.[133]

On October 7, from the Roosevelt Treaty Room, the President announced the launch of Operation Enduring Freedom. On September 14, Bush had said in his National Cathedral speech, 'War has been waged against us by stealth and deceit and murder. This nation is peaceful, but fierce when stirred to anger. This conflict was begun on the timing and terms of others. It will end in a way, and at an hour, of our choosing.'[134] For three weeks there had been a build up of expectations. What will Bush do? Now Bush said, 'We will win this conflict by the patient accumulation of successes rather than by a quick military victory.'[135] Rumsfeld had written in the *New York Times*, 'forget about "exit strategies"; we're looking at a sustained engagement that carries no deadlines.'[136] Bush's 'patience' would soon be tested again as the Air Force ran out of targets to bomb, while the ground operations remained invisible to the public and the Northern Alliance moved very cautiously toward Taliban lines of defense.

Operation Enduring Freedom was off to a quick start, with the Americans establishing air supremacy over Afghanistan almost immediately and within three days, the Air Force ran out of strategic targets. At the end of the war, it would become known that some 110 CIA officers and 300 Special Operations Forces did essentially all the ground operations, but these were invisible to the press, which had no permission to join US forces in combat. The Taliban used the media vacuum to claim that many humanitarian targets were being hit, such as a Red Cross supply depot, which later turned out to be a Taliban arms cache.

It appears that Bush had not thought enough about what would become of Afghanistan after the Taliban and Al Qaeda had been defeated, but had focused entirely on Operation Enduring Freedom. He was reluctant, as were Cheney and Rumsfeld, to commit American troops to nation building duties. The same gap in thinking would occur a year or so later in Iraq, yet it became clear early on that Musharraf could not settle for the Northern Alliance taking over Kabul. The majority of the people in Afghanistan and border areas of Pakistan were Pashtun (though with many internal differences), and if the Tajiks and Uzbeks would take control, a bitter civil war may ensue yet again. In the week of October 11, the President 'came around' to the idea of a broad-based new Afghan government and a UN role in Kabul.[137] Bush agreed that Powell should lay the groundwork for bringing the factions together in a type of national unity coalition. Powell appointed Richard Haass as his Special Assistant for Afghanistan. The 86 year old Afghan king, Mohammed Zadhir Shah was contacted to lend his support to a council of elders who would choose a unity government. The Bush administration needed a non-Taliban Pashtun who could form a moderate leadership. On October 26, one such leader, Abdul Haq, infiltrated into Afghanistan to begin this work. The Taliban, however, caught him almost immediately and executed him.

Before massive defections decimated their ranks, Taliban and Al Qaeda forces in Afghanistan were estimated at some 50,000.[138] The smaller forces of the Northern Alliance and of General Abdul Dostam were in no hurry to throw themselves into the fray. On October 14, a spokesman for the Northern Alliance said their forces would not be ready for another month. This did not go over well with the war planners in Washington. Perhaps the Northern Alliance expected regular US forces to join them soon, but the Pentagon's plan – which Rumsfeld and Wolfowitz devised with Tommy Franks – centered on Special Forces using sophisticated target designators in order to direct precision-guided munitions. General Franks spoke 'virtually daily' with his Special Operations Commander General Charles Holland.[139] The idea was to replace traditional artillery with instant and highly accurate air power, with the only regular troops in that plan coming from the Northern Alliance. It was not until the week of October 15 that Special Forces began to take over ground operations from the CIA, changing Operation Enduring Freedom from 'mostly covert to mostly military.'[140] As the Northern Alliance saw these forces putting real pressure on Taliban lines, they moved in alongside them, yet, the whole operation seemed to slow down, even stumble.

The press was coming at the Bush team in full force in late October and early November. William Kristol called Operation Enduring Freedom, 'a failed plan', while the tough-minded realist commentator, Charles Krauthammer, called the Bush operation 'half measures'.[141] Jacob Heilbrunn from the *Los Angeles Times* wrote that the President had 'bungled the campaign'[142] and R.W. Apple called it 'a quagmire, another Vietnam.'[143] Rumsfeld, whom the *New York Times* thought had 'cratered' at the Pentagon in early September, would later tease reporters with the word 'quagmire'.[144]

Several Bush advisers did worry about the strategy, and it was reported that Rumsfeld was working on a 50,000 troop contingency plan. Rice lived up to her job as guardian of the President's decision-making process. She alerted Bush to the 'handwringing' and urged him to put the existing strategy on the table for review. They all knew that once committed, Bush was not for second-guessing, but Rice wanted him to give a clear signal to his Secretaries one way or another. She did not want to exclude the possibility of overturning an earlier decision. The President found that they all still felt that the plan was sound, so at the NSC meeting of October 26, Bush rallied them. 'Be steady, don't let the press panic us,'[145] he said and, 'be patient people, it's going to work.'[146] He realized he was losing the public relations war, but he refused to throw out the agreed strategy merely to be seen to be doing something. That was a tough call. He had to have complete trust in Rumsfeld and Franks to stay the course. The President did order more humanitarian aid to the people of Afghanistan, totaling nearly $450 million by the start of November.[147]

After the low point in the end of October, the 'fog of war' lifted quickly. By November 5, the Northern Alliance was forcing the Taliban into defensive lines and this allowed the Special Forces in conjunction with the Air Force to direct the precision-guided bombs to Taliban positions. On November 9, the northern city of Mazar-i-Sharif was captured and by November 11, Special Forces and the Northern Alliance were approaching Kabul. Bush refused to pause for Ramadan, the Muslim holy month – a decision Rice defended by stating that most Muslim nations at war also did not pause and, more pertinently, 'we can't afford to have a pause.'[148] Blanket bombings and huge bombs, the so-called 'daisy cutters,' were wreaking havoc on the Taliban defenses. The much-diminished loyal Taliban and Arab forces now all headed for Kandahar, but Rumsfeld was ready for immediate pressure there. The Marines opened a base near that city and on December 7, Kandahar fell and the Taliban was defeated.

However, Mullah Omar and Osama Bin Laden escaped, robbing Bush of a public relations victory. Some felt the light footprint of American soldiers was the main reason why these leaders slipped through allied lines. On September 17, Bush had commented outside the Pentagon that he wanted Bin Laden 'dead or alive', but by late October, the Administration began to downplay his capture.[149]

With or without the capture of Bin Laden, the defeat of the Taliban was a major victory in the war on terror. When the people of Kabul celebrated their liberation, the President's moral campaign against the Taliban was vindicated. Laura took over one of Bush's radio addresses in November and became the administration's spokesperson for the plight of Afghan women. Putting together a stable government in Kabul was a complicated balancing act – United States forces rescued Hamid Karzai from the Taliban on November 2 and nearly a month later he escaped a friendly fire incident that killed several soldiers around him. He became the moderate Pashtun behind whom all factions eventually united. The European allies stepped forward with humanitarian and military aid and on December 20, the United Nations Security Council authorized the International Security Assistance Force for Kabul. The first 1,500 British troops arrived ten days later. Ultimately, ISAF would be under Tommy Franks' command, looking after

Kabul and governmental stability – always a tricky proposition in this warlord-ridden nation – while US and other Special Forces continued the hunt for Al Qaeda in the Tora Bora Mountains.

Operation Enduring Freedom was, by most counts, a success for the Bush administration. The Taliban were disposed of and Al Qaeda's network in Afghanistan was essentially dismantled, even though Osama Bin Laden's trail had gone cold. American and allied casualties had remained very low and the whole campaign affirmed Bush's key managerial principles: he set a clear goal, took his time to get the right strategy and then stuck with it regardless of the backseat drivers. While security in Kabul, remained precarious, the United States, with a wide coalition of allies, did make the conditions in Afghanistan better. A widely feared famine was averted and many refugees soon began to return. As the international security force tried to protect the new government of Karzai, American forces concentrated on 'hunting' Al Qaeda in the east of the country. What Bush could not have done with one military campaign was to remake Afghanistan's political culture – it was a fractious country before Operation Enduring Freedom and it remained so afterward. The President also could not do much to speed up economic aid, even though the United States provided 'the lion's share of money for rebuilding.'[150] Many other countries pledged economic assistance, but were slow in delivering. Perhaps even more significant in the long run than Afghanistan's stability was how Bush's enormous pressure on Pakistan led to Musharraf's radical turn and prevented what the *Economist* called the 'Talibanization' of Pakistan.[151] He continued the pressure on Musharraf after Pakistani terrorist groups killed 14 people in New Delhi on December 13, 2001.

The War on Terror and the International Coalition

There had been a worldwide outpouring of sympathy for what befell the United States on September 11. In the ensuing days, individual leaders and international organizations lined up to show their solidarity in an unprecedented manner. For the first time in history, the NATO alliance invoked its common defense clause, while the United Nations General Assembly and Security Council approved resolutions condemning the attacks. Australia's Prime Minister John Howard said the defense clause of the ANZUS Treaty would be used and instructed Australian forces to cooperate with American forces wherever needed. The Organization of American States invoked its reciprocal assistance clause and the European Union issued a statement of 'total solidarity'. The 56 nation Organization of the Islamic Conference condemned Al Qaeda and the attacks and even the Pope said that America could act in self-defense. The only national leader who did not join in was Saddam Hussein, who stated on September 12 that 'America was reaping the thorns of its foreign policy.'[152]

Hidden beneath the international solidarity lurked a good deal of suspicion about what the President meant by his 'war on terror.' In Western Europe, where he had had such a rough start, some leaders expressed more worry about what Bush would do than about what had been done to the United States. The French Premier Lionel Jospin said on September 13 that the US response should be 'reasonable', and his

Dutch counterpart asked for a 'dignified reaction', which prompted a State Department request for a 'clarification' on the Dutch position.[153] Wim Kok, then Dutch Prime Minister, quickly pulled in line. The German Defense Minister said, 'We do not face a war'. The European Union added to its 'total solidarity' that the US 'riposte' should be 'proportional'.[154]

The halting attitude of some in Europe was not lost on the White House. At the same time, most Europeans were suspicious of the President's usage of 'evil.' They also did not like his September 20 reference to every nation being either with or against America. Though the attacks brought emotional unity, they did not bring either a long-term rapprochement or a strategic re-alignment between Bush and the European continent. To be sure, France, Germany and all European states firmly supported the US War on Terror against Al Qaeda and the Taliban. The Security Council of the UN passed resolution 1373 on September 28. In this resolution, nations were not only 'required' to act against terrorists' movements, financing and operations, but they also agreed to report every 90 days to a 15 member compliance group with the UK in the chair.[155]

It did not help Bush and Europe that there simply was not much NATO could do. The United States was going to conduct a highly unusual campaign in Afghanistan for which Europeans (except Britain) and Canadians did not have the military wherewithal to participate. For over ten years, the United States had urged them to re-invest in modern military forces, but except for the UK and to some extent France, most NATO members had sidestepped that demand. Now Europe did not have the precision-guided munitions, the high-tech air power, nor the necessary logistics and intelligence to be a full partner. At the same time, the Pentagon was not really looking for a hands-on role for NATO, as its experience with NATO's command structure in the war in Kosovo in 1999 had been negative. The United States was acting in self-defense and did not want allied participation in determining what it could or could not bomb. In the end, NATO, and especially Germany, provided important base and logistical support. NATO also sent five of its AWAC airplanes to help patrol the skies over North America. September 11 did force more NATO reform as it finally settled the debate inside NATO whether the organization should act militarily outside the geographic space of Europe. When the Taliban fell, the United Nations authorized a robust peace support-force for Afghanistan. The International Security Assistance Force, or ISAF as it became known, was essentially a NATO operation. In the fall of 2002, NATO took responsibility for ISAF and moved its operations, for the first time in history, away from the European continent.

Homeland Security

In one of the houses in Kabul, American forces found a videotape of Osama Bin Laden celebrating the devastation wrought on September 11. While most governments had accepted the 'clear and compelling evidence', as NATO's Lord Robertson put it, of Bin Laden's involvement in early October, the tape allowed people across the world to see for themselves.[156] American forces also found crude plans by Al Qaeda to use biological and nuclear weapons, possibly distributing the biological agents with small crop duster planes. These plans only heightened homeland security concerns, which were already sky high.

On October 4, a 62 year-old photo-editor from Boca Raton, Florida suddenly died from Anthrax inhalation in the same city where some of the September 11 attackers had been hiding. Then on October 15, Senator Daschle's office, NBC studios and the office of the *New York Post* picked up spores of anthrax in their mailrooms – on October 29, the Supreme Court building was hit. Handwritten letters mailed from a New Jersey suburb were sending the deadly biological weapons into the upper echelons of government. 'Fear gripped Washington in October even more tightly than in September,' David Frum wrote.[157] Besides Russia and America, only Iraq was thought to possess this highly processed 'weapons grade' anthrax – of course there was immediate suspicion of Al Qaeda and Iraq. The Bush administration could not pinpoint the perpetrator and the President said, 'he would not put it past Bin Laden to have launched these attacks.' Ashcroft would not rule it out either, but acknowledged, 'There is no hard evidence.'[158] To its credit, the Bush administration did not simply lob anthrax into Al Qaeda's account or use it to hype up the war effort in Afghanistan.

The anthrax attacks showed again America's homeland vulnerability. It also showed that better interagency coordination and preparedness was needed. At the time of the first attack there was only enough anthrax vaccine for a few thousand people, and so on October 20 Bush requested $1.5 billion in emergency funds to stockpile antibiotics and medicine for Anthrax and smallpox. Tom Ridge's new office had started issuing 'red alerts' for domestic terror attacks when the intelligence seemed to warrant it, but neither Ridge nor Ashcroft had enough concrete information to say what type of attack was expected, nor when and where. In October, US intelligence picked up information that nuclear material was transshipped out of Pakistan. On October 29 there was a direct threat to the White House, reportedly in the form of a small 'dirty' nuclear bomb. Bush said, 'If they get me, they are going to get me right here,' so Cheney ended up spending more time in 'undisclosed locations'.[159]

Before the Anthrax threat faded away in December, there had been 18 infections and five deaths. Together with the general alarms of October 11, 29 and December 3, issued by Ridge, the public was spooked. For Ridge it was a dilemma: if he had a storm of intelligence and said nothing, and something happened, he would be delinquent; if he rang the alarm without knowing whether there would be a fire, he would eventually be ignored.

More important than Ridge's dilemma was what the anthrax and dirty bomb threats did to Bush and his immediate advisers in terms of their thinking about the war on terror. The nuclear and biological threat connected to the pre-September view that eventually terrorists would strike with asymmetrical weapons accentuated the need to go beyond the global financial, intelligence and diplomatic war on terror. The threat also showed the limits of the domestic war against terrorism. Later Powell explained this transition when he wrote: 'a strategy limited to dealing with immediate threats would in the end fail to defeat them – just as bailing water out of a boat would not fix a leak.'[160] This transition helped turn the 'second front,' after Afghanistan, into a campaign against weapons of mass destruction as the top priority, convincing the Bush administration that it needed both a defensive and an offensive option in the war on terror.

The amount of information that could be gathered from Al Qaeda suspects arrested in America, Germany and other nations revealed that sleeper cells were very difficult to discover in democratic societies with widespread privacy rights. It also showed that Al Qaeda struck with regular intervals and that it had made long-term preparations. Bush concluded that the disruption of the network after September 11 might just not be good enough to prevent the next round of attacks. If September 11 were 'only' the first round, the likelihood of weapons of mass destruction featuring in subsequent attacks would be high. As deterrence was almost useless and defense very limited, the administration had to go on the offensive against both the network *and* its next likely weapon.

Bush was 'floored' that in the week after September 11, the FBI swept up 417 people and that it had another 331 on its watch list.[161] If it could move so quickly after the attacks, he wanted to know how the agencies and departments could work better together to detect and prevent attacks. He did not want to create a new bureaucracy (more government) as some in Congress demanded – on October 8, Bush signed Ridge's office of Homeland Security into being with an executive order. Bush initially gave Ridge a small staff and budget (12 people and some $51 million dollars) and his formal powers did not go much beyond 'identifying priorities' and 'coordinating' what others should be doing.[162] The size of the staff and budget was seen by some as evidence that Ridge would lack the clout to make a real difference.[163] The President wanted him close by – he took over some of Josh Bolten's offices next door – to personally tutor him on what the key problems were. As Bush put it, 'I've given Tom ... a mission: to design a comprehensive, coordinated national strategy to fight terror here at home.'[164]

It was not long before Ridge became embroiled in various bureaucratic struggles with domestic and intelligence agencies that for decades had protected their own status in the complex myriad of American national security. Card found that 'the bureaucracy was resisting change at every turn,' and so Bush allowed him to conduct a secretive study on a 'sweeping re-organization plan'.[165] In June of 2002 Bush announced the outcome: a $38 billion, 170,000 employee Homeland Security Department that would bring together some fifty functions scattered throughout the executive government. The White House became embroiled in a political fight with Senate Democrats in the fall of 2002 over the civil service and union rights of the future employees of the new department. Bush won that fight, severely curtailing those labor rights when the lame-duck Congress passed his proposal in November 2002. He had begun to change the tide on bureaucratic impediments to information sharing inside the government.

It was plain that the FBI was one of the weakest links before September 11. Mueller was new in the job – Louis Freeh had left in June 2001 – and though Bush never criticized him, he gave Ashcroft the go ahead to take stronger control over the Bureau. Ashcroft brought his 'Patriot Act' forward, which the Congress passed on October 25. The Bill expanded domestic surveillance powers and allowed the FBI to put wiretaps on a person, rather than on one medium of that person (for example, a cell phone). It allowed the detention of foreign nationals for seven days (the Senate did not agree with Ashcroft's demand for an indefinite period) and it let the FBI share grand jury and wire tap information with the CIA. George Tenet testified in 2004 that the 'ironclad regulations' that existed between criminal investigations and intelligence had to be taken down in order to give the FBI and CIA a chance to share relevant information. He called the Patriot Act 'absolutely essential'.[166]

On October 31, Ashcroft announced that the government would monitor lawyer-client communications of suspected terrorists in custody, without specific court orders. The President's strong embrace of Islam did not mean he would be soft on suspects even if in practice it usually singled out Middle Eastern males. Ashcroft received a lot of criticism for his strong measures, but Bush was behind the strategy and was backing him up. At the same time, he told Ashcroft to do all he could to prevent a backlash against Muslims in general.

By November 2001, the government was holding over 1,100 people on suspicion of having links to Al Qaeda or other terrorist organizations; many were held on immigration violations. While the Patriot Act had a four-year sunset clause in it – a demand placed on it by the Senate – many civil libertarians from both the left and right end of the political spectrum worried that the Department of Justice was threatening to unravel America's civil liberties in its effort to question, monitor and detain every possible suspect. Some cities and states rebuffed Ashcroft's proposal to interview Middle Eastern young males on a voluntary basis.

The civil liberties debate will go on for some time. The vast majority of the detainees turned out not to have connections with terrorist groups though some were deported for immigration violations – by June 2002, only some 70 people were still left in custody. Given the threat level, the Bush administration could be forgiven for acting on the side of supreme caution. On June 17, 2003, a federal appeals court ruled that the Bush administration was justified in withholding the names and nationalities of the detainees after September 11. The detainees were not pushed through a hasty and biased legal system. The earliest cases of Al Qaeda suspects were not tried until June 2003. Of four men apprehended on September 17 for 'providing material support to terrorists', two were acquitted and two convicted.[167]

Bush made perhaps his most controversial move in the War on Terror when he announced that Al Qaeda fighters captured in Afghanistan would be held at a military prison in Guantanamo Bay, an American military base in Cuba, to be tried by secret military tribunals. Some 660 people were sent there. There was quite an initial outcry, especially by the European Press, who demanded that these suspects be given the protection of the Geneva Conventions on prisoners of war. There were reports that the suspects were treated inhumanely in Camp X-Ray – pictures of men in small outdoor cages accompanied the stories. Paul Wolfowitz explained in Congress that the Bush administration had in fact looked into historical precedent and that both Presidents Lincoln and Franklin Roosevelt had used military tribunals for non-lawful combatants. Roosevelt had ordered Nazi infiltrators and saboteurs tried by such tribunals and the Supreme Court had upheld those actions. The Defense Department made the case that the various Al Qaeda fighters captured in Operation Enduring Freedom did not belong to any legally constituted army and the Geneva Convention would give these detainees the right not to answer any questions.

Ashcroft was sharp in his defense of the military tribunals. He questioned whether the critics would want him to read 'these fighters' their Miranda rights, hire them a flamboyant defense lawyer and create a new cable network of Osama TV.[168] Neither Rumsfeld nor Tenet had much sympathy for the captives. On November 25 some 600 Al Qaeda prisoners staged a massive revolt in a prison complex near Mazar-i-Sharif. The only CIA officer lost in the entire campaign, Johnny Span, was killed in that revolt. Rumsfeld wanted the prisoners out of the theater of war and not dispersed in the civilian court system in the United States. The key issue for Bush in opting for military tribunals was that the court proceedings would not reveal CIA or other secrets about how the United States was fighting the war against Al Qaeda. Wolfowitz explained in Congress that the three objectives of the military tribunals were to better protect civilian judges, to allow more inclusive rules of evidence and to use classified information in a way that would not endanger 'sources and methods'.[169] This was Bush's bottom line – he wanted information without crippling the war on terror. Thus the administration seemed in no hurry to try any of the captives.

It seems that the decision on military tribunals was made without a thorough interagency debate. Soon after Bush's decision, a series of newspaper stories broke which showed pieces of a memo sent by the President's legal counsel, Alberto Gonzales, as well as memos by Colin Powell and Condi Rice. It looked like Bush had not fully consulted with all his principals, including Powell and the Chairman of the Joint Chiefs. He appeared to have acted mainly on the basis of Cheney and Ashcroft's recommendation for military tribunals.[170] The decision process looked incomplete on three counts: first, the decision was sketchy as most conditions and details were to be added later. This allowed unnecessary speculation about who might be tried – the critics said the captives were in 'legal limbo'.[171] Second, the decision had not fully considered the impact the tribunals would have on European and other allies, some of whose nationals were now being held in Camp X-ray, and how that might affect the cooperation between the United States and allied intelligence services. By January 2002 there were some 150 captives from 25 different nations in the camp. Third, the public relations fallout had also not been fully considered and the pictures looked bad.

In response, the administration announced that it would not try US citizens by military tribunal and would only send people to the military prison who were captured abroad. Second, the administration affirmed that it would treat the prisoners humanely as stipulated under the Geneva Conventions and that it would treat every case on its own merits. Three Supreme Court rulings in 2004 on the military tribunals affirmed Bush's constitutional authority, but also granted the prisoners the right to challenge their detention through the Federal Courts.

The Battle Lines for November 2002: The Budget and the 'Axis of Evil'

The attacks of September 11 brought an outpouring of bipartisan resolve. Members of Congress spontaneously sang 'America the Beautiful' on the steps of the Capitol. At the conclusion of his address to Congress on September 20, Bush gave Senator Tom Daschle 'a widely publicized bear hug'.[172] Bush visited New York four times in the fall and at a Veteran's day event, Mayor Rudolph Giuliani said, 'This city – it didn't vote for you, is in love with you.'[173]

Despite the initial goodwill, both political parties knew that the stalemate of the 2000 campaign would be settled in November 2002. The Clinton campaign in 1992 had successfully argued that Bush's father had neglected domestic politics – this President could not afford to pursue the war on terror by neglecting his home base. Both Bush and the Democratic leadership, especially in the Senate, returned to their pre-September 11 battle positions on domestic policy, but did so in more 'hushed, decorous tones'.[174] For a couple of months after September 11 Bush had stayed off the campaign trail, but by December he was back in swing. The battle lines for the Congressional midterm elections were drawn along two themes: Bush's handling of the war on terror and his handling of the economy. In late January and early February 2002, Bush staked out his position on both. He did so in the budget he submitted for fiscal year 2003 and in his State of the Union address, which became instantly known for three key words: 'axis of evil'.

The terrorist attacks caused America's gross domestic product to contract half a point. Mitch Daniels, Bush's Director of Office of Management and Budget, had forecast that the budget surpluses would almost be wiped out before recurring in 2004-2005, but now it looked like the Bush budget would go sharply into deficit numbers.[175] Most of Bush's economic advisers agreed that now was not the time to hold back on tax cuts, but rather to send a stimulus into the economy and worry about the deficit later. Congress agreed almost immediately on emergency domestic and national security spending to the tune of $20 billion for each. There also was agreement on the need to help out the worst hit industry, the airlines – it received $15 billion.

Bush proposed in early October an 'economic stimulus package' that included some $70 billion in corporate tax cuts. It looked to some Democrats like he was making use of the crisis to sneak in another type of tax cuts under the guise of stimulus. His package also included $12 billion in emergency aid to displaced workers and an acceleration of the existing cuts in personal income taxes (about $28 billion). The House passed the package on October 24 with a very narrow margin of 216 to 214, but it died in the Senate in January 2002.

The President's budget became a battle about tax cuts. If, in the aftermath of September 11, the Democrats could get him to go wobbly on the cuts, they would have the argument to undo his entire domestic agenda. This left two choices: do nothing more on tax cuts, or up the ante. If Bush now made the deficit his priority, again the Democrats could have returned to their argument that his tax cuts were to blame for the fiscal deterioration in the first place, so he chose to largely ignore the budget deficit. Bush, as Peggy Noonan put it, is by his political nature a 'high budget conservative'.[176]

Daschle called Bush's spending plans 'irresponsible', while at the same time adding to each one of Bush's bills his own spending priorities. The same dynamic that existed before the September 11 attacks continued into 2002; Daschle adding to the deficit and Bush refusing to veto. Perhaps, the Democrats were goading Bush into casting a veto, but he calculated that casting one before the mid-term elections in 2002 would gain nothing. It would be seen as Bush protecting corporate or other special interests from the Democrats' attempt to help the 'common man.'

On December 2, 2001, the energy giant Enron filed for bankruptcy. It went under amidst strong allegations of financial and accounting fraud, wiping out $60 billion in shareholder value. Kenneth Lay, Enron's CEO, and other top executives had sold their shares just before the company went down and several Congressional committees began hearings. At first the Bush White House was silent, then it fought back against the 'guilt by association' charge. Kenneth Lay, whom Bush once nicknamed 'Kenny Boy' had spent about half a million dollars in all of Bush's electoral campaigns.[177] Cheney's office admitted Enron had been in 'six times' during the energy task force deliberations.[178]

The President applied the lessons he had learned in his Congressional race against Kent Hance in the 1970s. If someone tries to define you, you must fight back – Bush said Enron had also supported his rival Ann Richards. The White House let it be known that Lay had visited Clinton at Camp David and golfed with him, and that Clinton's Secretary of the Treasury, Robert Rubin had recently lobbied for Enron. The company gave one out of every three dollars to Democratic candidates.[179]

It turned out that Bush's close friend and Commerce Secretary Don Evans had saved Bush from any embarrassment. Lay had come to Evans for help on October 29, 2001. Evans received sound advice from Paul O'Neill who told him not to help Enron in any way. Evans did not tell Bush, shielding him from any temptation to consider such help, so when it came to the point of '*really* needing' some influence, Enron found out it had not 'bought any influence' after all.[180] Even Cheney's Energy Task Force recommendations had not been that good for Enron as they featured nuclear and coal energy, which did not help Enron's gas operations. They did not set carbon-emission limitations, which was a line of business in which Enron wanted to expand, and they did not facilitate more access to interstate power lines. All Enron got was help with its offshore business in India, which is almost a given regardless of partisan politics.[181] By late January Bush joined in the call for criminal investigations into Enron's dealings.

On January 4, 2002, Daschle lamented the 'most dramatic fiscal deterioration in our nation's history' and said that Bush's tax cuts had 'probably' made the recession worse.[182] Daschle offered his own version of 'short-term tax relief' in the form of 'tax credits for businesses that add workers'.[183] Bush called the Democrats' plan to delay his tax cuts an actual tax increase. At a town hall meeting in California, he ad libbed, 'not over my dead body will they raise your taxes'.[184] Ari Fleischer said that the Democratic leadership 'aches in its bones to raise taxes'.[185]

On January 18, Karl Rove told campaign workers at a Republican National Committee meeting in Austin that they 'could go to the country' on Bush's handling of the war on terror and on homeland security because the voters 'trust the Republicans to do a better job of protecting America,' and of 'keeping our communities and families safe.'[186] Many Democrats who had loyally supported Bush throughout the war were understandably livid. In late February, Daschle criticized the President's pursuit of Bin Laden and the Al Qaeda network. 'We've got to find Osama Bin Laden,' he said, 'or we will have failed,' yet few Democrats followed his lead on that charge.[187]

Then one of Daschle's assistants told a *New York Times* reporter that the President looked 'disengaged and uninformed' at the weekly breakfast meetings with Congressional leaders. Such a personal comment is the kind of betrayal of trust that does not sit well with Bush. David Frum wrote, 'Relations between the two men never recovered.'[188] In February he scaled back his breakfast meetings with the Congressional leadership to once every two weeks.

On February 4, Bush sent a $2.13 trillion budget to Congress for the fiscal year 2003 that cut funding from the Departments of Labor, Transportation, Agriculture, from the Environmental Protection Agency, and the Corps of Engineers. He called for a ceiling of two per cent increase for all non-defense and homeland security spending and at the same time, Bush proposed nearly $40 billion more in Defense spending (an 11 per cent increase) and doubled the budget for homeland security to $18 billion.[189] From the Democrat's point of view it was a fighting budget as it cut funds from most of their priorities. This would be the second year the Pentagon had a budget increase of 11 per cent, again raising the question whether Rumsfeld was transforming the military or just adding to all its budget categories.

In the budget fight between Bush and Daschle, the deficit again took the brunt. For the previous fiscal year Bush had sought a cap of four per cent in spending, but ended up with an increase of seven per cent. Mitch Daniels admitted that even inside the Administration, it had been difficult to rein in spending after September 11, saying it had all the 'characteristics of a jailbreak' in which 'the first escapees were representatives of our own administration.'[190] Daniels had laid down a tight budget, but during the course of the election year, most of his limits were violated.

The President used his State of the Union Address on January 29, 2002 to present his vision for the second phase in the war on terror. Late 2001 and early 2002 were rife with speculation whether he had or had not yet decided to remove Saddam Hussein from power. Bush wanted to use the State of the Union Address to reset the boundary posts for American foreign policy. As is his style, he points to where he wants to go before heading in that direction. Before September 11, many people misinterpreted Bush's big speeches as mere rhetoric: the September 20 joint address had turned that trend around and now they were paying close attention.

Bush gave a preview of his thinking when he spoke at the Citadel on December 11, 2001. His 1999 campaign speech there had been about new military doctrines: missile and homeland defense and military transformation. Now his address was threat specific. 'A few evil men' intend to use weapons of mass destruction to threaten civilization, Bush said; his goal was to make sure they would never gain access to 'weapons of mass murder'. 'Our military has a new and essential mission,' he told the cadets. 'For states that support terror, it's not enough that the consequences be costly – they must be devastating.'[191] The most important conceptual step Bush made was to move the war from the sponsors of terrorism to the sponsors of the next weapons of terrorism. The prevention of these weapons coming into terrorist hands became the new strategy, and from prevention flowed the idea of preemption.

The President's personality has little propensity for what cognitive psychologists call 'procrastination' and 'value-conflict avoidance'.[192] Only days after September 11, he began to speak of this war as his calling to bring about world peace and as the defining mission of his presidency. Bush did not only see the conflict with moral clarity, he also needed to translate this newfound purpose into strategic clarity. Before September 11, Bush had already begun to challenge the strategic drift of the 1990s. Now he had the new chapter ready. America's military posture would be offensive and its main task would be the preemption of weapons of mass destruction falling into the hands of terrorist groups. Few allies realized what was coming: American foreign policy was about to take one of its most revolutionary turns ever.

The Axis of Evil speech caused quite a 'stir'. Some Europeans at first dismissed Bush's moral clarity as evidence of his 'relative ignorance of the outside world.'[193]

Especially so, as it named three specific countries as representatives of an 'axis of evil' that was 'threatening the peace of the world.'[194] Gerson and his staff were instructed to start drafting the speech in mid-December; David Frum who has been credited with coining the phrase 'Axis of Evil,' actually first proposed 'Axis of Hatred'.[195] It was Gerson who made it into 'Axis of Evil' and it is unlikely that Bush or any of his advisers anticipated that this phrase would become the symbol for his entire address. After all, the President used the term 'evil' quite regularly and used it five times in this address alone. Nor was it entirely clear what was meant by 'axis' in this context. To Frum it was a conceptual analogy: just as Japan, Nazi Germany and Fascist Italy had shared few things except 'resentment of the power of the West', so too Iraq, Iran and North Korea shared few characteristics, except their hatred of America.[196]

Fleischer said afterward that Bush meant 'no comparison' to the axis powers of World War II. According to Fleischer, the term was more 'rhetorical than historical.'[197] Indeed, Bush seldom used the phrase after this speech. The *more* revealing phrase of the speech was, 'I will not wait on events ..., I will not permit the world's most dangerous regimes to threaten us with the world's most destructive weapons.' It heralded the proactive nature of the second phase of the war on terror.

The war was 'only' the first part of the speech – in the second part, Bush tried to recast the entire economic and domestic debate as a derivative of the new national security environment: it was called economic security. Bush defined economic security with one word: jobs. Jobs would be secure if the nation followed the President's plans for education reform, more sources of energy, free trade, tax cuts, patient's rights and social security. It was another example how the Bush White House would link its political capital in the war on terror to its domestic agenda in light of the upcoming midterm elections. He ended his address with values – the volunteerism and self-sacrifice in the aftermath of the attacks showed a glimpse of 'what a new culture of responsibility could look like.' Now to his 'culture of responsibility,' he added seven worldwide, 'non-negotiable demands of human dignity,' including respect for women and religious tolerance.[198] Bush, an admirer of Abraham Lincoln, ended with something that sounded like Lincoln: 'Steadfast in our purpose, we now press on. We have known freedom's price, we have shown freedom's power ... we will see freedom's victory.' He had been inspired by Todd Beamer's last words on the doomed flight over Pennsylvania, 'let's roll'. In Beamer's words, Bush was on a roll.

One of the things Bush learned from Ronald Reagan was to speak directly to the people and over the heads of the media and the elites, and the people liked what they heard. It was all leadership, all the time. His unprecedented popularity ratings remained in the high 80s sixteen weeks after the September attacks. Some leading Democrats were peeved. To them Bush was using the war on terror, as one senator put it, as 'a gift that keeps on giving'.[199] *The Washington Post* called his address an 'overreach', and an 'unlimited hunting license'.[200] Knowing there would be a backlash from Western Europe, Powell called in his ambassadors and senior staff and told them 'The President meant what he said. I don't want anyone in this room to take the edge off it.'[201] Many allies in Europe as well as Canada, who still thought of terrorism as a crime and the threat of weapons of mass destruction as something to 'contain', were caught off guard.[202]

Conclusion

Over three thousand people lost their lives in the September 11 tragedy. The damage to New York and the national economy was enormous. Some 20 per cent of office space in Manhattan was rendered unusable, the New York Stock Exchange did not open until September 17 and the Dow Jones lost 13 per cent in the week after the attack. The Federal Reserve and offshore banks injected $120 billion into the money markets in the aftermath, but the airline and tourism industries suffered a huge blow. September 11 pushed the teetering economy into a clear recession. Bush had hoped that the first tax rebate checks coming to the people in August 2001 would give the economy a bit of a lift but instead, in the last quarter of 2001, one million Americans lost their jobs. The Gross Domestic Product contracted by nearly half a per cent. The Pentagon requested a total of $3.8 billion in extra funding for Operation Enduring Freedom in December 2001 and a year later, the estimate of the total cost for military operations was approximately $12 billion.

Did George W. Bush do enough to prevent the attacks? That became the key question in early 2004 for the 'National Commission on Terrorist Attacks Upon the United States'. Richard Clarke felt that Bush had not made the Al Qaeda threat an urgent issue, accusing the Bush administration of taking eight months to decide on a set of policy options he had basically ready in December 2000. That allegation begged the question why Clinton had not adopted such a policy if Clarke had it ready as early as 2000. Rice testified that the Bush policy differed strategically from Clarke's plans and that most of Clarke's immediate recommendations, such as arming the Predator, were already being implemented. The new strategy sought to build a regional alliance against the Taliban and Al Qaeda in order to go after the threat in a more holistic way.

It is fair to say that Bush's approach to Al Qaeda and the threat of international terrorism did not make it quick enough up the policy priority list. The reason was not wrongdoing or neglect, but he was preoccupied with other issues and did not yet have a war mentality. Without such total concentration it is not likely that Bush could have broken the 30-year old mindset on terrorism, and the legal impediments to criminal, immigration, and intelligence sharing. Richard Armitage perhaps put it most fairly when he said, 'Even if you're on the right track, you can get run over if you're not going fast enough.'[203]

The September 11 Commission chided Clinton and Bush for a failure of imagination. If Bush did too little before the attacks, he did an enormous amount in their immediate aftermath. Operation Enduring Freedom and the three weeks that led up to it will perhaps be recorded in history as his finest hour. Like John F. Kennedy during the 1962 Cuban Missile Crisis, Bush had the decision-making process working in an optimal manner, and his actions against Al Qaeda and the Taliban were both firm and proportionate. Bush's war on terror not only launched a revolution abroad, but he also challenged the bureaucratic impediments at home with the Patriot Act, the Department of Homeland Security, and several new interagency initiatives. Few realized how ready Bush was to take the next step in the 'war on terror'.

Notes

1   *Keesing's Worldwide News Digest*, September 2001, p. 44336.
2   As quoted in Bill Sammon, *Fighting Back: The War on Terrorism from Inside the Bush White House* (Washington, D.C.: Regnery Publishing, Inc., p. 362.)
3   Karen Tumulty, 'Behind all the Finger-Pointing', *Time Magazine*, May 27, 2002, p. 26.
4   Richard Morin and Dana Milbank, 'Bush and GOP Enjoy Record Popularity', *Washington Post*, January 29, 2002, p. 1.
5   Richard Armitage in Testimony before the National Commission on Terrorist Attacks Upon the United States, March 24, 2004 (http://www.9-11commission.gov/hearings/hearing8.htm).
6   Ivo H. Daalder and James M. Lindsay, *America Unbound: The Bush Revolution in Foreign Policy* (Washington, D.C.: Brookings Institution Press, 2003), p. 81.
7   Secretary of State Colin Powell, Prepared Statement on Counterterrorism, Senate Appropriations Subcommittee on Commerce, Justice, State, and the Judiciary, Washington, May 8, 2001.
8   'Testing Intelligence', *The Economist*, October 6, 2001, p. 31.
9   James Kitfield, 'A New and Colder War', *National Journal*, September 21, 2001.
10   Representative Schrock, House Budget Committee, US Congress, July 11, 2001, Washington, D.C.
11   Nicholas Lemann, 'The Quiet Man', *The New Yorker*, May 7, 2001, p. 61.
12   Donald H. Rumsfeld, 'Toward 21st Century Deterrence', *Wall Street Journal*, June 27, 2001, p. 16.
13   'No, Not Quite a Dictatorship', *Economist*, December 8, 2001, p. 30.
14   Seymour Hersh, 'What Went Wrong', *The New Yorker*, October 8, 2001, p. 35.
15   Richard K. Betts, 'Fixing Intelligence', *Foreign Affairs*, January/February 2002, p. 44.
16   *Final Report of the National Commission on Terrorist Attacks upon the United States*, Executive Summary, (Washington, D.C., Government Printing Office, 2004), p. 8.
17   Steve Hirsch, 'Insider Interview with Paul Pillar, former Deputy Chief of the CIA's Counterterrorist Center', *National Journal*, December 12, 2001.
18   Michael Elliot, 'How the US Missed the Clues', *Time Magazine*, May 27, 2002, p. 25.
19   Barton Gellman, 'A Strategy's Cautious Evolution: Before September 11, the Bush Anti-Terror Effort Was Mostly Ambition', *Washington Post*, January 20, 2002 (www.washingtonpost.com).
20   Bob Woodward, *Bush at War* (New York: Simon & Schuster), 2002, p. 34.
21   Richard A. Clarke, Testimony before the National Commission on Terrorist Attacks Upon the United States, March 24, 2004 (http://www.9-11commission.gov/hearings/hearing8.htm).
22   Gellman, 'A Strategy's Cautious Evolution'.
23   Idem.
24   Condoleezza Rice Testimony before the National Commission on Terrorist Attacks Upon the United States, April 8, 2004, (http://www.washingtonpost.com/wp-dyn/articles/A61252-2004Apr8.html).
25   Rice, 'Testimony', April 8, 2004.
26   Gellman, 'A Strategy's Cautious Evolution'.
27   Woodward, p. 4.
28   Clarke, 'Testimony', March 24, 2004.
29   Betts, p. 58.
30   Michael Elliot, p. 19.
31   Rice, 'Testimony', April 8, 2004.
32   'Text: President's Daily Brief on August 6, 2001', *Washington Post*, April 10, 2004.

33   Remarks by Condoleezza Rice on Terrorism and Foreign Policy, Paul Nitze School of Advanced International Studies, Washington, D.C., April 29, 2002, p. 1.
34   Sammon, p. 83.
35   Sammon, p. 86.
36   Sammon, p. 94.
37   Sammon, p. 128.
38   Karen Hughes, *Ten Minutes From Normal* (New York: Viking, 2004), p. 263.
39   James Fallows, 'Councils of War', *The Atlantic Monthly*, December 2001, p. 42.
40   Sammon, p. 102.
41   Woodward, p. 25.
42   Woodward, p. 10.
43   Derrick Z. Jackson, 'A Lesson from Condoleezza Rice', *Boston Globe*, November 20, 2002, p. 19.
44   Nicholas Lemann, 'The Options', *The New Yorker*, October 1, 2001, p. 72.
45   Elisabeth Bumiller, 'Pair of "Professional Friends" Form an Unlikely Partnership', *New York Times*, January 14, 2002, p. 11.
46   Sammon, p. 115.
47   Hughes, p. 241.
48   Lemann, 'The Options', p. 73.
49   Sammon, p. 119.
50   Woodward, p. 27.
51   Woodward, p. 28.
52   Christopher Andersen, *George and Laura: Portrait of an American Marriage* (New York: William Morrow, 2002), p. 268.
53   Carla Anne Robbins and Greg Jaffe, 'Counterattack', *Wall Street Journal*, October 18, 2001, p. 1.
54   Statement by the President in his Address to the Nation, Office of the Press Secretary, September 11, 2001 (http://www.whitehouse.gov/news/releases/2001/09/20010911-16.html).
55   George W. Bush, 'A Period of Consequences', The Citadel, September 23, 1999, (italics added).
56   Woodward, p. 31.
57   Woodward, p. 33.
58   James Carney and John F. Dickerson, 'Inside the War Room', *Time Magazine*, December 31, 2001-January 7, 2002, p. 104.
59   Mike Allen and Alan Sipress, 'Close Up: Who Meet When to Discuss What and Why', *Seattle Times*, September 28, 2001, p. 3.
60   Annie Leibovitz and Christopher Buckley, 'War and Destiny', *Vanity Fair*, February 2002, p. 84.
61   Alessandra Stanley, 'A Nation Challenged: The White House Spokesman', *New York Times*, October 27, p. 49.
62   Ryan Lizza, 'Spin Off', *The New Republic*, October 15, 2001, p. 16.
63   US Congress, 'Joint Resolution Authorizing the Use of Force Against Terrorists', September 14, 2001 (http://www.australianpolitics.com/usa/congress/sep11-joint-resolution.shtml).
64   Leibovitz and Buckley, p. 91.
65   Carla Anne Robbins and Jean Cummings, 'Powell's Caution Against Quick Strike Shapes Bush Plan', *Wall Street Journal*, September 21, 2001, p. 24.
66   Richard Armitage in Testimony before the National Commission on Terrorist Attacks Upon the United States, March 24, 2004 (http://www.9-11commission.gov/hearings/hearing8.htm).
67   Woodward, p. 52.

68   Howard Fineman and Martha Brandt, 'We Can Handle It', *Newsweek*, December 3, 2001, p. 30.
69   President's Remarks at National Day of Prayer and Remembrance, National Cathedral, Washington, D.C., September 14, 2001 (http://www.whitehouse.gov/news/releases/2001/09/20010914-2.html).
70   Howard Fineman and Martha Brandt, 'This is Our Life Now', *Newsweek*, December 3, 2001, p. 28.
71   Remarks by the President at the Islamic Center of Washington, D.C., September 17, 2001 (http://www.whitehouse.gov/news/releases/2001/09/20010917-11.html).
72   The White House, Office of the Press Secretary, 'Remarks by the President to the United Nations General Assembly', November 10, 2001.
73   Franklin Foer, 'Blind Faith', *The New Republic*, October 22, 2001, p. 14.
74   'National Day of Prayer Remarks', (emphasis added).
75   'Bush Pledges "Crusade" Against Evil Doers', *Associated Press*, September 17, 2001.
76   Margaret Carlson, 'A President Finds His Voice', *Time*, September 24, 2001 (www.time.com/time/columnist/carlson/article/0,9565,175437,00.html).
77   Office of the Press Secretary 'Remarks by the President to Police, Firemen and Rescue Workers', New York, September 14, 2001.
78   Sammon, p. 189.
79   Sammon, p. 198.
80   Woodward, p. 78.
81   Evan Thomas and John Barry, 'Evil in the Cross Hairs', *Newsweek*, December 24, 2001, p. 17.
82   Rowan Scarborough, *Rumsfeld's War: The Untold Story of America's Anti-Terrorist Commander* (Washington, D.C., Regnery Publishing, 2004), p. 30.
83   Fineman and Brandt, 'This is Our Life Now', p. 27.
84   Woodward, p. 303.
85   Fallows, p. 45.
86   Carney and Dickerson, p. 103.
87   Woodward, p. 87.
88   Carney and Dickerson, p. 103.
89   Woodward, p. 91.
90   Fineman and Brandt, 'This is Our Life Now', p. 27.
91   Woodward, p. 97.
92   Woodward, pp. 98-99.
93   Sammon, p. 232.
94   Woodward, p. 107.
95   Fallows, p. 42.
96   Woodward, p. 106.
97   'Seeing the World Anew', *Economist*, October 27, 2001, p. 19.
98   'Rumsfeld Urges NATO to Prepare for New Threats', Transcript, US Department of Defense (US Embassy Ottawa Electronic Documents), December 18, 2001.
99   'War Cabinet: Veterans on Familiar Ground', *Washington Post*, October 1, 2001.
100   Evan Thomas, 'Chemistry in the Cabinet', *Newsweek*, January 28, 2002, p. 29.
101   Woodward, p. 91; Sammon, p. 233.
102   'Weekly Compilation of Presidential Documents', September 24, 2001.
103   Treasury Under Secretary for International Affairs, John B. Taylor, 'Strengthening the Global Economy After September 11: The Bush Agenda', Kennedy School of Government, Harvard University, November 29, 2001.
104   'The United States and the Global Coalition Against Terrorism, September-December 2001: A Chronology', Office of the Historian, US Department of State (www.state.gov/r/pa/ho/pubs/fs/5889.htm)

105   Sammon, p. 206.
106   The White House, Office of the Press Secretary, 'President's Address to a Joint Session of Congress', September 20, 2001.
107   Peter J. Boyer, 'The Worrier', *The New Yorker*, November 26, 2001, p. 53.
108   David Frum, *The Right Man: The Surprise Presidency of George W. Bush* (New York: Random House, 2003), p. 125.
109   White House, Office of the Press Secretary, 'Remarks by the President at the Pentagon Memorial', October 11, 2001; 'Address to the Nation', World Congress Center, Atlanta, Georgia, November 8, 2001.
110   'A Leader is Born', *Economist*, September 24, 2001.
111   As quoted in Burt Solomon, 'National Security: All Leadership, All the Time', *National Journal*, December 1, 2001.
112   Fineman and Brandt, 'This is Our Life Now', p. 26.
113   Frank Bruni, *Ambling into History: The Unlikely Odyssey of George W. Bush* (New York: HarperCollins Publishers, 2002), p. 263.
114   'A Discussion with Karl Rove', American Enterprise Institute, Washington, D.C., December 11, 2001.
115   idem.
116   Hugh Heclo, 'The Political Ethos of George W. Bush', in Fred Greenstein (ed.), *The George W. Bush Presidency: An Early Assessment* (Baltimore: Johns Hopkins University Press, 2003), p. 19.
117   Peggy Noonan, '2001: A Bush Odyssey', *Wall Street Journal Online*, January 4, 2002. (http://www.opinionjournal.com/columnists/pnoonan/?id=95001687).
118   Bruni, p. 175.
119   Ann Gerhart, 'Laura Bush, Standing By Her Husband While Far Away', *Washington Post*, May 18, 2002, p. C1.
120   Andersen, p. 97.
121   Sarah Wildman, 'Portrait of a Lady', *The New Republic*, August 20, 2001, p. 20.
122   Leibovitz and Buckley, p. 92.
123   Ann Gerhart, *The Perfect Wife: The Life and Choices of Laura Bush* (New York: Simon & Schuster, 2004).
124   Andersen, p. 216.
125   Martha Brant, 'The Steel Behind the Smile', *Newsweek*, January 29, 2001, p. 31.
126   Ann Gerhart, 'Learning to Read Laura Bush', *Washington Post*, March 22, 2001, p. C6.
127   Andersen, p. 253.
128   Ellen Levine, 'We're Going to Be Okay', *Good Housekeeping*, January 2002, p. 102.
129   Martha Brant, 'Comforter in Chief', *Newsweek,* December 3, 2001.
130   Andersen, p. 264.
131   Woodward, p. 176 and p. 246.
132   Sammon, p. 223.
133   Sammon, p. 234.
134   'President's Remarks at National Day of Prayer and Remembrance', September 14, 2001.
135   'Presidential Address to the Nation', The White House, Office of the Press Secretary, October 7, 2001.
136   Donald Rumsfeld, 'A New Kind of War', *New York Times*, September 27, 2001.
137   Carney and Dickerson, p. 106.
138   Keesings News Digest, October 2001, p. 44392.
139   Thom Shanker, 'Conduct of War is Redefined by Success of Special Forces', *New York Times*, January 21, 2001, p. 8.
140   Woodward, p. 245.
141   Charles Krauthammer, 'Nice is Nice But This is War', *National Post*, October 30, 2001.

142 Sammon, p. 267.
143 R.W. Apple Jr., 'A Military Quagmire Remembered: Afghanistan as Vietnam', *New York Times*, October 31, 2001, p. B1.
144 Lexington, 'Old Hawk Learns New Tricks', *Economist*, October 13, 2001, p. 36.
145 Woodward, p. 262.
146 Carney and Dickerson, p. 109.
147 *Keesing's Worldwide News Digest*, October 2001, p. 44395.
148 'NSC Adviser Briefs on War on Terrorism', Information Resource Center, US Embassy, Ottawa, November 1, 2001.
149 Weekly Compilation of Presidential Documents, September 17, 2001.
150 'What September 11th Really Wrought', *Economist*, January 12, 2002, p. 25.
151 'The Saving of Pakistan?', *Economist*, January 19, 2002, p. 11.
152 Keesings Worldwide News Digest for September 2001, p. 44335.
153 John Vinocur, 'EU Solidarity Declaration Gives Both Sides a Victory', *International Herald Tribune*, September 24, 2001.
154 Keesings, pp. 44335, 44336.
155 Colin Powell, 'Statement for the Record', House International Relations Committee, US Congress, October 24, 2001.
156 'The United States and the Global Coalition Against Terrorism, September-December 2001: A Chronology', Office of the Historian, US Department of State (www.state.gov/r/pa/ho/pubs/fs/5889.htm).
157 Frum, 178.
158 'Anthrax isn't Contagious; Anxiety is', *Economist*, October 20, 2001, pp. 29-30.
159 Woodward, p. 270.
160 Colin Powell, 'A Strategy of Partnerships', *Foreign Affairs*, January/February 2004.
161 Woodward, p. 117.
162 Harold C. Relyea, 'Homeland Security: The Presidential Coordination Office', *Congressional Research Service* (Washington, D.C. October 10, 2001), pp. 1 and 6.
163 Sydney Freedberg, 'Shoring Up America', *National Journal*, October 19, 2001.
164 White House, Office of the Press Secretary, 'Remarks at the Swearing-In Ceremony for Tom Ridge as Director of Homeland Security', October 8, 2001.
165 Howard Fineman and Tamara Lipper, 'Bush's Homeland Shuffle', *Newsweek*, June 17, 2002, p. 31.
166 George Tenet in Testimony before the National Commission on Terrorist Attacks Upon the United States, March 24, 2004 (http://www.9-11commission.gov/hearings/hearing8.htm).
167 Danny Hakim, '2 Arabs Covicted and 2 Cleared of Terrorist Plot Against US', *New York Times*, June 4, 2003.
168 As quoted in Katharine Seelye, 'A Nation Challenged: The Military Tribunals', *New York Times*, December 8, 2001, p. B7.
169 Paul Wolfowitz, 'Testimony Before the Senate Armed Services Committee on Military Commissions', US Senate, Washington, D.C., December 13, 2001.
170 Katharine Seelye and David Sanger, 'Bush Reconsiders Stand on Treating Captives of War', *New York Times*, January 28, 2002, p. 1, 14.
171 'The Rights of Terrorists', *Economist*, January 19, 2002, p. 12.
172 Kirk Victor, 'Deconstructing Daschle', *National Journal*, June 1, 2002, p. 1614.
173 Elizabeth Bumiller, 'Multilateralist from Midland Takes the Stage', *New York Times*, November 12, 2001, p. B2.
174 Frum, p. 202.
175 Byron York, 'A Surplus of Anxiety', *National Review*, September 17, 2001, p. 17.
176 Noonan, January 4, 2002.
177 Karen Tumulty, 'Bush in the Glare', *Time*, January 21, 2002, p. 39.

178   Ryan Lizza, 'Lay Men', *The New Republic*, January 21, 2001, p. 12.

179   Ryan Lizza, 'Keep Away', *The New Republic*, January 28, 2002, p. 17.

180   Nicholas Lemann, 'Soft Money, Hard Lesson', *New Yorker*, January 28, 2002, p. 32.

181   Lexington, 'The Wrong Sort of Wall', *Economist*, February 2, 2002.

182   'Tom v. George', *Economist*, January 12, 2002, p. 27.

183   Alison Mitchell, 'First Salvo of Election Year: Daschle Speech on Economy', *New York Times*, January 4, 2002, p. 1.

184   Elisabeth Bumiller, 'Recent Bushisms Call for a Primer', *New York Times*, January 7, 2002, p. 14.

185   As quoted in Daniel Case, 'Back to Politics as Usual?', *Commentary*, March 2002, p. 28.

186   As quoted in Lou Dubose et al., *Boy Genius: Karl Rove, the Brains Behind the Remarkable Political Triumph of George W. Bush* (New York: PublicAffairs, 2003), p. 216, and in Thomas B. Edsall, 'GOP Touts War as Campaign Issue', *Washington Post*, January 19, 2002, p. 2.

187   Victor, p. 1614.

188   Frum quotes the *New York Times* source on p. 205 and made his conclusion on p. 206.

189   Richard Stevenson, 'President Submits $2 Trillion Budget That Raises Deficit', *New York Times*, February 5, 2002, pp. 1, 15.

190   Mitch Daniels, 'Remarks to the National Press Club', Washington, D.C., November 28, 2001.

191   White House, Office of the Press Secretary, 'President Speaks on War Effort to Citadel Cadets', Charleston, South Carolina, December 11, 2001.

192   Alexander George, *Presidential Decisionmaking In Foreign Policy* (Boulder: Westview Press, 1980), p. 32.

193   For example see Pierre Hassner, 'The United States: The Empire of Force or the Force of Empire', *Chaillot Papers*, No. 54, (Paris: EU Institute for Security Studies, September 2002), p. 38.

194   State of the Union Address, January 29, 2002.

195   Frum, p. 238.

196   Frum, p. 235.

197   David Sanger, 'Bush Aides Say Tough Tone Put Foes on Notice', *New York Times*, January 31, 2002, p. 12.

198   State of the Union Address, January 29, 2002.

199   Michael Hirsh and Roy Gutman, 'Powell's New War', *Newsweek*, February 11, 2002, p. 25.

200   'The Limits of Power', *Washington Post*, January 31, 2002, p. 26.

201   Hirsh and Gutman, p. 24.

202   'The Elusive Character of Victory', *Economist*, November 24, 2001, p. 11.

203   Armitage, 'Testimony'.

Chapter 6

The Iraq Nexus

George W. Bush's reason for removing Saddam Hussein is best explained by three threats forming a nexus in the eyes of the president and his close advisers. The threat of further terrorist attacks combined with the most deadly weapons, and supplied by the most hostile rogue state put Iraq in the cross hairs. The decision was made possible because military, diplomatic, and strategic reasons for taking on Iraq converged in late 2001. Bush made his 'in-principle' decision on regime change in January 2002, but followed it with a drawn-out strategy during which he persuaded the American public and Congress while fine-tuning his military options. The United Nations 'endgame' did not change Bush's goals but carried forward tenuous compromises among his advisers and Security Council members, which Bush resolved in January 2003.

The fast and highly successful war was followed by a most trying time of slow peace. Amidst increasing loss in life and growing costs, the administration's pre-war intelligence about weapons of mass destruction was found faulty. Bush's values in the war on terror and his vision for freedom and renewal in the Middle East became locked in a grueling battle with insurgents and terrorists in Iraq, and with skeptics nearly everywhere else for which the June 30, 2004 handover of Iraqi sovereignty would only be the end of the first chapter.

Early Signs

In 1998 Congress passed the Iraq Liberation Act and made regime change in Baghdad part of the law of the land. Of course, the law did not stipulate the use of military force but it was another expression, alongside the Missile Defense Act, of a strong Republican majority and a solid bloc of Democrats in Congress pointing American foreign policy into a specific direction. Bush's foreign policy advisers during the 1999-2000 campaign, the so-called Vulcans, considered Iraq 'unfinished business.' Several of these, such as Paul Wolfowitz, Richard Armitage and Robert Zoellick, had signed an open letter in 1998 warning the Clinton administration that Hussein's regime constituted an immediate threat and urging the government to do more to help Iraqi dissident groups to bring about the removal of Saddam Hussein's regime. By 2002, ten of the eighteen signatories served in senior positions in the Bush administration. The day George W. Bush nominated Colin Powell as his secretary of state, Powell commented to the press, 'Saddam Hussein is sitting on a failed regime that is not going to be around in a few years.'[1] In the fall of 2000, both Al Gore and Bush supported stronger opposition to Saddam Hussein, but Bush added that he would 'take him out if he continued to develop weapons of mass destruction.'[2] Paul O'Neill, the disgruntled former Secretary of the Treasury, revealed in early 2004, that Iraq had been an agenda item already during Bush's first National Security Council meeting on January 20.[3] At their first bilateral meeting at Camp David in February 2001, Bush and Britain's Tony Blair discussed the danger posed by Hussein's chemical and biological weapons.[4]

In early 2001, Bush's National Security Council set up an interagency policy review headed by Richard Haass, to examine options on how to deal with Iraq. Like a similar review on Al Qaeda and international terror, the paper process on Iraq never made it high up the President's policy agenda before the attacks of September 11, 2001. Meanwhile, Powell was given considerable room to try his hand at negotiating 'smart sanctions' – the idea was to make the United Nations' mandated 'Oil-for-food' program smarter by making Iraq's access to dual-use technology more difficult while easing the country's food requirements. Without a new policy, Bush continued Clinton's 'whack-a-mole' approach towards Saddam Hussein.[5] Every time the dictator would stick his head out, by targeting British or American planes enforcing the no-fly zones in the south and north, the President would whack him with air strikes, as he did on February 16, 2001. No one in the Bush administration felt that smart sanctions or air strikes would solve the Iraq problem.

Nexus and the Regime Change Decision

The first to put Iraq right at the top of the American policy agenda was Deputy Secretary of Defense Paul Wolfowitz, at the Camp David meetings in the wake of the September 11, 2001 attacks. Perhaps better than any other foreign policy adviser, Wolfowitz sensed very early that the emerging war on terror would require Bush to develop a strategic vision beyond missile defense and homeland security. Not only did this modern Pearl Harbor turn the tables of domestic and foreign policy priorities upside down, it also had to bring all of the President's main initiatives in foreign and national security into one overriding vision. Despite the burgeoning conspiracy theories, the Bush administration did not get 'hijacked' by Wolfowitz's ideas as so many critics have matter of factly concluded.[6] Quite pragmatically, Bush decided on first things first. Operation Enduring Freedom targeted Al Qaeda worldwide and the Taliban regime in Afghanistan, but 'Wolfie,' as Bush often calls him in private, did plant a mustard seed of strategic thought which found fertile soil in the President's own values on how to connect general principles enunciated during the 2000 campaign such as 'defenses beyond challenge', and 'a balance of power that favors freedom', with the monumental new tasks ahead in the war on terror.

Bush grew into this strategic vision little by little, mostly as a result of his own thoughts, sharpened or rounded by multiple sources of advice. He was the one who laid the foundation within hours of the planes hitting the buildings, by calling it a 'war', not a crime. Within days the President wiped out years of conventional knowledge on terrorism, namely that terrorists were stateless and faceless. It would not just be a war on terrorists but also on the states that gave them safe haven. He told Congressional leaders on September 12, 2001, 'These guys are like rattlesnakes; they strike and go back in their holes; we're not only going to go after the holes, we're going to go after the ranchers.'[7]

Bush's own feeling of right and wrong, his own sense of purpose in life laid the foundation of his first doctrine: international terror means war. By September 20, after hearing from all his advisers, Bush was completely clear about the first layer of construction upon his new foundation: states that harbor or assist terrorists were also terrorists, and would have to change their policies or face serious consequences. There was no consensus yet on what actions that would entail, nor did he naively intend one policy to suit all, but it was clear that the President's strategy would reach beyond the immediate perpetrators of the attacks. That is the essence of the second part of the Bush Doctrine.

The third layer of this doctrine grew gradually in the fall of 2001. Its essence is the nexus or connecting point between Bush's war on terror and the question: what would Al Qaeda do next? Powell expressed it in Congress as follows: 'A new reality was born. The world had to recognize that the potential connection between terrorists and weapons of mass destruction moved terrorism to a new level of threat. In fact, that nexus became the overriding security concern of our nation.'[8] The nexus between terrorists, countries that help them, and weapons that may make them spectacularly more successful created the governmental and policy conditions to go after Hussein's regime in Iraq. The doctrine combines the threats of weapon proliferation, rogue states, and international terror and includes countries beyond Iraq such as Iran, Syria and Libya.

In October 2001, American intelligence picked up considerable traffic about a plan to detonate a 'dirty bomb' in a major American city, possibly Washington, D.C.[9] Conventional explosives wrapped around a crude nuclear bomb would set off a nightmare of death and destruction. The anthrax attacks that gripped the nation during the same time acted like an echo; if it was not going to be nuclear, it could be a biological attack. A few months later, as American forces began to comb through Taliban and Al Qaeda buildings in Afghanistan, they found a lot of drawings and rudimentary plans to acquire nuclear, chemical and biological weapons. Osama Bin Laden had said it was his 'religious duty' to acquire weapons of mass destruction and Bush chose to believe him.[10]

The public attacks on the Bush Administration for not connecting the intelligence dots before the September 11 attacks did not come until the spring of 2002, but in the fall of 2001, the administration was already 'reviewing' this question in an informal way, spearheaded by Vice President Dick Cheney. Perhaps no one was as focused on a potential second attack as he was – in his interview with Nicolas Lemann, months before the attacks, Cheney was already deeply concerned about so called asymmetrical attacks where an undetected enemy uses biological or nuclear devices or computer sabotage to paralyze the nation. The fundamental questions before Bush after September was not rocket science – what was the essential objective of the Al Qaeda attacks? It was obvious: to wreak maximum destruction without warning. The loss of American life was the objective. Would they strike again? The only thing that seemed to limit them was capability. How could they better their 9/11 strike? Again, the answer appeared plain enough: by using some form, any form, of a weapon of mass destruction, especially biological and nuclear weapons, as chemical weapons are more difficult to disperse. What would happen if a second 9/11 with such a weapon were to take place? The gigantic economic costs, the national security paralysis, and the political crisis that such an attack would bring were truly astronomical. Bush, who is decisive in normal times, had no illusions but that he needed to consider the most robust form of preventive action.

This very stark calculation of interest during a period of time when the President and his advisers lived in what analysts of foreign policy call 'a psychological environment' of immediate threat produced a very robust, forward leaning nexus policy. Their 'definition of the situation' determined the direction of the next move in the war on terror.[11] Not only was the war bigger than Al Qaeda and the Taliban, it was also a race against the clock to prevent them from getting weapons of mass destruction. The war must thus be extended beyond merely ferreting out Al Qaeda and creating worldwide intelligence networks to dry up any supply line of terror weapons. The question was where they might acquire these. The big nuclear powers were ruled out early as a direct source for Al Qaeda, although Russia's supply of nuclear material to Iran remained a contentious issue. There was grave concern about Russian nuclear material getting mixed into the black market and so Bush led a $20 billion G-8 initiative in early 2002 to clean up these supplies.

Pakistani scientists and nuclear materials were at the top of the Bush Administration concerns – and in fact the focus of some intelligence – on 'dirty bombs,' but the Bush administration had succeeded in turning Pakistan's leader General Musharraf and his government into a close ally in September 2001. The President did not act naively. He knew that Pakistan was 'the most threatening' of failed states and 'a breeding ground for terrorism',[12] but he would work with and through Musharraf to deal with Pakistan as a source. Some called it a Faustian bargain, in which the hero of that medieval legend sells his soul to the devil in exchange for power and knowledge, but Bush had few good options in Pakistan and squeezing Musharraf tightly in a friendly embrace was the least bad choice. When it became clear that Pakistan's nuclear pioneer, Abdul Qadeer Khan, had also been a major supplier of nuclear materials to other states such as Libya, Musharraf helped Bush to shut off that supply line of illegal exports.

Next after Pakistan were the aspiring nuclear states, some of whom also had known stocks of biological and chemical weapons, or were suspected of having clandestine programs to get these. The list included Iraq, Iran, Syria, Libya, and North Korea. Libya and Syria were eliminated as urgent cases as their programs were deemed too rudimentary – they would be mentioned, however, a year later in Bush's National Security Presidential Directive-17 released in December 2002.[13] The critical next step in the nexus argument the Bush administration made was determining which of the remaining states would be most intent on harming the United States, and willing to take the greatest risk in so doing. Iran was a known sponsor of terrorism in Lebanon and Israel, moreover one of its clients, the terrorist group called Hezbollah, had taken American life before. The shipment of weapons on the vessel *Karina*, intercepted in early 2002 and destined for the Palestinian leadership, came from Iran. North Korea was locked in mortal diplomatic battle with the Bush Administration right from the start when the President told South Korea's leader that he would not continue Clinton's attempt to buy off North Korea's nuclear or missile violations without up front verification. No one of course needed to argue long that Iraq was right up there as Hussein's regime was widely believed to hold stockpiles of biological and chemical weapons, and was the only government in the world that openly celebrated the September 11 events.

The nexus argument put these three into the President's State of the Union Address in January 2002. They are 'evil' because of their stated hostility to the United States, the evil nature of their repressive government and because they could be the source of doomsday weapons for Al Qaeda. Following the now-famous 'Axis of evil' phrase, Bush devoted another paragraph to describing the specific threat posed by Iraq. It was clear that Iraq was singled out. Indeed, Mike Gerson, Bush's influential speechwriter had told his assistant, David Frum, in December to get him 'the best case for going after Iraq'.[14]

The Bush administration had few good options in North Korea as that evil regime held Seoul's population hostage with its guns only forty kilometers away. Unlike Iran and Iraq, who were both suspected of having some interaction with Al Qaeda people, there was no such link with North Korea. With both Russia and China right on North Korea's border, Bush could not lightly afford a Russian or Chinese veto over his actions. If he set out to overthrow the regime of Kim Jong Il and somewhere down the line China or Russia said 'no', he would have a nuclear standoff on his hands. Moreover, the administration was slowly making progress on bringing all North Korea's neighbors along in a strategy of combined diplomatic pressure. Despite his strong language on North Korea, neither he nor anyone in his circle of advisers was advocating a military option towards the 'hermit kingdom'. Iran's regime was 'rational' compared with the other two and also had a healthy and growing internal opposition, so a combination of outside and inside pressure seemed a smart choice to influence Tehran. In sum, a diplomatic strategy still had a chance in Iran and was the only option for North Korea. Powell called these two that part of the axis of evil 'we hope to talk to'.[15] No such calculations existed for Saddam Hussein who had defied coercive diplomacy for more than a decade.

What really completed the nexus argument on Iraq was intent. In his testimony before Congress in September 2002 Rumsfeld said, 'No living dictator has shown the murderous combination of intent and capability ...'[16] George Tenet, in late October 2001, told Bush that in terms of 'capability and malice' Iraq topped the list.[17] Even though Hussein's secular Baathist government had nothing in common with the fundamentalist militant vision of Al Qaeda, their mutual virulent hatred for America could turn them into fast friends. In the fall of 2001, there were reports about an Al Qaeda-friendly camp run by Ansar al-Islam in the north of Iraq and there was an on-again, off-again report that one of the September 11 hijackers had met with an Iraqi agent in Prague. In an interview with Nicolas Lemann in September 2002, Condoleezza Rice revealed the sentiment in the White House. She said, 'Saddam's regime and Al Qaeda have been orbiting each other quite a lot.'[18] This 'orbiting' is what sealed the nexus argument. If Bush wanted to 'lean forward' as Donald Rumsfeld had advised him right from his arrival in the White House[19] – and after 9/11 he wanted to lean with all his might – he had to take the risky step of knocking down the first outlaw state that might help terrorists in the new war on terror simply because it hated America and because it could.

The second reason why President Bush decided to put regime change in Iraq on the top of his list in late 2001 can be called a 'pile-on' argument. At issue here is how a large organization such as the US government with various interests can come together behind one common goal: Iraq was a case where different players inside the Bush administration came to support the same option for divergent reasons. The military came on board because the success in Afghanistan made the operation look doable; the diplomats joined (reluctantly) because the sanctions regime was showing few results and they had no good alternative options; and finally, the strategists saw an opportunity to send a strong signal to other rogue states that helping terrorism or making weapons of mass destruction would not pay.

The professional military engaged in a war in Afghanistan could be expected to have grave hesitations about taking on a middle-sized power in the heart of the Middle East, but by the end of January the military campaign against the Taliban was turning into a clear success. The CIA and Special Operation Forces, in coalition with the Northern Alliance and assisted by precision guided ammunitions from the air created a fast war with lots of surprise and 'a light footprint.' Relatively few troops were needed to rout the Taliban. It was a vindication of Rumsfeld's vision for military transformation. There would be military disappointments later in the Tora Bora region when US forces failed to capture Bin Laden, but in terms of defeating the Taliban, Rumsfeld's military operation was a huge success. The military knew that Iraq was only half as strong as in 1991. If Operation Enduring Freedom worked as well as it did, perhaps Hussein could be toppled more easily than was believed before. As one civilian official in the Pentagon commented, 'Afghanistan made the idea of regime change seem less exotic.'[20] Tommy Franks, the President's commander for the region that includes Afghanistan and Iraq, joined Bush at his Crawford ranch in December 2001 where Franks gave him an upbeat scenario on Iraq. After some initial tension, Franks and Rumsfeld had cemented a strong bond in the built-up to Afghanistan. A low-key son of Midland Texas, Franks had been able to make himself the bridge between the demanding transformer Rumsfeld and the military establishment. Franks, described by friends as 'a good ol' boy', low-key and unpretentious, would easily capture the respect and friendship of Bush. 'I really like Tommy. We speak the same language,' he said.[21]

In early September 2001, in a moment of exasperation over the tremendous opposition to his transformation plans he experienced from the Pentagon brass, Donald Rumsfeld had declared the Pentagon bureaucracy a 'mortal enemy', but September 11 changed the political dynamic of his struggle to modernize military strategy and equipment.[22] The war meant that Rumsfeld could impose new methods and strategy as part of the battlefield while Congress would appropriate for both conventional and new equipment. It was not good for Bush's budget in the long run as the pie was simply made bigger and trade-offs were postponed. In 2002 Rumsfeld managed to cancel only one major weapons program, the $11 billion Army Crusader artillery gun. Donald Rumsfeld had been a strong advocate of removing Saddam Hussein for some time and he needed no other arguments to bring him on board with one exception: if a war on Iraq would threaten to derail Rumsfeld's plans for transformation, he might perhaps hesitate. In fact the opposite would be the case, for if it came to war, Rumsfeld believed he could show the merits of his transformation plans in terms of reducing loss of life on both sides, revolutionizing strategy, and winning quickly.

Of all Bush's close advisers, Cheney took the 'most dire view of the terrorist threat' as his experiences had included enough close calls.[23] While he was secretary of defense in the early 1990s under Bush's father, US intelligence had told him repeatedly that Hussein was as much as ten years away from acquiring nuclear weapons. When arms inspectors went in after Desert Storm they found Iraq within a year or two of building such weapons. Given that fiasco and the failure of US intelligence to detect the hijackers of September 11, Cheney's counsel to the President was to act on the worst-case scenario, to not act rashly, but to connect the dots before rather than after the event. Those who knew Cheney for a long time noticed that he became more 'doggedly determined' and more 'secretive in his ways' in the lead up to Iraq.[24] A phrase was born in the White House, 'we don't want the smoking gun to be a mushroom cloud.'[25] For Rumsfeld and Cheney, removing Hussein was not a matter of vision or strategy, it was prudent, necessary, and ultimately, doable policy.

Various media reports about a profound and prolonged bureaucratic struggle between Powell and Cheney or Rumsfeld over Iraq must be looked at carefully.[26] First, there is no evidence that Powell ever opposed regime change in Iraq, as the questions for him was not 'whether' but 'how' and 'when'. Clearly, this leaves considerable daylight between Cheney and Powell, but it is not about continuing the existing policy versus regime change. At the same time, Powell's entire career makes it plain that he did not sign on to a single military solution early in the game. He was hesitant about using force in the first Gulf War, in Somalia and again in the Balkan Wars. For Wolfowitz, the 'pile on' dynamic behind targeting Iraq created an opportunity to tie toppling Hussein into a larger vision for Bush's foreign policy. But the debate about whether Iraq was a stand-alone policy or the beginning of a comprehensive approach to changing the politics of the Middle East did not have to be resolved when Bush decided on regime change in Iraq. Powell could favor regime change in Iraq without 'signing up' for Wolfowitz's larger vision or an inevitable war option.

The crucial decision on regime change appears to have come in January 2002.[27] There was no single meeting at which the president put the question on the table, asked for a recommendation and then made a decision. Rather, the decision evolved gradually. First, the nexus argument made regime change necessary, then, Bush was briefed by the CIA that Saddam could not be overthrown by covert means.[28] Bush had taken Rumsfeld aside as early as November 21, 2001 to look at what it would take to remove Saddam Hussein 'if we have to'. Bush wanted Rumsfeld and Franks to start on this without it being 'terribly noticeable'.[29] By late December, Franks briefed Bush in Crawford on the first version of a conceptual plan for attacking Iraq with all the other Principal advisers such as Cheney and Powell joined in by video conferencing. Thus Bush did not exclude any major player from this early option. On February 12, 2002, Powell testified before the Senate that there was 'an emerging consensus' to overthrow Hussein, and that the administration was considering 'a variety of options to topple Saddam Hussein'. 'We've finally jelled,' he commented.[30] On February 16, Bush signed a presidential decision that made the removal of Iraq's regime, America's strategic objective and requested $200 million from Congress for CIA operations to that effect.[31]

In March, Cheney made a trip to the key states surrounding Iraq such as Oman, Bahrain, Qatar, Jordan, Kuwait, United Arab Emirates, Saudi Arabia as well as the United Kingdom. He took no reporters along. Cheney briefed these allies on Bush's direction and tried to get from them a sense of their military contribution in any campaign against Iraq.

A Drawn-out Strategy

With Bush deciding as early as January to proceed with Iraqi regime change, it is a fair question why the rest of the decision making process (when and how) took so long. There are several answers to this question. First, contrary to a popular perception of this president as a rash and trigger-happy person, he is usually a disciplined decision-maker who tends to err on the side of a very deliberate process. The CEO in Bush likes to plan and strategize. Even under the greatest pressure right after 9/11, he took four weeks before launching his attack. In those weeks, he made the case to the American people, to Congress, and built an international coalition while his advisers were hammering out the best military package. In the case of Iraq, Bush followed a similar game plan: while his advisers worked on the options for his final decision, he went out to make the public case for his objectives, following the model for both his domestic and foreign policy. Given that war may result, Bush included a variety of military bases or functions as places to make his speeches. These speeches are not rhetoric as many at first believed,[32] but thoroughly prepared and rehearsed remarks – he typically means exactly what he says and says quite frankly what he means. The objectives are coined in terms of values and Bush uses rich value language not simply because focus group marketing tests have shown that people respond better to values than to intellectual terms, but also because he works with interests defined in terms of values. The President had a big job ahead convincing the American people that Iraq was the most important next chapter in the war on terror. He took his time, staying on message, and gradually winning over public opinion to his definition of the threat.

On April 17, at the Virginia Military Institute in Lexington, Bush said, 'we will not allow the world's most dangerous regimes to threaten us with the world's most dangerous weapons.' On June 1 during the graduation ceremony at West Point, Bush stated, 'Containment is not possible when unbalanced dictators with weapons of mass destruction can deliver those weapons on missiles, or secretly provide them to the terrorist allies.' He added, 'we must take the battle to the enemy,' and be 'forward looking', and 'be ready for preemptive action ...' This was the first time Bush used the term 'preemption'. Bush did not change his tone abroad. Addressing the German Parliament in Berlin on May 23, he explained, 'Wishful thinking might bring comfort, but not security. Call this a strategic challenge; call it, as I do, axis of evil; call it by any name you choose, but let us speak the truth.' On July 19, speaking to troops from the 10th Mountain Division at Fort Drum, New York, Bush said, 'We're threatened by regimes that have sought these ultimate weapons, and hide their weapons programs from the eyes of the world. The same regimes have shown their true nature by torturing and butchering their own people. We will use diplomacy when possible, and force when necessary.'[33] By the end of the summer, public opinion polls showed solid support for strong action against Iraq. Polls in August showed that almost 80 per cent of Americans believed Saddam Hussein was a threat, 67 per cent thought that military action was necessary, and some 59 per cent supported the use of US ground forces in such a campaign.[34]

There were other reasons why the process took so long: at Crawford, in December, Franks had shown the President the off-the-shelf version of a military attack on Iraq. It involved some 400,000 troops and was dubbed Gulf War II. Franks assured Bush that he was not contemplating this option, and promised something smaller, faster and riskier.[35] Rumsfeld let his advisers also look into a very light option, the so-called 'Afghanistan Redux'.[36] This option would use CIA and Special Ops forces in conjunction with a dissident Iraqi exile force. These forces would work with a Kurdish ground presence in the North, a very controversial option with a long history. Ahmad Chalabi, the leader of the Iraqi National Congress, had actually tried an insurrection in the north in 1995 and failed. Many officials in the CIA and in the Department of State believed that Chalabi did not represent Iraqis well, that his plans were naïve, and that he could not be trusted. Some of the people working with Wolfowitz wanted to take another look at 'Afghan Redux' or even lighter options. Their argument was that the Clinton administration had not supported the CIA and Iraqi National Congress well enough and that the lessons of Afghanistan showed the possibility of a light operation in Iraq. Richard Perle, the Chair of the Defense Policy Board was a strong supporter of Chalabi. General Richard Downing, whom Bush appointed to his National Security Council in October 2001 to combat terrorism, had just finished a career in Special Operations and played a key role in drawing up a plan while the State Department under Colin Powell remained skeptical.[37] General Anthony Zinni, who had been in Frank's position earlier, was the most outspoken critic, believing that this plan would lead to a repeat of the infamous 'Bay of Pigs' incident when President Kennedy sent a group of Cuban exiles to oust Fidel Castro in 1961. Castro pinned them on the beach and finished them off in short order. Zinni called the plan the 'Bay of Goats'.[38] Rumsfeld eventually rejected the plan as there simply was no equivalent of the Northern Alliance in Iraq and the Iraqi army, with six Republican Guard units in operation, was much stronger than the Taliban.

Bush had wanted a final military option by April 15 for a June decision.[39] In the early months of 2002, Rumsfeld kept boring into Frank's war plans like a 'dentist's drill that never ceased.'[40] On April 20, Franks presented the National Security Council with a Desert Storm Lite version, involving between 200,000 and 250,000 troops.[41] With strong coaching from Rumsfeld, Bush sent the plan back to Franks and his commanders at Central Command. Rumsfeld wanted a more nimble version with fewer troops, more strategic surprise, and more flexibility in logistics and speed of operations; Franks and Rumsfeld would work closely together to fine-tune this package. When Bush met with European colleagues and Russia's Vladimir Putin in May 2002, they expressed their concern that the President's strong speeches on Iraq seemed to indicate he was about to launch a war. He told them of the need for regime change, but also that he had made no final decision on how he would remove Saddam Hussein and that he had no 'war plans on his desk'.[42] The reason he did not was because he had sent them back. Pentagon planners had also told Bush that American stocks for precision guided munitions and cruise missiles would not be replenished until the early fall.[43] General Franks and Rumsfeld finished their fine-tuned plan in August.

The third reason for the lengthy process is that Bush's decision on regime change in Baghdad never excluded non-military options up front. In fact, soon after his 'axis of evil' speech, Baghdad contacted UN Secretary General Kofi Annan to start 'a new dialogue' on Iraq.[44] This open-ended approach allowed Powell to make a final push for smart sanctions and urge the Security Council to reinstate arms inspections, which had ended in 1998 when Hussein evicted the United Nations Special Commission on the destruction of Iraqi weapons of mass destruction (UNSCOM). It is often overlooked that the Bush administration actually made two attempts in 2002 to get United Nations inspections back in Iraq. The first effort was admittedly done without the personal imprint of Bush, as he let Powell push the UN Security Council process to see what would come out of it. It turned out to be not much since France and Russia were reluctant about the smart sanctions. They believed Hussein was sufficiently contained and were actually ready to normalize relations and therefore had no interest in starting another round of controversial inspections. Both French and Russian oil companies had big contracts to develop oil fields in Iraq and Hussein's regime owed both states a good deal of money.

In 1999, Bill Clinton and Tony Blair had pushed for a new weapons inspection program for Iraq called the UN Monitoring, Verification and Inspection Commission, known as UNMOVIC. However, neither Russia nor France had allowed the UN Security Council to put real pressure on Saddam to allow UNMOVIC inspectors into the country. Reports in 2004 that Saddam had engaged in billions of dollars of kickbacks in the 'Oil-for-Food' program raised questions whether countries such as France and Russia were hiding other substantial interests behind their rejection of further pressure on Iraq.

With Bush's strong language on Iraq in early 2002, and Powell's new demand that the Iraqi government must allow unfettered access to inspectors, the government in Baghdad began to stir.[45] On March 7, Kofi Annan announced that talks with Iraq would begin in mid-April; Hans Blix, a Swedish diplomat now in charge of UNMOVIC, joined Annan in the talks. Iraq negotiated with Annan and Blix, but sought clear limitations on the inspections, stalled the proceedings, and generally confirmed that it would only cooperate to the extent that pressure was exerted. For example, in April Hussein announced his representatives would not meet with Annan until May 'in order not to take attention away from the violence in Palestinian areas.'[46] At the Arab League Summit in Beirut in late March, Hussein pledged to respect the territorial integrity of his neighbors, but by July 5, talks between Iraq and Annan ground to a halt. Iraq was not going to give 'immediate, unconditional and unrestricted access' to Blix and his team.[47] It is very important to remember that in light of this stalling game, Cheney would in late August express his doubts about another UN inspections round making much difference. It was not just the experience of the 1990s he was referring to, but also Iraq's stalling tactics earlier in 2002.

The President's slow march on Iraq coincided with the preparation of his administration's National Security Strategy assessment that it must, by law, submit to Congress every two years. While this process did not per se halt progress on Iraq, it did draw out an internal discussion about the overall American strategic direction and how Iraq fit in. These discussions helped Bush to cement his approach on Iraq within an overall vision for freedom and prosperity in the Middle East. It made him more convinced and more determined that pushing for regime change was the key to bringing real progress to that part of the world. Wolfowitz wrote in the *Jerusalem Post* in early 2003 that 'the idea that we could live with another 20 years of stagnation in the Middle East that breeds this radicalism and breeds terrorism is, I think, just unacceptable.'[48]

On this vision, Wolfowitz was far from alone. Douglas Feith, his deputy, 'Scooter' Libby, Cheney's right hand man, as well as various people on the National Security Council, such as Elliot Abrams and increasingly, according to speech writer David Frum, Condi Rice herself, believed in this view.[49] She came, of course, from the school of Realism, which had always favored stability and security over democracy in the Middle East, but September 11, 2001 had truly changed the international system and the United States could no longer afford to be a mere 'status quo' great power as Henry Kissinger had once defined the term. Rather than being defensive, Bush had to turn American power into a revolutionary direction, just as Harry Truman had to take on the revolutionary task of stopping communism wherever he could and Reagan had to explain again to the American people that the Soviet Union was 'evil' to push for its final demise.

The vision that America had to foster real change in the Middle East rather than change its own policies in that region, as most critics contended, appealed to George W. Bush at multiple levels. He wanted to signal that it did not pay to have weapons of mass destruction, but he also wanted to be *for* something. Bush is not doctrinaire or Machiavellian. He is not a neo-conservative or 'neocon,' a much-abused term that presumably means someone who was once a liberal but now has turned into a strong conservative. If anything, Bush has some 'theocon', in him, deriving some of his ideas from principles of faith rather than from any ideology. The whole scheme, which in 2004 came to be known as the 'Greater Middle East Initiative,' appealed to him at another level also. Changing a region without hope into a beacon of light is what Bush likes best. Think of his education policy of 'leaving no child behind', or his compassionate conservatism. It is all about using revolutionary means to establish old truths of individual responsibility, freedom, security and prosperity. Liberals had practiced a type of soft bigotry by not testing inner-city black and Hispanic kids or letting them have lower standards, thus benevolently condemning them to second-class status. The liberal and secular argument that no faith-based institutions could be allowed in the field of welfare had left thousands of destitute people with enough government welfare money to buy drugs or alcohol, but with no hope or purpose in their hearts to turn their life around.

The same eternal truths could now be applied to international politics. At this junction, Wolfowitz's 'practical idealism' found common ground with Bush's optimistic beliefs in progress.[50] Intellectual and professional realists did with Islam and Arab peoples what Liberals had done to the urban poor at home. Bush would give the region a new lease on life; he would empower them. Responsible governments (Bush uses 'freedom' more often than democracy) would bring prosperity to the region and those two bastions would become the check on radical militant Islam. Even before the terrorist attacks, he had thought about big plans to free all the repressed people who lived in all remaining outlaw regimes. There is no bigger goal than 'world peace', he told Bob Woodward in August 2002.[51] He would begin with toppling Hussein in the Middle East and create out of that country the forerunner of a new Arab world in which people of Islamic faith could enjoy freedom and prosperity, as well as practice their faith. Iraq was oil-rich, had a well-educated population and something of a middle class. If not Iraq, then where? Why not let Arab democracy rather than American soldiers be the 'counterweight to Islamist extremism?'[52]

Powell was part of all these discussions in mid-2002 before the Strategy document was made public on September 20. It fell on him, Richard Armitage, his political director Marc Grossman and Richard Haass to temper the vision with a realist checklist and set it in the right multilateral perspective. Powell did not reject the vision, but again his point was that it mattered a great deal by what means Bush would pursue his vision. For Powell both the case of regime change in Iraq and the new strategic vision for the Middle East had to follow the path of America leading a broad coalition of its allies and partners down this new road. It must be a road in which all peaceful and diplomatic avenues are explored before military force is applied. Bush, in turn, had no problem with Powell's position. He never expressed a romantic notion of war as the agent of change and he could thus agree with both Wolfowitz's objectives and Powell's strategy. At the end of the day, however, the president would not break faith with his just goals if it meant only war could get him there. Of course this left a great deal of tension unresolved.

The last reason the entire Iraq process was so drawn out has to do with timing. Sometimes there is a 'sweet spot' in politics where what you want to do, how you do it, and the right timetable, all come together for good. Since his victory in Texas in 1994, Bush has always practiced the dictum that there is no use wasting the pursuit of good values by means of bad politics. Of course, the White House started planning for the November 2002 mid-term elections the moment it arrived in Washington. Karl Rove does not sit on the National Security Council, but he, like Karen Hughes, has ample access to the President before and after policy recommendations are made to him. Like Rice, Cheney and Card, Rove keeps his own counsel to the President completely confidential. Conspiracy theories about Rove's 'Rasputin-like' influence are all too easy to make. Many suspected Rove of orchestrating the entire Iraq decision and its timing, but Woodward, who did hundreds of hours of interviews with senior players, concluded that Rove 'took no direct part in the decision process for war planning.'[53] Not only is Bush in charge of his own strategy, it is also doubtful that people like Cheney or Rumsfeld would put their destiny into the hands of Rove. On the war against terror, it is more helpful to think of Rove as the senior adviser on the political impact of basic national security decisions.

Very likely, Bush and Rove, with the help of the 'Strategery group', devised a general game plan on the domestic aspects of the Iraq decision in early 2002. To what extent it actually played out we do not yet know. It is not inconceivable, given the strong consensus among Bush's national security advisers in January 2002, that the White House planned to move more quickly on Iraq but that the policy was slowed down by Rumsfeld and Franks going back and forth on the military plans. Also, Rove could not be sure what military option would finally come out of the Pentagon or how the talks between Annan and Iraq in the Spring of 2002 would turn out. Rove advised GOP campaign workers in Austin in January 2002 to make the war on terror and the issue of national security a top campaign item. The tax cuts were not yet turning the economy around and the jobless rate was still on the rise. As corporate scandals broke out in the spring of 2002, and the stock market dove down in their wake, Rove's logic would only become stronger. He was also organizing a nation-wide fundraising campaign, candidate selection for the House and Senate in key states and a very robust travel schedule for Bush and Cheney.

Decision Making: The Endgame

Every month Franks briefed Bush and his top advisers on the evolving military plan and by June, the version was nearing its final draft.[54] By July, Powell realized that talks with the Iraqi government to get an inspection team back into that country were going nowhere. He chose to make a final pitch for putting a new American-led UN initiative in front of the military option. Bush met with Powell and Rice at his White House residence on August 5.[55] Powell made the case that regime change without the diplomatic route held grave risks for the President that he did not need to take at this point. War would remove Saddam, and then 'You are going to be the proud owner of 25 million people,' Powell told Bush. Did Bush want his entire first term to be defined by Iraq?[56] Bush, who had enjoyed building the international coalition behind Operation Enduring Freedom in 2001, was open to Powell's suggestion. It was not a new option as Britain's Tony Blair had started advising as early as June that Bush needed to create a route to Baghdad via New York in order for Blair to pledge British troops in the campaign, if war was the last option.[57] The British Prime Minister received a lot of flak in the British press for being the President's 'poodle', or as one Member of Parliament dubbed him, 'the Honourable Member for Texas North.'[58] In fact Blair's influence on Bush was considerable and can be compared to that of a mainline secretary such as Powell. It was also the British Prime Minister who asked Bush to cast his policy in terms of disarmament rather than regime change.[59] The president obliged as perhaps he felt that at the end of the day there would be little difference between the two.

Bush took Powell's advice to his ranch, and in discussions with Rice, he came to see Powell's case as a win-win scenario. Why not 'Put the monkey on the UN's back,'[60] as Rice put it, to have its own resolutions enforced and in so doing obtain Iraq's disarmament? If the UN would not do it, at least Bush could not be accused of being unilateralist; if Iraq would not cooperate, at least the UN would join Bush in the fight. Both Blair and Powell were 'pushing an open door'.[61] On August 14, Rice chaired a Principal's meeting with all the main advisers in Washington to consider Powell's plan. Two days later they met again with Bush, now joining them by secure video. Cheney and Rumsfeld endorsed Powell's plan and the president told his advisers, 'He wanted to give the United Nations a chance.'[62]

Meanwhile a debate in the national newspapers broke out over the President's saber rattling on Iraq. Brent Scowcroft, national security adviser to Bush's father warned on August 15 in the *Wall Street Journal* about the dire consequences of going to war with Iraq. Such a war, according to Scowcroft, would detract from the 'real' war against Al Qaeda, and the controversy over such action would weaken if not break the international coalition supporting Bush, and the Middle East would turn into a more unstable and insecure region as a result, likely to produce more Al Qaeda recruits.

The public did not know that the Bush administration had already gone over these arguments and basically rejected them in favor of regime change. The Administration, including Powell, was closer to George Schultz who wrote in the *Washington Post* a few weeks after Scowcroft, 'if you know there is a rattlesnake in the yard, you don't wait for it to strike before you take action in self-defense.'[63] What the NSC did not resolve on August 16 was exactly what Bush would ask from the United Nations for the simple reason that Cheney had almost no faith in the UN route, while Powell had put all his weight on that option. Cheney's comments on August 26 were reported as signifying a split in the administration, which may be so, but the comments are also part of a strategic message from Bush's vantage point. After citing a long list of earlier Iraqi arms violations, discoveries and cover ups, Cheney said, 'Against that background, a person would be right to question any suggestion that we should just get inspectors back into Iraq, and then our worries will be over.'[64] He reinforced this by saying that a return of inspectors alone would thus not provide assurance of Hussein's compliance. Many in Washington believed Cheney's comments showed that an all-out bureaucratic war was raging between Powell and Cheney over whether Bush would go to the UN or not, but that issue had already been settled. Cheney was 'walking the point' for the President, signaling that while the United States would go to the UN, it was not looking for business as usual.[65] Bush had gone over the fine points with Cheney in a long private conversation. 'Cheney does not freelance,' one of his senior advisers commented.[66] Bush and his advisers now agreed that his scheduled speech at the UN for September 12 would be recast from a general vision speech to a specific case against Iraq.

Yet, some amount of tactical disagreement about what the President would ask from the UN was never resolved among the senior advisers. Powell made the case up till the very last draft of his speech (number 23) that Bush should ask for a new UN Security Council resolution. Both Cheney and Rumsfeld wanted to avoid a scenario in which the UN Security Council blocked such a request (after all there are four other veto members). If this happened, the legal case for the war would actually be weaker, for in their view, Iraq's repeated violations of numerous UN Security Council Resolutions since 1991 was all the legal and political ground needed to go to war. Alberto Gonzales, the President's legal counsel, released a statement to the effect that there already existed a legal *casus belli* against Iraq. Cheney preferred that Bush should ask a simple commitment from the United Nations to 'meet our mutual challenge'. In the end, Bush did both, asking the United Nations 'to act',[67] and ad libbing that he would 'work with the UN for the necessary resolutions.'[68] The plural 'resolutions' appears to have been a simple slip of the tongue, though in the end that is what happened.

There is no doubt that Bush scored a brilliant tactical victory with his address to the United Nations on September 12. Karen Hughes helped Mike Gerson and Condi Rice put a lawyer's brief into easy-to-understand language.[69] The nature of the public debate thus far had been stark threats and earnest values with critics saying that Bush 'the warmonger' was going after Iraq all by himself. Cheney's questioning the need for UN inspectors on August 26 had added to that perception. In a type of replay of his September 20, 2001 coherent and persuasive case for war on terror, the President now made an eloquent internationalist case for the United Nations to enforce its own resolutions. The *Economist* commented, 'Mr. Bush calmly pulled the rug from under his critics' feet.'[70] Those who had again underestimated him and believed Bush would defeat himself in his determination to topple Hussein now faced a much more difficult political battle to halt the momentum.

Chief of Staff Andy Card had said that the month of August was not a good time to market a new product. Now Bush was engaged on all levels. On August 29, he had signed off on the final military plan for toppling Saddam Hussein.[71] At the UN, President Bush not only made the diplomatic case, but also let his determination to act show through. He was about to ask Congress for a resolution allowing him to use 'all means necessary, including military force' to disarm Saddam Hussein. He set in motion the negotiations for a new 'super-tough' UN resolution and let Rumsfeld start the build up towards a military invasion. It was an impressive policy momentum which was not leaving any flanks uncovered, yet, there were internal differences that Bush was pushing into the future.

'Two Presidencies in One Week'

As Andy Card had suggested, there was a sort of 'Iraq rollout strategy' when Congress reconvened in September.[72] It was not a 'suddenly Saddam' shift in focus or a 'wag-the-dog' scenario in which a war is fabricated to win an election.[73] If simple political advantage was all Bush wanted, he should have stopped in the first week of November when his party gained two Senate seats, taking that chamber back and increasing his majority in the House by five seats. Two days later he scored a unanimous victory in the Security Council. He could have played an inspections and diplomatic game until 2004 if he wanted to play it safe politically, but this President tends not to err on the side of thinking small, but on thinking big.

On September 4, Bush met with Congressional leaders to tell them he would ask for a Congressional resolution authorizing the use of force against Hussein. On September 10, he briefed them again at the White House on his upcoming address to the United Nations. At this meeting, Democratic Minority Leader Dick Gephardt, who regretted his opposition to the 1990 Gulf War resolution and was again campaigning for the Democratic presidential nomination, came out strongly in support of the President's resolution, stating, 'You have my full support.'[74] James Carville, Bob Shrum and Stan Greenberg had written a political brief for Democratic leaders advising them to support such a resolution, forthwith, and change the voter's attention right back to the faltering economy.[75] After Bush's UN speech, his approval ratings rose from 60 per cent to 70 per cent. What was the point of fighting this war president on national security? Yet, no solid Democratic bloc formed as Senate Majority leader Tom Daschle and other senators hesitated and dragged out the process, with no strategy in place to actually defeat Bush's request. With Gephardt behind the President in the House, Daschle's hesitations were doomed from the start.

Senate Democrats had been uneasy about Bush's alleged propensity for unilateralism. On September 23, Al Gore gave his first foreign policy speech since the 2000 campaign. He agreed that this was Iraq's 'final reckoning', yet Gore accused Bush of a 'go-it-alone, cowboy-type approach'.[76] This seemed to energize some Democratic senators. Kennedy asked for proof of an 'imminent threat', but Bush never used that term, using instead 'grave and gathering danger'.[77] The reason is twofold: he did not want to meet the traditional legal requirements behind this term and, secondly, as Wolfowitz put it 'imminent assumes that we will know when it is imminent.'[78] The Nexus argument is not about a smoking gun, it is about avoiding a mushroom cloud. Barbara Boxer asked, 'why now?'[79] But most of the Democratic objections, except for Senator Robert Byrd who said he opposed the war on principle, were subsumed by Bush's UN speech. If indeed he would pursue his Iraq policy via the UN, he could no longer be accused of unilateralism or rash action.

On September 19 President Bush submitted the draft resolution to Congress. The same day, Powell testified before a House committee that a Congressional resolution would help the UN process. On September 24, the British Joint Intelligence Committee issued a major report on Iraq's forbidden arms, which included the assessment that there is 'no doubt that Iraq continues to develop chemical and biological weapons.'[80] Helped by Gephardt, Bush reached agreement with the bipartisan leadership of the House on the wording of the resolution on October 2. A National Intelligence Estimate that same week echoed the conclusions of the British report: 'Baghdad has chemical and biological weapons.'[81] The House passed the 'Authorization for Use of Military Force Against Iraq Resolution of 2002' on October 10, followed by the Senate the next day, after last minute maneuvers in the Senate to demand a two-step resolution (one for disarmament and another for war) were defeated soundly. The final version contained everything Bush wanted, including the key phrase in section 3, 'The President is authorized to use the Armed Forces of the United States as he determines to be necessary and appropriate ...' Bush received bigger majorities in both the Senate and House (77 and 296) than his father did in 1990. Less than a week later Congress adjourned in preparation for the November elections.

On September 13, Colin Powell and his British colleague, Jack Straw, began negotiations with the foreign ministers of the Security Council members. The President shared with his advisers a very strong concept of what that resolution should contain, about which Powell said to Larry King, 'We are knitted together as a cabinet team.'[82] In his September 12 address, Bush had made it plain that Iraq was already in material breach or violation on over a dozen UN resolutions and had a terrible record of hindering and eluding previous inspection efforts. The Bush administration wanted to make it crystal clear that what it sought was not another 'business-as-usual' resolution to be simply piled on top of all the others, but rather *one final* opportunity for Iraq to declare all in short order. The resolution would be both an offer and an instantaneous test for Iraq to come clean on all its weapons of mass destruction and related programs. This first half of the challenge – a test of Iraq's intent – was not some type of technicality, but the complete foundation of the entire resolution. Next, in Bush's view, the UN inspectors would quickly proceed to verify all that Iraq had declared and be there to witness the destruction of the entire WMD sector in that country.

From the very start, the Bush administration had a specific model of inspections in mind that it either was unable to communicate effectively to the rest of the world, or a good deal of the journalistic and international community simply failed to grasp or refuse to accept.[83] The model can be called 'inspections-as-verification', with precedents from the Ukraine, South Africa and Kazakhstan. These states decided to declare all weapons that they agreed not to have and then invited outside inspectors to come in and watch them being dismantled and destroyed. In 2004, Libya would adopt the same model after it was caught shipping nuclear material.

Because Iraq was able to impose another model of inspections immediately after Desert Storm and because the UN Security Council had not used military force right away to insist that the letter of the law be followed – in this case UN Security Council Resolution 687 which demanded a total declaration of Iraq's prohibited weapons – the world's perception about inspections in Iraq had taken on a different meaning. Call it the 'inspections-as-discovery' model. In this scenario, Iraq grudgingly admits it has some forbidden weapons and may declare some sites or stockpiles, but then proceeds to hide the rest and hinder and harass the inspectors in their work of finding them. As Rumsfeld told Congress on September 18, 2002, 'Iraq had gone to school on the inspectors.' Hussein was now a master at playing 'rope-a-dope-in-the-desert'.[84] Thus when the Americans started negotiating about a robust inspection regime in September, many people interpreted that to mean a set of very intrusive rules and capabilities which would allow UN inspectors to be very effective at beating him in his own 'hide-and-seek' game. Bush said that the inspectors were not sent 'on a scavenger hunt for hidden materials across a country the size of California.'[85] The onus was on Iraq to declare all and thus to declare where it all is and logically lead inspectors there to watch it being taken down. This was the crucial test Bush wanted up front in the new UN resolution.

The President wanted a clear-cut show of intent from Iraq that it had dropped the 'inspections-as-discovery' game and accepted the new 'inspections-as-verification' reality. Throughout August and September, Powell tried to make this clear, saying, 'inspections aren't the issue; disarmament is the issue.'[86] Thus, following a 'tell-it-all' WMD declaration that the Iraqi government needed to make, the UN inspectors would be completely free to go anywhere they wanted, see anything and talk to any person they chose. Bush was not looking for 'good' cooperation, he was insisting on perfect and complete cooperation; the value president wanted a value declaration. Not surprisingly, right after Bush's September 12 speech, Iraq indicated to Kofi Annan that it was now willing to let inspectors have 'unfettered access.' Most likely it sought to avoid a new UN resolution, but Powell made it clear that door was closed. On October 1, Blix announced an agreement had been reached with Iraq, allowing inspectors to go anywhere they wanted. However, soon thereafter, Hussein's regime informed Blix that 'anywhere' did not include presidential palaces. That sequence of events underscored exactly the negotiation trap Bush did not want to fall into. How many times are you going to step on the same rake?

There was a good deal of hard bargaining before the Security Council finally passed resolution 1441 on November 7. By all accounts, France was the toughest interlocutor, with Russia often agreeing with Paris, but letting France take the diplomatic heat. The fact that Germany was on the Council for a two-year elected term aided and abetted France's position enormously. With Germany's backing, France felt it could express the opinion of the European Union. France had been outspoken earlier about the need to restrain America's 'hyperpower'.

In a frank interview with the *New York Times* on September 9, French President Jacques Chirac expressed 'great reservations' about Bush's 'doctrine' of 'preemptive action'.[87] Unlike Tony Blair, who came to the same conclusion about the nexus argument as Bush, neither Chirac nor the German Chancellor ever bought into this logic. Certainly, the loose connection between terrorists, rogue states with weapons of mass destruction and hatred against America should not be used, in Paris's view, as a shortcut around the legal doctrine of 'imminent threat'. Chirac was concerned that Bush intended to use Resolution 1441 to legitimize his preemption strategy and that if he succeeded, it would set a dangerous precedent. 'A few principles,' the French President told the editors, 'and a little order are needed to run the affairs of the world.' Chirac could agree to the Security Council helping to disarm Iraq, but he reminded the interviewers that the Council had never decided on regime change in Iraq. 'If we go down that road,' he said, 'where are we going?' His approach was that 'one should go to see' if there are WMD in Iraq. 'And to see it,' Chirac said, 'Inspectors must be free, without any restrictions or conditions.' In other words, Chirac and Bush both wanted free and unrestricted inspections, but had different models in mind. Chirac's 'let's go see' is inspections-as-discovery but on the basis of existing intelligence and Hussein's past record of interference, Bush was well beyond the 'let's go see' mindset.

The President's National Security Strategy which was sent to Congress on September 20 made selling UN resolution 1441 more difficult, not because of the strategy's overall message, but because most observers focused on the idea of preemption. The strategy document called for an overall balance between political, economic and social instruments. It was far from unilateralist in tone and contained a mix of soft and hard power, but it did make the case that containment and deterrence alone were insufficient in the war on terror, that the 'crossroads of radicalism and technology' constituted the 'gravest danger'. It argued that conventional multilateral forums such as the Non Proliferation Treaty needed to produce better results, that the United States should pursue proactive counter proliferation and interdiction efforts to stop the threat of weapons of mass destruction. It noted that the 'overlap between states that sponsor terror and those that pursue WMD compels us to action.' It called for adapting the legal concept of 'imminent threat', and spelled out that if all else failed, the Bush administration might consider preemptive action to 'forestall or prevent' the new threat of rogue states with weapons of mass destruction.[88] It was this notion of preemptive action that spooked some of America's allies and made the case for regime change in Iraq more difficult at the diplomatic level, making some members, including the French, wonder whether America was really pursuing the disarmament of Iraq or if that was merely a cover for using force to change the government of one rogue state after another.

The second thing France wanted to avoid was a UN resolution that played into the hands of the Anglo-American military build up. Bush had agreed on a three-prong approach after the summer: Congressional support, a new UN resolution and the continuation of a military build-up on Iraq's borders. He believed that only with a military threat on his doorstep could Hussein be expected to pay attention to a UN resolution. By late September some 45,000 troops were already in theater and the construction of a new airbase and command center in Qatar was in progress. What the French and others wanted to preclude were 'hidden triggers' in the resolution which the United States could unilaterally pull as soon as the military build-up was complete. To be extra sure, France wanted two UN resolutions, one to set the disarmament regime and then another that would authorize 'serious consequences' (meaning war) if the Council believed Iraq was a threat to international peace and security. There was one thing on which Bush would not budge, there could be nothing in the resolution that restricted America's right to act according to Article 51 of the UN Charter whereby any member state is free to act in its self-defense.

The Bush administration had made this point right after the 9/11 attacks and was not about to compromise on it – France and all other Council members respected this right.

On October 23, Powell and Straw submitted a second-draft resolution and negotiations became intense. Powell had made a point of cultivating a personal friendship with the new French Foreign Minister Dominique de Villepin. Together, they worked out a compromise on the precise language: the third-draft on November 6 had all the ingredients of a deal in which the two sides split the difference. The key compromises are in paragraphs 4, 11 and 12 of the resolution.[89] Instead of two separate UN resolutions, there would be one resolution that contained two steps. If Blix or his colleague from the International Atomic Energy Agency were to report to the Council any 'failure to comply' or 'interference' by Iraq, the Council would 'convene' to consider what action to take. In other words, the United States could not decide on its own that there was no compliance, but the resolution also stated, as a result of American insistence, that Iraq 'has been and remains in material breach' of earlier resolutions (paragraph 1). Thus, if Washington wanted to invoke Article 51 in relation to these breaches it had technically already a legal case for war. In sum, the precise legal road to war remained clear as mud.[90]

France was afraid that Bush might seize on the declaration by Iraq to be submitted 30 days after the resolution as a 'further material breach' and thus a sufficient cause to invoke military action. Iraq was obliged to make a 'currently accurate, full and complete declaration.' Anticipating that Iraq would not comply and that Britain and the United States would declare this the final breach, France with Russian and German support insisted on changing one word: instead of 'false statements or omissions' in Iraq's declaration *or* 'failure to comply', with inspections, Villepin wrote 'false statements or omissions *and* failure to comply.' So Hussein had to violate both the declaration and the inspections to get called on the mat. Bush had initially wanted a zero-tolerance resolution, but in order to get Chirac and others on board, he had to settle for two Iraqi violations before he could pull the trigger and promise to go back to the Security Council for its consideration of the matter. France insisted on one more watering down. Instead of the Security Council deciding whether it should '*restore* international peace and security' – implying that Iraq had already violated this key phrase in the United Nations Charter, the United States and Britain agreed to the weaker phrase '*secure* international peace and security', which does not call for military action in the first place.[91] With these safeguards in place, France believed it had severely curtailed America's room for unilateral military action.

Chirac and Bush agreed on the same resolution, but had very different expectations about what that piece of paper would do. Just as Bush had stepped over a lack of precise agreement among his advisers on how a new UN resolution would eventually jell with the existing policy of securing regime change in Iraq back in August, he now added a second unresolved puzzle to his inventory.

Rather than acting arrogantly or unilaterally, Bush gave a good deal of freedom of action away in 1441, amounting to a genuine empowerment of the Security Council to disarm Iraq. If France and the other powers interpreted that accommodation to mean that Bush could be persuaded to water down his final objectives about Iraq, they underestimated him again. Yet, the tension about what the President's policy really amounted to was beginning to show. Blair and Powell had persuaded Bush that disarmament and a new UN resolution would help achieve his ultimate goal. But did the means begin to change the end? Was the goal disarmament or regime change? So long as Bush and his advisers believed they were the same thing, perhaps it would not matter, but what if the UN process would drive a wedge between the two goals?

The tension showed already in a speech Bush gave in Cincinnati on October 7. Modeled on his September 20, 2001 address to Congress, Bush raised the key questions; Why Iraq, why now, and will it detract from the war on terror? Why not use only diplomatic and economic pressure? Will it make the Middle East worse off? He used his usual strong words, calling Saddam Hussein a 'homicidal dictator addicted to weapons of mass destruction', a 'student of Stalin', driving towards 'an arsenal of terror', and guilty of having 'high-level contacts' with Al Qaeda operators. Most interestingly, for the first time he made the case that if the Iraqi regime met all of his demands, including disarmament and giving its own people freedom, such complete compliance would in effect be regime change. The regime could change itself he implied, and thus by inference avoid military action.[92] It is easy to dismiss the President's words as chimera, saying to Hussein, 'you can continue to be a fish if you get out of the water,' but Bush has no record of employing such cynicism.

For Bush, resolution 1441 would simply test Iraq's intent. Intent is a value and you show it or you don't, but to the other powers on the Security Council, intent is more difficult to measure. France and others were looking for progress. Robert Kagan and Bill Kristol, both critics of Bush from the right, predicted that he had been led into an 'inspections quagmire from which he may have difficulty escaping.'[93]

On November 5, Bush and Laura celebrated their 25th wedding anniversary amidst the euphoria of the best presidential first mid-term election since 1934. He stayed up past 1:00 am to watch the results, having campaigned as hard as any candidate and raised over $110 million dollars, finishing up with a whirlwind 15-state tour that was credited for making the difference in two senate races. Then to the surprise of many, he achieved unanimous Security Council support for Resolution 1441 two days later. Chief of Staff Andy Card could be excused for a bit of crowing. 'He had the equivalent of two presidencies in one week,' Card said. 'On Tuesday he showed he is leading the country,' and as another aide confided, the UN vote showed, 'he is leading the world.'[94]

The Villepin Coup and the Final Crunch

In late 2003 and early 2004, the Bush administration was widely accused of rigging the intelligence estimate, but rather than rigging, it seems that Bush and his advisers back in 2002 read old intelligence, but with new vigor. Their virility was based on the perception of the new threat environment after the attacks of September 11. In early 2003, towards the end of the standoff over UN Resolution 1441, senior officials began to bolster their case about weapons of mass destruction, even though Bush had said, 'Make sure no one stretches to make our case.'[95]

CIA Director George Tenet presented a National Intelligence Estimate on Iraq to the White House on October 4. Congress's Joint Select Committee on Intelligence also received a secret briefing on this dossier. A declassified version of the estimate was made public in 2003 that was similar to the British synopsis of September and essentially drew on existing conclusions about Iraqi weapons of mass destruction. Most of that record was already known during the Clinton Administration when Hussein's son-in-law defected in 1995 and forced Saddam to acknowledge that Iraq had biological and chemical weapons stockpiles. Two outstanding issues were at play: Western intelligence generally believed that Hussein had more than he actually declared and that he had not accounted for destroying the materials as he claimed. The American estimate was up front about the fact that intelligence agencies were 'not detecting portions of these programs,' yet, they also had 'high confidence' that Iraq was continuing these programs. Concerning nuclear weapon programs, the estimate said that if Iraq acquired sufficient 'weapons-grade fissile material, it could make a nuclear weapon in months to a year.' It turned out that there were significant footnotes in the estimate in which the Department of State's Bureau of Intelligence and Research disagreed with the other agencies on nuclear weapons. State's assessment was that there was 'no compelling case' that Iraq was 'pursuing an integrated and comprehensive approach to acquire nuclear weapons.'[96]

This disagreement on nuclear weapons would later play a role in the question whether the Bush administration had told the truth about these weapons, but right from the start, there was no serious disagreement inside the Bush administration or among Western intelligence agencies on chemical and biological weapons programs. Existing intelligence said that Hussein had them, destroyed some and did not account for the rest. Knowing that he hid these weapons while being watched, why would he not have them after the watchers were kicked out? That, Bush said in Cincinnati, was to 'hope against evidence'. The President used this basic intelligence information in his October 7 Cincinnati speech. He mentioned the unaccounted stocks of Anthrax, Mustard Gas, Sarin nerve gas, and VX nerve gas. Bush was less clear on nuclear weapons. How close is Saddam, he asked? 'Well, we don't know exactly, and that's the problem.'[97]

Rumsfeld and Cheney believed it would be imprudent to simply rely on conventional intelligence assessments. Rumsfeld set up a small Office of Strategic Plans run by Assistant Secretary of Defense for Near East and South Asian Affairs, William Luti. The idea actually came from Douglas Feith. As the senior policy adviser, he had struggled since late 2001 to get access to Rumsfeld's daily decision circle, called the 'Round Table'. This Round Table emerged after September 11, 2001 as the top forum inside the Pentagon in the war on terror. Rumsfeld and Wolfowitz met every morning with Richard Meyers and Peter Pace, the Vice Chairman of the Joint Chiefs. Rumsfeld had told Feith that he wanted his adviser 'to lob ideas ahead of him', but Feith responded that it was difficult to do, not knowing where Rumsfeld was on any given morning.[98] Thus Rumsfeld brought him into the 'Round Table' and Feith promptly delivered.

Feith put some of his staff in front of secure computers reading years of intelligence reports. Slowly they began to find a 'Baghdad-Bin Laden link' overlooked or underplayed by the CIA.[99] After a while, Luti was put in charge of the operation, tasked to provide Rumsfeld, Wolfowitz and Feith with an in-house assessment of existing and incoming intelligence. Luti had worked for Cheney in a previous position and now also coordinated OSP findings with Cheney's staff, especially 'Scooter' Libby. Cheney at times visited CIA headquarters to get a closer picture of how people there were putting the intelligence together. Condi Rice had put her deputy, Stephen Hadley in charge of an interagency committee that reviewed intelligence reports. Rice commented that intelligence estimates 'always underestimate capabilities.'[100]

As always, there were disagreements among the various agencies. The Defense Intelligence Agency, the CIA, and State's Bureau on Research and Intelligence would not arrive at the same conclusions. A key problem was that the US had poor human intelligence on the ground in Iraq. Before Bush's February 16 order to beef up CIA activity in Iraq, the CIA Iraq Section Chief had admitted that he could count all CIA reporting sources inside Iraq on one hand, 'and still pick my nose'.[101] The government relied heavily on satellites which cannot really read intent, fragmented signals intelligence, and Iraqi exile groups with their own reasons for feeding Washington the most dire reports. Most decisive in this intelligence issue was the fact that there was a climate of wanting to err on the side of the worst-case.

With this intelligence 'record' for Iraq in hand, everyone was eagerly awaiting Iraq's final declaration which came on December 7, just in time for the deadline set by 1441. The Bush administration took five days of study before it issued its preliminary assessment that the declaration 'failed to account for the chemical and biological weapons.'[102] Others were less careful, such as Democratic Senator Joe Lieberman who called it 'a 12,000 page, 100 pound lie'.[103] Jack Straw called it 'an obvious falsehood'.[104] On December 18, Bush convened a National Security Council meeting to review his advisers' assessment of the report. Powell delivered the official verdict the next day, calling Iraq's mandated declaration, 'anything but accurate, full and complete', and with great significance for the UN diplomatic standoff to come, he added that it was 'another material breach'.[105] Recalling the series of events in 2004, Powell remembered it as a 'ridiculous declaration',[106] a patchwork of recycled documents which stated that Iraq had no prohibited weapons or weapon programs.

Hans Blix, who tried to stick tenaciously to his mandate only to report facts, said that the declaration 'failed to answer many open questions', but then he added, 'I hope they provide it [sic] to us orally.'[107] Resolution 1441 had put Blix in a tough, maybe impossible, spot: if he chose the wrong words, he might become the first United Nations official responsible for the outbreak of war. In an October meeting with Condi Rice and Paul Wolfowitz, Blix had promised to be 'very aggressive' in his inspections.[108] There is no evidence that he ever reneged on that promise, but Bush and Blix parted company on what 1441 was meant to accomplish. The deal was that Hussein would declare *all* within 30 days, not some 'orally' later on. Still, Bush was hemmed in by his own diplomatic compromise. Paragraph 4 of the resolution said 'and' so he could not make this first breach by Hussein a cause for war, but on his mental shortlist of what would end the UN process on Iraq, the first box was checked off.

Since the declaration was the big indicator of whether Hussein had switched intent or not, the point of 1441 had already been proven to Bush. Since everyone, including France and Germany, were convinced that he had at least some weapons and programs, there was only one thing left, namely to show that he was unwilling to comply fully with Blix's mandate for full and unfettered inspections. Here again, Bush had to rely on Blix's reporting to the Council, and Blix's facts always revealed a cup half empty *and* half full. On January 9, 2003, he reported that Iraq was not complying fully *and* that inspectors had not found any evidence to disprove his declaration. Thus, if you believed in the 'inspections-as-verification' model, Iraq had failed to make a full declaration and failed to cooperate fully, but if you believed in the other model, nothing had yet been discovered. Even some administration members got the models mixed up, for example when Ari Fleischer said on January 13, that the inspectors were 'in the middle of their work'. How could they be, if they were supposed to verify a full declaration that had not been made? The media and public remained equally confused.[109] In an interview with Donald Rumsfeld on ABC 'This Week,' George Stephanopoulos noted that UN inspectors said they needed more time. Rumsfeld responded that it would be logical to take more time 'if one believed that we were sending in not inspectors but finders, discoverers, people going through that vast country ...' Stephanopoulos: 'But isn't that what they're doing?' Rumsfeld: 'Oh, no. My goodness, no! The test is not whether they can find something. The test is whether or not Iraq is going to cooperate.'[110] The idea that Saddam Hussein was not in compliance *and* that progress was being made in Iraq fixed itself firmly in the mind of American and world audiences. On January 14, Bush said, 'Time is running out,' while the same day, Kofi Annan said, 'The inspectors need more time.'

Blix's first report on January 9 was the final proof (if Bush needed it) that Saddam was not in compliance. In the narrow legal sense, Saddam had now violated both sides of the 'and' in UN resolution 1441. Bush knew the decision to go to war was near. He asked Condi Rice, 'Should we do this?' She answered that he could not let Saddam 'play volleyball with the international community.'[111] Bush had also asked Karen Hughes, and she advised him to 'exhaust all opportunities to achieve regime change peacefully,' which he felt he had done.[112] As with the decision on regime change in early 2002, Bush did not announce a final clear decision. He told Powell on January 13, 'I really think I am going to have to do this,'[113] which is not the same as a decision, but it would take a major change in the UN endgame to change the tide. France would close that door on January 20.

On January 24, 2003 Franks presented his final war plan. The military plan to invade Iraq, called OpPlan 1003 Victor, had reached its final version. On December 9, Rumsfeld had opened the new command center in Qatar, and nearly 135,000 US troops would be in the staging area (mainly Kuwait) by January 2003. Wolfowitz was intensifying his negotiations with Turkey to land another 40,000 troops from the north and Bush appointed one of his national security council directors, Zalmay Khalilzad, as special envoy for free Iraqis. In early January, the United States and Turkey asked the NATO alliance to provide Turkey with Patriot anti-missile systems, chemical and biological protective gear and air support. France, Germany and Belgium blocked this request, arguing in the words of the French Ambassador to Washington, that doing so would put 'the NATO cart before the UN horse'.[114] It would send the message that war was imminent and France above all did not want to send that message. On January 16, Rumsfeld, appearing on CBS, began speculating about Hussein leaving the country.

The turning point in the brewing fight over what 1441 really stood for came on January 20. On that day, Powell had to cancel his Martin Luther King Day appearances because his French colleague Dominique de Villepin had called for a special session on terrorism at the UN. After an uneventful session, and as Powell was traveling back home, Villepin called a press conference in which he pulled a 'bait and switch'.[115] Villepin, without warning Powell, laid down the French position on Iraq: 'nothing justifies envisaging military action'.[116] In other words, France would oppose any Security Council vote that would call Iraq in violation. Chirac, having gone on record against Bush's preemptive action doctrine had his minister pull off a preemptive diplomatic strike par excellence. In the negotiations leading up to 1441, Chirac and Villepin had always left the military option open as a last resort, as part of the entire rationale of 1441. In mid-December, a French military mission visiting the Pentagon had outlined France's plan to participate in a possible UN-led military action with 15,000 troops, 100 aircraft and an aircraft carrier.[117] Now, out of the blue from Powell's vantage point, France slammed that door closed. It would be inspections from here on till the end of time.

What caused France to pull this surprise on the Bush administration was the anticipation that Blix on January 27 would report to the Security Council that Iraq was not in full compliance with the inspection team. If so, Bush would then be in a position to claim that both sides of the 'and' in paragraph 4 had been violated and call for a Security Council meeting to consider using military force to redress Iraq's material breaches. On January 20, the Pentagon ordered the 4th Infantry Division to ship out (some 37,000 troops) which would make the military option near complete. Rumsfeld had told Franks to 'dribble' deployments 'out slowly'[118] so as to not send signals that war was inevitable, yet it seems France got word of this order and decided that Bush had made up his mind about war and Paris figured that it was better to prevent a Security Council meeting than have one in which it might have to cast a veto. France also feared that Bush might be able to quietly woo Putin to abstain, leaving France holding bag.[119]

Ironically, Villepin's coup drove Colin Powell straight into the arms of Cheney and Rumsfeld. Commenting on this incident, Richard Holbrooke, Clinton's former UN Ambassador, said 'It was a serious, maybe even unforgivable breach of diplomatic behavior from treaty allies.'[120] Senior aides to Powell said that he 'was very upset', even 'livid', and felt personally betrayed.[121] 'This building,' said one official referring to the Department of State, 'was furious'.[122] Whatever faith Powell had in the 1441 option evaporated in the wake of Villepin's stab in the back and from that day, relations between the Bush administration and France as well as Germany deteriorated sharply.

On January 22, Chirac and Schroeder celebrated the 25th anniversary of the Elysée Treaty, their bilateral defense relationship, by announcing that Germany and France were now united in opposing military action. Bush told Richard Lugar, the new chair of the Senate Foreign Relations Committee, that Schroeder had lied to him.[123] During the President's visit in May, Schroeder had not foreclosed support for possible military action, but during his election campaign in September, he had changed his position and staked his campaign on opposing a US-led move towards war calling it 'a military adventure'.[124] In early February 2003, Schroeder said that he would oppose military action even if the UN Security Council voted for it. This was a case of blatant unilateralism.

If France and Germany thought they could speak for the rest of Europe against Bush or simply get away with it, they were mistaken. In the fall of 2002, French Prime Minister Jean-Pierre Rafferin had said that 'young countries' like America should learn from 'old countries' in Europe. He chided those with a 'simplistic vision of war between good and evil,' in a fairly direct stab at Bush.[125] Rumsfeld now called the new Franco-German alliance 'old Europe'.[126] Tension between America, and France and Germany had been bubbling under the surface since early 2001 with Chirac and Schroeder resenting Bush's disregard for Kyoto and a host of other international treaties. They had used some of these endeavors to construct a stronger European common foreign policy. At the same time, Bush had been cultivating good relations with Italy's Sylvio Berlusconi and Spain's Jose Maria Aznar and both Bush and Rumsfeld had gone out of their way to help Eastern European countries get into NATO.

On January 31, eight European states led by Blair, Aznar and Berlusconi submitted an open letter of solidarity with the American position on Iraq in the *Wall Street Journal*. On February 5, the so-called Vilnius 10 (new European Union and NATO candidate countries on the outer edge of Eastern Europe) joined them. After an emergency EU summit on February 17, Chirac said that Eastern Europe had 'missed a great opportunity to shut up'.[127] Blair assured his Polish colleague, Leszek Miller on the phone that 'he [Chirac] has been clearly warned by us and the Americans that he can't do that.'[128]

On January 27, 2003, Blix reported that his team had found a 3,000-page report on laser enrichment of uranium in the house of an Iraqi scientist. Again, this was evidence of Hussein's failure to give a full declaration and that UNMOVIC was finding things. Blix further reported that Iraq was cooperating better in the process but not yet fully on the substance. Most of the unaccounted biological and chemical materials were still unaccounted, but there were Iraqi 'minders' who were hindering the inspector's interviews with scientists. Even before 1441 was signed, Bush had called upon the UN to take Iraqi scientists and their families out of the country in order to provide a safe environment for interviews, but in the Powell-Villepin negotiations, he agreed to give this discretion to Blix rather than to make it one of the resolution's stated demands. Blix had not yet insisted on using this power.

Knowing that France would now block military action in the Security Council, the Bush administration went all out to try and convince international opinion that Iraq had more than it declared. France had now forced America into the 'inspections-as-discovery' game beyond its own definition, leaving Bush only one option, namely to show the world as much intelligence on Iraq as he could and thus call upon the court of world opinion to expose Iraq's failure to comply. On January 26, Powell said that the United States would soon show its evidence against Iraq. He began to appear in numerous interviews on European TV and with European newspapers.

In 2004, Bush was accused of misrepresenting the case for weapons of mass destruction. There is no evidence that he forced intelligence agents to file false information or that he set out to make a false case or that he began to rely on the Office of Strategic Plan's version of intelligence rather than on the CIA. Still, the administration had its own difficulties with making the WMD case into a watertight public argument. CIA officers briefing Bush on December 21, 2002 did not impress him. 'Nice try,' he said, 'I don't think this is quite – it's not something that Joe Public would understand or gain a lot of confidence from.' Tenet had jumped up and assured Bush not to worry, that it was a 'slam dunk case', suggesting that the problem was with presentation.[129]

The Bush team did what many decision makers have done in similar cases; they started to bolster their arguments. The UN would no longer authorize war so they had to make the strongest indictment of Iraq and proceed to war with a few allies. Bush and his advisers, having been maneuvered out of their general nexus argument into a disarmament argument, began to make their case more compelling than the information at hand could support. As Political Scientist Alexander George has pointed out, such bolstering typically leads to distortions in information.[130] The administration knew about the British report that Iraq was trying to buy low-grade (yellow cake) uranium from Africa as early as October, though this was only one report. Plus, if it were low-grade, it would actually take several years before Iraq could fully enrich it. Bush left the story out of his October speech, but now he put it into his State of the Union Address on January 28. While bolstering makes one exaggerate the likelihood of an intended outcome, it may also lead to 'wishful thinking'.[131] Thus, Cheney, Rumsfeld and others started to drop 'likely and probably', replacing them with 'no doubt'. 'We have some leads' changed to 'We know where they are.'[132] Long after the war, in 2004, Chris Matthews asked Hans Blix if he felt the Bush administration had been 'dishonest'. Blix answered, 'I never felt that there was any bad faith. I think they were convinced of what they were saying. But I think that they were inclined to put exclamation marks where there should have been question marks.'[133]

Not since Adlai Stevenson had waved CIA pictures of missile site construction in Cuba in the Security Council in the early 1960s had there been so much anticipation about what Powell would show on February 5. He downplayed it a bit, saying he had no 'smoking gun', yet, he presented a smorgasbord of satellite and signals intelligence, showing suspected activities and sites with elaborate efforts at concealing, and played audio tapes of Iraqi conversations that appeared to be about thwarting UN inspectors. Powell strung it together with compelling analysis.[134] If Bush's most 'dovish' adviser was so concerned, there were few who remained in doubt. Dan Bartlett called it 'the Powell buy-in'.[135]

Blix went back to Iraq to follow up on some of Powell's leads and would report again on February 14. On February 6, Iraq accepted U-2 intelligence over flights 'under certain conditions'.[136] On February 10, it dropped all conditions. Powell had revealed information about Iraq building a drone to deliver chemical or biological weapons and also about Iraq's missiles exceeding their 150-kilometer range. Blix went in hot pursuit. On February 14, Blix reported to the UN Security Council 'a mixed picture of Iraqi disarmament.' Iraq did offer some missiles up that were indeed capable of going beyond their permitted range. On the deadly biological gasses there was still no word.

It appears that Blix's report on February 14 was the straw that broke the camel's back. Bush felt completely trapped in the old 'inspect-as-you-can-game.' In the third week of February, the calendar as stipulated in resolution 1441 would run out. Blix had had his 105 days to report on compliance and the pattern of Iraqi non-cooperation was now clearly in place. Bush had set his benchmark on 1441 and Hussein had failed it: case closed. The President now pulled the trigger on military action. He would ask the Security Council to convene to consider the matter and again, Tony Blair asked Bush for one more step. Given the tremendous public opposition to the use of force among European publics and the large amount of opposition to Blair's Iraq policy among his own Labour Party members of parliament, he asked Bush to negotiate a new UN resolution that would clearly identify Iraq's breach of 1441 and thus make Blair's going to war part of a UN mandated action. Spain's Aznar, who visited Bush at his Crawford ranch on February 22, agreed to be the third sponsor on such a draft resolution. On February 20, a senior official admitted that the second resolution was 'not dependent' on Blix's reporting.[137]

Meanwhile, French diplomacy went into overdrive to avoid a second resolution. France's ambassador in Washington had told Stephen Hadley that Paris would oppose the move, Hadley in turn said that the Bush administration believed it had nine votes on the Security Council. The British Prime minister had given Bush his pledge to be there at the crunch and he had kept his word. Now the President would try all he could to get the second resolution, but again Chirac beat him. Already before November 7, France had lobbied the so-called 'middle six' members of the Security Council, including Angola, Mauritius, Cameroon and Chile. If France could keep the number of countries in favor of a new resolution below nine (out of 15), it could avoid having to cast a veto against the United States. A brief diplomatic tug-of-war between Paris and Washington ensued until Bush gave up.

Beyond the hidden diplomacy, Iraq turned into a war for world opinion. On February 16, millions of people in numerous major cities of the Western world demonstrated against a war on Iraq. On February 20, Powell appeared on French, British, German and Russian television where he patiently and often under very hostile questioning, laid out the case that Iraq had blown its 'final opportunity' and that its gathering danger could no longer be stopped by diplomacy. At the same time, the United States forced NATO's stalled request on helping Turkey out of its North Atlantic Council forum where France is a member into the Defense Planning Committee where it is not. Washington leaned hard on Germany to stop the hold up. Germany, which had never opposed helping Turkey but had wanted to cover the diplomatic back of France, now relented.

On February 24, France, Germany and Russia floated an idea for faster inspections and a deadline in early summer. Blair might have considered it, but Bush dismissed the idea. When the Turkish Parliament on March 1, by the narrowest of margins, defeated a motion to allow American troops to land there in preparation for an invasion, some members thought this 'setback' could buy the Council a bit more time. Fleischer said, 'The government of Turkey did not expect this outcome, and neither did we.'[138] Canada proposed a compressed version of the German-French-Russian plan with an April deadline, but Canadian-American relations under Jean Chrétien were not much better than Bush-Chirac relations. In fact, Canada's position on Iraq had been nearly identical to Chirac's. Canada had ventured its foreign policy on the same international treaties as France and Germany, and Chrétien had not tried to build a close relationship with Bush. When Schroeder's justice minister likened Bush to Hitler, he fired her at once, but when Chrétien's communications director called Bush a 'moron', it took weeks of protests by Canadian media and two letters of resignation before the Prime Minister moved her to another spot. Canada had no political capital in the bank and Bush dismissed the gesture immediately. 'It is time,' the President said, 'for people to show their cards.'[139] On March 7, Bush, Blair and Aznar tabled a second draft that set March 17 as the final deadline for Iraq.

The same day, Blix reported that his team had found a drone, which had not been declared on December 8, and listed seventeen other instances of infractions against that declaration. An Iraqi Air Force document had been handed to the inspectors showing a higher missile count than had been declared. All together, Blix reported 29 clusters of problems unresolved. At the same time, Blix reported 'a substantial measure of disarmament'[140] as Iraq started to dismantle a good number of its Al Samoud 2 missiles. Knowing full well what Blix's further indictment meant, Chirac on March 10, for the first time in public, committed his country to a veto 'in all circumstances'.[141] Pushing 1441 beyond its own meaning, Chirac said, 'Disarmament must happen peacefully.'[142] Blair called it 'irresponsible'.[143] Meanwhile Bush and Blair were losing the diplomatic fight on getting nine members to support their new draft resolution and Blair was coming under tremendous pressure in his own party. 'The courage you have shown is admirable,' Bush said about his British colleague on March 3. 'You are a great leader,'[144] but that was not helping Blair at Westminster or among British voters.

Blair had committed himself to clear two hurdles; a second UN resolution and a House of Commons vote on going to war. On March 12, Blair aired a trial balloon in the chambers of the UN, proposing six very specific benchmarks for Hussein to meet, including a weapons declaration in Arabic and the surrender of all biological growth material and missiles. Because it included a deadline and a military consequence, France rejected this so-called non-paper, but it is unlikely that Bush would have accepted it. France's outright rejection got America off the hook of having to disagree with Blair who was facing a revolt in his Labour Party and strong public opinion against the war. Rumsfeld even mused about plans to proceed in the war without Britain. The amended draft of the proposed UN resolution now in play called for March 17 as the deadline for full Iraqi compliance. It was Hussein's 'last chance', but Bush and Blair soon dropped the UN hurdle as they could not get the nine votes.

In his address to the nation, on March 17, Bush said that the nations of the Security Council, 'share our assessment of the danger, but not our resolve to meet it.' The Security Council has not lived up to its responsibilities, 'so we will rise to ours.'[145] After a final war council in the Azores, Bush and Blair gave Hussein and his two sons 48 hours to leave Iraq. On March 18, 139 Labour MPs voted against their government, but Blair had enough of a majority to survive. UN staff began leaving Iraq on March 17.

A Fast War

When they started working together in 2001, Central Commander General Tommy Franks had said to Rumsfeld, 'If you can't work with anybody Bill Clinton has promoted, you need to get a whole new team. But if you want to work with me, I'll work my heart out for you.'[146] The two hammered out a bold and risky strategy: Franks would launch the attack with some 100,000 troops, mainly from the 3rd Infantry Division and the 1st Marine Expeditionary Force, while another 100,000 were in the pipeline. 'Speed kills,' Franks commented, and raises the possibility of 'catastrophic success'.[147] These two forces would rush towards Baghdad ahead of most of their supply lines while the British captured the south. Franks and Rumsfeld's main concern was how to maintain an element of tactical surprise for a war that everyone had seen coming for more than a year. They were confident they could deal with any chemical attacks and expected these would likely be used when US forces got to the 30-mile narrow Karbala Gap south of Baghdad. They would send Special Forces, including Australians in early to take care of the remaining SCUD missile launchers in Western Iraq that could target Israel.

Sensing already in early February that Turkey might not allow American forces a staging area, Franks nevertheless kept the ships with the 4th Infantry Division's equipment floating off the coast, and talking as if he could not start war without them. This way, Hussein might leave two Guard Divisions in the north of Iraq which he did until just before the sandstorm came on March 24. Rumsfeld and Franks turned the conventional wisdom of air attacks first, followed by ground forces on its head. The plan was to launch the ground attack almost immediately as command and control targets were being destroyed from the air. When Bush gave permission to hit Hussein's Dora Farms compound upon fresh intelligence from the CIA's new operations in Iraq that Saddam and his sons might be there, Franks decided to actually launch the ground attack before the bombardments. Seeing that Iraqi forces had not finished mining the oil wells in Rumalia, Franks rushed forces to the oil fields and in so doing averted an ecological disaster of the scale seen in Kuwait in 1991. Polish commandos took Iraqi oil platforms in the Gulf. 'Shock and Awe', which many thought was the war plan, was actually a ruse, trying to make Hussein think he would have a long time of bombing ahead of him. 'Sometimes even the critics can be deceived,' Franks commented wryly.[148]

Special Forces were mixed in with regulars as never before. Working together with CIA units and Kurdish troops in the north, these commandos opened a second front tying up Hussein's troops. Rumsfeld and Franks developed a careful plan to use precision targeting and munitions. The idea was not to destroy Iraqi infrastructure, not to send refugees fleeing Baghdad and even to spare as much of the Iraqi army, as possible as they could play a role in stabilizing Iraq in the aftermath. 'Do not fight for a dying regime,' was the message in millions of leaflets raining down on Iraqi troops.[149] The Project on Defense Alternatives, a left-leaning think tank, issued a report in October 2003 publishing calculations of various press investigations and hospital reports on casualties and found the number remarkably low, as 'low' as 10,000 on the Iraqi side.[150] When contrasted with Human Rights Watch's calculation that some 300,000 Iraqis had gone missing under Saddam Hussein,[151] the war could not be called unjust in terms of human toll.

Rumsfeld also changed the role of the media. Having been kept away from the frontlines for over a decade, he now allowed reporters to be embedded with US forces reporting a whirlwind of speed and progress in the first week of war. With few accidents or casualties, the British secured the south and the Americans rushed towards the Karbala Gap. Rumsfeld had predicted that pundits and critics would sooner or later call Operation Iraqi Freedom another 'quagmire' as they had done with the operation in Afghanistan. The pundits were not Rumsfeld's main concern, as there was a large body of discontent in the Army leadership who knew about Rumsfeld's and Frank's unconventional approach on the war plan, including its 'rolling start'.[152] Rumsfeld had scrapped the army's established procedure of troop and logistical build-up, demanding flexibility so that he could adjust strategy. Many former commanders, such as Generals Anthony Zinni and Norman Schwartzkopf and even Rumsfeld's then Army Chief of Staff, Eric Shinseki, as well as the Secretary of the Army, Thomas White, all believed that Franks had gone in on March 20 with too light a force. In fact, Franks had more troops in the pipeline than originally planned, due to the drawn-out diplomacy of UN Resolution 1441. Still, equipment and supplies were not ready and the 4th Infantry Division was two weeks away from engaging the enemy when the war begun. Schwartzkopf called Rumsfeld's meddling with army procedures 'scary'.[153]

The bad news started on March 23 when a supply convoy took a wrong turn and Americans were killed and captured. The next day, a sandstorm hit, grinding the speedy advance to a halt and making it very difficult to supply the troops who were running low on all supplies. Having the media embedded worked fine the first week. It offered another advantage as only Central Command's communication center at Doha could control the 'big picture'. Most of these reporters could not see more than what their unit was doing. Now, however, the reporters told the world about the bad condition of supplies and the forced halt while Doha was trying to say that it was only an 'operational pause' and all would be well. The critics of Franks' plan, such as former Gulf War General Barry McCaffrey, urged Rumsfeld to halt operations and wait for reinforcements. Critics argued that US troops were 'overextended and vulnerable to attack'.[154]

On March 29, in a videoconference, the President gave his commander the green light to do exactly the opposite. During the war, Condi Rice briefed Bush every morning at 6:00am by phone on overnight events. After his 8:00am intelligence meeting with George Tenet, he would hold an-hour long National Security Council meeting with Rumsfeld, Powell and others. In hindsight, the sandstorm was a blessing for Franks as the Iraqi military was busy reinforcing the Medina Republican Guard south of Baghdad. While his troops stood still, Franks ordered the most intense air campaign of the war. For the new Global Positioning Precision Guided Munitions the sandstorm was no cover and more than three quarters of the Iraqi division was put out of commission. Franks, benefiting from real-time intelligence, then staged a few feint attacks, while the 3rd Division raced past the remaining Iraqis towards Baghdad international airport. It took the Iraqi's somewhere on the order of 24 hours to react to any American move. As one American general put it 'For a commander that is a pretty good thing – fighting an enemy who can't really react to you.'[155]

Rumsfeld and Franks ditched one other piece of 'conventional' warfare: contrary to the lessons of urban warfare, they sent heavy armor right into the middle of the city. Franks had tried it in the city of Najaf and it worked. Bush and his advisers had worried about a 'Fortress Baghdad', but the speed of the advance did not allow the Iraqi military to finish preparations for a layered defense of Baghdad, thus, rather than besiege it, Franks ordered two battalions to make a 'thunder run' into the heart of the city, shooting at everything in sight.[156] Whatever defenses the Iraqis had planned soon melted away. Unfortunately, many of the Iraqi army regulars melted away with it. Soon thereafter Western reporters showed the pictures of Saddam Hussein's statue coming down in Firdos Square and Iraqi citizens welcoming the Americans as their liberators.

The war took only three weeks. It was Rumsfeld's finest hour as he and Franks had lifted American military strategy into a new dimension, overturning the risk adverse 'Powell doctrine.' It had been one of the smartest wars. Wolfowitz listed what could all have gone wrong, including environmental disasters, attacks on Israel, a war between Turkey and the Kurds, a long siege of Baghdad, Arab governments collapsing as a result of mass protests, and Iranian incursions in the south.[157] Bush, who had prevailed against all odds at the UN, seemed vindicated in his determined leadership and Cheney had said that Americans would be welcomed as 'liberators'.[158]

The former F-101 jet pilot could be forgiven for enjoying a landing in the co-pilot seat of a S-3B Viking on the aircraft carrier the Abraham Lincoln on May 1. Close aides said that the President spent a lot of time 'stewing about the families of the slain.'[159] Had Bush gone on a partial fast at the start of the war in solidarity with the troops and to focus his prayer, or, as most White House correspondents believed, because he was gaining too much weight and due to knee trouble could not run as much? 'Refusing to eat sweets' from the day the war started can be all these things, but at the core lies his close ties to the 'military family' and his tendency to turn to prayer in times of trial.[160] For now, it was a jubilant time and the big drape on the carrier's tower behind Bush said it all: 'Mission Accomplished'. That day, he exclaimed that, 'major combat operations in Iraq have ended,' but he also added, 'we have difficult work to do in Iraq.'[161]

A Slow Peace

The glow of Operation Iraqi Freedom did not last long. Following its brief celebration came a year of trouble upon trouble in which the Bush administration was continually put on the defensive. The President came under fire on four different fronts: first, Iraqi irregular forces fiercely loyal to Saddam Hussein, the so-called Fedayeen, regrouped early with the help of Islamic militants some coming from neighboring countries. They started a systematic campaign of terror, first against American troops, then against Iraqis who were cooperating with the occupation forces and finally against foreign civilian workers. Rocket attacks, ambushes, car bombs, and kidnappings became the staple of life, mostly within the so-called Sunni triangle area of Iraq. While only 169 US soldiers had died in the liberation of Iraq, of which some 60 in accidents, now between 4 and 14 troops lost their lives every week. November 2003 and April 2004 were especially bad months with over seventy soldiers killed in each and many wondered if the Bush administration had planned carefully enough for the military aftermath of the campaign. Was Rumsfeld's insistence on a light footprint in the war making the peace more difficult to keep now? Some reported that in early 2003, Franks and

Rumsfeld had hoped to bring US troops down to some 30,000,[162] but one year later, there were still 130,000 troops in Iraq and they would stay until the planned hand-over of Iraqi sovereignty in June 2004. Many would be needed much beyond that date, though at the request of the Iraqi government, and probably 'over the horizon' as a type of deterrence against civil war or political chaos.

The second controversy started up about a month after the war. Where were the weapons of mass destruction that had become the ostensible cause for going to war? By May 2003, two task forces searching for these weapons had come up empty handed, 'We came loaded for bear,' one member said, 'and found out the bear wasn't here.'[163] The occupation troops could be forgiven for focusing on immediate security issues for a while, but since Bush administration officials had sounded so confident just before the war about where the weapons or the productions facilities were, people started wondering why the 1,400 strong Iraq Survey Group was not finding anything. This drama would only grow in intensity. First, the White House cautioned patience, but by early 2004 a gale of controversy broke loose when David Kay, the head of the Iraq Survey Group, resigned and admitted to finding no weapons, nor even much evidence for weapon related program activities. Bush was accused of forging intelligence, misleading the people about the urgency of war and even the danger that Iraq posed to the United States. Blair experienced even worse political trouble in the wake of the suicide of one of Britain's intelligence specialists.

The third attack focused on the cost of the war and the reconstruction of Iraq. Bush officials had systematically low-balled or avoided questions in the fall of 2002 and early 2003 about how much the war would cost. On March 25, Bush requested a $75 billion defense supplemental bill from Congress while by October, he went back to Congress for another whopping $87 billion for Afghanistan and Iraq. In early 2004, Bush asked for another $25 billion. Many argued Bush had kept the Congress in the dark about the real costs. Wasn't Iraqi oil supposed to keep the costs down? Many Congressmen who voted for the war resolution now opposed the President's request for money. His alleged unilateralism, it was widely believed, cost the taxpayers dearly as few other nations contributed large sums. The high costs of rebuilding Iraq further pushed up the rapidly growing US budget deficit.

Finally, Bush's vision for Iraqi democracy – already decried by many 'realists' before the war as implausible – came under heavy scrutiny. What form of Iraqi government among the Kurds of the north, the Sunnis in the middle and the majority Shia in the south could provide both stability and democracy? Addressing Arab Americans at Dearborn, Michigan on April 28, Bush said, 'The goal is to help develop an Iraqi society that is first and foremost free.' He then cautioned on May 1, that it 'will take time, but it is worth every effort. Our coalition will stay until our work is done.' The official mantra became, 'we will stay as long as necessary, and leave as soon as possible.'[164]

By the fall of 2003, many observers felt that the Bush administration was woefully unprepared for the aftermath. James Fallows argued in early 2004, 'The Administration could not have known everything about what it would find in Iraq. But it could have – and should have – done far more than it did,' but being caught unprepared was not the whole story as the administration also stifled the debate on cost and risk before the war.[165] Thirdly, it was aware of a variety of post-combat recommendations offered by governmental reviews and think tanks, however, it rejected many of these for being too cautious and slow. As always, the Bush White House took risks. It knew, as Rumsfeld's close adviser Stephen Cambone put it, that things 'could go badly, ... especially if the United States and its allies do not manage the postwar period adeptly.'[166] Finally, some interagency debates between the Pentagon and the Department of State and the CIA were unresolved when the war ended. Compromises had to be forged that required multiple adjustments. While all four factors help explain the setbacks and slow progress, there is little evidence other approaches could have secured a quick and stable peace. Bush told Woodward in December 2003, 'I think I was pretty well prepared for a pretty long haul.'[167] The US-led coalition was in a cold-blooded race to do more good than the insurgents could do harm.

By all accounts, serious post-war planning started late. Though Condi Rice had run several interagency working groups in the fall of 2002, they seemed not to have produced concrete policy options.[168] Now, the President gave the task to the Department of Defense. The experience in Afghanistan had told the Bush administration that a multi-agency approach did not work. On top of that, so many people in the State Department were 'massively resisting the Iraq War,' that Bush could be forgiven for not entrusting them with the task of reconstruction after the invasion.[169] Still, State had a lot of expertise that he needed at the end of the day, but 'State felt shut out,' lamented one of its officials.[170] On January 20, 2003 Bush set up the Office of Reconstruction and Humanitarian Assistance under retired Lt-General Jay Garner.[171] Garner formerly headed 'Operation Provide Comfort' that helped the Kurds set up a semi-autonomous enclave after the first Gulf War. It was a strong signal to the Kurdish minority that Bush would not abandon them as previous American presidents had. The new office would have representatives from most departments, including State and the Office of Management and Budget. Barbara Bodine, a career diplomat from the Department of State became Garner's deputy.

Three factors hampered Garner from the start. First, brutal attacks by insurgents, saboteurs and terrorists made it difficult for Central Command to hand over much power to Garner. Second, the transition from 'Mission Accomplished' to reconstruction had gone very poorly. Extensive looting had done more damage than precision bombing had avoided, rendering some 17 out of 21 government buildings 'unusable'[172] while thousands of army regulars had disappeared with their weapons. An in-house Pentagon 'Strategic Lessons Learned' report in 2003 found that the military plan for stability operations, called Phase Four, was added late (January 2003) and was not well connected to the war plan. Rather than 'sequential' events, the report recommended that in the future the two be integrated.[173] Third, different factions among Iraqis with differing levels of support in Washington made the transition chaotic. An Iraqi Governing Council was eventually set up, composed of 25 members from both the exile and internal community, with a rotating chair. In May, Bush replaced Garner with Paul (Jerry) Bremer, a civilian administrator. Bremer dropped the policy of working with the old Iraqi army and disbanded it and went more aggressively after the leadership of the Baathist regime.

In the fall of 2002, the Bush administration had counted on far more international help for post-combat Iraq than it actually received. The damage of the acrimony surrounding UN resolution 1441 cannot be underestimated, affecting peacekeeping, humanitarian assistance and the political involvement of the UN. Peacekeeping was not part of Rumsfeld's transformation agenda and the tiny Peacekeeping Institute at the Pentagon was shut down in June 2002. It is likely that Bush, or at least Powell, had counted on major allies such as France and Germany to contribute peacekeeping forces after the war, but they, as well as India would not engage unless the US-led coalition handed over authority in Iraq to the United Nations. Some, like Canada, sent so many of its troops for peacekeeping to Afghanistan that there would be nothing left when Washington came asking. There was spite on both sides. From 'old' Europe's viewpoint, if Bush and Blair wanted to go to war alone, they should clean up after themselves. Thus, the Bush administration had to assemble a peacekeeping force from its new allies. It did better than expected, though American soldiers patrolled the most lethal areas. Poland sent some 6,000 troops, Italy 2,300, Ukraine 1,600, Spain 1,350, the Dutch 1,100 and late in 2003 even the Japanese joined in.[174] In early 2004, South Korea agreed to send 3,000 troops to the Kurdish area. Some 60 nations eventually pledged support in one way or another.

Blair urged Bush to involve the United Nations and he agreed to give it a 'vital role', though not a 'central role'. As with 'imminent threat', words matter. The 'central role', as Cheney put it, 'needs to reside with the coalition'.[175] Bush advisers were not about to handover Iraq to the UN, believing that 'if you were not with us on the take off, you don't deserve to be there for the landing.'[176] Many of his advisers were unimpressed, for good reasons, with the UN's record in Somalia and Kosovo. Still Bush sought a UN role in humanitarian assistance and in helping the various groups inside Iraq come to a governing consensus. UN efforts on the ground came to a halt when on August 19, 2003 the newly appointed Special Envoy Sergio Vieira de Mello together with 22 staff died in a massive suicide car bomb attack on the their building in Baghdad. Those who believed that simply handing over Iraq to a UN administration would quell the violence had something to think about. In September, Bush and Chirac disagreed openly when Chirac wanted sovereignty transferred to the UN immediately. 'If the French try to argue about taking things away from Jerry Bremer,' said one Bush official, 'that ain't gonna happen.'[177] This UN spat also frustrated the President's ability to bring in foreign donors. The Madrid donor conference in October produced meagre results with only a few major donors such as Japan ($1.5 billion) stepping forward. On December 15, at a press conference, Bush acknowledged that differences between him and Chirac and Schroeder on Iraq were far from over. Soon thereafter, the Pentagon announced that countries that did not form part of the coalition behind the war could not bid on some $20 billion in reconstruction contracts paid for by American taxpayers.

Before the war, Bush and his senior advisers simply did not want a debate about the cost of the war, the number of troops needed and the details of how an interim government should be set up and fare in the future. Bush's economic adviser Lawrence Lindsey inadvertently commented in September 2002 that the whole enterprise might cost $100 to $200 billion.[178] Both Powell and Rumsfeld had their reasons to be wary about an open debate as cost and future scenarios would inevitably play into the hands of those opposed to war. With the way things were going at the UN, Powell did not want more baggage. Open talk about 'Iraq after Hussein' would fuel the strong suspicion of countries such as France and Germany that war was predetermined and thus harm Powell's diplomatic efforts. When Shinseki testified on February 25 that it would take 'several hundred thousand troops', to secure Iraq afterwards, Wolfowitz two days later called Shinseki's comments, 'wildly off the mark'.[179] Suppressing a debate beforehand constitutes a calculated risk as it only comes back to bite you if the policy itself gets into deep water, but when it does, your credibility is on the line.

Cheney and Rumsfeld's senior staff were also weary about conventional studies about Iraq as these did not share the optimistic, forward-leaning vision for Iraqi democracy. The Department of State set up a 'Future of Iraq Project' as early as October 2001 that eventually produced thirteen volumes of findings and recommendations. The Chair of the group, Thomas Warrick, also happened to oppose war with Iraq. Needless to say, that did not exactly put him inside Bush's inner circle. The State Department should not have been surprised to find Warrick's volumes largely ignored. As one State Department official put it, 'State got shut out of the Iraq stuff.'[180] When Jay Garner initially put Warrick on his advisory team, Rumsfeld told Garner to take him off. Studies about post-combat Iraq flourished in late 2002 and early 2003: the CIA ran scenarios, USAID set up its 'Iraq Working Group' and think tanks such as Rand Corporation and the Council on Foreign Relations published reports. There were enough ideas around.

Powell, Rice, Rumsfeld and Cheney or their staffs knew about most of this material. Some of it was incorporated, such as the plan to quickly open schools and change the Iraqi currency which had Saddam's face on it. Other ideas were initially adopted but subsequently dropped, such as the plan to purge only the top of the Iraqi army and put the rest to good use in maintaining security (in 2004 that changed once again back to trying to work with the old leadership). Other ideas remained unresolved as a result of years of argument between different schools of thought on how to start a new government in Baghdad. Who would take the lead in such a government, Iraqi exiles or internals? Who among the splintered and contending factions of the Iraqi exiles should the United States promote? Bush had appointed Khalilzad as special envoy to the Iraqi exiles to bring them into a working coalition, but rivalries persisted.[181] Paul Wolfowitz and Douglas Feith had faith in Ahmed Chalabi while senior State and CIA officials tried to promote a moderate Sunni, named Ayad Allawi. State officials preferred to deal with Iraqis who were in the country rather than Chalabi who had been on the outside for years and whose reputation had been questioned. There was another line of disagreement between senior State and Defense officials: Wolfowitz was more optimistic about Iraqis constituting their own form of democracy quickly while State was more skeptical and wanted to bring stability and security first, with democracy coming later.[182] They eventually worked it out with a new Council of a mix of exiles and Iraqi internals and calling for regional caucuses first and popular elections later.

Just as important, the American influence over the council was limited. The Iraqi Governing Council turned out to be far from Bremer's lackey. Bremer was told in November that American plans for transferring sovereignty to Iraq should come no later than the summer of 2004 and would thus take place before Iraq could write its constitution. In early 2004, Shia leader Grand Ayatollah Ali al-Shistani blocked US efforts to transfer sovereignty to an Iraqi body chosen by regional caucuses and insisted on early popular elections.[183] Bush asked Kofi Annan to help the coalition and Annan sent an intermediary to broker a compromise. In late February 2004, Shistani agreed to elections after the transfer of sovereignty, possibly in early 2005. In early March, Iraqi leaders signed an interim constitution, a victory for Bush's timetable of handing over power to the Iraqis in the summer of 2004. Then the composition of the interim Iraqi government beyond the June 30 handover became a sensitive issue. Again, Bush asked Annan for more involvement. The UN sent Lakhdar Brahimi, who had also assisted the transition government in Afghanistan, to broker a deal among the various factions.

Near the end of 2003, Coalition forces had captured or killed almost all the 55 Saddam Hussein lieutenants that were on the most-wanted list. Gone were the notorious sons Uday and Qusay, but it was on December 14 that Bush got his biggest lift in the crisis since May 1; the capture of Saddam Hussein himself. Bearded and bedraggled, he was found in a small hole in the ground, ironically with nothing to show for, except a briefcase of US dollars. While Hussein's capture helped Bush for a moment, the missing weapons of mass destruction, the rising budget deficit – now projected to be some $500 billion in fiscal year 2005 – and the high jobless rates began to push Bush's approval rating down from the high 50s to the low 50s. Bush's troubles in Iraq had become a big part of the Democratic Party's primary campaign. The fiery former Vermont Governor, Howard Dean, practically built his rise on denouncing the President's war. When Democratic voters dumped Howard Dean after his disappointing showing in Iowa and opted for the more cautious and 'moderate' John Kerry in early 2004, polls showed Bush trailing the Massachusetts senator by some 5 points.

Conclusion

For political analysts, the war on Iraq caused 'justification fatigue'.[184] The trade in reasons and 'real' reasons why President Bush went to war has been brisk. They span from the ludicrous, such as settling Bush dynasty scores and stealing Iraqi oil, to the *realpolitik* of avoiding another North Korean nuclear standoff. The answer is more obvious: he chose regime change in Iraq because of his reading of Saddam Hussein's intent in a new, highly-charged psychological environment. It was his way of beating terrorism to the next front. All the other reasons why or why not to do Iraq could not put enough weight in the scales either way. Realist scholars John Mearsheimer and Stephen Walt argued that Hussein was 'eminently deterrable' and that a policy of 'vigilant containment' could do the job,[185] but even in terms of realist interest, American foreign policy was at a dead end in Iraq. Indefinite sanctions and no-flight zones are not a policy and no geopolitical argument could take away the possibility of Iraq assisting terrorist groups. Thomas Friedman argued that Bush went to war with Iraq to puncture the 'terrorism bubble' that had inflated in the Middle East.[186] Certainly, Bush wanted to dissuade rogues. No part of international law with its 'imminent threat' dogma was worth keeping if the terrorists could pull off another 9/11 with weapons of mass destruction. Yet, it was more than preventive, for Bush also felt strongly that removing Iraq's regime would be the beginning of a long-term cure for the region, a cure for neglect and oppression.

It was a bold choice, and a risky move. Writing about presidential leadership, Richard Brookhiser wondered whether Bush had enough 'imagination' to be president, and Bill Keller predicted that if he should fail, he would do so not as a result of caution but of 'overreaching'.[187] Brookhiser has his answer. Doing Iraq rather than just fighting Al Qaeda on its own terms was imaginative. Creating a launch pad for democracy in the Arab world and a homegrown alternative to pan-Arabic militant ideology is imaginative. Without ever saying so, Bush was working on the 'root causes' of Jihadist terrorism. Margaret Thatcher praised the President's 'all-embracing long-term strategy to defeat it'.[188] Some called it 'singular presidential leadership'.[189] It certainly was, but if you lean too far forward, you may fall on your face. That is the risk Bush was willing to take because the twin values of 'defenses beyond challenge' and freedom for all the people of the Middle East sealed his commitment.

Some concluded that the President's decision-making process was flawed. In this view, he consulted 'only a few, like-minded advisers', precluded the 'collective effort' of his war cabinet by his own impulses, and did not welcome 'ideas and alternatives',[190] but the evidence does not bear this out for most of this case study. Bush invited the debate on Iraq early and decided against widening the war in September 2001 after hearing both sides of the argument. Later that fall, he changed his mind and allowed a variety of arguments. General Zinni, who was working for Powell at some arms length, gave vigorous arguments why going after Iraq was a bad idea. One Bush official in the fall of 2002 quipped that there was more debate inside the administration, on Iraq, than between Republicans and Democrats.[191] He gave general policy direction but did not predetermine or ignore his National Security Council.

Throughout the drawn-out process, Condi Rice was able to keep both Powell and Rumsfeld's doors open to the Oval Office. Powell and Tony Blair gave strong divergent advice from Cheney and Rumsfeld and some of it was so strong that the 'decisive' Bush could not quite cut the knot. His September 12 call to the United Nations for both more commitment and a new resolution, and his acceptance of the watered-down version of resolution 1441 are examples of splitting the difference.

President Bush's open and deliberate decision process was not without flaws. Alexander George cautioned presidents to watch out when their advisers 'agree too readily on the nature of the problem facing them and on a response to it,'[192] and students of the psychology of decision making have found that '"Self evident beliefs" are involved in most intelligence failures.'[193] The decision process became vulnerable to this malfunction in the fall of 2002 when the public focus was shifted from regime change to disarmament. The Office of Strategic Planning was a classical 'Team-B' exercise in which a small group of advisers concentrate on second-guessing and pushing conventional intelligence and conclusions.[194] Wolfowitz and Perle had been involved in such analytical efforts as junior advisers, questioning Richard Nixon's and Gerald Ford's arms control policies and CIA estimates about the Soviet Union, but such exercises work best when done by a minority to challenge a majority view.

Just after 9/11 it was a good idea to challenge existing intelligence analyses that had failed to detect the attacks, but in the case of Iraq's illicit weapons, there was already a strong majority view. Most mainline advisers already shared the view of 'Team B.' As a result, Team B did not challenge the 'lazy consensus' but rather reinforced the existing view. Thus, it became more difficult for people in the State Department's Intelligence branch to argue caution about intelligence analyses. This took the critical edge off the debate, creating an atmosphere in which Bush and his advisers began to bolster their arguments about what Saddam Hussein allegedly possessed and what he was building. It may also have created a mild climate of 'groupthink' in which critical thinking is suppressed for fear of upsetting the predominant view. Had there been a tougher debate on the intelligence, the President's comments could have remained more 'hedged', which in turn would have insulated him somewhat from the harsh public criticism when no weapons were found in 2003. After all, when Bush decided in early 2002 on regime change in Iraq his reason was the Nexus threat, not just weapons of mass destruction. Blair and Powell thought that the WMD argument would be the more persuasive one, but in Bush's heart the real issue was the evil intent of Saddam Hussein. All of the bolstering was made easier by the fact that Hussein's credibility was at absolute zero and there were no reasons to give him the benefit of any rational doubt.

Even when accounting for over zealousness in the analysis of the Office of Strategic Plans and – what in 2004 became apparent were lies – in the intelligence forwarded by the Iraq National Congress under Chalabi, there never was any daylight among intelligence agencies in America and Europe about the firm conviction that Hussein had chemical and biological war materials. Kenneth Pollack, who had been an advocate for waging war against him in 2002, concluded in 2004 that Saddam must have decided to destroy his stockpiles and his 'just-in-time-production capacity' in the late 1990s in order to lure the international community away from further sanctions.[195] Keeping only a sliver of 'reconstitution capability' would also allow him to operate below the radar of future inspections, but rather than coming clean and complying with the UN, Pollack suggests, Hussein pretended he had more than he did in order to deter his domestic and regional rivals from toppling him.

Pollack's wasn't the only explanation. Based on interviews with Iraqi scientists after the war, *Washington Post* reporter, Barton Gelman, speculated that Iraqi scientists and senior military officials deliberately inflated their paperwork in order to make Saddam believe he had more than was the case, while Western intelligence ended up collecting 'the same false reports that fooled Hussein.'[196] On the other hand, deceiving Saddam Hussein was quite dangerous. Perhaps these scientists were trying to whitewash their own reputation. Hussein may have refused to cooperate with UNMOVIC because he feared Bush would use it as a cover for a CIA coup against him. Perhaps, as some Israeli sources believed, the illicit weapons were smuggled to Syria in the first weeks of the war when only one US artillery unit was trying to find them. Rumsfeld thinks they will still be found.

In early 2004, David Kay, the head of the Iraq Survey Group left his post, blaming the intelligence agencies for shoddy work. At the same time Lord Hutton cleared Tony Blair from misrepresenting the record as he knew it. Under pressure, Bush appointed an independent commission to look into how intelligence was gathered. Unlike the 9/11 Commission, its report would not come until after the 2004 election. Still, Iraq's missing weapons gave the Democrats a national security issue with which to attack the President's most valued commodity: his trustworthiness.

As the coalition neared the June 30 benchmark for the handover of power, the situation on the ground grew more chaotic. American and Iraqi forces fought and then settled on a truce around the insurgency stronghold of Falujah. A mixture of shuttle diplomacy by Brahimi and American show of force kept a breakaway Shia faction barely under control. Spanish Prime Minister and Bush's friend, Jose Maria Aznar, lost the March election and the new Socialist leader promptly withdrew Spanish forces from peacekeeping duties in what looked like a response to an Al Qaeda attack in Madrid. The scandal of American soldiers mistreating and grossly abusing Iraqi prisoners hurt Bush's moral cause. The race for freedom and hope was only just begun.

Notes

1   As quoted in William Schneider, 'The Cowboy and the Diplomat', *National Journal*, February 15, 2003, p. 550.

2   As quoted in Seymour Hersh, 'The Iraq Hawks', *The New Yorker*, December 24 & 31, 2001, p. 59. Glenn Kessler, 'US Decision on Iraq Has Puzzling Past', *Washington Post*, January 12, 2003, writes that Bush was saying take 'them' out; as in the weapons of mass destruction.

3   Ron Suskind, *The Price of Loyalty: George W. Bush, the White House, and the Education of Paul O'Neill* (New York: Simon & Schuster, 2004), pp. 72-75.

4   Peter Stothard, *Thirty Days: Tony Blair and the Test of History* (New York: Harper Collins, 2003), p. 86.

5   Evan Thomas, 'The 12-Year Itch', *Newsweek*, March 31, 2003, (http://mnsbc.msn.com/id/3068684).

6   Michael Lind, 'The Weird Men Behind George W. Bush's War', *The New Statesman*, April 7, 2003, pp. 10-13. See also Joshua Micah Marshall, 'Practice to Deceive', *The Washington Monthly*, April 2003, pp. 28-34.

7   As quoted in Karen Hughes, *Ten Minutes From Normal* (New York: Viking, 2004), p. 246.

8   Colin Powell, 'Statement for the Record', House Committee on International Relations, September 19, 2002.

9   Carla Anne Robbins and Jeanne Cummings, 'New Doctrine: How Bush Decided That Iraq's Hussein Must be Ousted', *Wall Street Journal*, June 14, 2002, p. 8.

10 Graham Allison, 'Could Worse Be Yet to Come?', *Economist*, November 3, 2001, p. 20.

11 Joseph de Rivera, *The Psychological Dimension of Foreign Policy* (Columbus, Ohio: Charles E. Merill Publishing Co., 1986), p. 17.

12 John Newhouse, *Imperial America: The Bush Assault on the World Order* (New York, Knopf, 2003), p. 77.

13 'National Strategy to Combat Weapons of Mass Destruction' (NSPD-17), December 2002.

14 David Frum, *The Right Man: The Surprise Presidency of George W. Bush* (New York: Random House, 2003), p. 224.

15 Michael Gordon and David Sanger, 'Powell Says US Is Weighing Ways to Topple Hussein', *The New York Times*, February 13, 2002, p. 14.

16 Donald Rumsfeld, 'Prepared Testimony', House Armed Services Committee Hearing, Washington, D.C., September 18, 2002.

17   Robbins and Cummings, 'New Doctrine', p. 8.

18   Nicolas Lemann, 'Without a Doubt', *The New Yorker*, October 14 & 21, 2002, p. 176.

19   Evan Thomas, 'He Has Saddam in His Sights', *Newsweek*, March 4, 2002, p. 20.

20   Author Interview with Department of Defense Official, March 15, 2004.

21   Peter J. Boyer, 'The New War Machine', *The New Yorker*, June 30, 2003, p. 55.

22   Mark Thompson and Michael Duffy, 'Pentagon Warlord', *Time*, January 27, 2003, p. 28.

23   Mark Hosenball et al., 'Cheney's Long Path to War', *Newsweek*, November 17, 2003. (http://mnsbc.msn.com/id/3403519).

24   Alexis Simendinger et al., 'Just the Ticket', *National Journal*, February 14, 2004, p. 452.

25   As quoted in Jeffrey Record, 'The Bush Doctrine and War with Iraq', *Parameters*, Spring 2003, pp. 4-21.

26   PBS Frontline devoted a 60 minute segment to this theme in March 2003, titled 'The War Behind Close Doors'.

27   Evan Thomas, 'Chemistry in the Cabinet', *Newsweek*, January 28, 2002, p. 28.

28   Bob Woodward, *Plan of Attack* (New York: Simon & Schuster, 2004), p. 73.

29   Woodward, *Plan of Attack*, p. 2.

30   Gordon and Sanger, 'Powell', pp. 1 and 14.

31   Rowan Scarborough, *Rumsfeld's War: The Untold Story of America's Anti-Terrorist Commander* (Washington, D.C., Regnery Publishing, 2004), p. 45; Woodward, *Plan of Attack*, p. 109.

32   See for example, Lewis H. Lapham, 'The Road to Babylon', *Harper's Magazine*, October 2002, p. 35.

33   Office of the Press Secretary, Washington, D.C., Remarks by the President at respectively Virginia Military Institute, Lexington, German Parliament, Berlin, West Point Graduation Speech, and Fort Drum, New York, April 17, May 23, June 1, July 19, 2002.

34   Morton Kondracke, 'Bush Begins Making Case for Iraq War', *Roll Call*, August 15, 2002.

35   Fred Barnes, 'The Commander', *Weekly Standard*, June 2, 2003, p. 22.

36   Evan Thomas, 'Rumsfeld's War', *Newsweek*, September 16, 2002, p. 25.

37   Ryan Lizza, 'Backfired', *The New Republic*, November 5, 2001, p. 16.

38   Thomas, '12-Year Itch',

39   Seymour Hersh, 'The Debate Within', *The New Yorker*, March 4, 2002.

40   Woodward, *Plan of Attack*, p. 98.

41   Woodward, *Plan of Attack*, p. 121.

42   Thomas Ricks, 'Bush Likens Terror to Nazism', *Washington Post*, May 24, 2002, pp. 1 and 26.

43   Seymour Hersh, 'The Debate Within', *The New Yorker*, March 4, 2002 (www.newyorker.com/printable/?fact/020311fa_FACT).

44   Carla Anne Robbins, 'Former Envoy Under Pressure as Showdown Looms with Iraq', *Wall Street Journal*, March 3, 2002, p. 31.

45   'First Iraq Weapons Talks "Useful", UN Says', (www.usis.it/file2002_03/alia/a2030709.htm).

46   'UN-Iraq Talks on Weapons Inspections to Begin May 1', ((www.usis.it/file2002_04/alia/a2042303.htm).

47   Testimony by George Tenet, CIA Director, Senate Armed Services Committee, March 19, 2002. (www.usis.it/file2002_03/alia/a2032008.htm).

48   As quoted in Thomas Ricks, 'Holding Their Ground', *Washington Post*, December 23, 2003, p. C. 1.

49   Frum, p. 200. Nicolas Lemann concurs with this view, describing Rice as becoming more 'moralistic'. 'Her Brilliant Career', *The New Yorker Online*, posted October 14, 2002 (www.newyorker.com/printable/?online/021014on_onlineonly02).

50   'Deputy Secretary Wolfowitz's Interview with Sam Tannenhaus', May 9, 2003 (http://defenselink.mil/transcripts/2003/tr20030).
51   Bob Woodward, *Bush at War* (New York: Simon & Schuster, 2002), p. 339.
52   Bill Keller, 'The Sunshine Warrior', *The New York Times Magazine*, September 22, 2002, p. 50.
53   Woodward, *Plan of Attack*, p. 90.
54   Christopher Marquis, 'Bush Officials Differ on Way to Force Out Iraqi Leader', *New York Times*, June 19, 2002.
55   Woodward, *Bush at War,* p. 333.
56   Woodward, *Plan of Attack*, p. 150.
57   Stothard, p. 13.
58   As quoted in Alex Danchev, 'Greeks and Romans: Anglo-American Relations After 9/11', *Royal United Services Institute Journal*, Vol. 148, Issue 2, April 2003.
59   Tamara Lipper et al, 'Selling the World on War', *Newsweek*, September 23, 2002, p. 29.
60   Woodward, *Plan of Attack*, p. 157.
61   Fred Barnes, 'The Dynamic Duo', *The Weekly Standard*, April 7, 2003, p. 12.
62   Woodward, *Bush at War*, p. 336.
63   George P. Schultz, 'The Danger is Immediate. Saddam Must Be Removed', *Washington Post*, September 6, 2002.
64   Richard Cheney, Speech Delivered at the Veterans of Foreign Wars 103rd Convention, Nashville, Tennessee, August 26, 2002.
65   Carl M. Cannon, 'The Point Man', *National Journal*, October 12, 2002, p. 2960.
66   Nancy Gibbs, 'Double-Edged Sword', *Time*, December 30, 2002-January 6, 2003, p. 77.
67   Woodward, *Plan of Attack*, p. 182.
68   Office of the Press Secretary, 'Remarks by the President in Address to the United Nations General Assembly', New York, September 12, 2002.
69   Elisabeth Bumiller, 'Still Advising, From Afar and Near', *The New York Times*, October 21, 2002, p. 12.
70   'Your Moves', *Economist*, September 21, 2002, p. 27.
71   Rowan Scarborough, 'US Rushed post-Saddam Planning', *Washington Times*, September 3, 2003 (www.washtimes.com/print_story.cfm?StoryID=20030903-120317-9393r).
72   William Scheider, 'A Question of Timing', *National Journal*, September 21, 2002, p. 2750.
73   James Moore and Wayne Slater, *Bush's Brain: How Karl Rove Made George W. Bush Presidential* (New York: John Wiley & Sons, 2003), p. 309.
74   As quoted in Morton Kondracke, 'Gephardt Pushes Consensus Action Against Iraq Threat', *Roll Call*, September 23, 2002.
75   As cited in Fred Barnes, 'Bush Speaks, Congress Salutes', *The Weekly Standard*, October 21, 2002, p. 10.
76   As quoted in Morton Kondracke, 'Congress Needs to Challenge Bush Doctrine', *Roll Call*, September 26, 2002.
77   For example in his September 12 address to the United Nations.
78   Remarks by Paul Wolfowitz, Fletcher Conference, Washington, D.C., October 16, 2002.
79   Barnes, p. 10.
80   *Iraq's Weapons of Mass Destruction: the Assessment of the British Government,* Issued September 24, 2002 (www.fco.gov.uk/files/kfile/iraqdossier.pdf).
81   As quoted in Woodward, *Plan of Attack*, p. 197.
82   Transcript, 'Powell: War with Iraq is Last Resort', Larry King Live, CNN October 9, 2002 (http://www.cnn.com/2002/ALLPOLITICS/10/09/powell.transcript/index.html).

83   One of the clearest cases is in 'Testimony by Donald Rumsfeld before the House Armed Services Committee', US Congress, September 18, 2002.

84   Rumsfeld Testimony, September 18, 2002.

85   State of the Union Address, Office of the Press Secretary, White House, January 28, 2003.

86   'Issue in Iraq is Not Inspections, Powell Says', August 3, 2002 (www.usis.it/file2002_08/alia/a2080202.htm).

87   Quotes below are from 'Jacques Chirac, French Leader Offers America Both Friendship and Criticism', *New York Times*, September 9, 2002, p. 9.

88   'The National Security Strategy of the United States', September 2002, pp. v and 15.

89   Press Background Briefing By Senior Administration Officials, Office of the Press Secretary, The White House, November 8, 2002.

90   Maggie Farley and Robin Wright, 'UN Debates Who Has Last Word on Iraq', *Los Angeles Times*, October 29, 2002 (www.latimes.com/news/printedition/asection/la-fg-uniraq29Oct290044442).

91   United Nations Security Council, Resolution 1441, November 8, 2002 (www.un.int/usa/sres-iraq.htm).

92   Office of the Press Secretary, 'President's Remarks at Cincinnati Museum Center', Cincinnati, Ohio, October 7, 2002.

93   'The UN Trap', *The Weekly Standard*, November 18, 2002, pp. 9-12.

94   Howard Fineman, 'How Bush Did It', *Newsweek*, November 8, 2002 (http://msnbc.msn.com/id/3067923).

95   Woodward, *Plan of Attack*, p. 250.

96   Federation of American Scientists, 'Iraq's Continuing Programs for Weapons of Mass Destruction', Excerpts from National Intelligence Estimate, October 4, 2002 as declassified on July 18, 2003. (www.fas.org/irp/cia/product/iraq-wmd.html)

97   President's Remarks At Cincinnati.

98   Scarborough, 'Rumsfeld's War', p. 40.

99   Idem, pp. 40-41.

100   Leman, 'Without a Doubt', p. 176.

101   Woodward, *Plan of Attack*, p. 105.

102   David Sanger, 'Iraq Arms Report Has Big Omissions, US Officials Say', *New York Times*, December 13, 2002.

103   As quoted in Joyce Howard Price, 'US Called to Get Tough on Iraq', *The Washington Times*, December 9, 2002.

104   As quoted in 'Bush Concerned with Omissions in Iraq Weapons Declaration', December 18, 2002 (www.usis.it/file2002_12/alia/a2121802.htm).

105   Powell as quoted in 'US Says Iraqi Declaration Constitutes "Material Breach"', December 19, 2002 (www.usis.it/file2002_12/alia/a2121903.htm).

106   Colin Powell, Press Conference, Department of State, January 8, 2004.

107   Blix quoted in 'US Says Iraqi Declaration Constitutes "Material Breach"', December 19, 2002 (www.usis.it/file2002_12/alia/a2121903.htm).

108   Steven R. Weisman, 'How Powell Lined Up Votes, Starting With His President', *New York Times*, November 9, 2002.

109   For example, Robert Wright, 'Verify First', *The New Republic*, March 31, 2003, p. 13, who wrote: 'UN inspectors would try to prove that he [Saddam] was lying, and, until they did, war would be put on hold.'

110   Transcript of Rumsfeld interview with George Stephanopoulos, January 19, 2003 (www.usis.it/file2003_01/alia/a3011713.htm)

111   Woodward, *Plan of Attack*, p. 251.

112   Woodward, *Plan of Attack*, p. 252.

113   Woodward, *Plan of Attack*, p. 270.

114 Jean-David Levitte as quoted in Lee Michael Katz, 'We Are Not a Pacifist Country', *National Journal*, March 8, 2003, p. 753.

115 James Kitfield, 'Damage Control', *National Journal*, July 19, 2003, p. 2340.

116 Glenn Kessler and Colum Lynch, 'France Vows to Block Resolution on Iraq War', *Washington Post*, January 21, 2003, p.1.

117 Kitfield, 'Damage Control', p. 2328.

118 Woodward, *Plan of Attack*, p. 233.

119 James P. Rubin, 'Stumbling Into War', *Foreign Affairs* (September/October 2003) http://foreignaffairs.org/20030901faesssay82504/james_p-rubin/stumbling-into-war.html).

120 As quoted in an interview by Lee Michael Katz, 'Sooner or Later, Iraq Had to Be Dealt With', *National Journal*, February 8, 2003, p. 461.

121 Kitfield, p. 2340. Stephen Haynes quotes an aide saying 'livid'. 'Time is Running Out', *Weekly Standard*, February 3, 2003, p. 12.

122 Author Interview with Department of State Official, March 16, 2004.

123 Elisabeth Bumiller, 'Just Another Bush Day, Except for its Conclusion', *New York Times*, March 18, 2003, p. 10.

124 As quoted in Quentin Peel et al., 'How the US Set a Course for War with Iraq', *Financial Times*, May 26, 2003 (http://www.globalpolicy.org/security/issues/iraq/attack/2003/0526course.htm).

125 As quoted in Steven Edwards, 'France Defies US With Iraq Resolution', *National Post*, October 9, 2002.

126 As quoted in 'Merci, M. de Villepin', *Weekly Standard*, February 3, 2003, p. 7.

127 As quoted in Max Boot, 'Europe 1, France 0', *Weekly Standard*, March 3, 2003, p. 18.

128 Stothard, p. 41.

129 Woodward, *Plan of Attack*, p. 249.

130 Alexander George, *Presidential Decision-Making in Foreign Policy*, (Boulder: Westview Press, 1980), p. 38.

131 George, p. 39.

132 Rowan Scarborough, 'Rumsfeld Says Iraq Likely Had Arms', *Washington Times*, February 5, 2004.

133 'Hardball with Chris Matthews', Transcript for March 15, 2004 (http://msnbc.msn.com/id/4540609/).

134 'Text of Powell's Address, Presenting "Deeply Troubling" Evidence on Iraq', *New York Times*, February 6, 2003, pp. 14-16.

135 Woodward, *Plan of Attack*, p. 312.

136 Julia Preston, 'France, Backed by Germany, Calls for Stronger Inspections, but the US is Unmoved', *New York Times*, February 6, 2003, p. 13.

137 Officials' Remarks to Reporters on Air Force One, Office of the Press Secretary, February 20, 2003 as quoted in (www.usis.it/file2003_02/alia/a3022114.htm).

138 Ari Fleischer, 'White House Report', March 3, 2003 (http://www.usis.it/file2003_03/alia/a3030301.htm).

139 Press Conference by the President, Office of the Press Secretary, March 6, 2003.

140 As quoted in 'Notebook', *The New Republic*, March 24, 2003, p. 10.

141 Mark Champion et al., 'How the Iraq Confrontation Divided the Western Alliance', *Wall Street Journal*, March 27, 2003.

142 As quoted in 'Waiting Game', *The New Republic*, March 17, 2003.

143 Stothard, p. 14.

144 Michael Elliot, 'Who's With Him?', *Time*, March 3, 2003, p. 17.

145 Remarks by the President to the Nation, Office of the Press Secretary, March 17, 2003.

146 As quoted in Boyer, 'The New War Machine', p. 58.

147 Barnes, 'The Commander', pp. 23-24.

148   As quoted in Boyer, p. 64.
149   'Counting Heads', *The New Republic*, April 7, 2003, p. 6.
150   Carl Conetta, 'The Wages of War: Iraqi Combatant and Noncombatant Fatalities in the 2003 Conflict', Project on Defense Alternatives, Research Monograph # 8, October 20, 2003 (www.comw.org/pda/0310rm8.html).
151   As quoted in David Remnick, 'Faith-Based Intelligence', *The New Yorker*, July 28, 2003, p. 28.
152   James Kitfield, 'The Army's Gamble', *National Journal*, March 29, 2003, p. 972.
153   Quoted in Boyer, p. 61.
154   Seymour Hersh, 'Offense and Defense', *The New Yorker*, April 7, 2003 (www.newyorker.com/printable/?fact/030407fa_fact).
155   Lt-General William Wallace, as quoted in James Kitfield, 'Always Attack', *National Journal*, April 26, 2003, p. 1295.
156   Barners, 'Commander', p. 25.
157   'Wolfowitz interview', (http://defenselink.mil/transcripts/2003/tr20030).
158   Cheney on NBC's 'Meet the Press', March 16, 2003, as quoted in (www.usis.it/file2003_03/alia/a3031604.htm).
159   Judy Keen, 'Strain of Iraq War Showing on Bush, Those Who Know Him Say', *USA Today*, April 2, 2003.
160   Stephen Mansfield, *The Faith of George W. Bush* (New York: Jeremy P. Tarcher/Penguin, 2003), p. 173.
161   'President delivers speech to nation from deck of carrier in Pacific', May 1, 2003 (http://www.usis.it/file2003_05/alia/a3050101.htm).
162   Lawrence Kaplan, 'Early Exit: Why the Bushies Want Out of Iraq', *The New Republic*, May 26, 2003, p. 18.
163   As quoted in Ivo H. Daalder and James M. Lindsay, *America Unbound: The Bush Revolution in Foreign Policy* (Washington, D.C.: Brookings Institution Press, 2003), p. 161.
164   Remarks by Donald Rumsfeld, Intrepid Sea-Air Space Museum, New York City, February 14, 2003.
165   James Fallows, 'Blind into Baghdad', *The Atlantic Monthly*, January-February, 2004, p. 54.
166   As quoted in Nicolas Lemann, 'After Iraq', *The New Yorker*, February 17, 2003.
167   Woodward, *Plan of Attack*, p. 424.
168   Michael Elliot, 'So What Went Wrong?', *Time*, October 6, 2003, p. 19.
169   Author Interview with State Department Official, March 16, 2004.
170   Idem.
171   Douglas Feith, 'Post-War Planning', Testimony before Senate Foreign Relations Committee, US Congress, February 11, 2003.
172   Romesh Ratnesar, 'Life Under Fire', *Time*, July 14, 2003, p. 33.
173   Scarborough, 'Rumsfeld's War', p. 54 and p. 178.
174   As of December 27, 2003 (www.washingtonpost.com/wp-srv/world/daily/graphics/iraq_security_123003.html)
175   Address to American Society of News Editors, New Orleans, April 9, 2003 (www.usis.it/file2003_04/alia/A3040904.htm).
176   Michael Duffy and Massimo Calabresi, 'Clash of the Titans', *Time*, April 14, 2003, p. 40.
177   As quoted in Michael Elliot, 'Facing Reality', *Time*, September 22, 2003, p. 21.
178   Fallows, p. 62.
179   Fallows, pp. 72-73.
180   Author Interview, Washington, D.C., March 16, 2004.
181   Eli J. Lake, 'Split Decision: The Bushies Two Plans for Iraq', *The New Republic*, May 5, 2003, p. 18.

182 Lawrence Kaplan, 'Federal Reserve', *The New Republic*, March 17, 2003, pp. 17-19.
183 Steven Weisman, 'Bush Team Revising Plans for Granting Self-Rule to Iraqis', *The New York Times*, January 13, 2004.
184 Lemann, 'After Iraq'.
185 'An Unnecessary War', *Foreign Policy*, January/February 2003 (www.foreignpolicy.com/wwwboard/walts.html).
186 Thomas Friedman, 'Because We Could', *New York Times*, June 4, 2003.
187 Richard Brookhiser, 'The Mind of George W. Bush', *Atlantic Monthly*, April 2003, p. 68; Bill Keller, 'Reagan's Son', *New York Times Magazine*, January 26, 2003, p. 62.
188 Margaret Thatcher, 'Advice to a Superpower', *New York Times*, February 11, 2002, p. 29.
189 Charles Krauthammer, 'Bush's Act of Political Courage', *National Post*, September 26, 2003.
190 For example, see William Crotty, 'Presidential Policymaking in Crisis Situations: 9/11 and its Aftermath', *Policy Studies Journal*, Vol. 31, No. 3, 2003, pp. 451, 457 and 460.
191 See Stephen Hayes, 'The State Department vs. Bush', *Weekly Standard*, September 9, 2002, pp. 12-14.
192 George, p. 122.
193 de Rivera, p. 55.
194 Hosenball et al. See also, Julian Borger, 'The Spies Who Pushed for War', *The Guardian*, July 17, 2003; Thomas Ricks, 'Iraq War Planner Downplays Role', *Washington Post*, October 22, 2003; Spencer Abraham and John Judis, 'The Operator', *The New Republic*, September 22, 2003, p. 27.
195 Kenneth M. Pollack, 'Spies, Lies, and Weapons: What Went Wrong', *Atlantic Monthly*, January/February 2004, p. 82.
196 Barton Gelman, 'Iraq's Arsenal Was Only on Paper', *Washington Post*, January 7, 2004.

Chapter 7

Bush's Style, Record, and Vision

Bush's Presidential Style

George W. Bush's presidential style is a study in contrasts. Behind the scenes, he is a 'stickler for being prepared', pushing briefers and speechwriters, but in public he makes it looks so easy.[1] His looks like a casual presidency, appearing for a brief press conference with Tommy Franks on December 28 around 10:00am in jeans and western shirt, making a few bland comments. What you didn't see was that he was up at 5:00, worked through a tone-setting video-conference with his national security team on Iraqi military plans and all that at his Crawford ranch, where people were assuming he was on holiday.

He is a conservative with a heart, but to half of the American electorate Bush looks like the 'Great Polarizer'.[2] He told Tim Russert in 2004 his 'biggest disappointment' was that he had not succeeded as a 'uniter'.[3] While visiting Britain in November 2003, Bush said he strove for 'open societies ordered by moral conviction', and 'private markets humanized by compassionate government', yet he did not get credit for his compassionate conservatism in foreign policy.[4] His Millennium Challenge Account plan for development aid, announced in March 2002 and his January 2003 initiative to fight HIV/AIDS would increase American foreign aid from $12 billion in 2002 to $18 billion in 2006, 'the largest increase in decades'.[5] It was Bush who insisted Rumsfeld and the military planners must have humanitarian assistance flowing on the first day of combat operations in both Afghanistan and Iraq.

Bush is a real faith president; he does not just say 'God bless America', at the end of his speeches as a kind of 'grace note', but, God, faith, and providence are the foundation of his speeches and at times the 'guts of the argument'.[6] He does not only pray for strength and direction, but also asks for 'forgiveness'.[7] Many people react harshly, calling him 'exclusionary', and brimming with 'messianic militarism',[8] but the claims are hollow for his faith does not exclude; what makes it stand out is that it is personal and practiced, and not just veneer. In Senegal in July 2003, Bush apologized for slavery and put his finger on Christian men and women becoming 'blind to the clearest commands of their faith'.[9] Yet, he does not make his faith look heavy, as he banters, and goofs, wisecracks and swaggers, making many think he cannot be serious.

Bush often looks and sounds impatient, even rash. He feeds the story that he is a gut player, and a quick draw. Funny thing that this 'impatient' man took eight months to coach Vladimir Putin out of the ABM Treaty and twelve months to change the regime in Baghdad. Even in the supercharged 9/11 atmosphere he took weeks to go after Al Qaeda and the Taliban.

This president is the consummate retail politician; he announces a big idea and rather than sit in the Oval Office to watch the national media and Congress take it apart, he gets on the plane and pitches the same theme in state after state. But when he has to play the national scene, his message control machine is under stress, as Bush cannot project his goofy seriousness onto TV; either he looks too stiff and brooding or he looks too casual. The same problem happens in press conferences. A president cannot do rigid message control in these because it makes him look programmed and robotic, even unthinking.

Bush has true vision. Rice's deputy, Steve Hadley, put it well: 'He loves to be a change agent.'[10] He is a 'romantic', just as Peggy Noonan described Reagan, and points to an absolute standard way over the horizon, leading his administration and country in that direction.[11] People will follow in the 'slipstream' of strong leadership, Bush told Woodward.[12] To his critics it looks like 'arrogance born of power, not principle', and they warn that 'few follow'.[13] Like Ronald Reagan, Bush has no ounce of arrogance or desire for hegemony in him, even though he may sound more brash than Reagan and needs Karen Hughes nearby to keep him from sounding too taunting. I 'don't do nuance', the President once told Senator Joe Biden.[14]

The Foreign Policy Vision

Bush, like Margaret Thatcher, believes in freedom-loving sovereign states working in partnership on the basis of shared values. Thatcher did not like the European Union because it was trying to take this identity away from Britain; Bush does not like the United Nations and the so-called multilateral world order with its treaties and regimes because it is trying to do the same thing to the United States. The President's value-based foreign policy rejects the standard model called neo-liberalism *and* the alternative model, neo-realism. He is not simply maximizing American national interest within a more or less accepted international regime structure. Instead, God-given, universal values, or as Bush calls them, the 'non-negotiable demands of human dignity,' such as 'the rule of law; limits on the power of the state; respect for women; private property; free speech; equal justice; and religious tolerance' must be the direct aim with states in the driver's seat.[15] He wants to use American purpose and power to make people free inside strong but accountable states. International treaties and organizations may or may not be of use depending on how they fit this bill. As Colin Powell put it, the President sees the goal of world politics as 'a family of nations that share basic values', and, as Rice stated, not 'a theory of rivalry, of competing interests'.[16] Just as Bush sought to persuade Putin out of the old mode, he rejects France's attempt to create a new multipolar world because in his view it is a distraction from the real struggle ahead.

The challenge to President Bush's vision, which focuses his foreign policy is the 'direct heir' to the Western fight against Nazism and Communism. Militant Islamic terror, in his eye, is a 'pseudo-religious tyranny' that does not respect any life, that seeks to enslave Muslims and cower the West.[17] Al Qaeda may have beaten Bush in the first charge, but it picked the wrong presidential character for an all-out fight. To use an historical analogy from the Cold War, Bush rejected the equivalent of George F. Kennan's limited containment strategy against communism and chose instead Paul Nitze's total countervalue strategy to fight the war on terror. In other words,

Harry Truman chose to resist the combination of communism and state power everywhere, always. It was North Korea's attack on its southern neighbor in 1950 that brought American troops back to Europe to stop communism. It was Al Qaeda's lust for weapons of mass impact that brought American soldiers into the Middle East. Bush believes that terrorism has to be pushed down and out everywhere because there is nothing to contain or deter it.

The President sees terrorism as a total threat, but he has no 'one-size-fits-all' strategy to deal with it. The monolithic threat is the nexus between terror, outlaw states that offer 'the quiet enjoyment of real estate' and materials or weapons of mass terror.[18] In the fall of 2001, Bush blended his pre 9/11 focus on rogue states with his post 9/11 goal to go after states that provide such havens or weapons. His tactics against this new armed-totalitarian doctrine vary, and preemption such as in Iraq is only one part of it. As Powell said, 'there is no such strategy of preemption. There is an option called pre-emption.'[19] Toppling Saddam showed all adversaries that they 'were in big trouble',[20] and that Bush would look not only for needles but also remove haystacks. This was followed with a massive attempt at reconstruction and nation building, as well as the Greater Middle East Initiative, to bring grassroots political and economic reforms to the entire region. Libya was rewarded for its change in intent.

Just as preemption is not a Bush dogma, neither is unilateralism for these 'process' words have no appeal for the President. He has no 'preference for going it alone' but instead, to coin a phrase, is 'missionlateral'.[21] His policy to North Korea, Iran, Libya and Syria is not as Richard Perle once put it: 'You're next', but is 'We have you surrounded with "effective multilateralism".'[22] When it comes to North Korea, you cannot find a more multilateral approach, yet Bush stands on his value; North Korea will not get away with a 'crime pays' policy, as James Baker put it.[23] First North Korea started into the plutonium business, against the law, and tried to extract American aid to build less dangerous nuclear facilities, then it tried for more Western payout to drop its missile business. Why would it not try for a third round of concessions to shut down its illegal uranium processing which was discovered in the summer of 2002? Bush sought instead the full pressure of Russia, China and Japan, combined with a fast missile defense capability and a new scheme of choking off North Korea's export of dangerous materials.

That 'choke off' – the Proliferation Security Initiative – is another example of the President's 'effective multilateralism.' Eleven states, including France and Germany, agreed in 2003 to share intelligence and coordinate the interception of suspicious shipments to or from rogue states. Bush sees this as a joint 'activity rather than an organization' without all the process and bureaucrats.[24] In 2003, joint efforts led to a seizure of chemical weapon materials going to North Korea and nuclear processing equipment bound for Libya.

The Decision-Making Process

Bush demands a tough brief and allows ample debate, but how does one influence him, even change his mind? Karen Hughes offers an example: early in the 1994 Texas race against Ann Richards, Bush had a standard expression he used at every rally: 'I am a capitalist'. Hughes tried to quietly reason him out of it but to no avail. One time after returning from a campaign stop he asked her when they were back on the plane how the speech went. She took the chance to stick it right to him, jumping in front of him she shouted, 'I am a capitalist – a *rich business* guy, and *you* – why *you* are *not!*'[25] He was a bit ticked off, but he got the point and never used it again. Hughes did this more often – and standing behind her one day in the fall of 2001 aboard Air Force One, Bush shook her shoulders and said, 'You correct me when I screw up, always. I want you to.'[26]

An effective adviser must have conviction. It is not about ideology, but is about pushing back without ever taking credit or second-guessing a final decision. To play, you have to be in the inner loyal circle. Loyalty is a contact sport for Bush and if the adviser does not jump ship, he will not toss him or her overboard. Losing New Hampshire, Michigan and worst of all, almost Florida, did not cost Karl Rove his job; not detecting the attacks of September 11 nor even getting the WMD intelligence in Iraq right does not end George Tenet's role; a devastating prison scandal in Iraq does not cost Donald Rumsfeld his job. Bush believes he extracts gold from this style and he is willing to pay a high political price for it. Powell argued hard for putting the UN in front of the war plan, and when Bush tried it without success, Powell came behind the president's decision; 'I don't quit on long patrols,' he said.[27]

Can this decision strategy provide the president with enough diversity of advice? All the front row foreign policy advisers and White House staff were both loyal and outspoken at the same time; they include Cheney, Rice, Card, Rove, Hughes, Rumsfeld, and Powell. These people enjoy open access to the President and he would invite them to argue sharply in front of him as they did just after September 11. Powell and Hughes advised a different tack from Cheney and Rumsfeld, but after Hughes left, that became more difficult for Powell. Still, Cheney told a reporter that he had tried 'to move Powell', but he had stood his ground.[28] Bush has a strong will and after September 11, George W. Bush 'the War President' had less time and energy for divergent advice; his decision process became more like a strung out strategy, dealing more with tactics than goals.

Would the advisers stop arguing once the President made his decision or would they engage in protracted bureaucratic battles in the implementation of the presidential decision? This tug-of-war dynamic appears to have taken place in implementing Iraq policy after the war with Richard Armitage taking the brunt of it and often feeling the Pentagon was stiffing him.[29]

The Bush Legacy

The sheer volume of things Bush accomplished in four years is astonishing; it was more than most two-term presidents achieve. On the domestic front, he persuaded Congress to make two deep tax cuts, a once-in-a-generation-education-overhaul and a huge prescription drug-benefit. The September 2001 terrorist attacks facilitated the President's actions, but even so, he had a paradigm changing Patriot Act passed and created the Homeland Security Department – the biggest governmental change since Harry Truman pushed the National Security Act in 1949.

The Bush foreign policy record does not lag behind. He ended the ABM treaty and signed a deep cuts agreement with Moscow on nuclear warheads. He only made moderate gains on free trade and military transformation, but fought and won two wars instead, transforming the military more than any strategy paper or budget could. Bush presided over the largest development assistance increase in decades, secured a peaceful end to Haiti's civil war and nearly completed a peace deal in Sudan. Relations with China and Russia are about the same as when he came in while ties with India and Pakistan have improved a great deal.

The President's big vision is matched by his willingness to take enormous risk. Washington and North Korea have been on the brink since early 2001; he has a stable vision on the Israel-Palestinian crisis (responsible Palestinian leadership will be rewarded with a real state) but no comforting results so far. In a good cop – bad cop scenario, Britain, France, Germany and Washington are pressuring Iran to dismantle its nuclear weapon potential. As the Greater Middle East Initiative begins to reward and help reforms, more political instability in the Middle East is likely to come before freedom.

At the end of his first term, Bush was prepared to stake his whole presidency on Iraq, saying, 'America did the right thing'.[30] With Iraq, the war on terror and the economy as the lead issues, the 2004 presidential race between Bush and John Kerry will likely remain close till the end.

In the early 1980s, Ronald Reagan shook up a sleepy consensus behind détente by calling the Soviet Union an evil empire, by insisting on helping the Solidarity movement in Poland, and by out competing the Soviet state on military arms. Many of America's allies at the time were as upset with Reagan's approach as they are with George W. Bush's approach today. In his second term, Reagan went on to consolidate his radical changes by engaging Mikhail Gorbachev's quest for change. The Cold Warrior signed some of the most effective arms accords. Eventually, many of Reagan's critics came to respect him.

George W. Bush has made his radical changes. He has declared war on terror and shown that he is willing to use the whole spectrum of power. If he gets a second term, he may achieve a modernized NATO, a new arms control approach that has the wherewithal to stop and reverse proliferation, and a new soft power front in the form of the Greater Middle East Initiative to help address the root causes of terror and assist real political and economic development in that region.

Notes

1   Karen Hughes, *Ten Minutes From Normal* (New York: Viking, 2004), p. 146.
2   John Dickerson and Karen Tumulty, 'The Love Him, Hate Him President', *Time*, December 1, 2003, p. 11.
3   Transcript, 'Interview with President George W. Bush', Meet the Press with Tim Russert, February 8, 2004 (http://www.msnbc.msn.com/id/4179618/).
4   'President Bush Discusses Iraq Policy at Whitehall Palace in London', Office of the Press Secretary, November 19, 2003.
5   Steven Radelet, 'Bush and Foreign Aid', *Foreign Affairs*, September/October 2003. For increases in fiscal year 2005 request, see 'Colin Powell: President's Budget Request for Fiscal Year 2005', Senate Appropriations Committee Hearing, Congress, Washington, D.C., April 8, 2004.

6   Deborah Caldwell, 'An Evolving Faith', August 29, 2003 (www.beliefnet.com/story/121/story_12112.html).

7   Bob Woodward, *Plan of Attack* (New York: Simon & Schuster, 2004), p. 379.

8   As quoted in David Frum, 'Iraq Will Test Bush's Spiritual Bond with America', *USA Today*, February 23, 2003 (http://www.usatoday.com/news/opinion/editorials/2003-02-23-frum_x.htm).

9   'President Bush Speaks at Goree Island in Senegal', Office of the Press Secretary, July 8, 2003.

10   Quoted in Hughes, p. 280.

11   Peggy Noonan, *When Character Was King: A Story of Ronald Reagan* (New York: Viking Press, 2001), p. 279.

12   Woodward, p. 377.

13   Ivo H. Daalder and James M. Lindsay, *America Unbound: The Bush Revolution in Foreign Policy* (Washington, D.C.: Brookings Institution Press, 2003), pp. 189 and 196.

14   Joe Klein, 'Why the 'War President' is Under Fire', *Time*, February 23, 2004, p. 11.

15   'State of the Union Address', Office of the Press Secretary, January 29, 2002.

16   Colin Powell, 'A Strategy of Partnerships', *Foreign Affairs*, January/February 2004; Rice quoted in Nicholas Kralev, 'Rice Tells Europe to Follow the US Lead on Nukes', *Washington Times*, June 27, 2003.

17   As quoted in 'Remarks by the National Security Adviser to the Reagan Lecture', Office of the Press Secretary, February 26, 2004.

18   Douglas Feith quoted in Rowan Scarborough, *Rumsfeld's War: The Untold Story of America's Anti-Terrorist Commander* (Washington, D.C., Regnery Publishing, 2004), p. 5.

19   In interview with James Kitfield, 'We Act with Patience and Deliberation', *National Journal*, February 1, 2003, p. 373.

20   Powell, 'A Strategy of Partnerships',

21   Max Boot, 'Think Again: Neocons', *Foreign Policy*, January/February 2004 (www.foreignpolicy.com).

22   'Effective Multilateralism' is the term used in 'US/UK Joint Statement on Multilateralism', Office of the Press Secretary, November 20, 2003.

23   James Baker, III, 'No More Caving on North Korea', *Washington Post*, October 23, 2002, p. 27.

24   John Bolton as quoted in Baker Spring, 'Backgrounder', *The Heritage Foundation*, March 18, 2004, p. 5.

25   Hughes, p. 87.

26   Hughes, p. 264.

27   As quoted in Dan Morgan, 'Powell Says He Was "Committed" to Iraq War', *Washington Post*, April 20, 2004, p. 9.

28   Mark Leibovich, 'In the Shadows of War and of Greatness', *Washington Post*, November 13, 2003, p. c1.

29   For example see, Woodward, pp. 414, 433, 441.

30   Nancy Gibbs, 'When Credibility Becomes an Issue', *Time*, February 16, 2004, p. 18.

Index